BILATERAL AND REGIONAL TRADE AGREEMENTS

The history of the world trading system and international trade agreements is characterised by shifts between bilateralism, regionalism and multilateralism. Bilateralism has recently returned, having gained momentum following the failed WTO negotiations at the 1999 Seattle Ministerial Conference. The result is that today's international trade rules are now a complex web of instruments and agreements. This volume contains case studies of selected bilateral and regional free trade agreements (FTAs), covering a wide range of countries, regions and key issues such as intellectual property and agriculture. Authored by leading scholars, practitioners and governmental officials, each case study provides a comprehensive review of the negotiating history and result of the selected agreement. Each study can serve as an in-depth examination of a particular FTA, and the group of case studies can be used to compare and contrast the coverage of different FTAs or to examine the FTAs signed by a particular country.

BILATERAL AND REGIONAL TRADE AGREEMENTS

CASE STUDIES

Edited by
SIMON LESTER and BRYAN MERCURIO

CAMBRIDGE UNIVERSITY PRESS
Cambridge, New York, Melbourne, Madrid, Cape Town,
Singapore, São Paulo, Delhi, Mexico City

Cambridge University Press
The Edinburgh Building, Cambridge CB2 8RU, UK

Published in the United States of America by Cambridge University Press, New York

www.cambridge.org
Information on this title: www.cambridge.org/9780521878289

© Cambridge University Press 2009

This publication is in copyright. Subject to statutory exception
and to the provisions of relevant collective licensing agreements,
no reproduction of any part may take place without the written
permission of Cambridge University Press.

First published 2009

A catalogue record for this publication is available from the British Library

Library of Congress Cataloguing in Publication Data
Lester, Simon.
Bilateral and regional trade agreements : case studies /
Simon Lester, Bryan Mercurio.
p. cm.
Includes bibliographical references and index.
ISBN 978-0-521-87828-9 (hbk.)
1. Commercial treaties. 2. Free trade. I. Mercurio, Bryan. II. Title.
HF1721.L47 2008
382'.9–dc22   2008012212

ISBN 978-0-521-87828-9 Hardback

Cambridge University Press has no responsibility for the persistence or
accuracy of URLs for external or third-party internet websites referred to in
this publication, and does not guarantee that any content on such websites is,
or will remain, accurate or appropriate. Information regarding prices, travel
timetables, and other factual information given in this work is correct at
the time of first printing but Cambridge University Press does not guarantee
the accuracy of such information thereafter.

CONTENTS

List of Tables   *page* vii

Notes on Contributors   viii

Acknowledgements   xii

Table of Abbreviations   xiii

Table of Cases   xvi

Table of Treaties and International Agreements   xviii

Introduction   1

1 Australia–United States Free Trade Agreement   6
   ANDREW D. MITCHELL AND TANIA VOON

2 Central American–Dominican Republic–United States Free Trade Agreement   44
   MAURICIO SALAS

3 Chile–China Free Trade Agreement   59
   LUZ SOSA

4 European Union–Mexico Economic Partnership, Political Coordination and Cooperation Agreement   74
   BRADLY J. CONDON

5 European Free Trade Association–Southern African Customs Union Free Trade Agreement   97
   PETER DRAPER AND NKULULEKO KHUMALO

6 Japan–Mexico Economic Partnership Agreement   111
   BRYAN MERCURIO

7 United States–Morocco Free Trade Agreement   144
JASON KEARNS

8 Association of Southeast Asian Nations–China Free Trade Agreement   192
JIANGYU WANG

Index   226

TABLES

3.1 Table II.1 Trade between Chile and China, 1994–2003   60
4.1 Antecedents and chronology of negotiations   87
7.1 US goods trade with Morocco   147
7.2 Total apparel exports   189

CONTRIBUTORS

Bradly J. Condon is Professor of International Trade Law at the Instituto Tecnológico Autónomo de Mexico (ITAM) and is Senior Fellow, Tim Fischer Centre for Global Trade and Finance, School of Law, Bond University, Australia. Dr Condon is author or co-author of five books and numerous academic articles on international trade law and economic integration. In 2006–2007, he held the position of visiting professor at the Permanent Mission of Mexico to the WTO in Geneva. He is listed in *Who's Who in the World*.

Peter Draper is Research Fellow and Head of the 'Development Through Trade' programme at the South African Institute of International Affairs. His areas of expertise are trade and investment policy and trade negotiations, with particular reference to the World Trade Organization, the Southern African region and South Africa's bilateral ties with key trading partners.

He is a member of 'Business Unity', South Africa's trade committee; lectures on international business part time at Wits Business School; and is a Research Associate of the Department of Political Science at the University of Pretoria. He is a board member and non-resident Senior Fellow of the Brussels-based European Centre for International Political Economy; a member of the IMD-Lausanne's Evian group including its 'Brains Trust'; and a board member-designate of the Botswana Institute for Development Policy Analysis.

Jason Kearns currently serves as Trade Counsel to the Committee on Ways and Means in the US House of Representatives. In that position, he advises Members of Congress on legislation concerning international trade and on oversight issues involving the Office of the US Trade Representative and other agencies involved in international trade policy and regulation. Before beginning his current position in October 2006, he served for three years in the Office of the General Counsel to the US Trade Representative. In that position he advised negotiators on issues that arose during bilateral and multilateral trade negotiations and represented the United States in several disputes in the World Trade Organization. From 2000 to 2003, Dr Kearns worked in the international trade group of Wilmer, Cutler & Pickering (now known as WilmerHale). Dr Kearns holds a Master in Public Policy from the Kennedy School of Government at Harvard University, a Juris Doctor from the University of Pennsylvania, and a Bachelor of Arts from the University of Denver.

Nkululeko Khumalo is Senior Researcher on Trade Policy at the South African Institute of International Affairs. He holds an LLM (*cum laude*) specializing in international trade and investment from the University of the Western Cape, South Africa, in collaboration with Amsterdam Law School in the Netherlands. His expertise is in trade facilitation, international trade and investment laws, trade in services and trade negotiations.

Since he joined SAIIA in September 2004, Mr Khumalo has managed a number of research projects including: Trade Facilitation in the WTO and Southern Africa, and Regional Integration and Liberalization of Trade in Services in Southern Africa. He is also involved in coordinating projects on the US–SACU FTA negotiations and International Trade, Food Security, and GMO Regulations in Africa.

Bryan Mercurio is a Professor of Law at the Chinese University of Hong Kong and Fellow of the Tim Fischer Centre for Global Trade & Finance. He previously held a faculty position at the University of New South Wales, where he was also the Director of the International Trade and Development Project at the Gilbert + Tobin Centre of Public Law. Prior to entering academia, Professor Mercurio worked in both the public and private sector and has practised international commercial law and international trade law in the United States and Australia. More recently, he has advised Members of both the Australian and New Zealand Parliaments on international trade law matters and has been a consultant on, among other issues, the Australia–United States Free Trade Agreement. Professor Mercurio has held visiting positions at the Center for International and Comparative Law at St Louis University School of Law, the George Washington University Law School, the Institute for International Economic Law at the Georgetown University Law Center and at the National University of Singapore. He is also on the Founding Committee of the Society of International Economic Law.

Andrew Mitchell is a Senior Lecturer at Melbourne Law School. He graduated from the University of Melbourne with First Class Honours in both his Bachelor of Laws and Bachelor of Commerce degrees. He subsequently obtained a Graduate Diploma in International Law from the University of Melbourne, a Master of Laws from Harvard Law School, and a PhD from the University of Cambridge. His dissertation is being published by Cambridge University Press in 2008 as *Legal Principles in WTO Disputes*. Dr Mitchell was previously a solicitor with Allens Arthur Robinson in Australia and worked briefly at Davis Polk & Wardwell in New York. He has also worked in the Trade Directorate of the Organization for Economic Cooperation and Development (OECD), the Intellectual Property Division of the WTO, and the Legal Department of the International Monetary Fund. Dr Mitchell has published in numerous journals and books on areas including WTO law, international law, international humanitarian law and constitutional law. He has taught WTO law at the University of Melbourne, the University of Western Ontario, Bond University,

Monash University, the International Development Law Organization and the Australian Department of Foreign Affairs and Trade.

Mauricio Salas is a partner at the law firm of BLP Abogados in San José, Costa Rica. He has served as Professor of International Trade at the University of Costa Rica. He holds degrees from the University of Costa Rica (both Bachelor and JD equivalent degrees) and from the Georgetown University Law Center (LLM). After obtaining his LLM, Mauricio worked as an intern at the Appellate Body Secretariat of the World Trade Organization. He is listed in the roster of arbitrators of the Mexico–Costa Rica free trade agreement. His work has been recognized by the *Guide to the World's Leading International Trade Lawyers* and by Latin Lawyer's *Leading International Trade Lawyers*. Mauricio Salas is also regularly included in *Chambers Global* and the *International Financial Law Review*.

Luz Sosa is an international legal trade adviser at the Agricultural Office in the Mission of Chile to the European Union in Brussels, Belgium. Previously, she served as a legal adviser in the Legal Affairs Division of the General Directorate of International Economic Affairs of the Ministry of Foreign Affairs of Chile. While there, she was directly involved in negotiating and implementing trade agreements on behalf of Chile, particularly in the area of dispute settlement. She was also involved in WTO dispute settlement proceedings as a member of the Chilean delegation. Prior to her work as a trade negotiator, Mrs Sosa was an international trade adviser in the Geneva office of Sidley Austin Brown & Wood LLP, where she focused her practice in the area of international dispute resolution. Luz Sosa is a Chilean lawyer and holds a Masters degree in international law and economics from the World Trade Institute, Berne, Switzerland.

Tania Voon is a Senior Lecturer at Melbourne Law School and a former Legal Officer of the Appellate Body Secretariat of the WTO. She completed her PhD at the University of Cambridge and her Master of Laws at Harvard Law School. She recently authored *Cultural Products and the World Trade Organization* (Cambridge: Cambridge University Press, 2007) and she has published numerous articles in leading journals on WTO law and public international law more generally. Dr Voon teaches international economic law, including advanced courses on WTO dispute settlement as well as dumping, subsidies and safeguards in the WTO. She has practised law with Mallesons Stephen Jacques and the Australian Government Solicitor and has also worked for the United Nations in New York and the Organization for Economic Cooperation and Development (OECD) in Paris.

Jiangyu Wang is an Associate Professor at the School of Law, the Chinese University of Hong Kong. He specializes in Chinese law, international economic law and international commercial law. Before coming to Hong Kong, Dr Wang taught at the Faculty of Law of the National University of Singapore for three years where he was an Assistant Professor of Law. He practised law in the Legal Department of the Bank of China and Chinese and American law firms. He served as a member of the Chinese delegation at the annual conference of the United Nations Commission on International Trade Law Conference in 1999. Dr Wang has published extensively in Chinese and international journals and newspapers on a variety of law and politics related topics. He is a member of the Chinese Bar Association and the New York Bar Association.

ACKNOWLEDGEMENTS

We would like to thank all the contributors to this volume as well as all of those who reviewed and commented on any of the chapters. We would also like to thank the governments from which a number of our authors are drawn for allowing them to contribute to this volume. We are also deeply indebted to Ms Nikki Chong for voluntarily providing countless hours of excellent research and editorial assistance to the authors and editors.

Bryan would also like to extend his thanks to his wife, Kate for her understanding and support and to young Kieran for his timely and necessary distractions.

Simon would also like to thank his wife, Kara Leitner for her understanding and assistance throughout the project.

All information given in the case studies was correct at the time of submission by the contributors.

ABBREVIATIONS

ACFTA	ASEAN–China Free Trade Agreement
AFTA	ASEAN Free Trade Area
ANZCERTA	Australia New Zealand Closer Economic Relations Trade Agreement
APEC	Asia-Pacific Economic Cooperation
ASEAN	Association of Southeast Asian Nations
AUSFTA	Australia–US Free Trade Agreement
BEE	black economic empowerment
BIT	Bilateral Investment Treaty
BLNS	Botswana, Lesotho, Namibia and Swaziland
BTA	Bilateral Trade Agreement
CAFTA	Central American Free Trade Agreement
CAFTA–DR–US	Central American–Dominican Republic–US Free Trade Agreement
CAP	Common Agriculture Policy
CBI	Caribbean Basin Initiative
CCP	Common Commercial Policy
CIE	Centre for International Economics
CRTA	Committee on Regional Trade Agreements
DFAT	Department of Foreign Affairs and Trade (Australia)
DIRECON	General Directorate of International Economic Affairs (Chile)
DSB	Dispute Settlement Body
DSM	Dispute Settlement Mechanism
DSU	Understanding on Rules and Procedures Governing the Settlement of Disputes
DTI	Department of Trade and Industry
EC	European Communities
ECOSOC	Economic and Social Council of the United Nations
EC Treaty	Treaty Establishing the European Communities
EEC	European Economic Community
EFTA	European Free Trade Association

EHP	Early Harvest Programme
EPA	Economic Partnership Agreement
EU	European Union
EU–SA TDCA	European Union–South Africa Trade, Development and Cooperation Agreement
EU Treaty	Treaty of the European Union
FDI	Foreign direct investment
FIRB	Foreign Investment Review Board (Australia)
FTA	Free Trade Agreement
FTAA	Free Trade Area of the Americas
GATS	General Agreement on Trade in Services
GATT	General Agreement on Tariffs and Trade
GDP	Gross Domestic Product
GPA	Agreement on Government Procurement (WTO)
GSP	Generalized System of Preferences
HS	Harmonized System
HSL	Highly Sensitive List
ICTSD	International Centre for Trade and Sustainable Development
ILO	International Labour Organization
IMF	International Monetary Fund
IP	Intellectual Property
IPR	Intellectual Property Rights
ITA	Information Technology Agreement (WTO)
JETRO	Japan External Trade Organization
JMEPA	Agreement between Japan and the United Mexican States for the Strengthening of the Economic Partnership
JSCOT	Joint Standing Committee on Treaties (Australian Parliament)
MEFTA	Middle East Free Trade Area
MERCOSUR	Common Market of the Southern Cone
METI	Ministry of Economy, Trade and Industry (Japan)
MEUFTA	Mexico–European Union Free Trade Agreement
MFN	most favoured nation
MOFA	Ministry of Foreign Affairs (Japan)
MRA	mutual recognition agreement
NAAEC	North American Agreement on Environmental Cooperation
NAFTA	North American Free Trade Agreement
NCM	non-conforming measure
NFTC	National Foreign Trade Council (US)

NT	National Treatment
OECD	Organization for Economic Cooperation and Development
PBS	Pharmaceutical Benefits Scheme (Australia)
PTA	Preferential Trade Agreement
ROO	rules of origin
RTA	Regional Trade Agreement
SACU	Southern African Customs Union
SCM	Subsidies and Countervailing Measures
SECOF	Secretaría de Economía (Mexico)
SIECA	Secretaría de Integración Económica
SL	Sensitive List
SME	square metre equivalent
SPS	Sanitary and Phytosanitary
TBT	Technical Barriers to Trade
TIG	Trade in Goods
TIS	Trade in Services
TPA	Trade Promotion Agreement
TPL	tariff preference level
TRIMS	Trade-Related Investment Measures
TRIPS	Trade-Related Aspects of Intellectual Property Rights
TRQ	tariff-rate quota
UK	United Kingdom
UN	United Nations
UNCTAD	United Nations Conference on Trade and Development
UNESCO	United Nations Educational, Scientific and Cultural Organization
US	United States of America
USITC	US International Trade Commission
USTR	United States Trade Representative
Vienna Convention	Vienna Convention on the Law of Treaties of 1969
WFOE	wholly foreign-owned enterprise
WIPO	World Intellectual Property Organization
World Bank	International Bank for Reconstruction and Development
WTO	World Trade Organization
WTO Agreement	Marrakesh Agreement Establishing the World Trade Organization

TABLE OF CASES

(1) Index of WTO Dispute Settlement Panel and Appellate Body Reports

Short title	Full title and citation
Australia – Automotive Leather II	Panel Report, *Australia – Subsidies Provided to Producers and Exporters of Automotive Leather*, WT/DS126/R, adopted 16 June 1999, DSR 1999:III, 951
Australia – Automotive Leather II(Article 21.5 – US)	Panel Report, *Australia – Subsidies Provided to Producers and Exporters of Automotive Leather – Recourse to Article 21.5 of the DSU by the United States*, WT/DS126/RW and Corr.1, adopted 11 February 2000, DSR 2000:III, 1189
EC – Asbestos	Panel Report, *European Communities – Measures Affecting Asbestos and Asbestos-Containing Products*, WT/DS135/R and Add.1, adopted 5 April 2001, modified by Appellate Body Report, WT/DS135/AB/R, DSR 2001:VIII, 3305
EC – Bananas III	Appellate Body Report, *European Communities – Regime for the Importation, Sale and Distribution of Bananas*, WT/DS27/AB/R, adopted 25 September 1997, DSR 1997:II, 591
EC – Sugar Subsidies	Appellate Body Report, *European Communities – Export Subsidies on Sugar*, WT/DS265/AB/R, WT/DS266/AB/R, WT/DS283/AB/R, adopted 19 May 2005, DSR 2005:XIII, 6365
Japan – Film	Panel Report, *Japan – Measures Affecting Consumer Photographic Film and Paper*, WT/DS44/R, adopted 22 April 1998, DSR 1998:IV, 1179
Mexico – Taxes on Soft Drinks	Panel Report, *Mexico – Taxes on Soft Drinks and Other Beverages*, WT/DS308/R, adopted 24 March 2006, as modified by the Appellate Body Report, WT/DS308/AB/R
Turkey – Textiles	Appellate Body Report, *Turkey – Restrictions on Imports of Textile and Clothing Products*, WT/DS34/AB/R, adopted 19 November 1999, DSR 1999:VI, 2345
US – Gasoline	Appellate Body Report, *United States – Standards for Reformulated and Conventional Gasoline*, WT/DS2/AB/R, adopted 20 May 1996, DSR 1996:I, 3

(1) (cont.)

Short title	Full title and citation
US – Lamb	Appellate Body Report, *United States – Safeguard Measures on Imports of Fresh, Chilled or Frozen Lamb Meat from New Zealand and Australia*, WT/DS177/AB/R, WT/DS178/AB/R, adopted 16 May 2001, DSR 2001:IX, 4051
US – Offset Act (Byrd Amendment)	Appellate Body Report, *United States – Continued Dumping and Subsidy Offset Act of 2000*, WT/DS217/AB/R, WT/DS234/AB/R, adopted 27 January 2003, DSR 2003:I, 375
US – Steel Safeguards	Appellate Body Report, *United States – Definitive Safeguard Measures on Imports of Certain Steel Products*, WT/DS248/AB/R, WT/DS249/AB/R, WT/DS251/AB/R, WT/DS252/AB/R, WT/DS253/AB/R, WT/DS254/AB/R, WT/DS258/AB/R, WT/DS259/AB/R, adopted 10 December 2003, DSR 2003:VII, 3117

(2) *Index of GATT Dispute Settlement Panel Reports*

Short title	Full title and citation
EEC – Oilseeds I	GATT Panel Report, *European Economic Community – Payments and Subsidies Paid to Processors and Producers of Oilseeds and Related Animal-Feed Proteins*, L/6627, adopted 25 January 1990, BISD 37S/86

TABLE OF TREATIES AND INTERNATIONAL AGREEMENTS

(1) *International Conventions and Multilateral Treaties*

Short Title	Long Title	Status
Brussels Satellites Convention	Convention Relating to the Distribution of Programme-Carrying Signals Transmitted by Satellite	signed at Brussels 21 May 1974; in force 25 August 1979
Budapest Treaty	Budapest Treaty on the International Recognition of the Deposit of Microorganisms for the Purpose of Patent Procedure	signed at Budapest 28 April 1977; in force 9 August 1980; amended 26 September 1980
Cultural Expressions Convention	Convention on the Protection and Promotion of the Diversity of Cultural Expressions	adopted in Paris by the United Nations Educational, Scientific and Cultural Organization (UNESCO) on 20 October 2005; in force 18 March 2007
Geneva Act	Hague Agreement Concerning the International Registration of Industrial Designs	adopted in Geneva 2 July 1999; in force 23 December 2003
ILO Declaration	International Labour Organization Declaration on Fundamental Principles and Rights at Work	adopted in Geneva by the General Conference of the International Labour Organization (ILO) during its 86th Session on 18 June 1998
Madrid Protocol	Protocol Relating to the Madrid Agreement Concerning the International Registration of Marks	adopted in Madrid 27 June 1989; in force 1 December 1995
PCT	Patent Cooperation Treaty	signed at Washington 19 June 1970; in force 21 January 1978; amended 2 October 1979; modified 3 February 1984 and 3 October 2001; in force 1 April 2002

(1) (cont.)

Short Title	Long Title	Status
PLT	Patent Law Treaty	adopted in Geneva 1 June 2000; in force 28 April 2005
TLT	Trademark Law Treaty	adopted in Geneva 27 October 1994; in force 1 August 1996
UPOV	International Convention for the Protection of New Varieties of Plants (*Union internationale pour la protection des obtentions végétales*)	adopted in Paris 2 December 1961; in force 10 August 1968; revised at Geneva 19 March 1991; in force 24 April 1998
Vienna Convention	Vienna Convention on the Law of Treaties	signed at Vienna 23 May 1969; in force 27 January 1980
WCT	WIPO Copyright Treaty	adopted in Geneva by the Diplomatic Conference on 20 December 1996; in force 6 March 2002
WPPT	WIPO Performances and Phonograms Treaty (1996)	adopted in Geneva by the Diplomatic Conference on 20 December 1996; in force 20 May 2002

(2) GATT/WTO Agreements

Short Title	Full Title	Status/Source
Agriculture Agreement	Agreement on Agriculture	Annex 1A of the WTO Agreement
Anti-dumping Agreement	Agreement on Implementation of Article VI of the General Agreement on Tariffs and Trade 1994	Annex 1A of the WTO Agreement
Customs Valuation Agreement	Agreement on Implementation of Article VII of the General Agreement on Tariffs and Trade 1994	Annex 1A of the WTO Agreement
DSU	Understanding on Rules and Procedures Governing the Settlement of Disputes	Annex 2 of the WTO Agreement
GATS	General Agreement on Trade in Services	Annex 1B of the WTO Agreement
GATT 1947	General Agreement on Tariffs and Trade 1947	signed 30 October 1947; in force 1 January 1948
GATT 1994	General Agreement on Tariffs and Trade 1994	Annex 1A of the WTO Agreement
GPA 1994	Agreement on Government Procurement 1994	Annex 4(b) of the WTO Agreement
Safeguards Agreement	Agreement on Safeguards	Annex 1A of the WTO Agreement
SCM Agreement	Agreement on Subsidies and Countervailing Measures	Annex 1A of the WTO Agreement
SPS Agreement	Agreement on the Application of Sanitary and Phytosanitary Measures	Annex 1A of the WTO Agreement
TBT Agreement	Agreement on Technical Barriers to Trade	Annex 1A of the WTO Agreement
TRIMS Agreement	Agreement on Trade-Related Investment Measures	Annex 1A of the WTO Agreement
TRIPS Agreement	Agreement on Trade-Related Aspects of Intellectual Property Rights	Annex 1C of the WTO Agreement
WTO Agreement	Marrakesh Agreement Establishing the World Trade Organization	signed 15 April 1994; in force 1 January 1995

(3) *Preferential Trade Agreements*

Short Title	Long Title	Current Parties (or membership immediately prior to extinction (unless otherwise indicated))	Status
ANZCERTA (*also referred to as* CER)	Australia–New Zealand Closer Economic Relations Trade Agreement	Australia, New Zealand	signed 28 March 1980; in force 1 January 1983
AUSFTA	Australia–United States Free Trade Agreement	Australia, United States	signed 18 May 2004; in force 1 January 2005
CAFTA–DR–US	Central America–Dominican Republic–United States Free Trade Agreement	Costa Rica, Dominican Republic, El Salvador, Guatemala, Honduras, Nicaragua, United States	signed 5 August 2004; in force 1 March 2006 (El Salvador, United States), 1 April 2006 (Honduras, Nicaragua), 1 July 2006 (Guatemala), 1 March 2007 (Dominican Republic)
Canada–Costa Rica FTA	Canada–Costa Rica Free Trade Agreement	Canada, Costa Rica	signed 23 April 2001; in force 1 November 2002
Chile–China FTA	Chile–China Free Trade Agreement	Chile, China	signed 18 November 2005; in force 1 October 2006
EFTA–SACU FTA	EFTA–SACU Free Trade Agreement	EFTA States, SACU States	signed 26 June 2006; not yet in force
EU/EC/EEC/European Treaty	Treaty of the European Union/ Treaty Establishing the European Communities	Austria, Belgium, Bulgaria, Cyprus, Czech Republic, Denmark, Estonia, Finland, France, Germany, Greece, Hungary, Ireland, Italy, Latvia, Lithuania, Luxembourg, Malta, Netherlands, Poland, Portugal, Romania, Slovakia, Slovenia, Spain, Sweden, United Kingdom	EEC (Treaty of Rome): signed 25 March 1957; in force 25 March 1957; EU (Maastricht Treaty): signed 7 February 1992; in force 1 November 1993; EU Enlargement (25): accession 1 May 2004; EU Enlargement (27): accession 1 January 2007

(3) (*cont.*)

Short Title	Long Title	Current Parties (or membership immediately prior to extinction (unless otherwise indicated))	Status
EU–Mexico FTA (*also referred to as* MEUFTA *or* Global Agreement)	European Union–Mexico Economic Partnership, Political Coordination and Cooperation Agreement	European Union, Mexico	signed 8 December 1997; in force 1 March 2001
EU–Morocco AA	European Union–Morocco Association Agreement	European Union, Morocco	signed 26 February 1996; in force 1 March 2000
EU–SA TDCA	European Union–South Africa Trade, Development and Cooperation Agreement	European Union, South Africa	signed 11 October 1999; partially in force 1 January 2000, fully in force 1 May 2004
FTAA	Free Trade Area of the Americas	Antigua and Barbuda, Argentina, Bahamas, Barbados, Belize, Bolivia, Brazil, Canada, Chile, Colombia, Costa Rica, Dominica, Dominican Republic, Ecuador, El Salvador, Grenada, Guatemala, Guyana, Haiti, Honduras, Jamaica, Mexico, Nicaragua, Panama, Paraguay, Peru, St. Kitts and Nevis, St Lucia, St Vincent and the Grenadines, Suriname, Trinidad and Tobago, United States, Uruguay, Venezuela	Ministerial Declaration of Miami, 8th Ministerial Meeting, adopted 20 November 2003
Japan–Brunei EPA	Japan–Brunei Economic Partnership Agreement	Brunei, Japan	signed 18 June 2007; not yet in force
Japan–Chile EPA	Japan–Chile Economic Partnership Agreement	Chile, Japan	signed 27 March 2007; in force 3 September 2007

Japan–Indonesia EPA	Japan–Indonesia Economic Partnership Agreement	Indonesia, Japan	signed 20 August 2007, not yet in force
Japan–Malaysia EPA	Japan–Malaysia Economic Partnership Agreement	Japan, Malaysia	signed 13 December 2005; in force 13 July 2006
Japan–Mexico EPA	Japan–Mexico Economic Partnership Agreement	Japan, Mexico	signed 17 September 2004; in force 1 April 2005
Japan–Philippines EPA	Japan–Philippines Economic Partnership Agreement	Japan, Philippines	signed 8 September 2006; not yet in force
Japan–Singapore EPA	Japan–Singapore New-Age Economic Partnership Agreement	Japan, Singapore	signed 13 January 2002; in force 30 November 2002
Japan–Thailand EPA	Japan–Thailand Economic Partnership Agreement	Japan, Thailand	signed 3 April 2007; in force 1 November 2007
NAFTA	North American Free Trade Agreement	Canada, Mexico, United States	signed 17 December 1992; in force 1 January 1994
North American Agreement on Environmental Cooperation (NAAEC) signed 14 September 1993; in force 1 January 1994
Singapore–Australia FTA	Singapore–Australia Free Trade Agreement	Australia, Singapore	signed 17 February 2003; in force 28 July 2003
Thailand–Australia FTA	Thailand–Australia Free Trade Agreement	Australia, Thailand	signed 5 July 2004; in force 1 January 2005
US–Chile FTA	United States–Chile Free Trade Agreement	Chile, United States	signed 6 June 2003; in force 1 January 2004
US–Colombia TPA	United States–Colombia Trade Promotion Agreement	Colombia, United States	signed 22 November 2006; not yet in force

(3) (cont.)

Short Title	Long Title	Current Parties (or membership immediately prior to extinction (unless otherwise indicated))	Status
US–Israel FTA	United States–Israel Free Trade Agreement	Israel, United States	signed 22 April 1985; in force 1 September 1985
US–Jordan FTA	United States–Jordan Free Trade Agreement	Jordan, United States	signed 24 October 2000; in force 17 December 2001
US–Morocco FTA	United States–Morocco Free Trade Agreement	Morocco, United States	signed 15 June 2004; in force 1 January 2006
US–Singapore FTA	United States–Singapore Free Trade Agreement	Singapore, United States	signed 6 May 2003; in force 1 January 2004

Introduction

The modern history of the world trading system, and in particular international trade agreements, is evidenced by shifts among bilateralism, regionalism and multilateralism. In the late nineteenth century and early twentieth century, bilateralism was clearly dominant. Trade agreements were negotiated on a bilateral basis between individual countries. In the 1860s and 1870s, England initiated much of this activity, pushing its trading partners to sign trade agreements that reciprocally lowered tariff rates. In the 1930s, it was the United States that made a big push in this area, through its Reciprocal Trade Agreements program, although a number of other countries were also active in negotiating bilateral agreements to lower tariff rates.

However, immediately after World War II, multilateralism and regionalism had replaced bilateralism as the dominant approach. From the late 1940s through the mid-1990s, multilateralism grew in strength as more and more nations joined the GATT or its successor the WTO. The GATT, which began with twenty-three countries, unquestionably came to dominate the world trading scene. It did not, however, completely replace regional and bilateral trade agreements. Regionalism remained a competing model, as nations in Europe, North America, South America and elsewhere all formed trading blocs during this period. East Asia was the only region to eschew regionalism, while Western Europe was the clear leader in terms of both the timing and the scope of its economic integration, with other regions following a bit behind. Bilateralism, on the other hand, diminished considerably during this period. Such agreements were extremely rare, and where they did exist could usually be explained mostly by political, rather than economic, factors.

In recent years, though, bilateralism has returned with a vengeance. The initial return to bilateralism can be traced to the breakup of the Soviet Union and the collapse of Communism in the early-1990s. The newly formed nations, along with several Eastern European economies in transition from a centrally planned to a market based economy, led a mini-revival of bilateralism in the mid-to late 1990s. Bilateralism, however, only significantly gained momentum following the failed WTO negotiations at the 1999 Seattle Ministerial Conference. Prior to 1999, it was rare for the major trading powers to negotiate and sign bilateral trade agreements. Following the failed Ministerial, all major trading nations (including the East Asian nations) almost immediately launched multiple negotiations. A large number of such agreements have now been negotiated and signed, and many more are currently being negotiated. The rapid increase in the total number of agreements has created a competitive process among nations, with all of the major trading powers pushing hard to conclude these agreements so as not to lose particular markets to their competitors.

In addition to bilateral agreements, there are also a growing number of what could be termed 'loose' regional trade agreements. These agreements are concluded among several countries in the same 'region', with the term region more loosely defined than in previous eras. These agreements are, in essence, plurilateral agreements among countries which may or may not be in somewhat close proximity to each other, but do not necessarily include all countries from that area. For example, the North American Free Trade Agreement (NAFTA), a more traditional RTA, was signed in 1993 between Canada, the United States and Mexico, three contiguous countries of North America. By contrast, in 2006 the CAFTA-DR agreement was signed between the United States, a few Central American countries, and the Dominican Republic. All are in the same general region, but there are many other countries within that region which were not included. On the other hand, the Trans-Pacific Strategic Economic Partnership Agreement (P4) between Brunei, Chile, New Zealand and Singapore cannot be said to even remotely resemble nations in close proximity to one another (although admittedly all members are linked by the Pacific Ocean).

The result of the proliferation of these agreements is that today's international trade rules now consist of a number of instruments. At the forefront, there is the multilateral WTO Agreement, which includes 151 countries or customs territories. In addition, there are the traditional regional trading blocs, each with their own agreements, some of which provide for deep integration or customs unions among the member countries. Then, there is the complex web of bilateral trade agreements between individual countries. Finally, there are a growing number of 'loose' regional agreements. All of these agreements – over 300 in total – exist together, creating a mish-mash of overlapping, supporting, and possibly conflicting, obligations.

Perhaps even more important than the sheer quantity of trade agreements is the scope of their coverage. While the 19th century and early 20th century bilateral agreements were often narrowly focused on reducing tariffs, the more recent ones contain obligations that are wide-ranging and controversial, from investment provisions to intellectual property rights affecting access to medicines to protections for labour/human rights and the environment. While the full impact that these agreements will have on domestic policy-making is uncertain, it is clear that a number of agreements are going beyond the coverage of the WTO as well as the regional and bilateral agreements negotiated prior to 1999 and reaching a new level of international policy-making.

The structure of the book

This volume consists of case studies of various free trade agreements (FTAs). At this stage, we are not offering a complete set of case studies of all trade agreements. Rather, we have tried to select a group that includes a good sampling in terms of countries and regions covered, and also a sampling of agreements that address key issues (such as intellectual property and agriculture). Authored by leading scholars, practitioners and governmental officials, each case study provides a comprehensive review of the selected agreement. The first case study, authored by Andrew Mitchell and Tania Voon, both of the Melbourne Law School, is the Australia–United States FTA. Mauricio Salas, of the law firm BLP Abogados in San Jose, Costa Rica, next reviews the CAFTA–DR–US FTA before Luz Sosa of the Agricultural Office in the Mission of Chile to the EU outlines the China–Chile FTA. Bradly Condon of the Instituto Tecnológico Autónomo de Mexico (ITAM) then provides a review of the EU–Mexico FTA. Next Peter Draper and Nkululeko Khumal, both of the South African Institute of International Affairs, review the EFTA–SACU. The México–Japan EPA is then reviewed by Bryan Mercurio of the Chinese University of Hong Kong, School of Law, before Jason Kearns of the US House of Representatives Committee on Ways and Means outlines the US–Morocco FTA. The book concludes with a review of the China-ASEAN FTA, authored by Jiangyu Wang of the Chinese University of Hong Kong, School of Law.

In future editions of the book, we plan to supplement this work by providing case studies of additional agreements, eventually compiling a comprehensive resource providing case studies of as many FTAs as is practicable. Such a resource should be useful in a number of ways. For example, each study can serve as an in-depth study of a particular FTA. Moreover, the group of case studies can be used to compare and contrast the coverage of different FTAs, or to examine the FTAs signed by a particular country.

The editors have also recently completed another collection, entitled 'Bilateral and Regional Trade Agreements' which is a companion to the 'Case Studies' series. In that volume, the contributors attempt to provide some preliminary answers to a number of interesting questions (in terms of politics, international relations, international law, economics and global governance) raised as a result of the spread of FTAs, including:

- What are the reasons for the recent interest in and growth of these agreements?
- How do the benefits of bilateral trade liberalization compare with those of multilateral trade liberalization?
- How do these new agreements relate to existing multilateral and regional trade agreements, and to international law more generally?

- What is the substantive scope of these agreements? That is, what policies do they promote and what obligations do they contain?
- How are these agreements negotiated among the various governments, and what is the role of non-State actors who have an interest in the agreements?

The term 'preliminary' is used intentionally, as the development of these agreements is still ongoing. The end does not appear to be in sight yet, especially as the Doha Round continues on (and on) with no set timetable for completion. Thus, the analysis offered here is necessarily limited to what has occurred so far.

The 'Commentary and Analysis' volume is structured as follows. Sections II and III will put these issues in context by providing some general background on the economics, politics, international relations and international law aspects of FTAs. For instance, Section II contains a chapter by Pravin Krishna of Johns Hopkins University, School of Advanced International Studies, evaluating the economics of FTAs. More specifically, Professor Krishna expands upon existing literature to find that the welfare effects of FTAs are ambiguous at best. The chapter also provides, inter alia, an interesting analysis on the design of FTAs with welfare-improving effects. Section II also contains a chapter on the political and international relations considerations of FTAs. Written by Olivier Cattaneo of the International Trade Department at the World Bank, the chapter asks the question 'why do countries conclude FTAs?' and provides a unique assessment of both the historical and present situation, ultimately concluding that the political economy of FTAs revolves more around politics than economics. The final chapter in Section II is a practical analysis of some of the differences between bilateral FTAs and multi-party ones. In the chapter, David Evans of the New Zealand Ministry of Foreign Affairs and Trade demonstrates how the 'new generation' of plurilateral FTAs are a break from traditional bilateral FTAs and offer some challenging issues, such as how are such agreements to be negotiated and structured to meet the needs (and ambitions) of all parties?

In Section III, we try to situate FTAs in the larger context in which they exist. There are two aspects to this: (1) how do FTAs fit with the WTO, which prohibits discrimination among WTO Members but has an exception for free trade agreements and customs unions? and (2) how do FTAs fit within international law more generally? The Section begins with a chapter by Andrew Mitchell of the Melbourne Law School, and Nicholas Lockhart of the law firm of Sidley Austin, examining the nature of the exception for FTAs under WTO rules. It outlines, in substantial detail, the conditions of the exception and concludes with an assessment of the likelihood of legal challenge to a FTA if it did not meet all of the conditions of the exception. In the following chapter, Andrew Mitchell and Tania Voon, also of the Melbourne Law School, provide a comprehensive analysis of the under-explored and often murky relationship of FTAs to international law. More specifically, Mitchell and Voon provide examples of difficult and unsettled issues surrounding the overlap between

FTAs and public international law, including the particularly thorny issues of conflicting norms between two treaties/agreements and multiple dispute settlement systems that are capable of hearing the same dispute.

Section IV provides a detailed look at specific subject areas that are part of FTAs. In essence, this section offers a comparison across the various agreements, examining the scope of the law that is being created in seven important policy areas. First, Tim Josling of the Stanford University, Food Research Institute, analyses the contentious area of agriculture with reference to historical data as well as differences between bilateral and regional FTAs. Next, Federico Ortino of King's College London provides a review of services in the multilateral forum before comprehensively detailing how certain FTAs are creating GATS-Plus obligations. Joshua Meltzer from the Australia Department of Foreign Affairs and Trade then contributes a thorough and detailed chapter on investment which particularly focuses on both the wide-ranging obligations undertaken in the area as well as specific areas which have caused much disagreement and dispute. Arwel Davies of University of Wales Swansea, Faculty of Law, next provides a chapter on government procurement which illustrates how many agreements are hesitant to move substantially beyond the WTO model. Michael Handler of the University of New South Wales, Faculty of Law and Bryan Mercurio next provide a chapter on intellectual property which looks at three TRIPS-Plus areas of intellectual property: copyright, geographical indications and patents. Lorand Bartels of Cambridge University then contributes an interesting article detailing the inclusion of social issues, such as labour, environment and human rights, into FTAs. Finally, Simon Lester of WorldTradeLaw.net and Victoria Donaldson of the WTO Secretariat conclude the Section with a detailed review of various dispute settlement provisions in FTAs, finding a general, but not perfect, correlation to the WTO model set out in the Dispute Settlement Understanding.

As mentioned above, the expansion of FTAs as a key part of the world trading system is a fairly recent development. As things continue to evolve, we will expand this study through future editions. For the chapters covering specific substantive areas, we will update these to take into account new agreements as they are signed. In addition, as noted, we will add more case studies with each new edition. In this way, we hope this book and its future editions will serve as a comprehensive and essential resource for understanding the role of FTAs in the international trade regime.

1

Australia–United States Free Trade Agreement

ANDREW D. MITCHELL AND TANIA VOON*

I. Introduction

Former Deputy Director-General of the World Trade Organization (WTO), Andrew Stoler has described the Australia–United States Free Trade Agreement (AUSFTA)[1] as a 'third wave' free trade agreement[2] (FTA) that goes 'beyond the envelope of the WTO',[3] in the sense that it ventures into areas barely covered in the WTO agreements, like competition, and expands on WTO disciplines in other areas, like services and intellectual property. Going beyond the existing WTO rules does not, of course, necessarily constitute progress, or even greater trade liberalization. In this chapter, we consider the extent to which the AUSFTA represents an improvement on the WTO bargain from the perspective of the two parties as well as the broader WTO membership.

Before considering how the AUSFTA came about, we now provide an introductory snapshot of the trading and broader relationship between these two countries. United States (US) trade data indicate that the value of US exports of goods to Australia in 2006 totalled around US$17.8 billion and the value of US imports of goods from Australia amounted to US$8.2 billion.[4] This put Australia

---

* This chapter was finalized in May 2007. An earlier version of this chapter was presented at the conference on 'Free Trade Agreements: Where is the World Heading?' hosted by the Bond University Faculty of Law and the Tim Fischer Centre for Global Trade and Finance, Gold Coast, Australia, 10 March 2007. We are grateful for the helpful comments made by participants at that conference. For valuable comments on an earlier draft of this chapter we also thank Ann Capling, Jürgen Kurtz, Simon Lester, Donald MacLaren, Bryan Mercurio and Matthew Rimmer. All opinions expressed here and any errors are ours.

[1] Signed 18 May 2004, in force 1 January 2005.
[2] We use the term 'free trade agreements' to refer to bilateral and regional agreements between States or customs territories that focus at least in part on liberalizing trade between the parties, as distinct from the multilateral system established under the WTO. 'FTAs' therefore include free trade areas and customs unions within the meaning of Article XXIV of the General Agreement on Tariffs and Trade 1994.
[3] Andrew L. Stoler, 'The Australia–United States FTA as a "Third Wave" Trade Agreement: Beyond the WTO Envelope' in Andrew D. Mitchell (ed.), *Challenges and Prospects for the WTO* (London: Cameron May, 2005), pp. 253–68 at p. 256.
[4] US Census Bureau, 'Foreign Trade Statistics: Trade in Goods (Imports, Exports and Trade Balance) with Australia', 2006, available at www.census.gov/foreign-trade/balance/c6021.html#2007 (last accessed 4 April 2007).

within the top 15 countries for US exports in 2006.[5] Services trade appears more balanced, with the Australian government reporting exports to the US at approximately AU$5.4 billion for 2005–6 and imports from the US at around AU$7.1 billion for the same period. The Australian government includes as Australia's 'major exports' to the US bovine meat, alcoholic beverages, personal travel, and 'other business services', and as 'major imports' from the US aircraft, motor vehicles for transporting goods, personal travel, and royalties and licence fees.[6]

In the WTO, Australia has complained against the US in two cases formally commenced in the dispute settlement system. Both proceeded to a Panel and then the Appellate Body, which found the US in violation of its WTO obligations,[7] and they were ultimately resolved when the US implemented the recommendations and rulings of the Dispute Settlement Body (DSB).[8] The US has complained against Australia in four cases, three of which were resolved before reaching the Panel stage,[9] and one of which was the subject of a mutually agreed solution[10] after a Panel had ruled against Australia.[11]

Why did Australia so vigorously pursue an FTA with the US?[12] Entry into the AUSFTA was consistent with Australia's general embrace of FTAs across the world in recent years, which is based on a perception that Australia relies on bilateral links

---

[5] US Census Bureau, 'Foreign Trade Statistics: Top Trading Partners – Total Trade, Exports, Imports', December 2006, available at www.census.gov/foreign-trade/statistics/highlights/top/top0612.html (last accessed 4 April 2007).

[6] Australian Department of Foreign Affairs and Trade (DFAT), 'United States Fact Sheet', available at www.dfat.gov.au/geo/fs/usa.pdf (last accessed 4 April 2007). For further historical discussion of the Australia–US trade and investment relationship, see Australian APEC Study Centre, Monash University, *An Australia–USA Free Trade Agreement: Issues and Implications: A Report for the Department of Foreign Affairs and Trade* (Canberra: Commonwealth of Australia, 2001), at pp. 9–18.

[7] Appellate Body Report, *US–Lamb*, paras. 1.97 and 1.98; and Appellate Body Report, *US–Offset Act (Byrd Amendment)*, paras. 318–19.

[8] WTO, *US–Safeguard Measures on Imports of Fresh, Chilled or Frozen Lamb Meat from New Zealand and Australia: Communication from the United States*, WT/DS177/12, WT/DS178/13, 2 October 2001; and WTO, *US–Continued Dumping and Subsidy Offset Act of 2000: Status Report by the US – Addendum*, WT/DS217/16/Add.24, WT/DS234/24/Add.24, 7 February 2006.

[9] WTO, *Australia–Measures Affecting the Importation of Salmonids: Notification of Mutually Agreed Solution*, WT/DS21/10, G/L/39/Add.1, G/SPS/W/40/Add.1, 1 November 2000; WTO, *Australia–Textile, Clothing and Footwear Import Credit Scheme: Request for Consultations by the United States*, WT/DS57/1, G/SCM/D7/1, 9 October 1996; US, *Subsidies Enforcement Annual Report to the Congress: Joint Report of the Office of the United States Trade Representative and the U.S. Department of Commerce* (February 1999), available at http://ia.ita.doc.gov/esel/seo99.htm (last accessed 4 April 2007); and WTO, *Australia–Subsidies Provided to Producers and Exporters of Automotive Leather: Request for the Establishment of a Panel*, WT/DS126/2, 11 June 1998 (the US withdrew its earlier request for establishment of a Panel while at the same time requesting the establishment of a new Panel regarding the same subsidies).

[10] WTO, *Australia–Subsidies Provided to Producers and Exporters of Automotive Leather: Notification of Mutually Agreed Solution*, WT/DS126/11, G/SCM/D20/2, 31 July 2000.

[11] Panel Report, *Australia–Automotive Leather II*, paras. 10.1–10.7; and Panel Report, *Australia–Automotive Leather II (Article 21.5–US)*, para. 7.1.

[12] Ann Capling, *All the Way with the USA: Australia, the US and Free Trade* (Sydney: University of New South Wales Press, 2005), at pp. 41–2 and 50–5.

to protect the national interest in international trade and investment as well as security.[13] Australia's Department of Foreign Affairs and Trade (DFAT) maintained that an FTA with the US was crucial in protecting national interests, given that the US 'is our largest single trade and investment partner and second-largest export market'.[14] DFAT also expressed the hope that the AUSFTA might prevent or mitigate harmful US policies such as 'Washington's past decisions to protect its lamb and steel industries' and increased subsidies to farmers,[15] and it indicated that the AUSFTA was particularly important given difficulties in the Doha Round of negotiations in the WTO.[16] However, according to the Australian Senate's Select Committee on the AUSFTA, 'Australia's pursuit of a free trade agreement with America ha[d] as much, if not more, to do with Australia's broader foreign policy objectives as it d[id] with pure trade and investment goals'.[17]

Why, then, did the US want the AUSFTA? Officially, among other things, the US was concerned with improving access to the Australian market for its agricultural exports, including by limiting Australia's use of sanitary and phytosanitary measures to restrict trade. It also sought to strengthen the US–Australia alliance for the purpose of the WTO's Doha Round negotiations, especially on agriculture. Like Australia, the US also linked the AUSFTA to its national security interests.[18] An unofficial suggestion is that the AUSFTA was 'payback' for Australia's support of the Iraq war:[19] September 11 may have been what finally led the US to agree to the AUSFTA.[20]

In this chapter we explain and evaluate the AUSFTA primarily from an Australian perspective, given that most countries will be in a more or less analogous position to Australia when negotiating an FTA with the US. The AUSFTA provides an illustration of the outcomes that countries with relatively little bargaining and economic power can expect from such an FTA. It also serves as a warning of how even an

---

[13] DFAT, *Advancing the National Interest: Australia's Foreign and Trade Policy White Paper* (Canberra: Commonwealth of Australia, 2003), at pp. 7, 9.
[14] Ibid., at p. 89.   [15] Ibid.
[16] See, e.g., Parliament of the Commonwealth of Australia, Joint Standing Committee on Treaties, *Report 61: The Australia – United States Free Trade Agreement* (June 2004), at para. 2.31 (quoting DFAT).
[17] Commonwealth of Australia, *Senate Select Committee on the Free Trade Agreement between Australia and the United States of America: Final Report* (Canberra, August 2004), at para. 1.24. See also Gavin Goh, *Regional Trade Agreements and Australia: A National Interest Perspective*, Australian APEC Study Centre, Monash University (May 2006), at p. 20; and Australian APEC Study Centre, Monash University, *An Australia – USA Free Trade Agreement: Issues and Implications: A Report for the Department of Foreign Affairs and Trade* (Canberra: Commonwealth of Australia, 2001), at pp. 72–7.
[18] Letters from Robert Zoellick, USTR, to Senator Robert Byrd and Dennis Hastert, Speaker, United States House of Representatives, 13 November 2002.
[19] M. Rafiqul Islam, 'The Australian Policy and Practice of Preferential Bilateral Trade: A Benign or Malign Alternative to the WTO Multilateral Free Trading System?' (2003) 2(2) *Journal of International Trade Law & Policy* 43–61 at 57. See also Linda Weiss, Elizabeth Thurbon and John Mathews, *How to Kill a Country: Australia's Devastating Trade Deal with the United States* (Crows Nest: Allen & Unwin, 2004), at pp. 141–2.
[20] Capling, above note 12, at pp. 53–4.

economically successful developed country may end up sacrificing its welfare, public policies and democratic processes in a dogged pursuit to cement relations with the US, in a manner that would be unlikely in the vigorous negotiating environment of the WTO. We begin by examining the way in which the AUSFTA was negotiated, before turning to some of the substantive outcomes of those negotiations in key areas such as goods, services, investment, and intellectual property.[21] Finally, we consider the impact of the AUSFTA to date and its future implications.

II. The negotiating process

The AUSFTA began with an announcement by Australia's Prime Minister, John Howard, then Trade Minister, Mark Vaile, and then United States Trade Representative (USTR), Robert Zoellick, on 14 November 2002, that negotiations on an FTA were commencing.[22] DFAT then invited public submissions on the proposed AUSFTA by 15 January 2003.[23] It received around 200 submissions from a range of individuals and bodies.[24] Negotiations then took place in five rounds: 17–21 March 2003 (Canberra), 19–21 May 2003 and 21–25 July 2003 (Honolulu), 27–31 October 2003 (Canberra), and from 1 December 2003 to 8 February 2004 (Washington, DC).[25]

The first round of negotiations covered framework issues and the scope of the negotiations, with working groups meeting on the following four broad areas: 'industrial products, agriculture, rules of origin, sanitary and phyto-sanitary measures; standards and technical barriers to trade, trade remedies; services, investment, intellectual property, competition policy; legal and institutional arrangements, including dispute settlement, environment and labour issues'.[26] In addition to the lead negotiators from the USTR and DFAT, officials involved in the negotiations included (for the US) 'representatives of the Departments of State, Commerce, Treasury, Agriculture, Justice and Labour, along with the US Customs Administration, the US Patents and Trademarks Office, the Federal Trade Commission, and the Environmental Protection Authority' and (for Australia) representatives from the Department of 'Agriculture, Fisheries and Forestry; Attorney-General's Department; the [Australian Competition and Consumer Commission]; Communications, Information, Technology and the

---

[21] Given space constraints, we are unable to consider all the most important or controversial issues raised by the AUSFTA.
[22] John Howard, Australian Prime Minister, 'Address to the Australian Chamber of Commerce and Industry', 14 November 2002; and Mark Vaile, Australian Minister for Trade, Media Release: 'Vaile Hails Breakthrough for Australia – US Trade Relations', 14 November 2002.
[23] DFAT, *Australia–United States Free Trade Agreement: Guide to the Agreement* (Canberra, March 2004), at p. 1; and DFAT, 'Australia–United States Free Trade Agreement: Call for Submissions', available at www.dfat.gov.au/trade/negotiations/us_aus_fta_public_submission.pdf (last accessed 4 April 2007).
[24] See www.dfat.gov.au/trade/negotiations/us_public_submissions.html (last accessed 4 April 2007).
[25] DFAT, *Guide to the Agreement*, above note 23, at p. 1.
[26] DFAT, *AUSFTA Briefing No. 1* (2003), at p. 1.

Arts (DCITA); Customs; Environment Australia; Health and Ageing (DOHA); Industry, Tourism and Resources (DITR); Intellectual Property Australia (IPA) and Treasury'.[27]

The second negotiating round took place in seventeen working groups and led to agreement on 'a broad working framework for the agreement, setting out its possible chapters'.[28] At a media briefing, chief negotiators from both sides expressed their desire for a comprehensive agreement by the end of 2003 and emphasized that the AUSFTA would not change the framework of Australia's Pharmaceutical Benefits Scheme[29] (discussed further below).[30] The third round focused on the provision by each side of market access offers for goods, services and investment and also achieved a 'composite text capturing the views of both parties on nearly all chapters'.[31] DFAT revealed that '[t]he initial US offer on agriculture was not as forward-looking as we had hoped, although the industrials offer had more positive elements'.[32] Following the fourth round of negotiations, which included three days on agriculture, DFAT indicated:

> Improved access for Australian beef, sugar and dairy will be essential elements of the agriculture package. . . .
>
> [T]he outcomes of an AUSFTA must not undermine Australia's capacity to continue to meet its social and cultural policy objectives, including maintaining local content rules and funding for Australian film production. . . .
>
> The issue of whether to include an investor-state dispute settlement (ISDS) mechanism in the chapter on investment in the FTA is still being discussed. The US has proposed that such a mechanism be included in the Agreement, but has not yet tabled draft text.[33]

During the fourth round of negotiations, the parties were somewhat more reluctant to reveal details of discussions on particular issues, although they indicated their confidence in reaching agreement and reiterated that they were making considerable progress.[34] The text of the AUSFTA was agreed on 8 February 2004 and then, in 'a departure from Australia's normal practice', released to the public before editing and signature.[35] This was an unusually fast negotiation – around one year from the

---

[27] Ibid., at p. 4.   [28] DFAT, *AUSFTA Briefing No. 2* (2003), at p. 2.
[29] DFAT, 'Media briefing on the second round of Free Trade Agreement negotiations between Australia and the United States, 19–23 May in Hawaii. Briefing conducted by Australia's chief negotiator Stephen Deady and the United States' chief negotiator Ralph Ives', 23 May 2003.
[30] See below section on 'Pharmaceuticals' under section IIIA.
[31] DFAT, *AUSFTA Briefing No. 3* (2003), at p. 2.   [32] Ibid., at p. 1.
[33] DFAT, *AUSFTA Briefing No. 4* (2003).
[34] DFAT, 'US–Australia Free Trade Agreement Negotiation Press Conference Embassy of Australia. Mr Ralph Ives – US lead negotiator and Mr Stephen Deady – Australian lead negotiator', 5 December 2003.
[35] DFAT, *Guide to the Agreement*, above note 23, at pp. 1–2.

start of negotiations until the completion of the final text: 'It does not happen much quicker when the governments of two complex economies seek integration'.[36] Nevertheless, more recently, the US reached an even faster agreement with Korea.[37]

According to one official, DFAT engaged in more consultation during the AUSFTA negotiations than it had in the previous ten years.[38] However, the AUSFTA has been subject to severe criticism, even apart from its substantive implications, due to the way in which it was concluded. In part this flowed from the Australian system of government, under which the executive branch negotiates and enters international treaties and the legislative branch subsequently implements those treaties through domestic legislation to the extent necessary.[39] Although some Parliamentary scrutiny of treaties occurs, this is usually only after Australia has signed the relevant treaty.[40]

The conclusion of the AUSFTA provides a typical example of the problems this approach may cause in practice. The Australian government agreed to the AUSFTA on 8 February 2004 and signed it on 18 May 2004; Australia's implementing legislation was passed in the House of Representatives on 24 June 2004. Parliamentary scrutiny, through the Joint Standing Committee on Treaties (JSCOT), did not commence until 2 April 2004, when it received its first official briefing on the AUSFTA.[41] That Committee concluded public hearings on 14 May 2004 and tabled its report in Parliament on 23 June 2004.[42] The awkward sequence of events is obvious: 'Within hours of the introduction of the JSCOT report's final presentation to the parliament, and without any debate or consideration of the report's contents, the implementing legislation had been introduced and passed'.[43] The report included a 'dissenting' portion by six members of the Committee (being those Committee members from the opposition: the Australian Labor Party), who:

> Believe[d] an extension of time should have been sought from the Minister for consideration of the Treaty to allow adequate time to review the evidence presented and to prepare the Report of the Committee. . . .
>
> Recommend[ed] that binding treaty action should not be taken until adequate opportunity ha[d] been given to consider the necessary legislative, regulatory and administrative action that underpins the implementation of

---

[36] Larry Crump, 'Global Trade Policy Development in a Two-Track System' (2006) 9(2) *Journal of International Economic Law* 487–510 at note 27 (see also p. 498).
[37] Office of the USTR, Press Release, 'United States and Korea Conclude Historic Trade Agreement', 2 April 2007 (negotiations commenced in June 2006 and the agreement was completed in April 2007).
[38] Crump, above note 36, at p. 506.
[39] Australian Constitution, sections 51(xxix) and 61; see also, e.g., *Minister for Foreign Affairs and Trade* v. *Magno* (1992) 37 FCR 298 at 303 (Gummow J); and Commonwealth of Australia, *Final Report*, above note 17, at para. 2.12.
[40] Commonwealth of Australia, *Final Report*, above note 17, at paras. 2.17 and 2.30.
[41] Parliament of the Commonwealth of Australia, above note 16, at para. 1.10.
[42] Commonwealth of Australia, *Final Report*, above note 17, at paras. 2.6–2.8.   [43] Ibid., at para. 2.9.

the Treaty in order to ensure the combination of the Treaty and the associated domestic action is ... in the national interest.[44]

Evidently, the dissenting members' concerns went unheeded. State and territory governments in Australia also complained that they were excluded from too much of the negotiation, particularly in its final stages.[45]

Several members of the Senate Select Committee on the AUSFTA (which received more than 500 submissions[46] – far more than DFAT did before concluding the AUSFTA) called for further consultation and Parliamentary debate before the executive signs treaties (especially those involving trade) in future,[47] echoing several previous Australian Parliamentary bodies.[48] However, this Committee was also split along party lines, with these recommendations being endorsed by Labor Senators, and Committee members from the government and other parties making separate statements and recommendations.[49] Not surprisingly, the Australian government largely dismissed most of the Labor Senators' recommendations regarding the consultation process, stating:

> The Government considers that the objective of ensuring both that the Government is able to energetically pursue opportunities for trade growth, and that appropriate consultation on negotiating objectives is undertaken with the broader community, are best met by current Parliamentary and consultation processes and practices.[50]

Ann Capling points to the AUSFTA negotiation as an illustration of the continued 'democratic deficit' in Australian treaty-making, emphasizing the partisan nature of discussions on its benefits, including the JSCOT and Senate investigations.[51]

---

[44] Parliament of the Commonwealth of Australia, above note 16, at pp. 301–2.
[45] Ibid. at paras. 3.53–3.61; see also Commonwealth of Australia, *Final Report*, above note 17, at paras 2.51–2.61 and 2.68; and Parliament of the Commonwealth of Australia, House of Representatives Joint Standing Committee on Foreign Affairs, Defence and Trade, *Australia's free trade agreements with Singapore, Thailand and the United States: Progress to date and lessons for the future* (Canberra, November 2005), at paras. 2.9 and 2.11.
[46] See www.aph.gov.au/senate_freetrade/submissions/sublist.htm (last accessed 6 April 2007).
[47] Commonwealth of Australia, *Final Report*, above note 17, at paras 2.30, 2.38, 2.75–2.76 and 2.91–2.92, and pp. 228–9 (Recommendations 2–5 of Labor Senators).
[48] Commonwealth of Australia, Senate Foreign Affairs, Defence and Trade References Committee, *Voting on Trade: the General Agreement on Trade in Services and an Australia–US Free Trade Agreement* (Canberra, November 2003), at para. 3.91 (Recommendation 2); Parliament of the Commonwealth of Australia, Joint Standing Committee on Treaties, *Report 42: Who's Afraid of the WTO? Australia and the World Trade Organisation* (Canberra, September 2001), at paras. 2.124–2.128; and Commonwealth of Australia, Senate Legal and Constitutional Affairs Committee, *Trick or Treaty? Commonwealth Power to Make and Implement Treaties* (Canberra, November 1995), at para. 17.4.
[49] Commonwealth of Australia, *Final Report*, above note 17, at. pp. 241–85.
[50] Government of Australia, *Response to the Final Report of the Senate Select Committee on the Free Trade Agreement between Australia and the United States of America* (Canberra, 2006), at p. 3 (responding to Recommendation 3 of Labor Senators).
[51] Ann Capling, 'Can the Democratic Deficit in Treaty-Making be Overcome? Parliament and the Australia – United States Free Trade Agreement' in Hilary Charlesworth, Madelaine Chiam, Devika Hovell and

III Substantive obligations

A. Goods

Key disciplines and scope

Chapter 2 sets out the general obligations of AUSFTA Parties regarding trade in goods. The national treatment obligation of Article III of the General Agreement on Tariffs and Trade 1994 (GATT 1994)[52] is 'incorporated into and made a part of this Agreement'.[53] Essentially, this means that an AUSFTA Party must not subject products imported from the other Party to internal taxes or charges 'in excess of those applied . . . to like domestic products'.[54] In addition, more generally, an AUSFTA Party must treat products imported from the other party 'no less favourabl[y]' than 'like products of national origin in respect of all laws, regulations and requirements affecting their internal sale, offering for sale, purchase, transportation, distribution or use'.[55] Obviously, these obligations apply between the US and Australia anyway, since both are WTO Members.

Article XI of the GATT 1994 is also incorporated in the AUSFTA. Under Article 2.9.1 of the AUSFTA, neither party may 'adopt or maintain any prohibition or restriction on the importation of any good of the other party or on the exportation or sale for export of any good destined for the territory of the other Party' except in accordance with Article XI. Article XI includes allowances for '[e]xport prohibitions or restrictions temporarily applied to prevent or relieve critical shortages of foodstuffs or other products essential to the exporting' Party, '[i]mport and export prohibitions or restrictions necessary to the application of standards or regulations for the classification, grading or marketing of commodities in international trade', and certain '[i]mport restrictions on any agricultural or fisheries product'.

Pursuant to Article 2.3, the Parties agree to eliminate customs duties on 'originating goods of the other Party' (identified according to the rules of origin discussed below) in accordance with Annex 2-B and not to increase existing duties or introduce new duties on imports of such goods. Under Annex 2-B, some products already received and will continue to receive duty-free treatment, while others received duty-free treatment from the date the AUSFTA entered into force (1 January 2005). Duties on other goods will be progressively removed by 2009, 2013 or 2015.

The obligations regarding national treatment, import and export restrictions, and elimination of customs duties do not apply to certain measures specified for each Party in Annex 2-A. For the US, the exempt measures include 'controls by the

---

George Williams (eds.), *The Fluid State: International Law and National Legal Systems* (Sydney: Federation Press, 2005), pp. 57–79 at p. 60.
[52] LT/UR/A-1A/1/GATT/1 (signed 15 April 1994, in force 1 January 1995). [53] AUSFTA, Article 2.2.
[54] GATT 1994, Article III:2. [55] Ibid., Article III:4.

United States on the export of logs of all species'. For Australia, they include certain 'controls on importation of second hand motor vehicles' and certain 'marketing arrangements' for wheat, grain, sugar and rice. For both Parties, actions are exempt where they are authorized by the DSB. This would cover actions taken pursuant to DSB authorization to 'suspend concessions' following a failure to implement adverse recommendations or rulings of the DSB in a WTO dispute.[56]

Chapter 5 sets out the general rules of origin for goods under the AUSFTA.[57] In particular, these rules apply in determining whether a good produced in the territory of one or both Parties using some materials produced elsewhere is an 'originating good' and therefore eligible for preferential treatment under the AUSFTA. The key criterion for determining whether a good is an originating good is whether 'each of the non-originating materials used in the production of the good undergoes an applicable change in tariff classification'[58] as prescribed in detailed product-specific rules.[59] In other words, have the non-originating materials gone through a sufficient change within the territory of a Party to alter the tariff classification according to which they are imported and exported? A good that fails this test may still be an originating good if the value of non-originating materials used in its production is *de minimis*[60] or if the good 'otherwise satisfies any applicable regional value content',[61] based on certain specified methods.[62]

Although Australia had refused the 'change in tariff classification' system in the Singapore–Australia Free Trade Agreement,[63] the US apparently managed to persuade Australia to accept its approach.[64] Australian stakeholders have criticized the outcome as variously over-inclusive[65] and under-inclusive, as well as unduly complex and thereby increasing compliance costs.[66] However, over time, the change in tariff classification system has generally come to be regarded as more certain and less costly than alternative approaches. It is now widespread, appearing in the Thailand–Australia Free Trade Agreement,[67] and also the Australia New Zealand Closer Economic Relations Trade Agreement[68] (ANZCERTA) following a recent amendment.[69]

---

[56] Understanding on Rules and Procedures Governing the Settlement of Disputes (DSU), LT/UR/A-2/DS/U/1 (signed 15 April 1994, in force 1 January 1995), Article 22.6.
[57] Chapter 4 contains rules of origin regarding textiles and apparel.   [58] AUSFTA, Article 5.1(b)(i).
[59] Ibid., Annex 5-A.   [60] Ibid., Article 5.2.   [61] Ibid., Article 5.1(b)(ii).   [62] Ibid., Article 5.4.
[63] Signed 17 February 2003, in force 28 July 2003, Article 3.1.
[64] Crump, above note 36, at p. 496.
[65] Parliament of the Commonwealth of Australia, above note 16, at para. 5.51.
[66] Ibid., at para. 5.50; and Commonwealth of Australia, *Final Report*, above note 17, at paras. 7.71–7.72.
[67] Signed 4–6 July 2004, in force 1 January 2005.
[68] Signed 28 March 1983, deemed to have entered into force 1 January 1983.
[69] *Exchange of Letters constituting an Agreement between the Government of Australia and the Government of New Zealand to Amend Article 3 of the Australia New Zealand Closer Economic Relations Trade Agreement (ANZCERTA) of 28 March 1983* (Wellington/Canberra, 12–19 December 2006) [2007] ATS 2.

Agriculture

Article 3.3.1 of the AUSFTA prohibits export subsidies on agricultural goods destined for the territory of the other Party. The Parties also agree to 'work together to reach an agreement on agriculture in the WTO that substantially improves market access for agricultural goods, reduces, with a view to phasing out, all forms of agricultural export subsidies, develops disciplines that eliminate restrictions on a person's right to export, and substantially reduces trade-distorting domestic support'.[70] However, the impact of the AUSFTA on agriculture is restricted because safeguard measures in the form of additional customs duties are allowed subject to certain conditions.[71] Further, the US retains the right to impose certain safeguards on horticultural products and beef, in particular circumstances set out in Annex 3-A.

Australia's tariffs on most agricultural products were already zero (although its quarantine system blocks many of them), and Australia agreed to eliminate the rest on agricultural imports from the US from the entry into force of the AUSFTA.[72] The US agreed to improve agricultural market access pursuant to several 'tariff rate quotas' under which limited quantities of imports of particular products from Australia are subject to preferential tariffs. The AUSFTA creates several new duty-free quotas (that is, tariff rate quotas with an in-quota tariff rate of zero) and progressively reduces the out of quota tariff rates for several agricultural products. The duty-free quota for beef will be very slowly increased to an unlimited amount and the out of quota tariff eliminated over seventeen to eighteen years.[73] Similarly long transition periods apply to the duty-free quotas for peanuts, tobacco, cotton and avocados until unlimited amounts are allowed free of duty.[74] The limited increase over time in duty-free quotas for dairy products and the absence of change in the out of quota tariff rate for most dairy products[75] may reflect US concerns about the effects of opening its dairy market to Australian producers. However, some research suggests these potential effects were exaggerated.[76]

According to Larry Crump, who interviewed 35 of the total of 150 AUSFTA negotiators, as well as other government officials and diplomats who 'did not sit at the table' but were involved in the negotiations,[77] '[a]griculture was the major AUSFTA issue for Australia', and Australia's most significant agricultural exports to

---

[70] AUSFTA, Article 3.1.1.   [71] Ibid., Article 3.4.
[72] Ibid., Article 2.3.1, Annex 2-B (Tariff Schedule of Australia).
[73] Ibid., Annex 2-B (General Notes to the Tariff Schedule of the US, para. 4(d), and Annex I, paras. 2 and 3).
[74] Ibid., Annex 2-B (General Notes to the Tariff Schedule of the US, Annex I, paras. 22–6).
[75] Ibid., Annex 2-B (General Notes to the Tariff Schedule of the US, Annex I, paras. 4–21 and 27).
[76] See generally Julian Alston, Joseph V. Balagtas, Henrich Brunke and Daniel A. Sumner, 'Supply and Demand for Commodity Components: Implications of Free Trade Versus the AUSFTA for the US Dairy Industry' (2006) 50(2) *Australian Journal of Agricultural and Resource Economics* 131–52.
[77] Crump, above note 36, at pp. 491–2 and 498.

the US are sugar, beef, and dairy products.[78] The importance of sugar to Australia is reflected in Australia's objectives in negotiating the AUSFTA, as identified in 2003. Then Minister for Trade Mark Vaile singled out sugar as one of five exports in relation to which Australia sought to remove tariff rate quota restrictions imposed by the US.[79]

Yet the AUSFTA does not improve Australia's market access for sugar, for example by increasing the lower tariff rate quota for Australian sugar exports to the US or reducing out of quota tariffs.[80] In explaining the exclusion of sugar from the agreement, DFAT maintains that it was '[f]aced with a decision of whether to walk away from the negotiations' and that 'the Government decided that the potential benefits from AUSFTA as a whole did not justify denying those benefits to the rest of the Australian community for the sake of one – albeit very important – agricultural sub-sector'.[81] In recognition of the AUSFTA's failure to realize expected gains in this sector, Australia has since provided a AU$444 million 'compensation package' to the sugar industry[82] ('a transfer from taxpayers to sugar producers'[83] that was not factored in to government calculations of the benefits to Australia of entering the AUSFTA).[84] However, Australia's capitulation on sugar was not necessarily a prerequisite to entering an FTA with the US, which has provided for a phasing in of unlimited duty-free sugar imports in FTAs with Singapore[85] and Chile[86] as well as steady increases in duty-free sugar imports from more competitive sugar-producing countries[87] of Central America.[88]

Philippa Dee notes that Australia's final stance on sugar under the AUSFTA contrasts with its position in the WTO, in particular its rejection of the proposal by the US and the European Communities on agriculture at the Fifth WTO Ministerial

---

[78] Ibid., at p. 496. [79] DFAT, *Guide to the Agreement*, above note 23, at p. 125.
[80] See ibid., at p. 16; and Centre for International Economics, *Economic Analysis of AUSFTA: Impact of the bilateral free trade agreement with the United States prepared for Department of Foreign Affairs and Trade* (2004), at p. 13.
[81] DFAT, 'AUSFTA: Frequently Asked Questions', available at www.dfat.gov.au/trade/negotiations/us_fta/faqs.html (last accessed 8 March 2007).
[82] Commonwealth of Australia, *Final Report*, above note 17, at para. 10.20; and John Howard, Prime Minister of Australia, Media Release: 'Sugar Industry Reform Programme', 29 April 2004.
[83] Philippa Dee, *The Australia – US Free Trade Agreement: An Assessment*, Pacific Economic Papers No. 345 (Canberra: Australian National University, 2005), at p. 22.
[84] Commonwealth of Australia, *Final Report*, above note 17, at paras. 7.67 and 7.68.
[85] United States–Singapore Free Trade Agreement (signed 6 May 2003, in force 1 January 2004), Annex 2B (Schedule of the US), Annex 1, para. 9(a).
[86] United States–Chile Free Trade Agreement (signed 6 June 2003, in force 1 January 2004), Annex 3.3 (General Notes: Tariff Schedule of the US), para. 9(a).
[87] Dee, above note 83, at p. 36 note 24 (referring to Costa Rica, El Salvador, Guatemala, Honduras and Nicaragua).
[88] Central America–Dominican Republic–United States Free Trade Agreement (CAFTA–DR–US) (signed 5 August 2004, in force for the US and El Salvador 1 March 2006, for Honduras and Nicaragua 1 April 2006, for Guatemala 1 July 2006, and for the Dominican Republic 1 March 2007), Annex 3.3 (General Notes: Tariff Schedule of the US) Appendix I, para. 3(a).

Conference held in Cancún in September 2003,[89] which she considers could have benefited Australia much more than the AUSFTA.[90] The importance of sugar for Australia is also revealed in its forceful challenge (together with Brazil and Thailand) under the WTO dispute settlement system of *EC–Export Subsidies on Sugar*.[91] Against this background, Australia's Joint Standing Committee on Treaties described the AUSFTA exclusion of sugar as 'disappointing' and recommended that Australia 'actively pursue . . . increased market access for Australian sugar into the United States' 'through all available channels and in all available fora including the Doha Round'.[92] But, despite DFAT's assurances to the contrary,[93] some query whether Australia's surrender on sugar in the AUSFTA may weaken its position when negotiating on agriculture in this Round.[94]

Pharmaceuticals

Australia's Pharmaceutical Benefits Scheme (PBS) was a sensitive issue for both countries during the AUSFTA negotiations. Australians were very keen to retain the scheme unchanged, while the US sought 'improvements' in this area.[95] The PBS is governed by the National Health Act 1953 (Cth) and associated regulations. Consumers pay a maximum amount for most medicines listed under the PBS, with the remainder of the price of the medicine being funded by an Australian government subsidy. The government currently spends around AU$6 billion on this scheme.[96] The Pharmaceutical Benefits Advisory Committee assesses applications to list drugs under the PBS (taking into account 'the effectiveness and cost of therapy involving the use of the drug . . . including by comparing the effectiveness and cost of that therapy with that of alternative therapies, whether or not involving the use of other drugs')[97] and makes corresponding recommendations to the Minister.[98] The Pharmaceutical Benefits Pricing Authority (an 'independent non-statutory body') reviews prices of items listed under the PBS 'to secure a reliable supply of pharmaceutical products at the most reasonable cost to Australian taxpayers and

---

[89] See ICTSD, *Agriculture Negotiations at the WTO: Post-Cancun Outlook Report* (Geneva: ICTSD, November 2003), at p. 14.
[90] Dee, above note 83, at pp. 13 and 38–9. [91] Appellate Body Report, *EC–Export Subsidies on Sugar*.
[92] Parliament of the Commonwealth of Australia, above note 16, at paras. 7.32, 7.35 and 7.37 (Recommendation 7).
[93] Commonwealth of Australia, *Final Report*, above note 17, at paras. 10.22–10.27.
[94] Ibid., at para. 10.21. Others suggest that the AUSFTA negotiation itself diverted Australia's negotiating resources and attention away from the discussions on agriculture in Cancún: Crump, above note 36, at pp. 506 and 507 (citing a 'Counsellor to the Delegation of the European Commission to Australia and New Zealand'); cf. Alan Oxley, *Free Trade Agreements in the era of globalization: new instruments to advance new interests – the case of Australia*, APEC Study Centre, Issues Paper No. 22 (2002), at p. 19.
[95] Commonwealth of Australia, *Voting on Trade*, above note 48, at paras. 6.90–6.98.
[96] Pharmaceutical Benefits Scheme, Data and Modelling Section Pharmaceutical Policy and Analysis Branch, *Expenditure and prescriptions twelve months to 30 June 2006* (Canberra, 2006), at p. 1.
[97] National Health Act 1953 (Cth), s. 101(3A). [98] Ibid., s. 101(3).

consumers and consistent with maintaining a sustainable pharmaceutical industry in Australia'.[99]

From the Australian government's perspective, the PBS is designed not to restrict trade but to ensure Australians have access to affordable medicines.[100] Indeed, it has been described as 'a highly effective and efficient public policy device that provides Australian citizens with some of the lowest pharmaceutical prices in the developed world'.[101] From the perspective of US drug manufacturers, the PBS interferes with market pricing and precludes sufficient rewards to encourage or fund research and development, leaving consumers in countries with higher priced drugs, such as the US, to subsidize Australian consumers in this regard.[102]

The AUSFTA contains obligations regarding pharmaceuticals and the PBS primarily in Annex 2-C (the goods chapter), an exchange of side letters, and Chapter 17 (the intellectual property chapter, as discussed further below). The concrete obligations relevant to the PBS in Annex 2-C include providing greater transparency and procedural fairness, for example by providing an 'independent review process' on request by applicants affected by recommendations or determinations.[103] Australia's Minister for Health and Ageing released details in February 2005 of how the independent review would work.[104] The Parties also agree to greater coordination between their relevant administrative bodies 'with a view to making innovative medical products more quickly available to their nationals'.[105]

Under the side letters, Australia provides several additional assurances to the US with express reference to the PBS. In particular, Australia agrees to grant procedural rights to applicants seeking to have a pharmaceutical listed under the PBS such as 'an opportunity to consult relevant officials prior to submission of an application for listing'. Australia also agrees to 'reduce the time required to implement

---

[99] Pharmaceutical Benefits Pricing Authority, *Annual Report for the Year Ended 30 June 2006* (Canberra: Commonwealth of Australia, 2006), at pp. 1 and 4.
[100] Commonwealth of Australia, *Voting on Trade*, above note 48 at para. 6.93 (quoting Minister for Health and Ageing, Tony Abbott in 'Drugs Threaten US Trade Deal', *The Australian*, 27 October 2003).
[101] Clive Hamilton, Buddhima Lokuge and Richard Denniss, 'Barrier to Trade or Barrier to Profit? Why Australia's Pharmaceutical Benefits Scheme Worries U.S. Drug Companies' (2004) 4(2) *Yale Journal of Health Policy, Law & Ethics* 373–85 at 382.
[102] Peter Sainsbury, 'Australia – United States Free Trade Agreement and the Australian Pharmaceutical Benefits Scheme' (2004) 4(2) *Yale Journal of Health Policy, Law & Ethics* 387–99 at 390. See also Maurice Rickard, 'Free Trade Negotiations, the PBS, and Pharmaceutical Prices', Parliament of Australia Research Note No. 32 (10 February 2004).
[103] AUSFTA, Annex 2-C, para. 2(f).
[104] Tony Abbott, Australian Minister for Health and Ageing, 'Australia – United States Free Trade Agreement (AUSFTA) & the Pharmaceutical Benefits Scheme (PBS): Statement on the Implementation of Australia's AUSFTA Commitments', February 2005, attached to Tony Abbott, Australian Minister for Health and Ageing, Media Release: 'Australia–United States Free Trade Agreement and the Pharmaceutical Benefits Scheme', 4 February 2005.
[105] AUSFTA, Annex 2-C, para. 4.

recommendations ... where possible' and to 'provide opportunities to apply for an adjustment to the price of a pharmaceutical under the PBS'.[106]

According to Crump, '[t]he US was very unsatisfied with this outcome, just as Australia was very unsatisfied with the outcome in agriculture'.[107] This is consistent with one commentator's conclusion that '[t]he fundamental principles that support the PBS remain virtually untouched by the *AUSFTA* and nothing can be read into the agreement that impairs Australia's ability to deliver fundamental healthcare policy objectives'.[108] Not surprisingly, the Australian government has emphasized that the AUSFTA did not require changes to the National Health Act 1953 (Cth) and that the changes that the AUSFTA did require actually improve the PBS by making it 'more accountable and more transparent for all stakeholders'.[109] Nevertheless, some regard the AUSFTA outcome for the PBS (or the fact that provisions relating to the PBS were included at all) as 'a major concession to the United States brand name pharmaceutical industry'.[110]

B. Services

Key disciplines and scope

Chapter 10 of the AUSFTA 'applies to measures adopted or maintained by a Party affecting cross-border trade in services by service suppliers of the other Party'.[111] Certain areas are excluded from this broad scope, such as air services. Like the General Agreement on Trade in Services (GATS),[112] Chapter 10 does not apply to 'services supplied in the exercise of governmental authority'[113] or government procurement,[114] nor does it impose obligations 'with respect to a national of the other Party seeking access to its employment market, or employed on a permanent

---

[106] Side letters from Mark Vaile (Australian Minister for Trade) to Robert Zoellick (USTR) and from Robert Zoellick to Mark Vaile dated 18 May 2004.
[107] Crump, above note 36, at p. 496.
[108] Bryan Mercurio, 'The Impact of the Australia–United States Free Trade Agreement on the Provision of Health Services in Australia' (2005) 26(4) *Whittier Law Review* 1051–100, at 1096.
[109] Abbott, Media Release, above note 104.
[110] Thomas A. Faunce, Kellie Johnston and Hilary Bambrick, 'The Trans-Tasman Therapeutic Products Authority: Potential AUSFTA Impacts on Safety and Cost-Effectiveness Regulation for Medicines and Medical Devices in New Zealand' (2006) 37(3) *Victoria University of Wellington Law Review* 365–90 at 366. See also Thomas A. Faunce, *Pharmaceutical Innovation in the AUSFTA: Implications for Public Health Policy in the US and Australia* (Canberra: Centre for Governance of Knowledge and Development, Australian National University, 2005), at p. 2; and Peter Drahos, Buddhima Lokuge, Tom A. Faunce, Martyn Goddard and David Henry, 'Pharmaceuticals, Intellectual Property and Free Trade: The Case of the US – Australia Free Trade Agreement' (2004) 22(3) *Prometheus* 243–57 at 246–7.
[111] AUSFTA, Article 10.1.1.
[112] LT/UR/A-1B/S/1 (signed 15 April 1994, in force 1 January 1995).
[113] AUSFTA, Articles 1.2.22 and 10.1.4(e); cf. GATS, Articles I.1, I.3(b) and I.3(c).
[114] AUSFTA, Article 10.1.4(b); cf. GATS, Article XIII:1 (excluding government procurement from the obligations of national treatment, MFN treatment, and market access).

basis in its territory'.[115] Unlike the GATS, Chapter 10 specifically excludes subsidies from its scope.[116]

The general approach of Chapter 10 involves a 'negative list' or 'top down' approach. In other words, the basic disciplines on trade in services apply to measures in all service sectors except where expressly excluded. The same approach applies in GATS with respect to the most favoured nation (MFN) obligation.[117] However, under GATS, national treatment and market access apply according to a 'positive list' or 'bottom up' approach, i.e. only in sectors for which and to the extent that the relevant WTO Member has included those commitments in its GATS Schedule.[118] This difference renders the services liberalization under the AUSFTA considerably more significant than that under GATS. Under the AUSFTA, a service sector or measure that is not mentioned is covered, whereas under GATS, an unmentioned sector is not covered by national treatment or market access. From an economic perspective, a negative list approach is generally preferable, but this may raise concerns about the compliance of future measures with the AUSFTA. In its report before the conclusion of the AUSFTA, the Foreign Affairs, Defence and Trade References Committee of the Australian Senate recommended against negative lists in future bilateral FTAs,[119] stating:

> A small error in the wording of a reservation, or an unanticipated technological development, or the devising of an entirely new service of major significance, could easily result in a country being deprived of the right, and a future government of its responsibility, to make policies about, and to regulate, that service in the national interest.

The primary AUSFTA disciplines on services are MFN treatment[120] and national treatment[121] (that is, respectively, according the other Party's service suppliers treatment no less favourable than that accorded to a non-Party's service suppliers or to a Party's own service suppliers in like circumstances). In addition, the obligation regarding local presence states that a Party may not require a service supplier of the other Party to establish an enterprise or to be resident in its territory as a condition for supplying cross-border services.[122] Finally, the market access obligation prohibits Parties from maintaining measures that limit the supply of services, for example limitations on the number of service suppliers, the total value of service transactions or assets, the total number of service operations, or the total number of natural persons who may be employed in a particular service sector.[123] At the same

---

[115] AUSFTA, Article 10.1.5; cf. GATS, Annex on Movement of Natural Persons Supplying Services under the Agreement, para. 2.
[116] AUSFTA, Article 10.1.4(d); cf. GATS, Article XV. [117] GATS, Article II.
[118] Ibid., Articles XVI:1 and XVII:1.
[119] Commonwealth of Australia, *Voting on Trade*, above note 48, at para. 6.89 (Recommendation 12).
[120] AUSFTA, Article 10.3. [121] Ibid., Article 10.2. [122] Ibid., Article 10.5. [123] Ibid., Article 10.4(a).

time, Parties may not 'restrict or require specific types of legal entity or joint venture through which a service supplier may supply a service'.[124]

In accordance with the negative list approach, the key services disciplines regarding MFN treatment, national treatment, local presence[125] and market access do not apply to 'existing non-conforming measures' that a Party maintains either at a local level of government or the central or a regional level of government to the extent set out in the Party's Schedule to Annex I[126] (with both Parties scheduling all existing non-conforming measures maintained at the regional level).[127] A 'ratchet' mechanism applies to these non-conforming measures,[128] such that if a Party amends a non-conforming measure to make it conform more closely with the relevant AUSFTA obligations, the exception continues to apply to the amended non-conforming measure. However, the exception will no longer apply to a non-conforming measure that is amended to become less conforming at any time.[129] Thus, in the words of DFAT, 'the liberalized measure becomes "bound" as part of the Agreement's treaty commitments'.[130] These key disciplines also do not apply to measures that a Party adopts with respect to sectors or activities as set out in its Schedule to Annex II.

Audiovisual services

Australia's Schedules to both Annex I and Annex II include reservations regarding measures affecting audiovisual services. Under Annex I, Australia includes as a non-conforming measure (contrary to the national treatment obligation) '[t]ransmission quotas for local content imposed on free-to-air commercial analogue and digital ... television broadcasting services ... up to 55 percent of programming transmitted annually between 6:00 a.m. and midnight'.[131] Under Annex II, Australia reserves the right to adopt or maintain, inter alia:

- '[t]ransmission quotas for local content, where more than one channel of programming is made available by a provider of free-to-air commercial television broadcasting services';[132]
- in the case of subscription television broadcasting services, '[e]xpenditure requirements for Australian production not exceeding 10 per cent of total program expenditure';[133] and

---

[124] Ibid., Article 10.4(b).
[125] On the 'local presence' obligation, see above note 122 and corresponding text.
[126] AUSFTA, Article 10.6.1(a).   [127] Ibid., Annex I (Australia, 1) (US, 12).
[128] DFAT, *Guide to the Agreement*, above note 23, at p. 47.
[129] AUSFTA, Article 10.6.1(c).
[130] DFAT, *Guide to the Agreement*, above note 23, at p. 47.
[131] AUSFTA, Annex I (Australia, 14). As indicated above, if Australia lowers the local content quota it cannot subsequently raise it (see above notes 129 and 130 and corresponding text).
[132] AUSFTA, Annex II (Australia, 5).   [133] Ibid., Annex II (Australia, 6).

- in the case of free-to-air radio broadcasting services, '[t]ransmission quotas for local content'.[134]

Australia also reserves the right to maintain 'preferential co-production arrangements for film and television productions', whereby works covered by such arrangements will receive national treatment,[135] potentially contrary to the MFN obligation. Australia maintains similar MFN exemptions under GATS.[136]

The audiovisual industry was reported to create '[t]he most contentious services issue',[137] reflecting the long-standing problem of trade and culture.[138] Indeed, the Foreign Affairs, Defence and Trade References Committee explained that it had:

> encountered vigorous advocacy from screen writers, producers, artists and media workers in favour of strong protection for cultural policies such as quotas of Australian production in television and interests related to audiovisual services, copyright and the development and delivery of the so-called 'creative industries.'[139]

Although Australia abstained from voting on the new Convention on the Protection and Promotion of the Diversity of Cultural Expressions in the United Nations Educational, Scientific and Cultural Organization (UNESCO) and has not acceded to the Convention,[140] prior to and within the WTO it has supported the notion of some form of special treatment for trade in audiovisual services in recognition of their cultural value.[141] In contrast, in both UNESCO and the WTO, the US has long opposed singling out audiovisual services in this way.[142] Australia therefore

---

[134] Ibid., Annex II (Australia, 6). [135] Ibid., Annex I (Australia, 8).
[136] WTO, *Australia–Final List of Article II (MFN) Exemptions*, GATS/EL/6, 15 April 1994. See also WTO, Council for Trade in Services, *Australia: Revised Services Offer*, TN/S/O/AUS/Rev.1, 31 May 2005, at p. 67.
[137] Crump, above note 36, at p. 496.
[138] For further discussion of the trade and culture problem in the context of the WTO, see generally Tania Voon, *Cultural Products and the World Trade Organization* (Cambridge University Press, 2007); Tania Voon, 'A New Approach to Audiovisual Products in the WTO: Rebalancing GATT and GATS' (2007) 14(1) *UCLA Entertainment Law Review* 1–32; Tania Voon, 'State Support for Audiovisual Products in the World Trade Organization: Protectionism or Cultural Policy?' (2006) 13(2) *International Journal of Cultural Property* 129–60; and Tania Voon, 'UNESCO and the WTO: A Clash of Cultures?' (2006) 55(3) *International & Comparative Law Quarterly* 635–52.
[139] Commonwealth of Australia, *Voting on Trade*, above note 48, at para. 6.112.
[140] States parties listed at http://portal.unesco.org/la/convention.asp?KO=31038&language=E&order=alpha (last visited 8 April 2007).
[141] GATT, Uruguay Round Group of Negotiations on Services, *Working Group on Audiovisual Services, Note on the Meeting of 5 and 18 October 1990*, MTN.GNS/AUD/2, 20 December 1990, at paras. 3 and 5; and Australian DFAT, 'Australian Intervention on Negotiating Proposal on Audiovisual Services', Council for Trade in Services Special Session, Geneva, July 2001.
[142] GATT, Uruguay Round Group of Negotiations on Services, *Working Group on Audiovisual Services, Note on the Meeting of 27–28 August 1990*, MTN.GNS/AUD/1, 27 September 1990, at paras. 2 and 26; WTO, Council for Trade in Services, *Communication from the United States–Audiovisual and Related Services*, S/CSS/W/21, 18 December 2000, at paras. 7 and 10(ii); WTO, Council for Trade in Services, *Communication from Hong Kong China, Japan, Mexico, the Separate Customs Territory of Taiwan, Penghu, Kinmen and Matsu, and United States: Joint Statement on the Negotiations on Audiovisual Services*, TN/S/W/49, 30 June

appeared to 'win' this issue in the AUSFTA negotiations, although the US has agreed to similar exceptions in other FTAs as well.[143] Some doubts remain as to whether Chapter 10 applies to Australia's public broadcaster, the Australian Broadcasting Corporation, or whether that body falls within the exclusions for subsidies or government-supplied services.[144]

Telecommunications, financial services, and electronic commerce

Separate chapters apply to telecommunications,[145] financial services,[146] and electronic commerce.[147] The telecommunications obligations in Chapter 12 include ensuring that suppliers of public telecommunications services provide number portability for fixed telephony[148] and dialling parity,[149] as well as a number of obligations regarding the conduct of 'major suppliers' of public telecommunications services.[150] These kinds of provisions go beyond the basic prohibitions on discriminatory and trade restrictive government measures to address private conduct (which is also covered in Chapter 14 on 'competition-related matters', another example of how the AUSFTA extends beyond the WTO).[151] Chapter 13 imposes specific national treatment,[152] MFN treatment[153] and market access obligations[154] in relation to financial services, as well as additional obligations on matters such as cross-border supply of financial services[155] and additional exceptions for measures such as 'measures for prudential reasons, including for the protection of investors ... or to ensure the integrity and stability of

---

2005, at para. 4; UNESCO, General Conference, *Preliminary Report by the Director-General Setting out the Situation to be Regulated and the Possible Scope of the Regulating Action Proposed, Accompanied by the Preliminary Draft of a Convention on the Protection and of the Diversity of Cultural Contents and Artistic Expressions*, 33 C/23 (4 August 2005), at paras. 58, 59, 61 and 70; and Robert Martin, 'Final Statement of the United States Delegation', Third Session of the Intergovernmental Meeting of Experts, UNESCO, Paris, 3 June 2005.

[143] See, e.g., United States–Chile Free Trade Agreement (signed 6 June 2003, in force 1 January 2004), Annex I (Chile-3); and North American Free Trade Agreement (NAFTA), 32 ILM 289 and 605 (signed 17 December 1992, in force 1 January 1994), Annex 2106.

[144] Commonwealth of Australia, *Final Report*, above note 17, at paras. 6.43–6.47.

[145] AUSFTA, Chapter 12.   [146] Ibid., Chapter 13.   [147] Ibid., Chapter 16.

[148] Meaning 'the ability of end-users of public telecommunications services to retain, at the same location, existing telephone numbers when switching between suppliers of like public telecommunications services': AUSFTA, Article 12.25.11.

[149] Meaning 'the ability of an end-user to use an equal number of digits to access a like public telecommunications service, regardless of the public telecommunications service supplier chosen by such end-user and in a way that involves no unreasonable dialing delays': AUSFTA, Article 12.25.3.

[150] As defined in AUSFTA, Article 12.25.8.

[151] See generally Jane Rennie, 'Competition Regulation in SAFTA, AUSFTA and TAFTA: A Spaghetti Bowl of Competition Provisions' (2007) 13(2) *International Trade Law & Regulation* 30; Jane Rennie, 'Export Exemptions and the Australia–United States Free Trade Agreement: Legitimate Domestic Protections or Self-defeating Protectionism' (2006) 12(1) *International Trade Law & Regulation* 21; and Andrew D. Mitchell, 'Broadening the Vision of Trade Liberalisation: International Competition Law and the WTO' (2001) 24(3) *World Competition: Law and Economics Review* 343–65.

[152] AUSFTA, Article 13.2.   [153] Ibid., Article 13.3.   [154] Ibid., Article 13.4.   [155] Ibid., Article 13.5.

the financial system'[156] and 'non-discriminatory measures of general application taken by any public entity in pursuit of monetary and related credit policies or exchange rate policies'.[157]

The negotiation of Chapter 16 on electronic commerce caused some consternation in Australia, particularly because of its potential relationship with audiovisual services: 'If e-commerce is defined as "all digital products" this is a clear back door way to include cultural industries in a trade agreement'.[158] Article 16.4 does impose non-discrimination obligations (both national treatment and MFN treatment) in relation to digital products, which is defined broadly as 'the digitally encoded form of computer programs, text, video, images, sound recordings, and other products, regardless of whether they are fixed on a carrier medium or transmitted electronically'.[159] However, Article 16.4.4 makes clear that these obligations do not prevent Parties from maintaining measures pursuant to exceptions they have listed in the general services and investment chapters, 'including measures in the audiovisual and broadcasting sectors'. Also, perhaps recognizing the ongoing debate in the WTO over the treatment of audiovisual products,[160] a footnote emphasizes that '[t]he definition of digital products should not be understood to reflect a Party's view on whether trade in digital products through electronic transmission should be categorized as trade in services or trade in goods'.[161]

The second major discipline imposed in Chapter 16 involves an agreement not to 'impose customs duties, fees, or other charges on or in connection with the importation or exportation of digital products, regardless of whether they are fixed on a carrier medium or transmitted electronically'.[162] This corresponds with but goes significantly further than the WTO informal moratorium on imposing customs duties on electronic transmissions.[163]

C. Investment

> The loudly proclaimed benefits to Australia arising from a liberalised foreign investment regime and from dynamic productivity gains are based on a series of inferences and educated guesses.[164]

---

[156] Ibid., Article 13.10.1.   [157] Ibid., Article 13.10.2.
[158] Commonwealth of Australia, *Voting on Trade*, above note 48, at para. 6.121.
[159] AUSFTA, Article 16.8.4 (footnote omitted).   [160] See above note 138 and corresponding text.
[161] AUSFTA, Chapter 16, note 7.   [162] Article 16.3 (footnote omitted).
[163] WTO, Ministerial Conference, *Doha Work Programme: Ministerial Declaration Adopted on 18 December 2005*, WT/MIN(05)/DEC, 22 December 2005, at para. 46; and Sacha Wunsch-Vincent, *WTO, E-commerce, and Information Technologies: From the Uruguay Round through the Doha Development Agenda*, A Report for the United Nations Information and Communication Technologies Task Force (19 November 2004), at para. 40. See also Andrew D. Mitchell, 'Towards Compatibility: The Future of Electronic Commerce Within the Global Trading System' (2001) 4(4) *Journal of International Economic Law* 683–723.
[164] Commonwealth of Australia, *Final Report*, above note 17, at para. 8.52.

Key disciplines and scope

Chapter 11 on investment goes much further than the corresponding WTO provisions.[165] The whole of Chapter 11 of the AUSFTA applies to measures of a Party relating to investors of the other Party[166] (including nationals and enterprises)[167] or to 'covered investments',[168] which are very broadly defined as 'every asset that an investor owns or controls, directly or indirectly, that has the characteristics of an investment, including such characteristics as the commitment of capital or other resources, the expectation of gain or profit, or the assumption of risk', including assets such as enterprises, shares, intellectual property rights and construction contracts.[169]

Measures caught by Chapter 11 are subject to a wide range of obligations. The national treatment and MFN treatment obligations apply with respect to the 'establishment, acquisition, expansion, management, conduct, operation, and sale or other disposition of investments'. Thus, with respect to those matters, each Party must accord investors of the other Party and covered investments 'treatment no less favourable than that it accords, in like circumstances', to its own investors or their investments (national treatment)[170] and to investors of any non-Party or their investments (MFN treatment).[171] In addition, even apart from these non-discrimination obligations, each Party must accord 'covered investments treatment in accordance with the customary international law minimum standard of treatment of aliens, including fair and equitable treatment and full protection and security'.[172]

Chapter 11 also imposes significant prohibitions on performance requirements. In general,[173] this means that a Party may not impose requirements 'in connection with the establishment, acquisition, expansion, management, conduct, operation, or sale or other disposition of an investment of an investor of a Party or of a non-Party in its territory' to, inter alia, export a certain amount or proportion, use a certain amount or proportion of domestic content, or transfer a particular technology.[174] Additional prohibitions are imposed on conditioning the receipt of an advantage with certain other performance requirements.[175]

---

[165] See Agreement on Trade-Related Investment Measures, LT/UR/A-1A/13 (signed 15 April 1994, in force 1 January 1995).
[166] AUSFTA, Article 11.1.1(a).
[167] Ibid., Article 11.17.4. Nationals are defined to include permanent residents: AUSFTA, Article 1.2.16, Annex 1-A, para. 1.
[168] Ibid., Article 11.1.1(b).   [169] Ibid., Article 11.17.6.   [170] Ibid., Article 11.3.   [171] Ibid., Article 11.4.
[172] Ibid., Article 11.5.1 (see also Annex 11-A).
[173] This is subject to certain exceptions, including some analogous to those found in Article XX of GATT 1994; AUSFTA, Article 11.9.3(c).
[174] AUSFTA, Article 11.9.1.   [175] Ibid., Article 11.9.2.

Article 11.7.1 imposes the key discipline in relation to expropriation, as follows:

> Neither Party may expropriate or nationalise a covered investment either directly or indirectly through measures equivalent to expropriation or nationalisation ('expropriation'), except:
>
> (a) for a public purpose;
> (b) in a non-discriminatory manner;
> (c) on payment of prompt, adequate, and effective compensation; and
> (d) in accordance with due process of law.

As with the minimum standard of treatment, these conditions on expropriation are 'intended to reflect customary international law concerning the obligation of States with respect to expropriation'.[176] They also correspond in part to provisions in the Australian and US Constitutions. The former takes the form of a limitation on legislative power, in that the Parliament is granted power to make laws with respect to '[t]he acquisition of property *on just terms* from any State or person for any purpose in respect of which the Parliament has power to make laws'.[177] The latter forms part of the Bill of Rights, stating, 'nor shall private property be taken for public use, without *just compensation*'.[178]

Article 11.7 does not apply to certain actions taken in connection with intellectual property rights.[179] In addition, actions cannot constitute expropriation unless they 'interfer[e] with a tangible or intangible property right or property interest in an investment'.[180] A determination of whether an action constitutes an 'indirect expropriation ... requires a case-by-case, fact-based inquiry'.[181] In recognition of each Party's right to regulate within its territory for legitimate policy objectives, Annex 11-B makes clear that, '[e]xcept in rare circumstances, nondiscriminatory regulatory actions by a Party that are designed and applied to achieve legitimate public welfare objectives, such as the protection of public health, safety, and the environment, do not constitute indirect expropriations'.[182] This provision suggests that an action that adversely affects an investment will fall outside Article 11.7.1 as long as it is for a legitimate regulatory objective and is non-discriminatory. Of course, it may be difficult to distinguish legitimate objectives and to assess whether a given action is in fact designed and applied to achieve such an objective. Therefore, some investors may be put off by the apparent uncertainty that this provision introduces.

Chapter 11 also contains explicit exceptions for certain specified measures. Similar to the position under the services chapter, obligations such as those regarding national treatment, MFN treatment and performance requirements do

---

[176] Ibid., Annex 11-B, para. 1. [177] Australian Constitution, Article 51(xxxi) (emphasis added).
[178] United States Constitution, Fifth Amendment (emphasis added). [179] AUSFTA, Article 11.7.5.
[180] Ibid., Annex 11-B, para. 2. [181] Ibid., Annex 11-B, para. 4(a). [182] Ibid., Annex 11-B, para. 4(b).

not apply to 'existing non-conforming measure[s]' that a Party maintains either at a local level of government or at the central or a regional level of government to the extent that the measure is included in the Party's Schedule to Annex I.[183] Moreover, a ratchet mechanism similar to that under the services chapter also applies to investment measures.[184] These key obligations also do not apply to measures a Party adopts with respect to sectors or activities as set out in its Schedule to Annex II. Thus, Australia 'reserves the right to adopt or maintain any measure with respect to investment that accords preferences to any indigenous person or organisation'.[185]

Australia's non-conforming measures pursuant to Annex I include limits on foreign interests in Telstra (the country's dominant telecommunications provider, formerly a State monopoly), 'commercial television broadcasting licensee[s]', newspapers, and Australian international airlines including Qantas (the former State airline).[186] Furthermore, perhaps more controversially, the Parties agreed that Australia would list the non-conforming measure involving review by the Australian Foreign Investment Review Board (FIRB) of foreign investments in Australia. However, whereas previously the FIRB reviewed investments in businesses or corporations with assets valued at above AU$50 million, the deal struck under the AUSFTA meant that the FIRB would review such US investments only in certain sectors (such as telecommunications, transport, and military equipment) and in most other cases only where the relevant business or corporation had assets above AU$800 million (with both thresholds indexed annually).[187] Several Australians have raised concerns about this increased threshold, which they argue means that US companies may now acquire the vast majority of Australian companies without review.[188]

Investment disputes

On one view, the AUSFTA investment provisions are, in any case, 'largely unenforceable'.[189] In contrast to several other FTAs,[190] the AUSFTA contains no

---

[183] Ibid., Article 11.13.1(a).
[184] DFAT, *Guide to the Agreement*, above note 23, at p. 56; and AUSFTA, Article 11.13.1(c).
[185] AUSFTA, Annex II (Australia, 1).
[186] Ibid., Annex I (Australia, 13, 15–16 and 19–20). In relation to Telstra, see also side letter from Mark Vaile (Australian Minister for Trade) to Robert Zoellick (USTR) dated 18 May 2004.
[187] AUSFTA, Annex I (Australia, 2–5). See also side letters on the FIRB from Mark Vaile (Australian Minister for Trade) to Robert Zoellick (USTR) and from Robert Zoellick to Mark Vaile dated 18 May 2004; Foreign Acquisitions and Takeovers Regulations 1989 (Cth), reg. 13; and www.firb.gov.au/content/US_thresholds.asp (last accessed 29 May 2007).
[188] Commonwealth of Australia, *Final Report*, above note 17, paras. 8.38–8.40.
[189] William S. Dodge, 'Investor-State Dispute Settlement between Developed Countries: Reflections on the Australia–United States Free Trade Agreement' (2006) 39(1) *Vanderbilt Journal of Transnational Law* 1–37 at 26.
[190] See, e.g., NAFTA, Chapter 11B; Singapore–Australia Free Trade Agreement (signed 17 February 2003, in force 28 July 2003), Article 14; and Thailand–Australia Free Trade Agreement (signed 4–6 July 2004, in force 1 January 2005), Article 917.

mechanism for resolving disputes between one Party and the investor of the other Party regarding the second Party's AUSFTA obligations (that is, 'investor-state dispute settlement'). Article 11.16.1 merely provides that, if circumstances affecting dispute settlement under AUSFTA Chapter 11 change, the Parties should be open to consultations with a view to establishing procedures to allow an investor of one Party to submit a Chapter 11 claim to arbitration with the other Party. This provision does not prevent an investor of one Party from submitting to arbitration an action against the other Party to the extent already allowed under the second Party's domestic legal system.[191] However, this avenue is not generally available under US[192] or Australian law.[193]

Accordingly, for now, investor-state disputes have to be resolved through the general 'state-state' dispute settlement mechanism established for resolving AUSFTA disputes between the Parties.[194] In other words, Australian investors will need to rely on the Australian government to bring AUSFTA disputes on their behalf regarding US compliance with AUSFTA obligations, and vice versa[195] (a step that Australia may be unwilling to take in any given case, for a variety of broader political or diplomatic reasons unrelated to the particular dispute).[196] Moreover, the international rule on exhaustion of local remedies[197] would probably require these investors to seek a resolution through Australian courts (for example, under section 51(xxxi) of the Australian Constitution)[198] before resorting to state-state AUSFTA dispute settlement.[199]

DFAT contends that the Parties decided not to include an investor-state dispute settlement mechanism in the AUSFTA '[i]n recognition of the Parties' open

---

[191] AUSFTA, Article 11.16.2.
[192] Dodge, above note 189, at 25 (referring to United States–Australia Free Trade Agreement Implementation Act, 19 United States Code 3805 (2004), s. 102(c)(1)).
[193] See *Minister for Immigration and Ethnic Affairs* v. *Teoh* (1995) 183 CLR 273, paras. 25–9 and 34 (Mason CJ and Deane J), paras. 21–3, 29 and 32 (Toohey J), and paras. 3 and 6 (Gaudron J) (treaties that Australia has ratified do not create a direct and independent source of individual rights and obligations under Australian law, although domestic statutes and regulations are to be interpreted, to the extent consistent with their language, in conformity with international law. In addition, treaties may affect the development of the common law in Australia, and ratification of a treaty gives rise to a legitimate expectation, in the absence of contrary statutory indications, that administrative decision-makers will act in accordance with the treaty.); cf. *Re Minister for Immigration and Multicultural Affairs ex parte Lam* (2003) 214 CLR 1, paras. 98–102 (McHugh and Gummow JJ), paras. 120–22 (Hayne J), and paras. 141–8 (Callinan J). See also Acts Interpretation Act 1901 (Cth), s. 15B(1).
[194] This mechanism is discussed in section IVB below.   [195] AUSFTA, Article 11.16.2.
[196] Dodge, above note 189, at 8–9 and 27–8.
[197] See generally C. F. Amerasinghe, *Local Remedies in International Law* (2nd edn, Cambridge University Press, 2004).
[198] This provision states that 'The Parliament shall, subject to this Constitution, have power to make laws for the peace, order, and good government of the Commonwealth with respect to: – . . . The acquisition of property on just terms from any State or person for any purpose in respect of which the Parliament has power to make laws'.
[199] Dodge, above note 189, at 22–3 and 26.

economic environments and shared legal traditions, and the confidence of investors in the fairness and integrity of their respective legal systems'.[200] Given significant US interests pushing for such a mechanism[201] (other than State government interests who may see investor-state dispute settlement as an intrusion into their spheres of autonomy),[202] this outcome is often perceived as a victory for the Australian negotiators.[203] Australia apparently feared having to defend before a supra-national tribunal large numbers of challenges by US investors[204] (the US being more accustomed to these kinds of challenges through its experience with the North American Free Trade Agreement (NAFTA)).[205] The question nevertheless arises whether Australia paid too high a price, in other areas of the agreement, for this perceived benefit, particularly given that neither US support for nor Australian opposition to an investor-state dispute settlement mechanism was uniform. Alan Oxley, for example, a former Australian Ambassador to the General Agreement on Tariffs and Trade 1947 (GATT 1947)[206] and GATT Chairman, argued vigorously for the inclusion of such a mechanism,[207] while Noah Rubins contends that 'political forces in the US Congress threatened to derail negotiations if investor-state arbitration provisions were not removed',[208] at least in part due to negative experiences in the NAFTA context.[209]

D. *Intellectual property*

> The negotiation between the US and Australia of a free trade agreement ... was a negotiation between the first and 15th biggest economies in the world. On the key issue of intellectual property rights one might have expected

---

[200] Australian DFAT, *Guide to the Agreement*, above note 23, at p. 59.
[201] See letters from Robert Zoellick, USTR, to Senator Robert Byrd and Dennis Hastert, Speaker, United States House of Representatives, 13 November 2002; William H. Cooper, *The U.S.–Australia Free Trade Agreement: Provisions and Implications*, CRS Report for Congress (Library of Congress, 12 January 2005), at p. 16; and Parliament of the Commonwealth of Australia, above note 16, at para. 4.22.
[202] Intergovernmental Policy Advisory Committee, 'The US–Australia Free Trade Agreement', Report to the President, the Congress, and the USTR (12 March 2004), at pp. 2, 6, 10–11 and 14–15.
[203] See, e.g., David Richardson, 'Foreign Investment and the Australia–United States Free Trade Agreement', Parliament of the Commonwealth of Australia Current Issues Brief No. 7 (8 March 2004).
[204] Commonwealth of Australia, *Voting on Trade*, above note 48, at paras. 6.130, 6.132 and 6.134(b); Dodge, above note 189, at 24–6; and Ann Capling and Kim Richard Nossal, 'Blowback: Investor-State Dispute Mechanisms in International Trade Agreements' (2006) 19(2) *Governance* 151–72 at 157–60.
[205] For more information on the US experience with dispute settlement tribunals under NAFTA, see www.naftaclaims.com/disputes_us.htm, a comprehensive website administered by Canadian trade lawyer, Todd Grierson-Weiler.
[206] LT/UR/A-1A/1/GATT/2 (signed 30 October 1947). [207] Capling, above note 12, at pp. 71–2.
[208] Noah Rubins, '*Loewen v. United States*: The Burial of an Investor-State Arbitration Claim (2005) 21(1) *Arbitration International* 1–36 at 34.
[209] Capling and Nossal, above note 204, at 161–5.

Australia to do better than Chile (47th), Jordan (90th) or Honduras (101st) did in their respective FTAs with the US. It did not.[210]

Intellectual property was the area in which the AUSFTA had perhaps the greatest impact on Australian laws, although the community protest may have been less pronounced than that in relation to agriculture and pharmaceuticals. It was a relatively one-sided outcome, in the sense that Chapter 17 significantly strengthens intellectual property rights, from which the US clearly has more to benefit than Australia, a net importer of intellectual property.[211] For example, in 2004, 1,170,447 patents for which applicants were US residents were in force. The corresponding number for Australian residents was 22,502.[212] Many of the provisions of Chapter 17 also required Australia to bring its intellectual property laws closer in line with existing laws in the US.

The AUSFTA exemplifies the trend towards 'TRIPS-plus' FTAs (particularly in FTAs of the US),[213] meaning FTAs including stronger or more rigorous intellectual property provisions than those contained in the Agreement on Trade-Related Aspects of Intellectual Property Rights (TRIPS Agreement).[214] Each TRIPS-plus FTA tends to increase the protection of intellectual property rights not only between the FTA partners but more broadly across the WTO Membership, because the TRIPS Agreement does not include a general exemption from the MFN rule[215] for FTAs of the kind found in GATT 1994 and GATS.[216] This means that, in general, a WTO Member that provides stronger intellectual property protections to one country must provide these protections to all WTO Members. This strengthening of intellectual property rights risks upsetting the delicate balance between providing sufficient incentives for innovation, on the one hand, and preventing anti-competitive conduct and ensuring access to new products and technologies, on the other.[217]

Chapter 17 has been described as 'the largest chapter in the AUSFTA in content and substance'.[218] It is not possible here to discuss all the important aspects of the chapter. However, we wish to mention a few of the chief provisions regarding copyright and patents from Australia's perspective.

---

[210] Drahos et al., above note 110, at 243 (footnote omitted).
[211] See generally David Richardson, *Intellectual Property Rights and the Australia–US Free Trade Agreement*, Department of Parliamentary Services Research Paper No. 14 (Canberra, 31 May 2004).
[212] World Intellectual Property Organization, *WIPO Patent Report: Statistics on Worldwide Patent Activities*, WIPO Publication No. 931(E) (Geneva: WIPO, 2006), at p. 35.
[213] See generally Carsten Fink and Patrick Reichenmiller, *Tightening TRIPS: The Intellectual Property Provisions of Recent US Free Trade Agreements*, World Bank Trade Note No. 20 (7 February 2005); and Bryan Mercurio, 'TRIPS-Plus Provisions in FTAs: Recent Trends' in Lorand Bartels and Federico Ortino (eds.), *Regional Trade Agreements and the WTO Legal System* (Oxford University Press, 2006), pp. 215–37.
[214] LT/UR/A-1C/IP/1 (signed 15 April 1994, in force 1 January 1995). [215] TRIPS Agreement, Article 4.
[216] See below section IVC.
[217] Fink and Reichenmiller, above note 213, at p. 8; and Richardson, above note 211, at p. 6.
[218] Commonwealth of Australia, *Final Report*, above note 17, at para. 3.1.

In relation to copyright, the TRIPS Agreement generally requires the term of protection of a work to be no less than 50 years from first authorized publication, where calculated 'on a basis other than the life of a natural person'.[219] However, as a result of the AUSFTA, Australia had to extend its term of copyright protection for literary, dramatic, musical and artistic works from 50 to 70 years after the death of the author or first publication.[220] The principal beneficiaries of this change are US copyright owners such as the Disney Corporation, yet it is difficult to see how it can affect their incentives to create.[221] Crump writes that a 'Senior Advisor to the Australian Prime Minister reported that this ... issue was sufficiently sensitive to include the judgement of the Prime Minister in the final decision'.[222] This is not surprising, given that the Australian government had previously accepted a recommendation by the Intellectual Property and Competition Review Committee that the term of copyright protection not be extended.[223]

The AUSFTA also imposes obligations in connection with civil and criminal liability for certain copyright-related breaches,[224] some of which Australia recently implemented.[225] For example, AUSFTA strengthens copyright protection by requiring the Parties to impose liability for circumvention of 'effective technological measure[s]', being devices intended to control access to protected works or copyright[226] and by establishing stringent conditions that internet service providers must fulfil if they are to avoid liability for copyright infringements.[227]

We turn to the impact of the AUSFTA on patents. One of the biggest concerns about the intellectual property chapter of the AUSFTA was that it would allow the pharmaceutical industry to engage in 'evergreening' or prolonged extension of

---

[219] TRIPS Agreement, Article 12.
[220] AUSFTA, Article 17.4.4; Copyright Act 1968 (Cth), ss. 33(2) and 33(3); and US Free Trade Agreement Implementation Act 2004 (Cth), Schedule 9, para. 120.
[221] Richardson, above note 211, at p. 14. For further discussion, see Matthew Rimmer, 'Robbery under arms: Copyright law and the Australia–United States Free Trade Agreement' (2006) 11(3) *First Monday* 1–45 at 5–12; and Matthew Rimmer, *The United States–Australia Free Trade Agreement & the Copyright Extension*, A Submission to the Joint Parliamentary Standing Committee on Treaties (12 April 2004).
[222] Crump, above note 36, at p. 505.
[223] Intellectual Property and Competition Review Committee, *Review of Intellectual Property Legislation under the Competition Principles Agreement*, Final Report to Senator the Hon Nicholas Minchin, Minister for Industry, Science and Resources, and the Hon Daryl Williams AM QC MP, Attorney General (Australian Capital Territory: Commonwealth of Australia, September 2000), at p. 13; and *Government Response to Intellectual Property and Competition Review Recommendations: Information Package*, p. 1, attached to IP Australia, News Item: 'Release of Government Responses to Recent Reviews of Intellectual Property Legislation', 28 August 2001.
[224] AUSFTA, Articles 17.4 and 17.11.
[225] Copyright Amendment Act 2006 (Cth); and Commonwealth of Australia, *Senate Standing Committee on Legal and Constitutional Affairs: Copyright Amendment Bill 2006 [Provisions]* (Canberra, 2006), at para. 1.2.
[226] AUSFTA, Article 17.4.7. See the discussion in Rimmer, 'Robbery under arms', above note 221, at 12–21.
[227] AUSFTA, Article 17.11.29. See the discussion in Rimmer, 'Robbery under arms', above note 221, at 21–9.

patent rights.[228] This concern stemmed in part from Article 17.9.8 of the AUSFTA, which requires Parties to allow adjustment of a patent term to compensate for 'unreasonable delays in [the] Party's issuance of patents' and, in the case of patented pharmaceutical products, for 'unreasonable curtailment of the effective patent term as a result of the marketing approval process'. This adds to the duration of patents even though Australia had already extended its patent term generally from 16 to 20 years upon the establishment of the WTO[229] and, subsequently, its pharmaceutical patent term for up to five additional years.[230]

The TRIPS Agreement obliges WTO Members to prevent 'unfair commercial use' of 'undisclosed test or other data, the origination of which involves a considerable effort' when they require the submission of such data as a condition of approving the marketing of certain pharmaceutical products.[231] The AUSFTA goes further, requiring Parties to prevent third persons (such as generic drug manufacturers) from marketing without consent the same or a similar product on the basis of such data for at least five years from the date that marketing approval is granted for the original product.[232] Parties must also prevent generic drug manufacturers from marketing generic products that are claimed in a patent without the patent owner's consent or acquiescence, for the term of that patent.[233] This may raise the price of PBS and non-PBS drugs in Australia and unnecessarily delay the introduction of generic versions of patented drugs as the patent reaches an end.[234]

The AUSFTA also prohibits parallel imports of patented products. In other words, each Party's laws must provide that the sale or distribution of a patented product outside that Party's territory does not necessarily exhaust the patent owner's rights in that product: the patent owner may prevent the importation of the product without its consent by 'plac[ing] restrictions on importation by contract or other means'.[235] This means that neither Party could in future allow parallel imports in the face of restrictions imposed by the patent owner without violating the AUSFTA, even though the TRIPS Agreement allows WTO Members to decide whether to adopt a national or international exhaustion approach.[236] Australia did not allow parallel imports of patented products anyway, but the AUSFTA now prevents it from reforming patent laws to do so.[237]

Finally, the AUSFTA restricts the circumstances in which a Party may issue a compulsory licence of a patent to enable a third party to manufacture or export

---

[228] Matthew Rimmer, 'The Jean Chrétien Pledge to Africa Act: patent law and humanitarian aid' (2005) 15(7) *Expert Opinion on Therapeutic Patents* 889–909 at 900–2.
[229] Patents (World Trade Organization Amendments) Act 1994 (Cth), s. 4.
[230] Intellectual Property Laws Amendment Act 1998 (Cth), Schedule 1.
[231] TRIPS Agreement, Article 39.3.   [232] AUSFTA, Article 17.10.1(a).   [233] Ibid., Article 17.10.4(a).
[234] Drahos et al., above note 110, at 250–1; and Mercurio, above note 108, at 1083.
[235] AUSFTA, Article 17.9.4.   [236] TRIPS Agreement, Article 6.
[237] Commonwealth of Australia, *Final Report*, above note 17, at pp. 259–60 (Australian Democrats Dissenting Report).

a product without the consent of the patent holder, for example to address a public health crisis within the territory of the Party or in another country. Whereas the TRIPS Agreement does not prescribe the circumstances in which a WTO Member may grant such a licence (provided that a number of stringent conditions are fulfilled, such as payment of adequate remuneration),[238] the AUSFTA precludes such licences except to remedy anti-competitive practices or 'in cases of public non-commercial use, or of national emergency, or other circumstances of extreme urgency'.[239] Again, Australian law did not make full use of the flexibilities built into the TRIPS Agreement in any case,[240] but the AUSFTA removes the possibility of doing so in future.[241]

In sum, the restrictions that the AUSFTA places on marketing approval for new products, parallel imports, and compulsory licensing all threaten to diminish the potential of generic pharmaceutical products to promote public health within and outside Australia. Ironically, this comes at a time when WTO Members have reached a crucial agreement on allowing compulsory licensing to enable manufacture and export of pharmaceutical products to address the public health needs of Members with insufficient manufacturing capacity in the pharmaceutical sector.[242] At the least, several of the AUSFTA's TRIPS-plus provisions seem contrary to the 'spirit of the Doha Declaration, and will limit the capacity of States to progressively realize the human right to health'.[243] Unlike some other FTAs of the US, the AUSFTA contains no side letter confirming the importance of public health and the intention not to interfere with public health objectives.[244]

As in the WTO, intellectual property rights are arguably out of place in an FTA, given that they are not necessarily trade-liberalizing.[245] On the other hand,

---

[238] TRIPS Agreement, Article 31(h).
[239] AUSFTA, Article 17.9.7. In contrast, Article 31(b) of the TRIPS Agreement provides that in those circumstances the Member may waive the requirement to 'ma[k]e efforts to obtain authorization from the right holder on reasonable commercial terms and conditions'. These circumstances are not a prerequisite to compulsory licensing per se.
[240] See Patents Act 1990 (Cth), s. 133 (as amended by Intellectual Property Laws Amendment Act 2006 (Cth), Schedule 8); and Commonwealth of Australia, *Final Report*, above note 17, at para. 4.119.
[241] See Rimmer, above note 228, at 902–3.
[242] WTO, Ministerial Conference, *Declaration on the TRIPS Agreement and Public Health Adopted on 14 November 2001*, WT/MIN(01)/DEC/2, 20 November 2001; WTO, General Council, *Implementation of Paragraph 6 of the Doha Declaration on the TRIPS Agreement and Public Health: Decision of 30 August 2003*, WT/L/540, 2 September 2003; and WTO, General Council, *Amendment of the TRIPS Agreement: Decision of 6 December 2005*, WT/L/641, 8 December 2005. See generally Frederick M. Abbott, 'The WTO Medicines Decision: World Pharmaceutical Trade and the Protection of Public Health' (2005) 99(2) *American Journal of International Law* 317–58.
[243] Carlos M. Correa, 'Implications of Bilateral Free Trade Agreements on Access to Medicines' (2006) 84(5) *Bulletin of the World Health Organization* 399–404 at 402. See also Fink and Reichenmiller, above note 213, at p. 3.
[244] As summarized in Fink and Reichenmiller, above note 213, at pp. 3 and 5.
[245] Thomas Cottier, 'The Agreement on Trade-Related Aspects of Intellectual Property Rights' in Patrick F. J. Macrory, Arthur E. Appleton and Michael G. Plummer (eds.), *The World Trade Organization: Legal,*

Chapter 17 may be seen as one of several areas in which the AUSFTA moves beyond trade liberalization and towards deeper integration through harmonization of regulations and the imposition of positive obligations.

Other such areas include telecommunications, as discussed above, competition,[246] labour and environment. In relation to the latter two areas, each Party agrees to 'strive to ensure that its laws provide for labour standards consistent with [certain] internationally recognised labour principles and rights',[247] to 'ensure that its laws provide for and encourage high levels of environmental protection',[248] and not to 'fail to effectively enforce' its labour or environmental laws 'in a manner affecting trade between the Parties'.[249] This differs considerably from the treatment of labour and environment in the WTO. Although WTO Members recognize the 'objective of sustainable development' and the need 'to protect and preserve the environment',[250] most concrete provisions regarding labour or environment in the WTO simply allow departures, in certain circumstances, from the usual WTO disciplines like national treatment and MFN treatment, for instance, for measures 'relating to the products of prison labour' or 'relating to the conservation of exhaustible natural resources'.[251]

IV. Implementation, impact and prospects

A. Economic and political effects and review

The AUSFTA is implemented and enforced by DFAT and the Office of the USTR.[252] A Joint Committee was established under the AUSFTA 'to supervise the implementation of this Agreement and to review the trade relationship between the Parties'.[253] The Joint Committee met for the first time on 7 March 2006 in Washington, DC, co-chaired by Mark Vaile (the Australian Deputy Prime Minister and, at that time, Minister for Trade) and Rob Portman (USTR).[254] At that meeting, the Joint Committee identified gains from the AUSFTA to date and reviewed

---

Economic and Political Analysis (New York: Springer, 2005), vol. I, pp. 1041–120 at pp. 1045 and 1054; and Richardson, above note 211, at p. 3.

[246] See above note 151 and corresponding text.   [247] AUSFTA, Article 18.1.2.   [248] Ibid., Article 19.1.
[249] Ibid., Articles 18.2.1(a) and 19.2.1(a).
[250] Marrakesh Agreement Establishing the World Trade Organization, LT/UR/A/2 (signed 15 April 1994, in force 1 January 1995), Preamble.
[251] GATT 1994, Articles XX(e) and XX(g).
[252] Committee on Regional Trade Agreements and Council for Trade in Services, *Free Trade Agreement between the United States and Australia: Notification from the Parties*, WT/REG184/N/1, S/C/N/310, 23 December 2004.
[253] AUSFTA, Article 21.1.1.
[254] 'Australia–United States Free Trade Agreement: Inaugural meeting of the AUSFTA Joint Committee', 7 March 2006, Washington, available at www.fta.gov.au/default.aspx?FolderID=416&ArticleID=992 (last accessed 2 March 2007).

bilateral discussions on specific areas that had been taking place since the AUSFTA entered into force, namely agriculture,[255] SPS measures,[256] professional services,[257] financial services,[258] competition law,[259] and medicines.[260] Unfortunately, the Australian Senate's Select Committee on the AUSFTA found little information available to it (let alone the public) regarding the work of the various monitoring groups established under AUSFTA.[261]

According to official reports following the Joint Committee meeting, the AUSFTA has led to substantial economic gains in both countries, including, from the Australian perspective: a 4.5 per cent increase in Australian services exports to the US in 2005; Australian export gains of 19 per cent to 229 per cent in industries from lamb and mutton to co-axial electric conductors; and the creation of a new E-3 visa category for Australians and their spouses to work in the US.[262] From the US perspective, the USTR reported a 10.9 per cent increase in US goods exports to Australia since the AUSFTA entered into force, including exports of pork, fruit and vegetables, rice, wine, machinery, trucks and parts, and aircraft.[263]

These official statements may not tell the whole story, just as Australian government studies supporting entry into the AUSFTA in the first place may present a skewed version of the numbers. For example, DFAT commissioned a study by the Centre for International Economics (CIE) that found that the AUSFTA would increase Australia's net national income by AU$359 million per year,[264] whereas Philippa Dee of the Australian National University (in a study commissioned by the Australian Senate's Select Committee on the AUSFTA)[265] made various criticisms of the CIE's modelling and calculated the gain as only AU$53 million per year.[266]

---

[255] See AUSFTA, Article 3.2 (Committee on Agriculture).
[256] See ibid., Article 7.4 (Committee on Sanitary and Phytosanitary Measures) and Annex 7-A (Standing Technical Working Group on Animal and Plant Health Measures).
[257] See ibid., Annex 10-A (Working Group on Professional Services).
[258] See ibid., Article 13.16 (Financial Services Committee).
[259] See ibid., Article 14.2.4 (Joint Working Group on Competition Law and Anti-Competitive Business Conduct).
[260] See ibid., Annex 2-C, para. 3 (Medicines Working Group).
[261] Commonwealth of Australia, *Final Report*, above note 17, at para. 1.56.
[262] See above note 254. In relation to the E-3 visa, see Department of State, 'Visas: Treaty Trader, Treaty Investor, or Treaty Alien in a Specialty Occupation', United States Federal Register, Vol. 70, No. 170 (2 September 2005) at p. 52292.
[263] Office of the USTR, Press Release: 'USTR Portman Meets with Australian Deputy Prime Minister Mark Vaile', 7 March 2006.
[264] Centre for International Economics, *Economic Analysis of AUSFTA: Impact of the bilateral free trade agreement with the United States prepared for Department of Foreign Affairs and Trade* (Canberra: CIE, 2004), at p. 82.
[265] Commonwealth of Australia, *Final Report*, above note 17, at para 1.71.
[266] Dee, above note 83, at pp. 24–33. Garnaut also identifies assumptions and limitations of the modelling exercises on which DFAT based its predictions: Ross Garnaut, *An Australia–United States Free Trade Agreement*, Australian National University School of Pacific and Asian Studies, Research Paper (2001), at pp. 14–16. Cf. Alan Oxley, *Free Trade Agreements in the era of globalization: new instruments to advance new interests – the case of Australia*, APEC Study Centre, Issues Paper No. 22 (2002), at pp. 12–15; and

'Overall', according to Siriwardana, 'there is a modest welfare loss amounting to U.S.$179 million to the world as a result of the AUSFTA'.[267] These are nevertheless prospective estimates, based on a number of variables and assumptions, and we may have to wait several more years to determine the full and precise impact of the AUSFTA on Australia's economy. Similarly, Australia's Joint Standing Committee on Foreign Affairs, Defence and Trade concluded in November 2005 that it was 'too early to assess the performance of Australia's free trade agreements' with Singapore, Thailand and the US.[268]

Certain areas covered by the AUSFTA may be subject to additional obligations, deeper integration, or at least further negotiations in the future. For example, the US has agreed to 'initiate a review of measures affecting cross-border trade in the higher education sub-sector for the purpose of providing greater transparency' with respect to certain States.[269] A side letter to the AUSFTA also identifies the 'shared objective of a more liberal air transport agreement between our two countries' and the US 'wish to promote continued liberalization in international air transportation bilaterally'.[270]

What about Australia's trade in its own region? On one view, from a diplomatic perspective, the AUSFTA 'send[s] a message across Asia that Australia remains largely a traditional trading ally of the western world'.[271] A concrete economic concern is that the AUSFTA will cause trade diversion, entailing increased imports from the US at the expense of more efficient producers (facing higher trade barriers) in Australia's Asian trading partners,[272] with Australian consumers benefiting from only slightly lower prices and all the tariff revenue forgone by the Australian government remaining instead with the US producers.[273] On the other hand, Australia has recently entered FTAs with Singapore and Thailand,

---

Australian APEC Study Centre, Monash University, *An Australia–USA Free Trade Agreement: Issues and Implications: A Report for the Department of Foreign Affairs and Trade* (Canberra: Commonwealth of Australia, 2001), at pp. 50–60.

[267] Mahinda Siriwardana, 'The Australia–United States Free Trade Agreement: An economic evaluation' (2007) 18(1) *North American Journal of Economics and Finance* 117–33 at 125.

[268] Parliament of the Commonwealth of Australia, House of Representatives Joint Standing Committee on Foreign Affairs, Defence and Trade, 'Australia's free trade agreements with Singapore, Thailand and the United States: Progress to date and lessons for the future' (Canberra, November 2005), at para. 2.1.

[269] Side letters on education from Mark Vaile (Australian Minister for Trade) to Robert Zoellick (USTR) and from Robert Zoellick to Mark Vaile dated 18 May 2004.

[270] Side letters from John Byerly (Deputy Assistant Secretary for Transportation Affairs, United States Department of State) to Peter Yuile (Deputy Secretary, Department of Transport and Regional Services) and from Peter Yuile to John Byerly dated 18 May 2004.

[271] Islam, above note 19, at 59.

[272] Mahinda Siriwardana, 'Australia's Involvement in Free Trade Agreements: An Economic Evaluation' (2006) 35(1) *Global Economic Review* 3–20 at 13; Siriwardana, above note 267, at 118–19 and 130; Garnaut, above note 266, at pp. 21–4; and Parliament of the Commonwealth of Australia, above note 16, at para. 2.33 (quoting submission by Garnaut).

[273] Dee, above note 83, at pp. 16–18 (see also pp. 37–9).

and it is currently negotiating FTAs with China,[274] Japan[275] and Malaysia.[276] In addition, Australia is investigating the possibility of an FTA with Korea,[277] and Australia and New Zealand have launched negotiations on a joint FTA with the Association of Southeast Asian Nations (ASEAN).[278] These steps may partially mitigate the political message of the AUSFTA (although not the problem of trade diversion).

B. Resolving disputes[279]

Disputes between the Parties regarding the existing AUSFTA rules are governed by Section B of Chapter 21. This section covers disputes 'regarding the interpretation or application' of the AUSFTA or where one Party considers that the other has failed to carry out its AUSFTA obligations or has adopted a measure inconsistent with those obligations.[280] Some matters are excluded from the dispute settlement system, for example certain competition-related disputes.[281] In addition, a form of 'non-violation complaint'[282] is contemplated in relation to the AUSFTA chapters on national treatment and market access for goods, agriculture, rules of origin, cross-border trade in services, government procurement, and intellectual property rights[283] (arguably among the most important chapters of the agreement).[284] Specifically, a Party may bring a dispute where it considers that a 'benefit' that it

---

[274] Memorandum of Understanding between the Department of Foreign Affairs and Trade of Australia and the Ministry of Commerce of the People's Republic of China on the Recognition of China's Full Market Economy Status and the Commencement of Negotiation of a Free Trade Agreement between Australia and the People's Republic of China (signed 18 April 2005), para. 3.

[275] John Howard, Prime Minister of Australia, Media Release: 'Australia–Japan Free Trade Agreement', 13 December 2006; and Joint Consultative Committee, *Joint Study for Enhancing Economic Relations between Japan and Australia, including the Feasibility or Pros and Cons of a Free Trade Agreement: Final Report* (December 2006). See also Ippei Yamazawa, 'Australia–United States Free Trade Agreement and its Implications for Japan', in Muhammed A.B. Siddique (ed.), *Regionalism, Trade and Economic Development in the Asia-Pacific Region* (Cheltenham: Edward Elgar, 2007), pp. 71–82.

[276] John Howard, Prime Minister of Australia, Media Release: 'Prime Minister of Malaysia', 7 April 2005; and Australian Department of Foreign Affairs and Trade, *An Australia–Malaysia Free Trade Agreement: Australian Scoping Study* (February 2005).

[277] Warren Truss, Australian Minister for Trade, Media Release: 'Australia–Korea FTA Study', 6 December 2006.

[278] Joint Declaration of the Leaders at the ASEAN–Australia and New Zealand Commemorative Summit (signed 30 November 2004), para. 2.

[279] See also the discussion of investor-state dispute settlement in section IIIC above.

[280] AUSFTA, Articles 21.2(a) and 21.2(b).   [281] Ibid., Article 14.11.

[282] This concept derives from the WTO. See generally Frieder Roessler and Petina Gappah, 'A Re-appraisal of Non-Violation Complaints under the WTO Dispute Settlement Procedures', in Macrory, Appleton and Plummer, above note 245, pp. 1371–87; Gail E. Evans, 'A Preliminary Excursion into TRIPS and Non-Violation Complaints' (2000) 3(6) *Journal of World Intellectual Property* 867–88; and Sungjoon Cho, 'GATT Non-Violation Issues in the WTO Framework: Are They the Achilles Heel of the Dispute Settlement Process?' (1998) 39(2) *Harvard International Law Journal* 311–56.

[283] These are Chapters 2, 3, 5, 10, 15 and 17 respectively.   [284] Dee, above note 83, at p. 2.

could 'reasonably have expected to accrue to it' under one of those chapters 'is being nullified or impaired as a result of a measure that is not inconsistent with this Agreement'.[285] This formulation broadly accords with the concept of non-violation as developed in the WTO, including the wording and interpretation of the equivalent WTO provisions.[286]

Aside from the provisions detailing the coverage of the dispute settlement mechanism, certain other provisions affect the scope of AUSFTA dispute settlement. First, an exclusive choice of forum clause provides that, once a Party has chosen the forum for settling a dispute arising under both the AUSFTA and another trade agreement between the Parties (such as the WTO agreements) by requesting a Panel under either agreement, the dispute settlement forum provided under the other agreement may no longer be used.[287] Second, neither Party may provide for private rights of action under its domestic law enabling claims that a measure of the other Party violates the AUSFTA.[288]

In certain respects, the AUSFTA dispute settlement mechanism mirrors that of the WTO. For example, disputes begin with mandatory consultations between the Parties[289] and may be resolved by Panels comprising three individuals appointed on an ad hoc basis,[290] who are to interpret the agreement 'in accordance with applicable rules of interpretation under international law as reflected in Articles 31 and 32 of the *Vienna Convention on the Law of Treaties*'[291] and then prepare an 'initial report' for consideration by the Parties, followed by a 'final report'.[292] If a Panel rules in favour of the complainant, the AUSFTA contemplates proceedings by the same Panel to determine whether the responding Party has complied with the ruling,[293] the provision of mutually acceptable compensation,[294] and the suspension of benefits by the complaining Party,[295] the level of which may need to be determined by the original Panel.[296]

However, dispute settlement under the AUSFTA is different from that under the WTO in several ways. After consultations and before the establishment of a Panel, the Joint Committee will attempt to resolve the matter.[297] Panel hearings are public,

---

[285] AUSFTA, Article 21.2(c). On the prevalence of and problems associated with non-violation complaint mechanisms in FTAs, see generally Locknie Hsu, 'Non-violation Complaints – World Trade Organization Issues and Recent Free Trade Agreements' (2005) 39(2) *Journal of World Trade* 205–37.
[286] GATT 1994, Article XXIII:1(b); GATS, Article XXIII:3; WTO Panel Report, *EC–Asbestos*, para. 8.283; WTO Panel Report, *Japan–Film*, paras. 10.41 and 10.61; and GATT Panel Report, *EEC–Oilseeds I*, para. 144.
[287] AUSFTA, Article 21.4.   [288] Ibid., Article 21.15.   [289] Ibid., Article 21.5 (cf. DSU, Article 4).
[290] AUSFTA, Article 21.7 (cf. DSU, Articles 6–8 and 11).
[291] AUSFTA, Article 21.9.2 (cf. DSU, Article 3.2); and WTO Appellate Body Report, *US–Gasoline*, pp. 16–7.
[292] AUSFTA, Articles 21.9.1, 21.9.3 and 21.9.4 (cf. DSU, Article 15).
[293] AUSFTA, Articles 21.11.3(b) and 21.13 (cf. DSU, Article 21.5).
[294] AUSFTA, Article 21.11.1 (cf. DSU, Article 22.2).
[295] AUSFTA, Articles 21.11.2 and 21.11.4 (cf. DSU, Articles 22.2–22.6 and 22.8).
[296] AUSFTA, Articles 21.11.3(a) and 21.11.4 (cf. DSU, Articles 22.6–22.7).   [297] AUSFTA, Article 21.6.

subject to the protection of confidential information.[298] This differs from the situation in the WTO, where Panel 'deliberations' and Appellate Body 'proceedings' are to be confidential[299] and only two Panel hearings have been partially open to the public by consent of the disputing Parties[300] (although Members including the US support a more open process in WTO dispute settlement generally).[301] The AUSFTA also has no equivalent to the WTO's Appellate Body.[302]

Implementation of adverse rulings under the AUSFTA also differs somewhat from the WTO system. AUSFTA Panels may only recommend how to resolve the dispute at the request of the Parties.[303] In turn, the Parties are to 'agree on the resolution of the dispute, which normally shall conform with the determinations and recommendations, if any, of the panel'.[304] However, normally the resolution would be 'to eliminate the non-conformity or the nullification or impairment',[305] which is similar to the usual requirement under the Understanding on Rules and Procedures Governing the Settlement of Disputes (DSU) to 'bring the measure into conformity' with the relevant agreement.[306] As an alternative to suspension of benefits, the AUSFTA provides for the non-complying Party to pay to the complaining Party an 'annual monetary assessment'.[307] Certain WTO Members have called for a similar system of monetary compensation in WTO dispute settlement,[308] which would at least remove the ideological and economic problems associated with suspending 'concessions' against a non-implementing Member (that is, the fact that this kind of retaliation is directly contrary to the theory of comparative advantage on which the WTO is based,[309] and that it hurts consumers and industrial users in the retaliating Member). However, some commentators 'argue that monetary assessments are typically very blunt and poorly targeted ways of correcting particular breaches'.[310]

---

[298] Ibid., Article 21.1(a). See also Bryan Mercurio and Rebecca Laforgia, 'Expanding Democracy: Why Australia Should Negotiate for Open and Transparent Dispute Settlement in its Free Trade Agreements' (2005) 6(2) *Melbourne Journal of International Law* 485–514 at 494–5.

[299] DSU, Articles 14.1 and 17.10.

[300] USTR, *Notice of Public Meeting in the WTO Dispute: European Communities and Certain Member States – Measures Affecting Trade in Large Civil Aircraft (DS316)*, available at www.ustr.gov/assets/Trade_Agreements/Monitoring_Enforcement/WTO_Airbus_ Case/asset_upload_file527_10870.pdf (last accessed 6 April 2007); and WTO, *United States–Continued Suspension of Obligations in the EC–Hormones Dispute (WT/DS320); Canada–Continued Suspension of Obligations in the EC–Hormones Dispute (WT/DS321): Communication from the Chairman of the Panels*, WT/DS320/8, WT/DS321/8, 2 August 2005.

[301] See, e.g., DSB (Special Session), *Contribution of the United States on Some Practical Considerations in Improving the Dispute Settlement Understanding of the WTO Related to Transparency and Open Meetings*, TN/DS/W/79, 13 July 2005.

[302] DSU, Article 17.   [303] AUSFTA, Article 21.9.2 (cf. DSU, Article 19.1).

[304] AUSFTA, Article 21.10.1 (cf. DSU, Articles 21.1 and 21.3).   [305] AUSFTA, Article 21.10.2.

[306] DSU, Article 19.1.   [307] AUSFTA, Articles 21.11.5–21.11.7.

[308] See, e.g., DSB (Special Session), *Negotiations on the Dispute Settlement Understanding: Proposal by the LDC Group*, TN/DS/W/17, 9 October 2002, para. 13.

[309] See generally Alan O. Sykes, 'Comparative Advantage and the Normative Economics of International Trade Policy' (1998) 1(1) *Journal of International Economic Law* 49–82.

[310] Dee, above note 83, at p. 11 (cf. p. 13).

Where the dispute arises from a Party's failure to enforce labour or environmental laws in a manner affecting trade between the Parties,[311] the monetary assessment may be up to US$15 million per annum (adjusted for inflation)[312] and is to be paid into a fund used for 'appropriate labour or environmental law initiatives, including efforts to improve or enhance labour or environmental law enforcement ... in the territory of the Party complained against, consistent with its law'.[313] This provision strengthens the AUSFTA's focus on labour and environmental matters as creating positive obligations rather than merely justifying exceptions from the usual trade liberalizing rules, as discussed above.

Several differences between the AUSFTA and the WTO can be seen as granting more power to the Parties rather than the Panels (which may be seen as quasi-judicial decision-makers, as in the WTO). This applies to the inclusion of the additional step of referral to the Joint Committee between consultations and Panel establishment, the absence of an appellate tribunal, and the general approach to leaving the resolution of the dispute to the Parties after the final Panel report is issued. These differences may make the AUSFTA a good illustration of William Davey's suggestion that 'WTO dispute settlement is viewed as more legitimate because it is less power-based and more rule-based than RTA dispute settlement'.[314] Although some WTO Members, such as the US in particular, continue to call for increased Member control over WTO disputes,[315] from the perspective of the rule of law this is undesirable. In this sense, the Parties' greater control of AUSFTA disputes may represent a move backwards, towards the more diplomatic system of resolving disputes under the GATT 1947.[316] And the beneficiary of a more power-based dispute settlement system under the AUSFTA will be, of course, the US (as it would be in the WTO).

C. Conformity with WTO rules

Turning to the broader WTO context, on 22 December 2004, the Permanent Missions of the US and Australia to the WTO jointly notified other WTO Members,

---

[311] AUSFTA, Articles 18.2.1(a) and 19.2.1(a).   [312] Ibid., Article 21.12.2.   [313] Ibid., Article 21.12.4.

[314] William Davey, 'Dispute Settlement in the WTO and RTAs: A Comment' in Lorand Bartels and Federico Ortino (eds.), *Regional Trade Agreements and the WTO Legal System* (Oxford University Press, 2006), pp. 343–57 at p. 356.

[315] See, e.g., DSB (Special Session), *Negotiations on Improvements and Clarifications of the Dispute Settlement Understanding on Improving Flexibility and Member Control in WTO Dispute Settlement: Contribution by Chile and the United States*, TN/DS/W/28, 23 December 2002; DSB (Special Session), *Further Contribution of the United States on Improving Flexibility and Member Control in WTO Dispute Settlement*, TN/DS/W/82/Add.1 and Corr.1, 25 October 2005; and DSB (Special Session), *Further Contribution of the United States on Improving Flexibility and Member Control in WTO Dispute Settlement*, TN/DS/W/82/Add.2, 17 March 2006.

[316] See generally, e.g., Joseph H. H. Weiler, 'The Rule of Lawyers and the Ethos of Diplomats: Reflections on the Internal and External Legitimacy of WTO Dispute Settlement' (2001) 35(2) *Journal of World Trade* 191–207.

pursuant to Article XXIV:7 of GATT 1994, the Understanding on the Interpretation of Article XXIV of GATT 1994, and Article V:7(a) of GATS, that they had 'signed and completed their respective domestic procedures for approval and implementation of the United States–Australia Free Trade Agreement'.[317] On 11 March 2005, the Committee on Regional Trade Agreements (CRTA) adopted terms of reference to examine the AUSFTA 'in light of the relevant provisions of the GATT 1994 ... and to submit a report to the Council for Trade in Goods'.[318] The Working Party will assess the consistency of the AUSFTA with Article XXIV of GATT 1994 (particularly paragraphs 5 to 8),[319] and the Council for Trade in Services has also referred the AUSFTA to the CRTA for examination under GATS[320] (especially paragraphs 1 to 2 and 4 to 6 of Article V). The secretariat's factual presentation reports regarding the goods and services aspects were released on 11 and 4 June 2007, respectively.[321]

Little WTO jurisprudence exists on the meaning of Article XXIV of GATT 1994 and Article V of GATS, probably because WTO Members prefer not to challenge each other's FTAs for fear of facing such challenges in return. Moreover, these provisions are exceedingly complex and ambiguous.[322] This makes it extremely difficult to assess with any certainty whether the AUSFTA complies with these WTO exceptions for FTAs. The two main conditions that the AUSFTA must

---

[317] Committee on Regional Trade Agreements and Council for Trade in Services, *Free Trade Agreement between the United States and Australia: Notification from the Parties*, WT/REG184/N/1, S/C/N/310, 23 December 2004. See also Council for Trade in Services, *Report of the Meeting Held on 9 February 2005: Note by the Secretariat*, S/C/M/77, 16 February 2005, paras. 8 and 10.

[318] Committee on Regional Trade Agreements, *Free Trade Agreement between the United States and Australia: Terms of Reference of the Examination*, WT/REG184/2, 21 June 2005.

[319] See, eg, *Working Party on the Enlargement of the European Communities: Accession of Austria, Finland and Sweden*, WT/REG3/1, 13 March 1995. On the many difficult issues surrounding the exception in Article XXIV of GATT 1994, see generally Nicolas Lockhart and Andrew D. Mitchell, 'Regional Trade Agreements under GATT 1994: An Exception and its Limits', in Mitchell, above note 3, pp. 217–52. See also James H. Mathis, *Regional Trade Agreements in the GATT/WTO: Article XXIV and the Internal Trade Requirement* (The Hague: TMC Asser Press, 2002); and Joel P. Trachtman, 'International Trade: Regionalism' in Andrew T. Guzman and Alan O. Sykes (eds.), *Research Handbook in International Economic Law* (London: Edward Elgar, 2007), pp. 151–76 at pp. 160–72.

[320] Council for Trade in Services, *Report of the Meeting Held on 9 February 2005: Note by the secretariat*, S/C/M/77, 16 February 2005, paras. 11 and 12.

[321] Committee on Regional Trade Agreements, *Factual Presentation: Free Trade Agreement between the United States and Australia (Goods) – Report by the secretariat*, WT/REG184/3 (11 June 2007); Committee on Regional Trade Agreements, *Factual Presentation: Free Trade Agreement between the United States and Australia (Services) – Report by the secretariat*, WT/REG184/4 (4 June 2007).

[322] See generally Lockhart and Mitchell, above note 319; and Mathis, above note 319. See also Trachtman, above note 319, at pp. 160–72; Sungjoon Cho, 'Breaking the Barrier between Regionalism and Multilateralism: A New Perspective on Trade Regionalism' (2001) 42(2) *Harvard International Law Journal* 419–65 at 450–2; and Roberto V. Fiorentino, Luis Verdeja and Christelle Toqueboeuf, *The Changing Landscape of Regional Trade Agreements: 2006 Update*, WTO Discussion Paper No. 12 (Geneva: WTO Publications, 2007), at p. 27.

satisfy to fall within the exception for a 'free-trade area' in Article XXIV of GATT 1994 are:

> [T]he duties and other regulations of commerce maintained in each of the constituent territories and applicable at the formation of such free-trade area ... to the trade of Members not included in such area ... shall not be higher or more restrictive than the corresponding duties and other regulations of commerce existing in the same constituent territories prior to the formation of the free-trade area ...[323]

> [T]he duties and other restrictive regulations of commerce (except, where necessary, those permitted under Articles XI, XII, XIII, XIV, XV and XX) are eliminated on substantially all the trade between the constituent territories in products originating in such territories.[324]

A conclusion as to the consistency of the AUSFTA with these conditions would require an economic analysis of the effect of the AUSFTA on duties and regulations of commerce imposed on non-AUSFTA WTO Members, as well as its effect on duties and regulations of commerce between the US and Australia. The exclusion of particular areas such as sugar from the AUSFTA and the absence of any agreement to refrain from imposing anti-dumping duties on each other's imports[325] mean that the agreement evidently does not eliminate duties and restrictive regulations of commerce on all trade between the Parties, but since elimination is required only with respect to '*substantially* all the trade', this would not necessarily prevent the AUSFTA from falling within Article XXIV of GATT 1994. Similar but potentially more flexible requirements apply under the Article V exception of GATS.[326]

V. Conclusion

A common sentiment in Australia regarding the AUSFTA is that Australians were the losers in the agreement and that the government surrendered more than was necessary in a bid for political favour with the US. This feeling, which stems largely from the substance of the bargain in areas such as agriculture and intellectual property, was exacerbated by the manner in which the Australian government appeared to rush the agreement through, paying insufficient attention to community interests and concerns. Although, in the end, Australia managed to retain the substance of public policy mechanisms such as the PBS and local content quotas for audiovisual services, while resisting the US push for an investor-state dispute settlement mechanism, this was not enough to satisfy many Australians of the worth

---

[323] GATT 1994, Article XXIV:5(b).   [324] Ibid., Article XXIV:8(b).
[325] See AUSFTA, Article 2.10.1. This differs from the situation, for example, under the Protocol to the Australia New Zealand Closer Economic Relations–Trade Agreement on Acceleration of Free Trade in Goods (signed and in force 18 August 1988), Article 4.2.
[326] GATS, Articles V:1 and V:4.

of the AUSFTA overall for consumer or industry welfare. Instead of highlighting the benefits of liberalized trade as a platform for more ambitious progress at the multilateral level, the AUSFTA may have made Australians wary of further FTAs, particularly with developed countries, as well as trade liberalization more generally, including through the WTO. It has not, on the other hand, curtailed the government's taste for FTAs. We can only hope, as some DFAT officials have assured us, that this was a unique deal based on the particular status of the US and not a preview of bilateral or multilateral agreements to come.

2

Central American–Dominican Republic–United States Free Trade Agreement

MAURICIO SALAS[*]

I. Introduction

The prehistory of the Central American–Dominican Republic–United States Free Trade Agreement (CAFTA–DR–US) can be traced back to the failed efforts of twice Secretary of State, James G. Blaine 'The Plumed Knight from Maine'.[1] At the close of the nineteenth century, Blaine actively sought to elbow out European influence in Central America[2] by the promotion of the then innovative devices of tariff reciprocity and arbitration treaties. Blaine also pushed hard for a meeting of Latin American leaders held in 1890 during his second tenure as Secretary of State, under President Harrison. The agenda of the meeting was dominated by trade issues.[3] Nothing much came of the meeting, and his tariff reduction project came to naught as a result of the McKinley Tariff Act. Nevertheless, the effort still stands out in the middle of this hundred-year period of United States–Central American history marked by direct military intervention and other forms of gunboat diplomacy.

After the 1898 Spanish–American war, the influence of the United States (US) in the region quickly began to overtake that of the United Kingdom (UK) and Germany, not only in geopolitical terms, but also in terms of trade and investment.[4] The UK's investment peaked in 1913, and by 1929 the US was the leading export market for most countries in the region.[5]

---

[*] The opinions expressed in this chapter are strictly of a personal nature. The author is grateful to Liz Westbrook for her help in preparing this article.
[1] David Healy, *James G. Blaine and Latin America* (Columbia: University of Missouri Press, 2001), at p. 252.
[2] Joseph A. Fry, 'Book Review, James G. Blaine and Latin America' (2003) 108 *American Historical Review* 202–3 at 202.
[3] Michael Devine, 'Was James G. Blaine a Great Secretary of State?' (2003) 27(5) *Diplomatic History* 689–93 at 691.
[4] See generally, Raymundo Brenes Rosales, *Antecedentes Históricos de las Tensiones Políticas en Centro América* (San José: Alma Mater, 1987).
[5] Walter La Feber, *Inevitable Revolutions: The United States in Central America* (2nd edn, New York: W.W. Norton & Co, 1993), at p. 62.

American investment not only grew in terms of quantity during the early twentieth century. It also had very different characteristics from European investment. Where UK investment had been mostly channelled in terms of government bonds and other financial instruments, the American investment was much more 'hands-on'.[6] Railway, mining and fruit companies appeared under strong-willed American entrepreneurs who moved in to undeveloped areas and directly exploited concessions. Such was the story of the pioneers of the banana trade: the Vacarro brothers and Samuel Zemurray in Honduras, and Minor C. Keith in Costa Rica.[7] The fruit companies in Central America were established on the sides of the new railway lines that penetrated virgin lands from coastal starting points, creating semiautonomous enclaves in those remote areas. The acquisitions and mergers of these entities in time produced the mighty United Fruit Company, which was influential not only in terms of trade, but also in regional politics.

Banana production, coffee beans and a few other exports of raw materials dominated Central American trade during the better part of the nineteenth century.[8] As was common in the developing world, local economies based on monocultures (disparagingly referred to as 'dessert economies'), were very susceptible to variations in international commodity prices. Regional efforts were made in the 1960s to reorient development towards the creation of a local industry base. The efforts were inspired by the development theories of import substitution formulated by Raul Prebisch and his group of Comisión Económica para América Latina y el Caribe (CEPAL) economists.[9] This led to the creation of the Central American Common Market in 1960.[10] The regional integration efforts were successful in increasing intraregional trade, and in creating a light industry base for manufacturing that was previously non-existent.

The upsurge of political violence during the 1970s and mid 1980s caused stagnation in intraregional trade,[11] and generally, in the Central American integration process. During this violent period, cold war issues dominated the regional agenda. It was at this juncture that the US passed the Caribbean Basin Economic Partnership Act of 1984 (the regulatory framework for the initiative known as the Caribbean Basin Initiative (CBI)). This unilateral grant of tariff free access is still in force today in an amended form.[12] CBI grants duty free access to a sizeable portion of the Central American exports destined for the US. CBI permitted the establishment of

---

[6] Rodrigo Facio, *Estudio Sobre Economía Costarricense* (San José: Editorial Costa Rica, 1972), at p. 53.
[7] La Feber, above note 5, at p. 43.   [8] Facio, above note 6, at p. 101.
[9] José Antonio Ocampo, 'Raúl Prebisch and the Development at the Dawn of the Twenty-First Centruny' (2001) 75 *Cepal Review* 23–36 at 24.
[10] Laura Quinteros de Aguilera, *La Integración Económica Centroamericana Desde sus Inicios en 1950 Hasta la Firma del Protocolo de Guatemala* (Guatemala: SIECA, 2004).
[11] Manuel R. Agosin and Ennio Rodríguez, *Libre Comercio en América Central: ¿Con Quién y Para Qué? Las Implicancias del CAFTA Documento de Divulgacion 37* (Washington, DC: Inter American Development Bank, 2005), at p. 5.
[12] The Caribbean Basin Trade Partnership Act (CBTA) of 2000, 19 USC 2703 (2000).

the textile assembly industry commonly known as '*maquila*'. Despite the recent relocation of textile production to China and other Asian States, textile assembly is still a very important export product in certain Central American countries like Honduras and El Salvador.

Trade policy changed again in the mid 1990s, when an open trade policy replaced the ailing import substitution programme. The new era of open trade was heralded by the passing of the North American Free Trade Agreement (NAFTA)[13] in 1994. At that time, Central American nations were finishing accession to the General Agreement on Tariffs and Trade (GATT), and becoming members of the new World Trade Organization (WTO). NAFTA caused great concern in Central America, since it was thought that there would be significant trade and investment diversion towards Mexico and out of Central America. At that time, the nations of the isthmus lobbied strongly for 'NAFTA parity', meaning same terms of access to the US market as those enjoyed by México.[14] A formal proposal was presented to US President, Bill Clinton during his visit to Costa Rica in May 1997.[15] Still reeling from its experience in persuading Congress to approve NAFTA and subsequent failure to renew Fast-Track authority, the Clinton administration showed little desire to seek further trade agreements in general[16] and certainly not with smaller economies such as those of Central America. After 1997, Central American nations resigned themselves, and promoted free trade agreements amongst themselves, and with other important economic players in the region, such as Canada, Mexico and Chile.

It came as a surprise, then, that on 16 January 2002, President George W. Bush announced his administration's intention to seek a free trade agreement with the nations of Central America. During a speech at the Organization of American States, Bush said:

> Today I announce that the United States will explore a free trade agreement with the countries of Central America. My administration will work closely with Congress towards this goal. Our purpose is to strengthen the economic ties we already have with these nations; to reinforce their progress toward economic and political and social reform; and to take another step toward completing the Free Trade Area of the Americas.[17]

---

[13] North American Free Trade Agreement, signed at Ottawa, Canada, on 11 and 17 December 1992, Mexico City on 14 and 17 December 1992, and Washington, DC, on 8 and 17 December 1992; in force 1 January 1994, available at www.nafta-sec-alena.org.

[14] José M. Salazar-Xirinachs and Jaime Granados, 'The US-Central America Free Trade Agreement: Opportunities and Challenges' in Jeffrey J. Schott (ed.), *Free Trade Agreements, US Strategies and Priorities* (Washington: Institute for International Economics, 2004), at p. 226.

[15] Ibid.

[16] Pablo Rodas-Martini, 'Tras la búsqueda de El Dorado. El TLCCA con Estados Unidos', *Foreign Affairs en Español*, October–December 2004, p. 1.

[17] Quoted in Salazar-Xirinachs and Granados, above note 14, at p. 225.

The stated purpose of the negotiation for the US was thus threefold: strengthening economic ties, bolstering political reform and a stepping stone toward the very elusive Free Trade Area of the Americas. Other, more implicit, objectives have been cited: signal US commitment to free trade, an effort to control drug traffic, preventing terrorism, and reducing immigration.[18]

CAFTA–DR–US originally included the US, Guatemala, El Salvador, Honduras, Nicaragua and Costa Rica. As will be seen, it later grew to include the Dominican Republic. For historical reasons, Belize and Panama, although neighbours in the Caribbean basin, are not encompassed by the concept of Central America, and were not included in the CAFTA negotiations.[19]

From the Central American perspective, CAFTA–DR–US offered the possibility of securing CBI concessions in a more definite form. The treaty also offered opportunities to attract direct investment, export growth and export diversification.[20] Despite efforts in diversification, notably those of Costa Rica, Central American countries export to the US a relatively small number of products.[21] For Central American policy makers, the launching of CAFTA–DR–US represented the capstone in a long effort towards reform and free trade in the region.[22] The social, political and economic conditions across the six Latin American countries vary widely,[23] but they still share a common background and a similar process of opening markets during the last decades.

For the historical reasons mentioned above, trade in the region is very intense. Intraregional trade in percentage terms, taking into account the US, is above 70 per cent, which is similar to that existing between members of the European Union (EU).[24] More than half of Central American exports are currently destined for the US, and 44 per cent of all imports coming into Central America originate there.[25] Moreover, investment flow of US capital into the region is key for economic growth. US investment has been very important since the late nineteenth century, as

---

[18] Ibid. at p. 230.
[19] Panama entered bilaterally into a Trade Promotion Agreement with the US as of late 2006. See www.mici.gob.pa and www.ustr.gov/Trade_Agreements/Bilateral/Panama_FTA/. It also has ongoing trade negotiations with Central America.
[20] Eduardo Lizano and Anabel González, *El Tratado de Libre Comercio entre el Istmo Centroamericano y los Estados Unidos de América Documento de Divulgación 9* (Washington: Inter-American Development Bank, 2003), at p. 5.
[21] Salazar-Xirinachs and Granados, above note 14, at p. 235.
[22] Inter-American Development Bank, *DR-CAFTA: Challenges and Opportunities for Central America* (Washington: Inter American Development Bank, 2006), at p. 3.
[23] For a detailed analysis and contrast of socioeconomic conditions in Central America, see Jorge Nowalski Rowinski (ed.), *Asimetrías económicas, laborales y sociales en Centroamérica* (San José: FLACSO, 2002). See also Proyecto Estado de la Nación – PNUD, *Segundo Informe sobre Desarrollo Humano en Centroamérica y Panamá* (San José, Estado de la Nación, 2003).
[24] Agosin and Rodríguez, above note 11, at p. 1.
[25] J.F. Hornbeck, 'The Dominican Republic-Central America-United States Free Trade Agreement (CAFTA-DR)', CRS Report for Congress, Congressional Research Service – The Library of Congress (5 April 2007), p. 11.

described above. It accounts for more than 35 per cent of foreign investment in most CAFTA–DR–US countries.[26]

II. The negotiating process

The trade negotiations carried out by the US with Chile and Singapore, and the resulting agreements with these nations, served as a precedent, and almost as the template, for the CAFTA–DR–US negotiations. The sequence and content of these two previous experiences were closely followed. It has been said that the United States Trade Representative (USTR) had received Congressional approval for the Chile–Singapore model, as being compliant with the Trade Promotion Authority mandate, and was very hesitant to deviate from that self-imposed standard.[27]

CAFTA–DR–US as an end product is thus very similar to its Chilean and Singaporean predecessors, and part of this modern version of an FTA with the US. It is not a 'hub and spokes' agreement where every country enters into single undertakings with the US, but rather a multilateral agreement where every country, in principle, assumes the same set of obligations. Exceptions and particular undertakings of a single State were included in an annex to each relevant chapter. Additionally, schedules of commitments for each country in the market access chapters are listed individually in the treaty. For the negotiation, each Central American State involved had its own negotiating team, broken up by subject matter sub-teams and experts.

The Central American countries had high expectations for the subject of immigration, one of the main topics of the regional foreign policy agenda. Between 1990 and 2005, immigration of Latin American people to the US increased by 130 per cent. Of the 19.3 million migrants, 71 per cent originated from Mexico and Central America.[28] The US refused to bring the topic into the negotiations, producing considerable disappointment early in the process.

The timeline of the negotiation was very tight, putting enormous pressure on Central American negotiating teams. During 2002, six technical or preparatory workshops were conducted involving all negotiating parties. Negotiations started in earnest in 2003. Nine rounds of negotiation were held in different cities. The negotiation groups toured the capital cities of all signatories, as well as Houston, Cincinnatti and New Orleans.[29] The process was wrapped up by December 2003. At

---

[26] United States International Trade Commission (USITC), 'U.S.-Central America-Dominican Republic Free Trade Agreement, Potential Economywide and Sectoral Effects', USITC Publication 3717 (2004), at p. 128.
[27] Rodas-Martini, above note 16, at p. 2.
[28] Comisión Económica para América Latina y el Caribe (CEPAL), *Espacios Iberoamericanos* (Santiago de Chile: CEPAL, 2006), Chapter VI at pp. 129–30. See also M. Villa, 'El Cambiante Mapa Migratorio de América Latina y el Caribe' (Mexico: CEPAL, 2001), p. 2.
[29] For a summary of each negotiation round, see www.comex.go.cr/negociaciones.

that point, El Salvador, Honduras, Nicaragua and Guatemala concluded their negotiations, but surprisingly Costa Rica stated that the text of the resulting Agreement contained several unacceptable provisions, especially related to access of agro-industrial products. After several weeks of suspense, the USTR and Costa Rica held 30 additional hours of negotiations during the month of January 2004, which ended up with a successful conclusion.

It was then, when it appeared to be too late to add a new party, that the Dominican Republic joined the table as a negotiator. The negotiation between the Dominican Republic vis-à-vis the rest of the Latin States was not complicated, as it already had free trade agreements in force with all of them. It was then an issue of taking the finished treaty and determining the exclusions and special commitments applicable to the Dominican Republic. This was done at an amazing speed. The only points of contention involved agricultural products, such as sugar.

The inclusion of the Dominican Republic was wrapped up by August 2004, at which time the agreement was signed by the seven parties involved, subject to subsequent Congressional approval in each nation. It has been suggested that the inclusion of the Dominican Republic would facilitate the approval of the treaty in the United States Congress, since it could bolster support from representatives with a large Latino constituency.[30]

III. Substantive obligations

A. Market access

CAFTA–DR–US will eliminate tariffs for virtually all goods. Most tariffs will be eliminated immediately, especially those applied by the US. On average, duties on 80 per cent of US exports are eliminated immediately by all CAFTA–DR parties, with the rest phased out over a period of up to 10 years.[31] In the case of Central America, cuts will be phased out over time, with sensitive agricultural goods left to last. Options for tariff elimination were: immediate, 5 years, 10 years, 12 years, 15 years and some extra long 20-year periods for the critical lines of poultry parts, rice and dairy products which were the result of powerful lobbying by strong political interests in Central America. Politically sensitive goods were either excluded or made subject to zero tariff quotas. Examples of politically sensitive goods are sugar for entry into the US, corn for entry into Central America and potatoes and onions into Costa Rica.

Tariff-rate quotas were used to grant or expand access to the US for certain sensitive agricultural products, such as peanuts, peanut butter, beef, pork, poultry and dairy products. A special agricultural safeguard was included to protect against

---

[30] Hazel Feigenblatt, 'El Peso del voto latino en el pulso', *La Nación*, 12 April 2005, available at www.nacion.com.
[31] Hornbeck, above note 25, at p. 18.

sudden import surges, triggered on the basis of volume. An agricultural safeguard of this type cannot be in force for more than four years.

B. Sanitary and phytosanitary measures

Reference is made in CAFTA–DR–US to the obligations of the WTO Agreement on Sanitary and Phytosanitary Measures (SPS), which in any case, are already applied by the CAFTA–DR–US parties. An SPS working group will oversee and report on technical issues and national rules. Technical assistance on this subject will be critical to the proper implementation of the agreement, as technical issues dealing with plant approvals and other sanitary procedures have been one of the most cited non-tariff barriers to trade not only for access to the US market, but also in other CAFTA–DR–US parties, such as Honduras. Problems for access of poultry and poultry parts have been recurrent.

C. Agricultural export subsidies

CAFTA–DR–US detractors in Central America pointed to US agricultural export subsidies as the main reason not to enter into the agreement. The subject was much discussed, but few significant commitments were made by the US, probably because it would only commit to this subject in multilateral trade negotiations where the EU is present.

D. Sugar and the prospects for ethanol

CAFTA–DR–US includes commitments to increase the zero-tariff import quota of sugar from Central America, from 99,000 metric tons in the first year to about 140,000 metric tons over fifteen years. This will permit very interesting opportunities for Central American producers, who will be able to increase sales in the US, where import prices have been very attractive. The new market access will mean that Central America will double the share of current production that is exported to the US from an average of 4 per cent to 8 per cent. Sugar was the most controversial agricultural issue to resolve in the negotiations, with US producers strongly and consistently opposing even its inclusion as a negotiating topic.[32]

Moreover, ethanol, produced in the region using sugar cane, also has very good prospects under CAFTA–DR–US. The treaty will not increase current access from regional feedstocks materially, but would make CBI preferences permanent, and would additionally establish ample country-specific shares for Costa Rica and El Salvador. Ethanol imports have grown an average of 11 per cent per year and, due to

---

[32] Ibid., at p. 21.

recent gasoline blending rules, demand is set to increase. This context has already encouraged ethanol-related investments in Central America.[33]

E. Rules of origin and textile access

Textile rules in CAFTA–DR–US include more accommodating rules of origin, addressed to the decline in US market share of textile imports from Central America, which have been displaced by Asian products.[34] Special rules will permit 'coproduction' of goods, in which different stages of manufacture can take place in the US or other CAFTA–DR–US members, and still qualify for duty-free access as a regional product. Complicated rules persist for the sensitive lines of apparel and textiles, which carefully control and restrict *maquila* production destined for the US.

CAFTA–DR–US expands on the preferences previously made by the US under CBI. There will be allowances for unlimited use of regional inputs, meaning yarn produced in the region. This differs from current CBI rules, which mostly require 'US only' inputs. CAFTA–DR–US also allows a list of short supply inputs, which may be sourced from a third country without losing the zero-duty status.

Less restrictive rules of origin were negotiated for selected products, such as underwear and sleepwear. For these products, the use of fabric made in third countries will be accepted as long as 'substantial transformation' takes place in Central America.

Producers of textiles in the region expected more from the treaty in terms of access to the US market, and even the United States International Trade Commission (USITC) stated that CAFTA–DR–US benefits 'will likely have a negligible impact on U.S. production or employment'.[35]

F. Services

The service chapter in CAFTA–DR–US contains substantial obligations for Central American nations, especially Costa Rica. CBI contains no reference to services, and WTO commitments in this area by Central American countries were generally minimal. It was understood that Costa Rica was entering into the negotiations with few offers in the services area. Nevertheless, the last days of the negotiation proved to contain some important commitments. During the final weeks of the negotiation, in January 2004, the US pressed for the opening up of the government monopolies in the Costa Rican insurance and telecommunications industries. The Costa Rican delegation caved in, warning that these commitments, which would require substantial legal reform in order to be implemented, would be difficult to approve in Congress. The warnings made by the Costa Rican delegation turned out to be quite

---

[33] Mauricio Salas, 'Down with Diesel', *Project Finance Magazine*, September 2005, 1.
[34] Hornbeck, above note 25, at p. 18.
[35] Cited in Hornbeck, above note 25, at p. 19.

an understatement, as the attitude towards CAFTA–DR–US of important groups of civil society in Costa Rica immediately turned from cautious to incendiary.

In concrete terms, the obligations assumed by Costa Rica in these areas are only to allow the private sector to compete in specific telecommunication sectors, namely cellular bands, internet and private networks.[36] More generally, CAFTA–DR–US provides for broader market access and greater regulatory transparency.[37] There are rules demanding that local regulations be applied in a non-discriminatory manner. Costa Rica will also need to enact new regulatory frameworks and oversight bodies for the insurance and telecommunications markets. These have not been necessary so far, in light of the above mentioned government monopolies.

It remains to be seen whether this access to services, especially to telecommunications, will ultimately prevent the agreement from entering into force in Costa Rica. What is clear is that the end result derailed the Congressional approval of CAFTA–DR–US in Costa Rica. At the time of writing, the treaty has not been approved by the Costa Rican Congress. The legal reforms on services have unified local opposition against the treaty. Leading political opponents have even suggested wrongdoing, indicating that the telecommunications issue was brought to the table by Costa Rican negotiators without the US even asking for it, as a part of a hidden agenda of privatization on the part of that Central American government.[38]

G. Distribution laws/dealer and agency contracts

During the 1970s, specific statutes were enacted in the region for the protection of local distributors in their dealings with foreign manufacturers. Several of these statutes are still on the books, and during the CAFTA–DR–US negotiations commitments were obtained from the jurisdictions in question to obtain their repeal or amendment. The problematic provisions in these laws included termination indemnities based on statutory formulas, and injunctions against the foreign litigants' imports during the term of the proceedings. It was not the actual effect or application of these laws which turned them into a persistent point of contention in international business transactions, but the lack of transparency in the system. For example, it was common for foreign companies to enter into distribution contracts unaware that statutes rendered certain contract provisions invalid.

Five of the Latin signatories still have provisions of this type in their laws, and have committed to amend them.[39] Amendments are focused on improving transparency, liberty of contract and promoting alternative dispute resolution methods.

---

[36] CAFTA–DR–US, Annex 13, section III.2. [37] Hornbeck, above note 25, at p. 24.
[38] Asociación Nacional de Empleados Públicos, 'Arias Reconoce Mentiras en Torno al TLC y que Costa Rica dio más de lo Pedido por Estados Unidos', Asociación Nacional de Empleados Públicos Comuniqué (6 February 2007).
[39] See CAFTA–DR–US, Annex 11.13.

H. Intellectual property

Countries in the CAFTA–DR–US region had intellectual property legislation in line with the WTO TRIPS Agreement standards. Nevertheless, intellectual property was one of the issues where the US decided to push the envelope, pressing its Latin counterparts to adopt 'TRIPS Plus' provisions. Piracy and enforcement issues were cited as criticism of the Central American system.

CAFTA–DR–US members committed themselves to ratify a number of international agreements on the subject, such as the Budapest[40] and International Union for the Protection of Plants (UPOV)[41] treaties, which touch on the sensitive issues of patents over micro-organisms and plant varieties.[42] There were also commitments to displaying 'best efforts' to ratify other instruments, such as the Madrid Protocol, which would centralize trademark filings in a single point of registration.[43] During negotiation, the US sought to make the Madrid Protocol ratification a mandatory obligation. The final text, however, was limited to requiring 'best efforts' to join such an instrument. The toning down of the obligation was probably due to the opposition of established law firms and practitioners dedicated to trademark work.

The issue of pharmaceutical data protection deserves to be highlighted. CAFTA–DR–US favours big pharmaceutical companies by forcing an amendment of local health and drug legislation to mimic US rules on the subject. To bring a patented drug to market in the US, a drug company must demonstrate through clinical trials that the drug is safe and effective. Under US patent law, the data used to establish these claims are protected from use by generic manufacturers for five years from the time when the drug is introduced in a country's market. A similar system has been imposed on CAFTA–DR–US members, much to the chagrin of the local generic industry, which seemed to be totally taken by surprise by the commitments. Guatemala tried to backtrack on the CAFTA–DR–US language, with an amendment of its health regulations using WTO language during November 2004. The USTR picked up on this and pointed out the change as a breach of CAFTA–DR–US obligations.[44] Guatemala reversed the amendment.[45]

---

[40] Budapest Treaty on the International Recognition of the Deposit of Micro-organisms for the Purposes of Patent Procedure, done at Budapest on 28 April 1977, amended on 26 September 1980, available from www.wipo.int.
[41] International Convention for the Protection of New Varieties of Plants, done at Paris on 2 December 1961, available from www.upov.int.
[42] CAFTA–DR–US, Article 15.1.2.   [43] Ibid., Article 15.1.6(c).
[44] Martín Rodríguez P., 'Peligra TLC con EE.UU. por ley sobre genéricos', *La Prensa Libre*, 27 December 2004, available at www.prensalibre.com. See also, 'Consideran injusto atribuir a Guatemala no ratificación del TLC', *La Nación*, 29 December 2004, available at www.nacion.com.
[45] Martín Rodríguez P. and Eduardo Smith, 'Ejecutivo pedirá al Congreso proteger patentes médicas', *La Prensa Libre*, 28 December 2004, available at www.prensalibre.com. See also, Eduardo Smith, 'Datos de Prueba se protegerán nuevamente', *La Prensa Libre*, 4 February 2005, available at www.prensalibre.com.

I. Labour

Labour and environmental issues received a lot of attention during the negotiation of CAFTA–DR–US, especially from American interest groups and politicians. Their presence in the treaty text was assured, as the Trade Promotion Authority legislation so requires.

There was some debate as to whether Central American countries had appropriate labour legislation in force, pursuant to basic International Labour Organization (ILO) principles. This view probably arose out of ignorance or political interest, as it did not seem to be the case. The countries of the region have a relatively homogenous legal system, similar to that of other civil law systems with which the US has previously negotiated FTAs, such as Chile and Mexico. The discussion was then more properly framed as a problem of enforcement, or lack thereof, of existing rules.

In an attempt to curtail the questions and criticisms, the Central American nations requested from the ILO a report on the level of compliance of their internal laws with the organization's standards.[46] Central American nations were confident that they would get good marks. A very comprehensive report was issued by the ILO, mostly confirming compliance with dozens of international agreements on labour issues, but pointing out several non-conforming statutes.[47] The document was then used by both sides in the debate as support for their respective arguments. Most of the criticism in the ILO report is nevertheless targeted at freedom of association protection. This also echoes past American Federation of Labor and Congress of Industrial Organizations (AFL-CIO) criticism of the stagnation of the union movement in the region. Similarly, a 2005 report by the Inter-American Development Bank focused on the enforcement issue, as the main shortfall of the labour laws in Central America.[48] Those two issues, namely the unionization movement and enforcement generally, thus became the key issues in relation to labour.

The resulting labour chapter in CAFTA–DR–US closely follows TPA language, and has three main rules: (1) effective enforcement of domestic labour laws; (2) reaffirmation of commitments to the ILO basic principles; and (3) 'non-derogation' from domestic standards to encourage trade and investment.[49] Only an alleged contravention of the first rule, namely a 'failure to enforce domestic law' can be challenged under CAFTA–DR–US's dispute settlement rules.[50]

---

[46] Hornbeck, above note 25, at p. 28.
[47] International Labour Organization (ILO), *Fundamental Principles and Rights at Work: A Labour Law Study: Costa Rica, El Salvador, Guatemala, Honduras, Nicaragua* (Geneva: ILO, 2003).
[48] Working Group of the Vice Ministers Responsible for Trade and Labor in the Countries of Central America and the Dominican Republic, *The Labor Dimension in Central America and the Dominican Republic. Building on Progress: Strengthening Compliance and Enhancing Capacity* (San José: Ministerio de Trabajo y Seguridad Social, April 2005).
[49] Hornbeck, above note 25, at p. 29.
[50] Leonor Echeverría Hine, 'El Tratamiento del Tema Laboral en las Negociaciones Comerciales Internacionales: El Caso del Tratado de Libre Comercio entre República Dominicana, Centroamérica y

J. Environment

Environmental obligations were included as a chapter in the agreement itself, and not as a side agreement, as had been the experience in earlier negotiations of the signatories.[51] The chapter starts by recognizing each Party's right to establish its own level of protection. CAFTA–DR–US demands that each party must maintain high levels of environmental protection and, furthermore, must improve on those levels.[52] That is the main point and fundamental obligation of the environment chapter. As in the labour chapter, the treaty contains an obligation to enforce environmental norms effectively, and the commitment not to derogate from environmental laws in order to attract investment. Dispute settlement provisions only apply, however, to a sustained and recurring non-enforcement of environmental norms affecting trade.

The public submission process included in CAFTA–DR–US[53] deserves mention, as an innovative and improved public access mechanism. The process is considered to be an improvement on the citizen submission mechanism in Articles 14 and 15 of the North American Agreement on Environmental Cooperation (NAAEC), cousin to NAFTA. Any national of a signatory State can file a submission at the appropriate secretariat, which actually works under the umbrella of the Secretaría de Integración Económica (SIECA) a technical secretariat formed under the aegis of the Central American Common Market instruments, denouncing a failure to enforce environmental law in any signatory State. If any member of the CAFTA–DR–US Environmental Affairs Council so requires, the secretariat will prepare a factual record for review by the full Council. Environmental experts can assist the Council. The mechanism does not entail economic or other hard core sanctions, but the resolutions will certainly carry political and moral weight. In this respect, the NAAEC has handled some interesting cases[54] in its 10 years of existence. It is expected that access to the CAFTA–DR–US mechanism would also produce interesting actions by civil society, and be somewhat easier for the petitioner to pursue if compared with NAAEC.

A side Environmental Cooperation Agreement was also negotiated.[55] This agreement complements the treaty text with a more general and wider scope of coverage, as it is not limited to the restrictions of the area of trade and environment interaction.[56] The Environmental Cooperation Agreement includes a list of priority

---

Estados Unidos' in Anabel González (ed.), *Estudios Jurídicos sobre el TLC entre República Dominicana, Centroamérica y Estados Unidos* (San José: ASE-TLC, 2005), at p. 673.

[51] Such as NAFTA, or as the Canada–Costa Rica Free Trade Agreement, signed 23 April 2001, in force 1 November 2002, available from www.comex.go.cr.
[52] CAFTA–DR–US, Article 17.1.   [53] Ibid., Article 17.7.
[54] Commission for Environmental Cooperation of North America, *Citizen Submissions on Enforcement Matters* (Montreal: Editions Yvon Blais, 2004).
[55] CAFTA–DR–US, Article 17.9.
[56] Jorge Cabrera Medaglia, 'El tratamiento de los temas ambientales en el Tratado de Libre Comercio', in González, above note 50, at p. 708.

areas for cooperation between the parties. Areas identified in the agreement include environmental management systems and market-based incentives for natural resource protection.

IV. Implementation and prospects for the future

CAFTA–DR–US needed Congressional approval in all seven jurisdictions before coming into effect. The history of international trade agreements indicates that opposition to such agreements tends to crystallize in these Congressional settings. CAFTA–DR–US was no exception.

The governments of El Salvador, Honduras, Nicaragua and Guatemala were able to move CAFTA–DR–US through Congress quickly and easily. By the spring of 2005, the treaty had received Congressional approval in those three States. The Dominican Republic followed in August 2005. The story in the US and Costa Rica was much more complicated.

The US Senate approved CAFTA–DR–US by a 54 to 45 vote on 30 June 2005. When the Bill was presented to the House of Representatives, however, the future of CAFTA–DR–US seemed uncertain. After much political work by the White House, the Bill was voted on in the House of Representatives late at night on 27 July 2005, but analysts still upheld their 'too close to call' outlook. The House floor received a surprise visit from President Bush, an unfamiliar show of support in Congressional voting. Close to midnight, the House passed its counterpart Bill by a vote of 217 in favour to 215 against, with two Congressmen abstaining.[57] It was the closest vote ever on a trade agreement.

The complications in Costa Rica proved to be more serious, and are ongoing at the time of writing, more than three years after the conclusion of negotiations. As of February 2008, the Costa Rican Congress still has not granted approval to CAFTA–DR–US and its complementary set of legal reforms.

Costa Rica is the only party to the treaty that has to enact major legal reforms as a result of the negotiations. As discussed above, telecommunications reform derived from CAFTA–DR–US commitments ignited the controversy, and served to catalyse opposition from different sectors.

The administration of Costa Rican President, Abel Pacheco, which negotiated CAFTA–DR–US back in 2004 did not have the political weight, or rather the acumen, to present the implementation Bill to Congress during its term in office. More than one year was lost with CAFTA–DR–US at a standstill during the last stage of Pacheco's administration. Support for the treaty eroded during this time.

The Bill was sent to Congress as one of the first actions of the new government of Oscar Arias in mid 2006. During the early months of the administration, approval of CAFTA–DR–US seemed close at hand, since pro-CAFTA–DR–US votes in the

---

[57] 'Congreso de EE.UU. aprueba el TLC', *La Nación*, 27 July 2005, available at www.nacion.com.

Costa Rican Congress far outnumbered those set to vote against the treaty. The treaty was discussed at length by the international affairs committee amid strong opposition from civil society. A very heterogeneous group of public servants, middle-class groups and university students were at the core of the opposition, in which the runner-up to the Presidential elections, Ottón Solis from Partido Acción Ciudadana, acted in a credible leadership role. Opposition voices presented all sorts of arguments against the CAFTA–DR–US, including constitutional, social and environmental reasons. At this point, the political cost of the CAFTA–DR–US issue made even pro-trade legislators hesitate in the decision to move the matter to a plenary vote. Costa Rican decision-makers have traditionally recoiled from decisions that provoke open social conflict, and CAFTA–DR–US turned out to be the most divisive legal Bill in the country's modern history.

In order to break the political deadlock and surrender the matter to the ultimate democratic test, President Arias presented a Bill to Congress asking for a 'Yes or No' vote in a national referendum. Congress was happy to consent and get the explosive Bill off its floor. The referendum was held 7 October 2007. It was the first time a national referendum had been called for in Costa Rica, and probably the first time a bilateral trade agreement had been ratified by popular vote by any nation.

As part of every treaty approval process in Costa Rica, the Constitutional Court has to issue on opinion on the draft Bill of implementation. The decision of the Costa Rican Constitutional Court on the CAFTA–DR–US Bill was much anticipated, as opponents had presented a series of constitutional claims on the treaty content. International arbitration of investment disputes, for example, was claimed to be unconstitutional in certain respects. Anti-CAFTA–DR–US legislators presented a long list of constitutional claims before the Court. The Constitutional Court issued its decision in preparation for the referendum by majority opinion, ruling in favour of the treaty's constitutionality (five in favour, two against). All constitutional objections were rejected by the majority opinion.

The CAFTA–DR–US referendum marked a 'before and after' in Costa Rican politics. The campaign itself polarized the nation between the supporters of the 'Yes' and the supporters of the 'No'. The 'Yes' party started out with a comfortable lead in the polls. Nevertheless, a few months before the vote, an email sent by Costa Rican Vice President and Minister Kevin Casas leaked out to the press. According to the press, in this email memorandum to a group of collaborators, Casas apparently pressed the idea of curtailing budgetary allocations to local governments whose governors were not campaigning for the 'Yes' vote. Casas publicly accepted drafting the email while being upset with progress in the campaign. After the scandal, Casas resigned his position as Minister, and has since been removed from the government. The Casas email scandal influenced the undecided voters towards the 'No', and the referendum was held in a very tense atmosphere and under a virtual tie according to most polls.

59.4 per cent of all registered electors cast their votes in the referendum. Only 40 per cent was necessary for a binding result. The supporters of the 'Yes' to

CAFTA–DR–US won with a slim 51.6 per cent of the vote.[58] With this result, CAFTA–DR–US will be signed into law by Congress. Costa Rica is expected to proceed to implementation talks shortly afterwards. Only the text of the agreement itself was covered in the referendum of 7 October 2007. This means that certain implementing legislation, such as the approval of telecommunications reform, still needs to be approved through normal Congressional action. At the time of this writing, the relevant Bill is being discussed on the floor of the Costa Rican congress, amid strong opposition by certain political forces such as Partido Acción Ciudadana.

CAFTA–DR–US has meanwhile entered into force for the six nations that have followed the approval and ratification process. The implementation process in the rest of the Central American States was not without its glitches, as evidenced by the Guatemala patent regulation issue described above.

One of the tangible, albeit indirect, effects of CAFTA–DR–US will be the acceleration of the Central American integration process. A new set of rules and dispute settlement procedures is expected to increase transparency and the rule of law. This will probably be felt first in problematic areas such as sanitary and phytosanitary measures, where complaints have been numerous. New commitments, extending beyond WTO obligations in areas such as intellectual property, services and government procurement, will also be areas to watch.[59]

Since trade in intraregional terms is already quite strong, and Central American exports generally receive duty free treatment in the US, the effects of CAFTA–DR–US will probably not be dramatic in economic terms. It can surely be argued, however, that CAFTA–DR–US will serve to bolster the growing trade and investment trend in the region to the benefit of the local population.

---

[58] Official referendum results can be obtained from www.tse.go.cr.
[59] For a detailed analysis of the application process of the CAFTA–DR–US, see Anabel González, *The Application of the Dominican Republic-Central America-United States Free Trade Agreement* (Washington: Organization of American States, 2005).

3

Chile–China Free Trade Agreement

LUZ SOSA

I. Introduction

Chile and China have a long history of positive relations in trade and other matters. Chile was one of the first Latin American countries to engage in trade and economic exchanges with China. After the establishment of diplomatic relations in 1970, bilateral trade developed quickly.

In this context, in 1999, Chile was the first among Latin American countries to reach a bilateral agreement with China on China's entry to the World Trade Organization. In 2002, China supported Chile running for non-permanent member of the United Nations (UN) Security Council for the period 2003–2004.

Furthermore, Chile and China have signed a number of governmental agreements on trade, science and technology, culture, mutual visa exemption for diplomatic and service passports and investment protection. The two countries have conducted consultations in international affairs and enjoyed satisfactory cooperation in international organizations and conferences.

As noted by a group studying the prospects for a Chile–China free trade agreement:

> In 2003, bilateral trade between Chile and China reached a record high of 3.155 million dollars. This places China as Chile's third global trading partner, behind Argentina and the United States, but also above countries like Japan, Brazil and all of the European Union economies. The latter strongly diverge from what was recorded a decade ago, when bilateral trade flows ranked in the fifteenth place.
>
> The strong growth in trade between Chile and China is the result of a dynamic evolution in exports and imports, thus generating an increase in bilateral exchange of no less than 662% between 1994 an 2003, surpassing in more than six times the growth of Chile's global trade in the same period (94%).
>
> The trade balance, exports minus imports, in 2003, also marked a record high with a surplus for Chile of 575 million dollars, [a] sum that is far from the 147 million dollar deficit of 1994. The traditional deficit in favor of Chile dates to 2001 and has increased since then.

Table 3.1 Table II:1 extracted from Chilean High Level Study Group, *Joint Feasibility Study on a Free Trade Agreement Between Chile and China* (Santiago: Gorierno De Chile, October 2004), p. xlii

TABLE II.1

TRADE BETWEEN CHILE AND CHINA, 1994–2003
(millions of dollars and %)

	1994	1995	1996	1997	1998	1999	2000	2001	2002	2003
I. China										
Exports (FOB)	133,3	287,9	354,1	433,4	459,7	359,1	907,2	1.021,8	1240,1	1865,4
Imports (CIF)	280,7	390,3	515,0	659,1	753,1	660,1	951,4	1.013,7	1102,4	1290,2
Trade Balance	(147,4)	(102,4)	(160,9)	(225,7)	(293,4)	(301,0)	(44,1)	8,1	137,7	575,2
Trade Exchange	414,0	678,3	869,1	1.092,5	1.212,8	1.019,1	1.858,6	2.035,4	2342,5	3155,6
II. Global										
Exports (FOB)	9198,7	11604,1	15.394,6	17.017,0	14.753,9	15.914,6	18.425,0	17.668,1	17.676,3	20.627,2
Imports (CIF)	10543,6	11149,1	16.810,0	18.111,6	17.087,4	14.022,0	16.842,5	16.233,9	15.753,2	17.663,6
Trade Balance	(1.344,9)	455,0	(1.415,4)	(1.094,6)	(2.333,5)	1.892,6	1.582,5	1.434,2	1.923,1	2.963,6
Trade Exchange	19.742,3	22.753,2	32.204,6	35.128,6	31.841,3	29.936,6	35.267,5	33.902,0	33.429,5	38.290,8
III. Participation										
Exports	1,4	2,5	2,3	2,5	3,1	2,3	4,9	5,8	7,0	9,0
Imports	2,7	3,5	3,1	3,6	4,4	4,7	5,6	6,2	7,0	7,3
Trade Exchange	2,1	3,0	2,7	3,1	3,8	3,4	5,3	6,0	7,0	8,2

Source: Dirección de Estudios, DIRECON (May 2004), based on data from Banco Central de Chile.

As in total trade exchanges, in 2003, the Chinese economy represented the third destination of Chilean exports, accounting for 1.865 million dollars. Between 1994 and 2003 Chilean exports destined to China grew in an accumulated amount of 1,299%, meaning an average of 130% annually, growth that is ten times greater than that shown by total Chilean exports.

Imports coming from China in 2003, reached a sum of 1.290 million dollars, placing China as the fourth supplier of imported goods to Chile. Although imports from the Asian giant haven't shown the spectacular surges as those in imports, these do not cease to amaze given that between 1994 and 2003 imports reached a growth rate of 360%, [a] fact that is of no minor importance considering that global imports only grew by 124% in the same period.[1]

For detailed statistical information on the growth of Chilean–Chinese trade since 1994, see Table 3.1. Chilean exports to China are concentrated mainly in the sectors of mining and industry, which account for 98.9 per cent of total exports to China. Within the mining sector, copper exports represent the largest share of the exports for this sector. In terms of the industrial sector, the main export products are cellulose and fishmeal. In recent years, China has begun importing wine and fruits.

China mainly exports to Chile industrial products such as textiles, clothing, chemicals (including plastics and metal products), hand tools and electromechanical equipment, together with the exports of machinery and electronic products (televisions, chips, computers and cellular phones) and home appliances.

II. The negotiating process

Chile and China always attached great importance to developing good mutual trading relations. During the negotiating process both countries were ready to push pragmatic cooperation in economy, trade and other areas to a higher level.

The initiative to negotiate the Free Trade Agreement between the Government of the People's Republic of China and the Government of the Republic of Chile[2] (Chile–China FTA or 'the Agreement') was proposed by China in June 2002. Chile responded positively to the proposal, as China is an important part of Chile's Asian policy and developing bilateral ties was supported by a consensus among the Chilean government, Parliament and business.

The first step taken by both countries was to perform a joint feasibility study in order to evaluate the merits of deepening trade relations among them. This joint study was initiated on April 2004 and its main conclusion was the approval of negotiating an FTA, the first stage of which was aimed at the liberalization of trade in goods.

---

[1] Chilean High Level Study Group, *Joint Feasibility Study on a Free Trade Agreement Between Chile and China* (Santiago: Gorierno De Chile, October 2004), at p. xlii.
[2] Signed 18 November 2005, in force 1 October 2006.

The official announcement of the launching of the negotiations was made during an Asia-Pacific Economic Cooperation (APEC) Summit on 18 November 2004 by Chilean President, Ricardo Lagos and Chinese President, Hu Jintao.

The negotiating process lasted eleven months, at which point the first stage of the FTA between Chile and China was concluded. This first stage consists solely of the liberalization of trade in goods. It has been agreed by both countries that future negotiations will take place for the liberalization of trade in services and investment.[3]

During the negotiating process there was a positive and transparent collaboration between the government agencies[4] of both countries in charge of the negotiations and private sectors. Representatives of labour unions, industry associations, civil society in general were permanently consulted and informed of the different aspects involved during the negotiations.

Particularly in the case of Chile, different society groups have stated their interest in expressing their views with respect to ongoing negotiations that can eventually affect their areas of economic, political and social integration. In this context, the General Directorate for International Economic Affairs has always had a close dialogue with companies and trade associations related to international trade. This wide variety of companies has been consulted through their respective trade associations representatives every time Chile has engaged in international trade negotiations.[5] As a result, valuable contributions have been collected and transmitted directly to the entities engaged in a particular negotiating process.

The First Round of Negotiations was held in Beijing from 25–27 January 2005. At this time, the Trade Negotiations Committee was created in order to discuss the terms of reference of the Agreement (scope and coverage of the Agreement), timetable for the negotiating process and exchange views on trade in goods.

The Second Round of Negotiations took place in Santiago from 27–29 April 2005. On this occasion, the Technical Expert Group (composed of senior government representatives of both countries) was created in order to facilitate the outcome of

---

[3] Article 120 of the Agreement.

[4] The Chilean delegation was headed by the Director General of the General Directorate for International Economic Affairs of the Ministry of Foreign Affairs of Chile. Chilean government agencies involved include: General Directorate for International Economic Affairs, Ministry of Finance, Central Bank, Chile Foreign Investment Committee, Ministry of Labour and Social Security, National Customs Service, Ministry of Agriculture, Ministry of Education, Ministry of Economy.

Chinese government agencies involved include: Ministry of Commerce, Ministry of Foreign Affairs, Ministry of Finance, National Development and Reform Commission, Ministry of Agriculture, Customs General Administration, General Administration of Quality Supervision, Inspection and Quarantine and State Administration for Industry and Commerce.

[5] The participation of civil society is also open to non-governmental organizations, professional associations, academic entities, indigenous organizations, entities and individuals of the world of culture, who are willing to express their opinion and participate in the open debate related to the trade negotiations undertaken by Chile in the most diverse areas.

the negotiations and with the aim of solving any particular issue that could arise during the negotiating process.

The Third Round of Negotiations was held in the city of Wuxi, China from 28–30 June 2005. During this meeting, progress was made particularly in relation to the chapters on Cooperation, Market Access, Rules of Origin and Customs Procedures, Technical Barriers to Trade, and Sanitary and Phytosanitary Measures.

The Fourth Round of Negotiations was held in Santiago from 12–16 September 2005. At these meetings, negotiations related to the Chapters on Sanitary and Phytosanitary Measures and on Technical Barriers to Trade were concluded. Progress was made in the areas of Cooperation, Dispute Settlement and Rules of Origin.

The Fifth and last Round of Negotiations took place in the city of Beijing from 24–28 October 2005, where the remaining aspects of the negotiations were concluded.

Finally, the Agreement was signed by the Foreign Minister of Chile, Ignacio Walker and the Minister of Commerce of China, Bo Xilai on behalf of their respective governments on 18 November 2005 during the 2005 APEC Summit in Korea, and entered into force on 1 October 2006 after the completion of necessary domestic legal procedures by each country.

III. Analysis of noteworthy substantive obligations

This Agreement consists of 14 chapters, including Market Access, Rules of Origin, Trade Remedies, Sanitary and Phytosanitary Measures, Technical Barriers to Trade, Dispute Settlement and Cooperation, and has 8 annexes.[6]

A Memorandum of Understanding between the corresponding labour and social security authorities of both countries was also signed along with the Agreement, mainly due to Chile's policy of incorporating social matters in its Agreements and consistent with its posture of including labour issues in international trade negotiations. In this section, some of the key provisions are analysed.

A. Market access

As described by Chile's General Directorate for International Economic Affairs:

> With respect to tariff reductions, there is consensus for the immediate reduction of tariffs on 92% of Chilean exports to China, applicable as from

---

[6] Annex 1: Elimination of Import Customs Duties
Annex 2: Geographical Indications
Annex 3: Product Specific Rules
Annex 4: Certificate of Origin
Annex 5: Competent Government Authorities of Chile
Annex 6: Model of Certification and Verification Networking System on Certificate of Origin
Annex 7: Rules of Procedure of Arbitral Panel
Annex 8: Implementation of Modifications approved by the Commission.

the first day the Agreement entered into force. For China, this percentage amounts to 50% of its current trade.

The agreement also considers tariff reductions after 1, 5, and 10 years for Chilean products imported into China, and terms of 1, 2, 5, and 10 years for Chinese exports to Chile. Product exclusions for 1% of Chilean exports and 3% of Chinese shipments to our country were agreed to protect certain sensible sectors.[7]

The Chilean products considered by China for immediate and five-year tariff reductions that will benefit most include: copper and other minerals, vegetables, fish oils, poultry, fresh cherries, fresh peaches and fresh nectarines, wood panels, smoked salmon, cheese, canned peaches, chocolates and tomato paste.

Additionally, it was agreed that the tariff reduction for products that had been declared by China as highly vulnerable, such as fresh and frozen salmon, grapes and apples, would occur in 10 years.

Chile was able to achieve its objective of keeping certain products which are sensitive, such as cements, some chemicals, surgical gloves, certain areas of the textile and clothing sector, within the 10-year category. Exceptions were also established for agricultural products subject to a price band system (wheat, flour, and sugar), tyres, metallurgical products and household appliances. In total, Chile excluded from the Agreement 152 products, all considered sensitive for its production sectors.

The Chinese products that will have immediate access to the Chilean market include machinery, computers, vehicles, DVDs and printers, among others.

With respect to agricultural export subsidies, the Parties agreed that they will not introduce or maintain any export subsidy on any agricultural good destined for the territory of the other Party.[8]

Additionally, the Agreement creates a Committee on Trade in Goods comprising representatives of each Party, the functions of which include:

(a) promoting trade in goods between the Parties, including through consultations on accelerating tariff elimination[9] under this Agreement and other issues as appropriate; and

---

[7] Asia and Oceania Department/General Directorate for International Economic Affairs, '*Characteristics of the Free Trade Agreement Negotiation Between Chile and China*' (June 2006), at www.direcon.cl/documentos/China2/Antecedentes_de_la_Negociación_China_Junio2006_ING.pdf (last visited 11 June 2007).

[8] Article 12.2 of the Agreement. It is important to highlight that both Parties share the objective of the multilateral elimination of export subsidies for agricultural goods and have agreed to work together toward an agreement in the World Trade Organization to eliminate those subsidies and prevent their reintroduction in any form.

[9] The Agreement allows that, on the request of either Party, the Parties shall consult to consider accelerating the elimination of import customs duties set out in their Schedules. An agreement between the Parties to accelerate the elimination of an import customs duty on a good shall supersede any duty rate or staging

(b) addressing barriers to trade in goods between the Parties, especially those related to the application of non-tariff measures.

B. Rules of origin

The Chapter on rules of origin is composed of a normative text and an annex that contains specific rules of origin for certain groups of products.

The normative aspects of this chapter include the following elements:

(a) criteria to determine if a good shall be regarded as originating in Chile or China
(b) operations that do not confer origin
(c) accumulation[10]
(d) de minimis[11]
(e) neutral elements used in the production of a good
(f) packing materials for retail sale or shipment
(g) transit through third countries
(h) exhibitions.

Three main criteria are established so that a good shall be regarded as originating in Chile or China:

(a) the good is wholly obtained or produced entirely in the territory of one Party;
(b) the good is produced in the territory of one or both Parties, using non originating materials that conform to a regional value content not less than 40 per cent;
(c) specific rules for a group of products which shall comply with the corresponding origin criteria specified in the respective Annex.[12]

Additionally, the agreement provides that the certificates of origin shall be the responsibility of government bodies of both countries. Moreover, within a period of two years, both countries agreed to implement an electronic certification system that will improve the processes' efficiency.

---

category determined pursuant to their Schedules for such good when approved by each Party: Article 8.3 of the Agreement.

[10] Where originating goods or materials of a Party are incorporated into a good in the other Party's territory, the goods or materials so incorporated shall be regarded to be originating in the latter's territory: Article 20 of the Agreement.

[11] A good that does not conform to the tariff classification change (product specific rules) shall be considered to be originating even if the value of all non-originating materials used in its production not meeting the tariff classification change requirement does not exceed 8 per cent of the value of the given good: Article 21 of the Agreement.

[12] Annex 3 of the Agreement settles specific rules for groups of products. It is necessary to highlight that some sectors considered sensitive are subject to a stricter rule of origin than the general rule.

C. Trade remedies

This Chapter contains provisions on bilateral safeguards and global safeguards, anti-dumping and countervailing duties.

Provisions on bilateral safeguards[13] were established so as to allow both countries to protect themselves in the event that, as a result of the reduction or elimination of a duty provided in the Agreement, a product benefiting from preferential tariff treatment under the Agreement is being imported in such increased quantities which could distort or which could have negative effects threatening the domestic industry.

Where this occurs, a Party may, to the extent necessary to prevent or remedy serious injury, or threat thereof, and to facilitate adjustment:

(a) suspend the further reduction of any rate of duty on the product provided for under this Agreement; or
(b) increase the rate of duty on the product to a level not to exceed the lesser of
  (i) the MFN applied rate of duty in effect at the time the action is taken; or
  (ii) the MFN applied rate of duty in effect on the date of entry into force of this Agreement.

A Party may apply a definitive safeguard measure for an initial period of one year, with an extension not exceeding one year. Regardless of its duration, such measure shall terminate at the end of the transition period. A bilateral safeguard measure may not be imposed more than once on the same product.

However, in the case of a product for which the transition period is over five years, a Party may impose a safeguard measure for a second time on the same product, provided that a period equal to that of the previously imposed measure has elapsed.

With respect to global safeguards, both Parties maintain their respective rights and obligations under Article XIX of the General Agreement on Tariffs and Trade 1994 (GATT l994) and the World Trade Organization (WTO) Safeguards Agreement.

Additionally, with respect to anti-dumping and countervailing duties, the Parties maintain their rights and obligations under the Agreement on Implementation of Article VI of the GATT 1994 and the WTO Agreement on Subsidies and Countervailing Measures.

D. Sanitary and phytosanitary measures (SPS)

The main objectives of this Chapter are to:

(a) promote and facilitate the trade of animals, products of animal origin, plants and products of vegetal origin between the Parties, protecting at the same time public health, animal and vegetable health;

---

[13] Articles 44–50 of the Agreement.

(b) improve between the Parties the implementation of the SPS Agreement;[14]
(c) provide a forum to approach bilateral sanitary and phytosanitary measures, to solve the problems of trade that derive from them, and to expand trade opportunities; and
(d) provide mechanisms of communication and cooperation to resolve sanitary and phytosanitary issues in a prompt and efficient manner. [15]

The Parties agreed to increase the exchange of information, including the rule-making procedures that are necessary for the establishment of sanitary and phytosanitary measures that need to be undertaken as well as information regarding non-compliance with sanitary and phytosanitary requirements of an importing Party. Also, the Parties will exchange information related to the sanitary and phytosanitary condition in their territories and will provide the necessary information to develop risk assessment and equivalence processes.

In order to implement this Chapter appropriately, the Parties agreed to establish a Committee on Sanitary and Phytosanitary matters that will be composed of representatives of each Party who have responsibility for sanitary and phytosanitary matters. It will meet at least once a year unless the Parties otherwise agree.

This Committee[16] will provide a forum to:

(a) enhance mutual understanding of each Party's sanitary and phytosanitary measures and the regulatory processes related to those measures;
(b) consult on matters related to the development or application of sanitary and phytosanitary measures that affect, or may affect, trade between the Parties;
(c) consult on issues, positions, and agendas for meetings of the WTO SPS Committee, the various Codex committees (including the Codex Alimentarius Commission), the International Plant Protection Convention, the World Organization for Animal Health, and other international and regional fora on food safety and human, animal and plant health;
(d) coordinate technical cooperation programmes on sanitary and phytosanitary matters;
(e) improve bilateral understanding related to specific implementation issues concerning the SPS Agreement;
(f) review progress on addressing sanitary and phytosanitary matters that may arise between the Parties' agencies with responsibility for such matters; and
(g) hold consultations on the disputes concerning sanitary and phytosanitary matters that may arise.

---

[14] The WTO SPS Agreement is considered an integral part of the SPS Chapter in this Agreement.
[15] Article 53 of the Agreement.
[16] Article 58 of the Agreement.

E. Technical barriers to trade (TBT)

The main objectives of this Chapter are to increase and facilitate trade, and to fulfil the objectives of this Agreement, through the improvement of the implementation of the WTO TBT Agreement, the elimination of unnecessary technical barriers to trade and the enhancement of bilateral cooperation.

The Chapter contains transparency provisions that include the provision of information regarding the objective of, and rationale for, a technical regulation or conformity assessment procedure that the Party has adopted or is proposing to adopt.

Additionally, the Parties agreed to start a mutual recognition agreement (MRA) feasibility study within six months following the date of entry into force of this Agreement, referring to the APEC framework, if applicable.

Special attention is granted to bilateral technical cooperation. In this respect, the Parties will study the possibility of strengthening the relationship and links between compulsory and voluntary certification and strengthen the bilateral communication in this regard, as a means to facilitate market access. The Parties will also work towards increasing the information exchange, particularly regarding bilateral non-compliance with technical regulations and conformity assessment procedures.

Just as in the SPS chapter, it was agreed to create a Committee on Technical Barriers to Trade comprising representatives of each Party which shall meet at least once a year unless the Parties otherwise agree.

This Committee is the relevant forum for:

(a) monitoring the implementation and administration of this Chapter;
(b) promptly addressing any issue that a Party raises related to the development, adoption, application or enforcement of technical regulations and conformity assessment procedures;
(c) enhancing cooperation in the development and improvement of technical regulations and conformity assessment procedures;
(d) where appropriate, facilitating sectoral cooperation among governmental and non-governmental conformity assessment bodies in the Parties' territories;
(e) exchanging information on developments in non-governmental, regional and multilateral fora engaged in activities related to standardization, technical regulations and conformity assessment procedures;
(f) taking any other steps which the Parties consider to assist them in implementing the TBT Agreement and in facilitating trade in goods between them;
(g) consulting on any matter arising under this Chapter, upon a Party's request;
(h) reviewing this Chapter in light of any developments under the TBT Agreement, and developing recommendations for amendments to this Chapter in light of those developments; and
(i) exchanging information on charge parameters or services fees of compulsory conformity assessment procedures performed by governmental bodies.

F. Dispute settlement

It was agreed to include an expedited mechanism on dispute settlement that will allow both parties to resolve their trade disputes effectively within the Agreement.

This mechanism has a wide coverage and is applied to all the provisions of all the chapters in the Agreement, unless specifically excluded (as in the case of the Chapter on Cooperation). It shall apply with respect to the avoidance or settlement of all disputes between the Parties regarding the interpretation or application of this Agreement and wherever a Party considers that a measure of the other Party is inconsistent with the obligations of this Agreement or that the other Party has failed to carry out its obligations under this Agreement.

This chapter includes a choice of forum provision. In this respect, where a dispute regarding any matter arises under this Agreement and under another free trade agreement to which both Parties are parties or the WTO Agreement, the complaining Party may select the forum in which to settle the dispute. Once the complaining Party has requested a panel, the forum selected shall be used to the exclusion of the others.[17]

The procedure is composed of the following stages:[18]

(a) Consultations   Any Party may request consultations in writing with respect to any measure that it considers might affect the operation of the Agreement. Its main objective is to allow the Parties to arrive at a mutually satisfactory resolution of any matter. They shall be confidential and are without prejudice to the rights of any Party in any further proceedings.

(b) Intervention of the Commission[19]   If the Parties fail to resolve a matter, a Party may request in writing a meeting of the Commission. The Commission shall convene within 10 days of receipt of the request and shall endeavour to resolve the dispute promptly. In this respect, the Commission may assist the Parties to reach a mutually satisfactory resolution of the dispute. Additionally, it can call on such technical advisers or create such working groups or expert groups as it deems necessary; have recourse to good offices, conciliation, mediation; or make recommendations.

---

[17] Article 81 of the Agreement.   [18] Articles 82–93 of the Agreement.

[19] The Parties have in fact established the Free Trade Commission (Commission), which comprises representatives of the Parties. (China is represented by its Ministry of Commerce (MOFCOM) Chile is represented by its General Directorate of International Economic Affairs (DIRECON)). This Commission shall:

(a) supervise the implementation of this Agreement;
(b) oversee the further elaboration of this Agreement;
(c) seek to resolve disputes that may arise regarding the interpretation or application of this Agreement;
(d) supervise the work of all committees and working groups established under the Agreement;
(e) establish the amounts of remuneration and expenses that will be paid to panellists; and
(f) consider any other matter that may affect the operation of this Agreement.

(c) Establishment of an arbitral tribunal   If the Parties still fail to resolve the matter, either Party may request in writing the establishment of an arbitral panel to consider the matter. An arbitral panel shall be composed of three members.[20] The function of an arbitral panel is to make an objective assessment of the dispute before it, including an examination of the facts of the case and the applicability of and conformity with the Agreement. Where an arbitral panel concludes that a measure is inconsistent with the Agreement, it shall recommend that the responding Party bring the measure into conformity with the Agreement. In addition to its recommendations the arbitral panel may suggest ways in which the responding Party could implement the recommendations.

(d) Implementation of the final report   The Parties shall implement the recommendations contained in the final report of the arbitral panel. In case there is disagreement as to the existence or consistency with the Agreement of measures taken to comply with the recommendations of the arbitral panel, such dispute shall be referred to an arbitral panel proceeding, including wherever possible by resort to the original arbitral panel.

(e) Non-implementation – suspension of benefits   If the Party concerned fails to bring the measure found to be inconsistent with the Agreement into compliance with the recommendations of the arbitral panel, that Party shall, if so requested, enter into negotiations with the complaining Party with a view to reaching a mutually satisfactory agreement on any necessary compensatory adjustment. If there is no agreement, the complaining Party may suspend the application of benefits of equivalent effect to the responding Party if the arbitral panel decides the responding Party has not implemented the recommendations contained in the final report to bring the inconsistent measure into conformity. The complaining Party shall notify the responding Party 30 days before suspending benefits.

Compensation and the suspension of benefits shall be temporary measures. Neither compensation nor the suspension of benefits is preferred to full implementation of the recommendations to bring a measure into conformity with this Agreement. Compensation and suspension of benefits shall only be applied until such time as the measure found to be inconsistent with this Agreement has been removed, or the Party that must implement the arbitral panel's recommendation has done so, or a mutually satisfactory solution is reached.

---

[20] Each Party will designate one member of the arbitral tribunal. The third member will be designated by common agreement and will be the chair of the panel. If any member of the arbitral panel has not been designated, at the request of any Party to the dispute the necessary designations shall be made by the Director-General of the WTO.

G. Cooperation

The Parties agreed to establish close cooperation aimed at:

(a) promoting economic and social development;
(b) stimulating productive synergies, creating new opportunities for trade and investment and promoting competitiveness and innovation;
(c) increasing the level of and deepening cooperation actions while taking into account the association relation between the Parties;
(d) reinforcing and expanding cooperation, collaboration and mutual interchanges in the cultural areas;
(e) encouraging the presence of the Parties and their goods and services in their respective markets of Asia, Pacific and Latin America; and
(f) increasing the level of and deepening collaboration activities among the Parties in areas of mutual interest.

In this respect, this chapter embraces the following areas: Economic Cooperation; Research, Science and Technology; Education; Small and Medium Size Enterprises; Cultural Cooperation; Intellectual Property Rights; Investment Promotion; Mining and Industrial Cooperation.

The Parties shall enhance their communication and cooperation on labour and social security through the Memorandum of Understanding on Labour and Social Security Cooperation signed between the Parties (Article 108).

In this respect, both Parties commit to carry out cooperation activities in the fields of employment and labour policies and social dialogue, including decent work, labour laws and labour inspection; improvement of working conditions and worker training; globalization and its impact on employment, the working environment, industrial relations and governance and social security.

The cooperation activities mentioned above will be carried out by exchanges of information and expertise in the fields covered by the Memorandum; reciprocal visits of experts and delegations; joint organization of seminars, workshops and meetings for experts, regulatory authorities and other persons concerned; and consultations within the framework of multilateral discussions on employment, training, labour and social security issues.

Additionally, with a view to guaranteeing the implementation of this Memorandum, to establishing a cooperation programme to be carried out within a specified period and to coordinating the cooperation activities referred to in the Memorandum, each Party will appoint a coordinator who will meet on a regular basis every two years.

IV. Impact and prospects for future application

The Agreement entered into force on 1 October 2006 and, as noted, in its first stage covers the liberalization of trade in goods only. However, both Parties are aware of the importance of trade in services in the world economy, both overall and in developing countries. To a great extent, modern economies rely more on trade in services than on trade in goods. Due to the importance and increase of world exports in trade in services, the Parties agreed to a future work programme to broaden the scope of the Agreement and include provisions on trade in services and investment.[21]

In this respect, both Parties met in Beijing from 15–17 January 2007 and initiated negotiations to incorporate in the Agreement chapters on trade in services and investment.

Additionally, the Parties reviewed the impact of the Agreement since its entry into force, and observed that there is a positive impact on bilateral trade. Chilean exports to China, for example, increased by 37 per cent with respect to the same period in 2005. Chilean export products that have registered increases are wines, red meat, Pacific salmon and trout.

At the time of writing, only a few months have elapsed since the Agreement entered into force. Currently, along with considering a broadening of the scope of the Agreement to include trade in services and investment, the Parties are implementing the FTA and expanding bilateral goods trade commitments. The aim with respect to trade in goods is to lower and cut tariffs and non-tariff barriers and improve market access conditions. Its implementation will continue to facilitate bilateral trade in goods and stimulate the development of related industries in both countries. Both Chile and China are making full use of the conditions created by the Agreement in order to improve the commodity trade structure, diversify trade commodities, strengthen the exchange of information on markets, products and trade, promote their goods in the Asian and Latin American markets, broaden their bilateral ties and raise their bilateral economic and social cooperation level.

Sources

Antecedentes_de_la_Negociación_China_Junio2006_ING.pdf, Government of Chile, General Directorate for International Economic Affairs.

Asia and Oceania Department/General Directorate for International Economic Affairs, *Characteristics of the Free Trade Agreement Negotiation Between Chile and China* (June 2006), at www.direcon.cl/documentos/China2/ (last visited 11 June 2007).

Asia and Oceania Department/General Directorate for International Economic Affairs, *China–Chile Trade* (June 2006), at www.direcon.cl/documentos/China2/intercambio_comercial_chile_china_marzo_ING.pdf (last visited 11 June 2007).

'Chile, China Ratify Free Trade Accord', *Houston Chronicle, USA*, 9 August 2006.

'Chile, China to Sign Free Trade Accord', *Associated Press*, 28 October 2005.

'Chile–China Trade Pact Could Be Signed in November', *Reuters*, 20 September 2005.

---

[21] Article 120 of the Agreement.

Chilean High Level Study Group, *Joint Feasibility Study on a Free Trade Agreement Between Chile and China* (Santiago: Gorierno De Chile, October 2004).

DIRECON, 'Chile y China Evalúan Impactos de un Acuerdo de Libre Comercio' (15 Junio 2004).

DIRECON, 'Chile y China Inician Estudio Para Un Eventual Tratado de Libre Comercio' (26 Abril 2004).

DIRECON, 'Chile y China Inician Primera Ronda de Negociaciones' (25 Enero 2005).

DIRECON, 'Cierre de Negociación de TLC Chile–China' (28 Octubre 2005).

DIRECON, 'Concluyó Cuarta Ronda de Negociaciones Para un Tratado de Libre Comercio' (20 Septiembre 2005).

DIRECON, 'Concluyó la Tercera Ronda de Negociaciones Para un Tratado de Libre Comercio' (30 Junio 2005).

DIRECON, 'Revisan Estado de Avance de Estudio de Factibilidad' (16 Septiembre 2004).

Jiang Wei, 'China–Chile FTA Talks Smooth', *China Daily*, 31 January 2005.

'Latest China–Chile FTA Talks Complete', *China Daily*, 1 November 2005.

Memorandum of Understanding on Labour and Social Security Cooperation Between the Ministry of Labour and Social Security of the People's Republic of China and the Ministry of Labour and Social Security of the Republic of Chile.

Ministerio Secretaría General de Gobierno de Chile, 'residentes de Chile y China Suscribieron Tratado de Libre Comercio' (18 Noviembre 2005).

Prochile, 'TLC Chile–China Comienza a Regir a Partir de 1 de Octubre' (29 Septiembre 2006).

Zhao Huaxin, 'China, Chile Launch Free Trade Talks', *China Daily*, 19 November 2004.

4

European Union–Mexico Economic Partnership, Political Coordination and Cooperation Agreement

BRADLY J. CONDON

I. Introduction

Relations between Europe and Mexico have been dramatic ever since Hernán Cortez conquered the Aztec empire and established New Spain in the early sixteenth century. Along with many other Latin American countries, Mexico gained its independence from Spain in 1810 in a war of independence, after almost three centuries of Mexican gold and silver financing Spanish wars in Europe. Half a century later, Napoleon installed Maximilian von Hapsburg and his wife, Carlotta, as Emperor and Empress of Mexico in a dispute over debts owed to France. The Mexicans later shot Maximilian by firing squad in Querétero, while Carlotta went mad and died a ward of the Vatican (only to be resurrected decades later by Bette Davis in the black-and-white Hollywood movie, *Juárez*).

Trade liberalization and foreign investment were welcomed for three decades under Mexican dictator, Porfirio Díaz. That cycle of economic opening ended with the Mexican Revolution in 1910. The twentieth century witnessed the nationalization of the oil industry under President Lázaro Cárdenas in 1938 and of the banking industry under President José López Portillo in 1982, before swinging back to trade liberalization and a reopening to foreign investment under President Carlos Salinas de Gortari in the 1990s. On 1 July 2000, the new century marked the entry into force of the Mexico–European Union Free Trade Agreement (MEUFTA or Global Agreement), the most comprehensive trade agreement between Europe and Mexico since the Spanish conquistadores first established transatlantic trade relations almost half a millennium earlier.[1]

---

[1] Free Trade Agreement between the European Communities and Mexico, Decision No. 2/2000 of the EC–Mexico Joint Council of 23 March 2000, entered into force 1 July 2000 (with respect to trade in goods), available at www.worldtradelaw.net/fta/agreements/ecmexfta.pdf. MEUFTA was notified to the WTO in August 2000. See WTO document WT/REG/109/1, 3 August 2000. Decision No. 2/2000 (with respect to trade in services) entered into force 1 March 2001. See Edna Ramírez Robles, 'Political & quasi-adjudicative dispute settlement models in European Union Free Trade Agreements: Is the quasi-adjudicative model a trend or is it just another model?', WTO Staff Working Paper No. ERSD-2006–09 (November 2006), at p. 27, available at www.wto.org/english/res_e/reser_e/ersd200609_e.htm. Also see the text in Spanish at Diario Oficial de la Federación, 26 June 2000, where the provisions relating to

As a large, developing country, Mexico's market has more future growth potential than the mature markets of the European Union (EU)(15),[2] making it attractive to producers of goods, providers of commercial services and foreign investors. Indeed, the Mexican economy is forecast to be the fifth largest in the world by 2040, after China, the United States (US), India and Japan, and ahead of Russia, Brazil, Germany, Britain and France (all in that order, using market exchange rates).[3] Mexico's membership in the North American Free Trade Agreement (NAFTA) is a key element in its future growth prospects, its economic stability and its attractiveness as a destination for foreign direct investment (FDI). However, Mexico now has a network of free trade agreements with 43 countries on three continents (including the 25 members of the EU and Japan).

As of July 2006, Mexico had a trade deficit of US$4.1 billion for the previous twelve months and a current account deficit of US$600 million.[4] Foreign direct investment inflows for 2006 were forecast to be around US$14 billion for 2006, putting Mexico in sixth place among emerging markets, just behind Brazil.[5] The Euro area had a trade deficit of US$13.5 billion and a current account deficit of US$52.1 billion as of June 2006.[6] In the second quarter of 2006, Mexico's GDP grew 4.7%, while the Euro area's GDP grew at 2.4%.[7] For 2006 and 2007, Mexico's GDP was forecast to grow at 4% and 3.7%, respectively, while the Euro area was forecast to grow at 2.4% and 2%, both below the forecast of 5.1% and 4.9% for the global economy.[8] In 2006, inflation rates in Mexico and the Euro area were 3.5% and 2.3%, respectively.[9]

Mexico's key economic indicators (inflation, GDP growth and exchange rate fluctuations) have converged with those of its NAFTA partners in recent years. One result is that international markets now view Mexico as part of North America, rather than Latin America. This has insulated Mexico from the effects of economic instability elsewhere in Latin America (for example, in Brazil and Argentina) and has enhanced economic stability in Mexico, particularly compared with the high inflation and currency devaluations of the 1980s and early 1990s.

---

services, investment and intellectual property can be found, including the provisions and reservations regarding financial services, available at www.economia.gob.mx/work/snci/negociaciones/tlcuem/pdfs/sre2a.pdf.

[2] I will refer to the developed country members of the EU as the EU(15) and to the members as of 2006 as the EU(25). In 2007, the EU membership increased to 27, with the accession of Bulgaria and Romania.

[3] 'The New Titans: A survey of the world economy', *The Economist*, 16 September 2006, p. 12, citing the IMF and Goldman Sachs as sources. Also see Goldman Sachs, Global Economics Paper No. 134, at https://portal.gs.com.

[4] 'Emerging market indicators', *The Economist*, 16 September 2006, p. 116. [5] Ibid.

[6] 'Economic and financial indicators', *The Economist*, 16 September 2006, p. 115.

[7] Ibid., p. 114; and 'Emerging market indicators', above note 4, at p. 116.

[8] 'Economic and financial indicators', above note 6, at p. 114.

[9] Ibid.; and 'Emerging market indicators', above note 4, at p. 116.

A. The merchandise trade statistics are revealing

Mexico and the EU(25) both rank in the top ten globally in merchandise trade and in the top twenty in commercial services trade. In 2004, the EU(25) and Mexico ranked first and eighth, respectively, in world merchandise trade exports (excluding intra-EU(25) trade), and second and eighth, respectively, in world merchandise trade imports.[10] In 2004, the EU(25) and Mexico ranked first and twentieth, respectively, in world commercial services exports (excluding intra-EU(25) trade), and first and seventeenth, respectively, in world commercial services imports.[11]

Merchandise exports from the EU(25) to Mexico were worth US$18 billion in 2004, having grown 12% per year in 2003 and 2004 and making Mexico the destination of 0.5% of EU(25) exports in 2004, the same percentage as in 2000. Mexico's merchandise exports to the EU(25), at US$8.5 billion, were less than half as much, representing only 0.3% and 0.2% of EU(25) imports in 2000 and 2004, respectively. Mexico's exports to the EU grew at a faster rate than EU exports to Mexico in 2003 and 2004, increasing by 19% and 15%, respectively. However, Mexican exports to the EU grew more slowly than those from other major emerging economies in 2003 and 2004, such as China (41% and 33%), the Russian Federation (31% and 33%), Brazil (25% and 24%), and India (23% and 28%).[12]

In 2005, 11.6% of Mexico's imports came from the EU(25), compared with 8.6% in 2000 (the year that MEUFTA entered into force) and 12% in 1993 (the year before NAFTA entered into force).[13] The percentages for Mexico's NAFTA partners (the US plus Canada) for the same three years were 56.3% (2005), 75.4% (2000) and 71% (1993).[14] These figures suggest that NAFTA had the effect of increasing the percentage of Mexico's imports from its NAFTA partners, at the expense of the EU. Indeed, in the late 1990s, European business people complained that they were losing market share to the Americans, due to the tariff elimination under NAFTA. For Mexico, the strategy of signing free trade agreements (FTAs) around the globe appears to have achieved the objective of diversifying trade relations, with imports now growing faster with its newer FTA partners, such as Central America, Japan and the EU(25) (and World Trade Organization (WTO) members such as Korea, China and Taiwan with which Mexico does not have trade agreements), than with its

---

[10] 'Leading exporters and importers in world merchandise trade (excluding intra-EU (25) trade)' (2004), at www.wto.org/english/res_e/statis_e/its2005_e/section1_e/i06.xls.

[11] 'Leading exporters and importers in world trade in commercial services (excluding intra-EU (25) trade)' (2004), at www.wto.org/english/res_e/statis_e/its2005_e/section1_e/i08.xls.

[12] 'Merchandise trade of the European Union (25) by region and economy' (2004), at www.wto.org/english/res_e/statis_e/its2005_e/section3_e/iii37.xls.

[13] Secretaría de Economía, Subsecretaría de Negociaciones Comerciales Internacionales, Inteligencia Comercial, 'Importaciones totales de México', available at www.economia.gob.mx/?P&=2261#, with author's own calculations.

[14] 'Importaciones totales', above note 13, with author's own calculations.

NAFTA partners.[15] The result is that the percentage of Mexico's total imports that come from its NAFTA partners has decreased significantly.

The statistical pattern of downs and ups for its EU(25) trade is similar for Mexico's exports, but Mexico's exports remain destined for North America in their overwhelming majority. Of Mexico's total exports, 4.6% were destined for the EU(25) in 2005, compared with 3.4% in 2000 and 5.4% in 1993.[16] North America received the following percentages of Mexican exports in these years: 88.2% (2005), 90.7% (2000), and 85.7% (1993).[17] Thus, Mexico has clearly been less successful in diversifying destinations for exports than it has been in diversifying sources of imports. One possible reason for the high percentage in the export category is high oil prices, which increase the value of Mexican exports to the US. Currency fluctuations are an unlikely cause of fluctuations in Mexican trade with the US in recent years, since the exchange rate has been fairly stable. The appreciation of the euro against the peso in recent years should have the effect of reducing EU exports to Mexico and increasing Mexican exports to the EU. Indeed, currency fluctuations may have a greater impact on trade than tariff elimination.

Both the EU(25) and Mexico are major producers of automotive goods. Mexico ranks sixth in exports and fourth in imports, while the EU(25) ranks first in both categories (although, excluding intra-EU trade, the EU ranks only third in imports, remaining first in exports).[18] Moreover, they are each major trade partners for the other in automotive goods. Mexico is the eighth largest supplier of automotive goods to the EU(25), while the EU(25) is the second largest supplier of automotive goods to Mexico. However, growth in automotive exports slowed dramatically in 2004, compared with 2003. The growth rate for Mexico's exports to the EU went from 59% to −7%, while the EU's went from 13.8% to −4%. In the North American market, the EU and Mexico are close competitors, ranking third and fourth, respectively, as suppliers in both the Canadian and American automotive markets.[19]

In office and telecom equipment, both the EU(25) and Mexico are leading exporters (ranking fourth, for extra-EU exports, and tenth) and importers (ranking second, for extra-EU imports, and tenth).[20] In the category of office machines and telecom equipment, Mexico represents only 0.4% of EU(25) imports, ranking just 18th as a supplier to the EU. In contrast, Mexico ranks second as a supplier to the US, with 12.6% of US imports.[21]

---

[15] 'Importaciones totales', above note 13.   [16] Ibid., with author's own calculations.   [17] Ibid.
[18] 'Leading exporters and importers of automotive products' (2004), at www.wto.org/english/res_e/statis_e/its2005_e/section4_e/iv66.xls.
[19] 'Imports of automotive products of selected economies by region and supplier' (2004), at www.wto.org/english/res_e/statis_e/its2005_e/section4_e/iv65.xls.
[20] 'Leading exporters and importers of office and telecom equipment' (2004), at www.wto.org/english/res_e/statis_e/its2005_e/section4_e/iv46.xls.
[21] 'Imports of office and telecom equipment of selected economies by region and supplier' (2004), at www.wto.org/english/res_e/statis_e/its2005_e/section4_e/iv45a.xls.

In the broader category of manufactures, Mexico ranks ninth in exports and seventh in imports, while the EU(25) ranks first in both categories.[22] Both the EU(25) and Mexico saw exports of manufactures grow rapidly in 2004, at 18% and 13%, respectively, as well as imports, at 18% and 15%.[23] However, Mexico represents only 0.2% of EU(25) imports of manufactures, ranking just twenty-fifth as a supplier to the EU.[24] In contrast, Mexico ranks fifth as a supplier of manufactures to the US, with 10.6% of US imports.[25]

Globally, Mexico ranks thirteenth in exports and tenth in imports of iron and steel, while the EU(25) ranks first in both categories.[26] Mexico does not even rank in the top thirty suppliers of iron and steel and thus represents less than 0.1% of EU(25) imports.[27]

The EU(25) is a distant second in exports of textiles to Mexico, with 6.1% of Mexican imports, after first-place US, with 76% of Mexican imports. Mexico ranks thirty-fourth in EU(25) textiles imports.[28] In contrast, Mexico is the fifth largest supplier of textiles to both Canada (with 3% of Canadian imports) and the US (with 8.2% of US imports).[29] Mexico is the sixth largest supplier of clothing to Canada (with 5.2% of Canadian imports) and the second largest to the US (with 9.2% of US imports).[30] However, Mexico does not even make it into the top forty suppliers of clothing to the EU(25), with less than 0.1% of EU clothing imports.[31]

The EU(25) and Mexico are both major traders of agricultural goods. However, agricultural trade between them represents a small percentage of overall trade. The EU(25) ranks first and Mexico ranks thirteenth in agricultural exports.[32] However, agricultural exports form a greater share of EU exports (9.3%) than

---

[22] 'Leading exporters and importers of manufactures' (2004), at www.wto.org/english/res_e/statis_e/its2005_e/section4_e/iv26.xls.
[23] Ibid.
[24] 'Imports of manufactures of selected economies by region and supplier' (2004), at www.wto.org/english/res_e/statis_e/its2005_e/section4_e/iv25a.xls.
[25] Ibid.
[26] 'Leading exporters and importers of iron and steel' (2004), at www.wto.org/english/res_e/statis_e/its2005_e/section4_e/iv34.xls.
[27] 'Imports of iron and steel of the European Union (25) and the United States by region and supplier' (2004), at www.wto.org/english/res_e/statis_e/its2005_e/section4_e/iv33.xls.
[28] 'Textile imports of selected economies by region and supplier' (2004) (*continuation*), at www.wto.org/english/res_e/statis_e/its2005_e/section4_e/iv73b.xls.
[29] 'Textile imports of selected economies by region and supplier' (2004), at www.wto.org/english/res_e/statis_e/its2005_e/section4_e/iv73a.xls.
[30] 'Clothing imports of selected economies by region and supplier' (2004), at www.wto.org/english/res_e/statis_e/its2005_e/section4_e/iv81a.xls.
[31] 'Clothing imports of selected economies by region and supplier' (2004) (*continuation*), at www.wto.org/english/res_e/statis_e/its2005_e/section4_e/iv81b.xls.
[32] 'Leading exporters and importers of agricultural products' (2004), at www.wto.org/english/res_e/statis_e/its2005_e/section4_e/iv08.xls.

Mexican exports (6%).[33] The EU(25) also ranks first and Mexico ranks eighth in agricultural imports.[34] As with exports, agricultural imports form a greater share of EU imports (9.9%) than Mexican imports (7.8%).[35] However, Mexico's share of EU imports is only 0.1%, placing Mexico in thirty-seventh place among suppliers of agricultural goods to the EU.[36] Mexico receives 0.8% of EU agricultural exports, ranking twentieth as an export market for EU agricultural products.[37] However, Mexico's agricultural exports to the EU are growing faster (19%) than EU agricultural exports to Mexico (7%).[38]

While Mexico is a major oil producer, fuels do not make up a significant portion of Mexican exports to the EU (less than 1%). Rather, Mexico's fuel exports go to the US, where it is the fourth largest supplier (at 9.4%), just behind Saudi Arabia (10.1%) and Venezuela (10.9%). Canada is the top supplier of fuels to the US (23%). This is not surprising, given the EU's geographic proximity to its major suppliers (Russia, Norway, Saudi Arabia and Libya).[39]

The EU(25) and Mexico are both leading exporters and importers of pharmaceuticals, although there is huge gap in their shares of world trade. In exports, they rank first and ninth, with 72% and 0.7% of world exports, respectively. In imports, they also rank first and ninth, with 14.9% and 1.2% of world imports. (The EU ranks first in both categories whether including or excluding intra-EU trade.) However, Mexico's trade in pharmaceuticals is growing at a faster rate than the other leading exporters (at 32%, exceeded only by Israel among the top fifteen) and importers (at 35%, in first place).[40]

The EU(25) and Mexico are leading exporters of chemicals in the world, ranking first (with extra-EU exports at 19.6% of global trade) and thirteenth (0.8%). As importers they rank first (with extra-EU imports at 10.9% of global trade) and seventh (2.1%). The growth rate in exports was high in 2004 for both the EU (18%) and Mexico (28%), as well as for imports to the EU (20%) and to Mexico (16%).[41]

The picture that emerges from the foregoing statistics suggests that a primary motivation for Mexico to enter into the FTA with the EU was to diversify its trade relations beyond North America, with which Mexico has traditionally conducted

---

[33] 'Exports of agricultural products of selected economies' (1990–04), at www.wto.org/english/res_e/statis_e/its2005_e/section4_e/iv09.xls.
[34] 'Leading exporters and importers of agricultural products', above note 32.
[35] 'Imports of agricultural products of selected economies' (1990–04), at www.wto.org/english/res_e/statis_e/its2005_e/section4_e/iv10.xls.
[36] 'Imports of agricultural products of selected economies by region and supplier' (2004), at www.wto.org/english/res_e/statis_e/its2005_e/section4_e/iv07b.xls.
[37] Ibid.   [38] Ibid.
[39] 'Imports of fuels of selected economies by region and supplier' (2004), at www.wto.org/english/res_e/statis_e/its2005_e/section4_e/iv18.xls.
[40] 'Leading exporters and importers of pharmaceuticals' (2004), at www.wto.org/english/res_e/statis_e/its2005_e/section4_e/iv40.xls.
[41] 'Leading exporters and importers of chemicals' (2004), at www.wto.org/english/res_e/statis_e/its2005_e/section4_e/iv39.xls.

the overwhelming majority of its trade. With only 0.5% of EU merchandise imports coming from Mexico and only 0.2% of EU merchandise exports destined for Mexico, bilateral trade volume is relatively insignificant for the EU. When viewed from Mexico's perspective, bilateral trade with the EU(25) is more significant, at 11.6% of imports and 4.6% of exports, and has returned more or less to pre-NAFTA percentages of Mexico's trade. For the EU(25), a strong motivation for the FTA would have been to compete more effectively with the US in the Mexican market and it appears to have achieved this goal.

In terms of the products traded, the automotive trade between the EU and Mexico is significant for both and likely represented the most significant source of industry pressure for a trade agreement with respect to merchandise trade. Trade in manufactures, iron and steel, and chemicals are insignificant for Mexico. Bilateral agricultural trade is insignificant for both. Trade in fuels is insignificant and likely to remain so due to geography. Trade in textiles is significant for the EU, but not for Mexico. In pharmaceuticals, Mexico represents an attractive emerging market for the EU. While the EU and Mexico are both major traders in goods, they have not developed commensurate trade relations. Thus, for both, another motivation for the FTA is to pursue numerous unexploited opportunities to expand trade in goods.

Given the relatively insignificant amount of bilateral trade between Mexico and the EU in most major product categories, it comes as no surprise that there have been few trade disputes. As at the date of writing, there has only been one case between Mexico and the EU at the WTO that has progressed beyond the consultations stage. At the WTO, most of Mexico's trade disputes have involved the US.[42] This is not surprising, since Mexico conducts the overwhelming majority of its trade with the US. Mexico has been involved in sixteen WTO disputes as complainant, of which seven were against the US and three were against the EU (however, the three EU cases have been different incarnations of the bananas dispute).[43] Mexico has been involved in fourteen WTO disputes as respondent, of which six were with the US and three were with the EU. However, two of the three cases involving the EU as complainant involved olive oil at different stages of a countervailing duty investigation and none of the three cases had progressed past the consultations stage at the time of writing (although the most recent olive oil case appeared ripe for litigation).[44]

---

[42] See www.wto.org/english/tratop_e/dispu_e/dispu_by_country_e.htm.

[43] WTO Appellate Body, *EC–Bananas III* (two other cases on the same topic have not got past the consultations stage: DS16 and DS158).

[44] *México–Customs Valuation of Imports*, DS53 (consultations stage, requested 27 August 1996); *México–Provisional Countervailing Measures on Olive Oil from the European Communities*, DS314 (consultations stage, requested 18 August 2004); and *México–Definitive Countervailing Measures on Olive Oil from the European Communities*, DS341 (consultations stage, requested 31 March 2006).

B. Mexico's FTAs stimulate foreign direct investment

In the decade following the signing of NAFTA (1992–2001), Mexico became the second favourite destination for foreign direct investment among the Organization for Economic Cooperation and Development (OECD) countries in terms of cumulative net flows, after the US.[45] After NAFTA entered into force in 1994, Mexico became the second largest destination of foreign direct investment worldwide among the developing countries, after China.[46] However, Mexico's relative attractiveness as a destination for FDI has had its ups and downs since, in part due to the rise in the attractiveness of other major emerging markets, such as Poland, India, Russia and Brazil.[47] Mexico's FTAs with the EU and Japan have helped Mexico to compete for FDI with these other emerging markets.

Mexico's attractiveness as a destination for FDI has been influenced by MEUFTA and, indeed, attracting FDI was a key motivation for Mexico to seek the FTA in the first place. Mexico ranked as the fifth most attractive destination for FDI worldwide in 2001. It dropped to ninth place in 2002 (its lowest rank since A.T. Kearney began its survey of FDI attractiveness), primarily due to a decline in the interest of European multinationals (ahead of the 2004 expansion of the EU).[48] Outside Europe, Mexico remained a highly attractive destination for FDI. Canada ranked Mexico number two, the US ranked Mexico number six, and Japan ranked Mexico in the top five.[49] In 2003, Mexico moved up to third place, after China and the US. What increased Mexico's attractiveness in 2003, apart from its proximity to the US and its economic stability, were acquisitions in Mexico's financial sector and lower tariffs for goods from Europe under MEUFTA.[50] In 2004, Mexico dropped dramatically, to twenty-second place, rising to sixteenth place in 2005, just behind Japan.[51]

Mexico has pursued a hub-and-spoke strategy with respect to its FTA policy, signing a series of FTAs in order to increase its attractiveness as a hub for FDI in the manufacturing sector.[52] Manufacturing and financial services rank first and second as destinations for FDI in Mexico, together accounting for almost three-quarters of FDI flows over the past twelve years. From 1994 to 2005, inclusive, 48.9%

---

[45] OECD, *International Investment Perspectives: 2002 Edition* (Paris: OECD, September 2002); and Bradly J. Condon and Tapen Sinha, *Drawing Lines in Sand and Snow: Border Security and North American Economic Integration* (New York: M.E. Sharpe, 2003), Table 4.9.
[46] UNCTAD, *World Investment Report 2002: Transnational Corporations and Export Competitiveness* (Geneva: UNCTAC, 17 September 2002); and Condon and Sinha, above note 45, at Chapter 4.
[47] A.T. Kearney Foreign Direct Investment (FDI) Confidence Survey (various years), at www.atkearney.com. This survey asks the world's largest 1,000 firms about their opinions and their investment intentions regarding the 68 countries that receive 90 per cent of global FDI flows. These companies are responsible for about 70 per cent of global FDI flows.
[48] A.T. Kearney FDI Survey (2002), above note 47. [49] Ibid.
[50] A.T. Kearney FDI Survey (2003), above note 47. [51] A.T. Kearney FDI Survey (2005), above note 47.
[52] This term was coined by Canadian economist, Richard Lipsey to describe the effect on FDI decisions where one country (the 'hub') has bilateral FTAs with other countries (the 'spokes').

(US$80,794.1 billion) of Mexico's total FDI (US$165,112.1 billion) was destined for the manufacturing sector.[53] During this same period, 23.4% (US$38,691.2 billion) was destined for the financial services sector.[54] FDI in manufacturing has been more or less evenly spread across this twelve-year period, with 53.7% taking place in the second half.[55] However, FDI in financial services has been concentrated in the flows from 2000 to 2005, when 85% of the total flowed into Mexico's financial services industry.[56] This coincides with Mexico allowing up to 100% foreign ownership of financial services firms in 2000 for firms from NAFTA and MEUFTA countries.

NAFTA and MEUFTA countries account for over 90% of the sources of FDI in Mexico in the seven-year period from 1999 to 2005.[57] The US is the top source of FDI in Mexico, making up 63.6% of the total.[58] Spain is second (12.2%), the Netherlands third (8%), Canada fourth (2.7%), the United Kingdom fifth (2.3%) and Germany is sixth (2.2%).[59] During this period, French FDI in Mexico declined by US$688.1 billion.[60] Much of this FDI can be accounted for in large investments made by multinational firms. For example, in 2001, the American financial services firm Citigroup paid US$14 billion for the Mexican bank Banamex, which represented half of Mexico's FDI inflows that year and two-thirds of the US total. Similarly, over this period there were large investments from the automobile manufacturer Volkswagen (Germany) and from several multinational financial services firms: BBVA and Santander (Spain), ING (Netherlands), Scotiabank (Canada) and HSBC (United Kingdom).

Both NAFTA and MEUFTA have had a significant impact on both Mexico's attractiveness as a destination for FDI and in terms of the actual FDI flows, particularly in manufacturing and in financial services. More recently, the MEUFTA effect on Mexico's attractiveness has been repeated with the Japan–Mexico Economic Partnership Agreement (Japan–Mexico EPA). In 2005, the year that the Japan–Mexico EPA entered into force, Japanese investors ranked Mexico their fifth most attractive market, up from below the top twenty-five in 2004.[61] Thus, the Mexican government's strategy of using FTAs to diversify its trade and investment ties beyond the US appears to be working with respect to both FDI and trade. Over the long term, Mexico will remain a highly attractive destination for FDI due to its geographic location, the size and potential of its internal market and its network of free trade agreements. However, the FDI and trade boost that Mexico gets from its FTAs may fade if other major emerging markets pursue similar FTA strategies or if

---

[53] Author's calculations based on figures from Inversión extranjera directa según sector económico, Secretaría de Economía, 'Dirección General de Inversión Extranjera', at www.inegi.gob.mx/est/contenidos/espanol/rutinas/ept.asp?t&=sext04&c&=5006.
[54] Ibid.   [55] Ibid.   [56] Ibid.
[57] Author's calculations based on figures from 'Inversión extranjera directa anual según principales países de origen', at www.inegi.gob.mx/est/contenidos/espanol/rutinas/ept.asp?t&=sext03&c&=5005 (last visited 2 March 2006).
[58] Ibid.   [59] Ibid.   [60] Ibid.   [61] A.T. Kearney FDI Survey (2005), above note 47.

multilateral trade negotiations dilute the effect of Mexico's FTAs. Nevertheless, the relatively long-term nature of FDI, together with the long-term attractiveness of the Mexican market, means that a significant portion of the recent FDI flows to Mexico are likely to remain there, provided Mexico's domestic economic policies promote its promise as a major emerging economy.

C. Mexico's automotive sector: emerging markets and the FDI-trade linkage

Trade and FDI barriers affect the location decisions of firms that import inputs and export finished products. Mexico has attracted considerable FDI in automobile production for this and other reasons. Mexico enjoys a labour cost advantage over the other NAFTA members, Japan and the EU(15). Mexico improved treatment of foreign investors through amendments to its Foreign Investment Law, the signing of NAFTA, and the negotiation of foreign investor protection agreements. Mexico reduced political risk (through democratic reforms prior to the 2000 election) and economic risk (through the introduction of a floating exchange rate in 1994). Prior to these reforms, Mexico had attracted automobile producers by making access to its domestic market conditional upon FDI in local manufacturing and the use of local inputs. However, as Mexico liberalized its trade and investment regimes, car manufacturers chose to locate or expand operations in Mexico for other reasons.

Mexico enjoys a strategic geographic location. Its proximity to both the sizeable North American car market and the emerging Latin American car markets (including Mexico's large emerging market) makes Mexico's location very attractive for a product that is expensive to transport. In addition, Mexico's Atlantic and Pacific ports facilitate transportation of inputs and finished products to both Asia and Europe. When one adds to this Mexico's FTAs with North America, Europe, Japan and Latin America, Mexico begins to look like a very attractive location for FDI in car manufacturing. With its network of FTAs, Mexico now provides preferential access to all the major car markets.

The NAFTA rules of origin for automobiles required the percentage of NAFTA content to rise (from 50% of net cost in 1994 to 60% or 62.5% in 2003, depending on the type of vehicle), in order to qualify for duty-free treatment. This gave North American based manufacturers an advantage over those based in Europe and Asia. To compete in the North American market, European and Asian car manufacturers had to produce cars in North America. While many already did, those which did not, or which chose to expand North American production, have had several incentives to choose Mexico over the US or Canada (of course, protectionist rules of origin in other FTAs have the potential to throw a spanner into the works).

For Mexico, a clear motivation for the MEUFTA negotiations was to attract more FDI from European automobile manufacturers. For the EU, the elimination of tariffs on automotive inputs in Mexico would make it easier to compete with North American based automotive manufacturers whose tariffs on inputs were eliminated under NAFTA. Increased investment in automobile manufacturing in Mexico from the EU and Japan will help to diversify Mexico's trade relations, by increasing intra-firm trade in inputs. Thus, in the automotive industry, MEUFTA helps Mexico achieve key trade policy objectives: to increase and diversify sources of FDI and to expand and diversify trade relations. For the EU, it facilitates competition with North American producers by lowering the cost of North American manufacturing operations.

D. Trade in commercial services

NAFTA opened up the Mexican financial services market to a greater degree than did the WTO financial services agreements.[62] Under the WTO General Agreement on Trade in Services (GATS), market access commitments must be applied without discrimination to all WTO Members, unless exceptions are listed in an annex on most favoured nation (MFN) exemptions in the lists of specific commitments of WTO Members. Article V of the GATS permits WTO Members to enter into agreements that liberalize trade in services beyond GATS, just as Article XXIV of the GATT permits Members to create free trade areas and customs unions. Thus, preferential treatment granted to NAFTA members does not have to be extended to other WTO Members, nor be listed in the MFN exemptions.[63] With NAFTA, Mexico permitted up to 100% foreign ownership of financial services providers by Canadian and American investors, compared with a limit of 49% for foreign investors from other jurisdictions in Mexico's WTO commitments.[64]

With MEUFTA, companies from the EU gained the same degree of access to the Mexican financial services market that Canadian and American firms received in NAFTA.[65] MEUFTA contains provisions for financial services that mirror those of

---

[62] See Bradly J. Condon, *NAFTA, WTO and Global Business Strategy: How AIDS, Trade and Terrorism Affect Our Economic Future* (Westport: Quorum Books, 2002), Chapter 3. See also Joel P. Trachtman, 'Trade in Financial Services under GATS, NAFTA and the EC: A Regulatory Jurisdiction Analysis' (1995) 34(1) *Columbia Journal of Transnational Law* 37–122.

[63] See Bradly J. Condon, 'Smoke and Mirrors: A Comparative Analysis of WTO and NAFTA Provisions Affecting the International Expansion of Insurance Firms in North America' (2001) 8 *Connecticut Insurance Law Journal* 97–130.

[64] México, Lista de compromisos específicos, Suplemento 3, GATS/SC/56/Suppl.3, 26 de febrero de 1998. Mexico's WTO commitments are limited to the provision of financial services by foreign companies through a commercial presence in the country, that is, through foreign investment.

[65] For a more detailed discussion of the obligations of the NAFTA countries in financial services under NAFTA and WTO, see Condon, above note 62, at Chapter 3. Regarding the Mexican insurance market specifically, see Bradly J. Condon, Joyce C. Sadka and Tapen Sinha, *Insurance Regulation in North America: Integrating American, Canadian and Mexican Markets* (London: Kluwer Law International, 2003); and Bradly J. Condon and Tapen Sinha, 'The Mexican Insurance Sector under the Shadow of the North American Free Trade Agreement (NAFTA)' (2001) 20 *Journal of Insurance Regulation* 207–19. Regarding the interaction of NAFTA and MEUFTA in the North American insurance market, see Bradly J. Condon and Tapen Sinha, 'Digesting the Regulatory Layer Cake in the North American Insurance Market', *Global Reinsurance* 64–71, London, December 2001/January 2002.

NAFTA, except for two important differences. First, the MEUFTA contains no equivalent to NAFTA Chapter 11 (which applies to foreign investment generally). The majority of the EU members have negotiated bilateral investment treaties with Mexico that provide substantially the same protection for foreign investors as NAFTA Chapter 11. Second, Mexico's MEUFTA reservations limit foreign investment in financial services firms to 49%. However, Mexico allows European investors to avoid this restriction by establishing or acquiring a financial holding company, through which they may establish or acquire financial services firms.[66]

For the EU, as in the automotive sector, a key reason for MEUFTA was to provide the European financial services industry the same opportunities as those enjoyed by North American firms in the emerging Mexican market. The Mexican financial services industry is now dominated by European firms (such as BBVA, Santander, HSBC, and ING) and North American firms (such as Citigroup and Scotiabank). For Mexico, major investments from these multinational firms increased FDI and, as noted above, increased Mexico's attractiveness for further FDI.

II. The negotiating process

On 2 May 1995 Mexico and the European Union signed the Paris Declaration and announced their decision to create a new, global agreement (1) to strengthen political dialogue, (2) to establish a free trade area and (3) to intensify cooperation. On 8 December 1997, Mexico and the EU signed the Economic Partnership, Political Coordination and Cooperation Agreement and the Interim Agreement on Trade and Accompanying Measures, which included a mandate for the negotiation of a free trade area. The Mexican Senate and the European Parliament ratified these agreements on 23 April and 13 May 1998, respectively.[67] This step allowed the parties to negotiate merchandise trade issues, which came under EU jurisdiction, without having to await the approval of the Global Agreement by the Member States and the EU. It also authorized the EU to negotiate issues that fell under the jurisdiction of the Member States (services, investment and intellectual property).[68]

The trade negotiations successfully concluded on 24 November 1999. The Global Agreement was signed on 8 December 1997 and was ratified by the Mexican Senate on 20 March 2000 and completed the ratification process in European national

---

[66] See Condon, Sadka and Sinha, above note 65, at Chapter 3. See the text in Spanish at Diario Oficial de la Federación, 26 June 2000, where the provisions relating to services and investment can be found, including the provisions and reservations regarding financial services.

[67] Jaime Zabludovsky K. and Sergio Gómez Lora, 'The European Window: Challenges in the Negotiation of Mexico's Free Trade Agreement with the European Union', Intal Working Paper SITI-09, July 2005, available at www.iadb.org/intal/aplicaciones/uploads/publicaciones/i_IECI_WP_09_Zabludovsky_ Lora. pdf.

[68] Ibid. See also Edna Ramírez Robles, *Solución de controversias en los acuerdos celebrados entre México y la Comunidad Europea* (Guadalajara: University of Guadalajara, 2003), at p. 89; and Robles, above note 1, at p. 27.

Parliaments in February 2001. On 23 March 2001, the President of Mexico, Ernesto Zedillo signed the Lisbon Declaration and the Global Agreement with the European Union at the summit of EU leaders in Lisbon.[69] The Mexican Senate and the European Parliament approved the trade agreement before the Global Agreement had been ratified by the Parliaments of the 15 Member States. For this reason, the trade agreement entered into force in July 2000, whereas the non-trade portions of the agreement (on political dialogue and cooperation) did not enter into force until March 2001.[70]

Table 4.1 sets out the chronology of the context and the negotiations.[71] The entry of Portugal and Spain into the EEC raised the profile of EU relations with Latin America and coincided with the beginning of Mexico's economic opening in 1986. The NAFTA served as a motive for both sides to seek a counterweight in the MEUFTA. Table 4.1 notes some of the differences that had to be resolved during the different stages of the negotiations.

The key challenges in the trade negotiations were with respect to tariff elimination schedules for industrial products, agricultural trade, rules of origin and services and investment.[72] The EU sought NAFTA parity with tariff elimination on most industrial goods by 2003, whereas Mexico sought longer transition periods. The result was that the EU eliminated its tariffs by 2003, while Mexico eliminated its tariffs by 2007, with tariffs on certain products of interest to the EU eliminated by 2003 (such as automotive goods). With respect to agricultural trade, Mexico's objections to EU export subsidies under the Common Agricultural Policy (CAP) were addressed in two ways. First, cereals, dairy products and meat products that benefited from CAP subsidies were placed in a special category for sensitive products. Second, the liberalization of trade in these products was made contingent upon CAP reforms (which ultimately did not take place, leaving these products excluded from the liberalization process). The parties accommodated Mexico's export interests in agricultural products by creating preferential quotas and seasonal windows. Finally, tariff elimination for covered agricultural products was scheduled to occur over ten years. With respect to rules of origin, the EU negotiators were instructed to follow the standard 'single European list of rules of origin', whose aim was to harmonize EU rules across its various trade agreements. However, these rules were designed with Eastern European and North African countries in mind; their production chains were more integrated with Europe's, while Mexico's was more integrated with US production chains. The EU therefore agreed to flexibility in the sectors of greatest interest to Mexico (automotive, chemicals, electronics, textiles and clothing and footwear). With respect to investment and services, Mexico gave

---

[69] See www.embamex.co.uk/Update/2000/01/free_trade.htm.
[70] Zabludovsky and Gómez Lora, above note 67.
[71] The sources for this table are Ramírez Robles, *Solución de controversias*, above note 68; and Zabludovsky and Gómez Lora, above note 67.
[72] Zabludovsky and Gómez Lora, above note 67, at pp. 19–24.

Table 4.1 Antecedents and chronology of negotiations

Place	Date	Subject	Stumbling blocks
–	1986	Portugal and Spain join EEC. Mexico joins GATT	
–	July 1989	Mexican President, King of Spain, PM of Spain agree to organize Iberian and Latin American Leaders Summit	
Guadalajara	July 1991	First Ibero-American Leaders Summit	
–	Oct 1991	Mexico–EU Cooperation Framework Agreement enters into force	
–	Sept 1992	NAFTA signed	
–	Jan 1994	NAFTA enters into force	
Paris	May 1995	Decision to create new global Mexico–EU agreement	Differences arise regarding the goal. Mexico's main interest is the FTA
–	Dec 1997	Economic Partnership, Political Coordination and Cooperation Agreement signed	Differences over wording of democratic clause resolved in favour of EU when Mexico recognizes that the wording is standard in all EU association agreements
–	Dec 1997	Interim Agreement on Trade signed, including mandate to negotiate FTA	FTA mandate uses term 'preferential' and refers to GATT Article XXIV, avoiding explicit mention of the FTA to accommodate EU
–	Nov 1999	Trade negotiations conclude after nine rounds	Key challenges: tariff elimination schedules, agricultural trade, rules of origin, services and investment
–	July 2000	FTA enters into force	
Lisbon	March 2001	Mexican President and EU leaders sign Lisbon Declaration and Global Agreement following ratification by Mexican Senate and European national Parliaments	
–	March 2001	Non-trade elements enter into force	

the EU the same access for financial services as that enjoyed by the NAFTA countries. However, in the other areas of services and investment, the parties are only obliged to not introduce new restrictions in national legislation. Commitments to revisit this area have been overtaken by the WTO Doha Round negotiations.

While Mexico had been using the NAFTA as a model for other FTAs, the EU used a format that reflected the combination of supranational and national jurisdiction over the issues under negotiation and, therefore, Mexico decided to abandon the NAFTA format.[73] The EU's share of Mexico's total trade had dropped under NAFTA; this provided a motivation for both Mexico and the EU to negotiate the FTA. In addition, Mexico's NAFTA obligation to end its duty drawback and duty free programmes for inputs used in products exported to NAFTA countries was to enter into force 1 January 2001. This would make Mexico a less attractive destination for EU FDI, because Mexico had higher MFN tariffs than Canada or the US; without the MEUFTA or the duty drawbacks, Mexico would be a relatively less attractive base for the EU's North American manufacturing plants, particularly in the automotive sector. In addition, Mexico's access to the EU market had been eroded by unilateral changes to the EU's Generalized System of Preferences (GSP) programme in 1995 and the extension of preferential treatment under the EU FTAs with other countries.[74]

Under the Mexican Constitution, international treaties are negotiated and signed by the President and ratified by the Senate. Once ratified, treaties become self-executing and do not require an act of transformation, such as implementing legislation; in other words, Mexico's is a monist system, rather than a dualist system like the US or Canada. This means that treaties can be applied or invoked directly before the Mexican courts.[75]

However, the hierarchy of treaties in the domestic legal system is a debatable issue in Mexico. The Supreme Court of Mexico has interpreted Article 133 of the Mexican Constitution to find that treaties rank below the Mexican Constitution, but above federal and state law.[76] However, this ruling does not constitute binding precedent in the Mexican legal system and many legal scholars consider that treaties are at the same level as federal law.[77] Nevertheless, in practice, the Mexican government is treating the Supreme Court decision as an accurate statement of the law.[78]

While some federal legislation is amended in Mexico to reflect changes brought about by treaties, this does not always occur. For example, in the case of financial

---

[73] Ibid., at p. 18.   [74] Ibid.
[75] See Condon, Sadka and Sinha, above note 65, at Chapter 2. Also see Ramírez Robles, *Solución de controversias*, above note 68, at pp. 60–1.
[76] See Mexican Supreme Court Tesis P.LXXVII./99. See also Condon, Sadka and Sinha, above note 65, at Chapter 2; and Robles, *Solución de controversias*, above note 68, at p. 62.
[77] In the Mexican legal system, in order to create binding 'jurisprudencia', the Supreme Court must consistently rule on the same point in five cases.
[78] See Condon, Sadka and Sinha, above note 65.

services, the Foreign Investment Law continued to limit foreign investors to a maximum of 49%. However, NAFTA and MEUFTA allowed up to 100% in this sector. In practice, the government agency charged with approving the investments allowed up to 100% for NAFTA and MEUFTA investors, treating the treaties as superior to the federal law.[79]

In Mexico, the Secretaría de Economía (formerly SECOFI) is charged with formulating trade policy and conducts trade negotiations, on behalf of the executive. However, given the Senate's role in approving treaties, the Senate plays an active role in formulating views on trade policy (through formal committees) and influencing negotiations (through political means). Moreover, as in many countries, industry associations hire consultants to advise them on trade policy and to lobby the federal government regarding their interests. For example, in the MEUFTA negotiations, the Mexican cattle producers lobbied the Mexican senate and SECOFI to minimize the liberalization of trade in beef.[80] The result of this lobbying was that beef made it into a limited list of sensitive products and was excluded from tariff elimination. The Mexican Chamber of Deputies (Cámara de Diputados) also plays an important political role in trade policy and has legislative authority to initiate laws that can affect trade. For example, the Chamber of Deputies was responsible for the legislation that introduced a tax on soft drinks that use high fructose corn syrup, legislation that became the subject of a WTO dispute between Mexico and the US.[81] As in other presidential systems, such as the US, it can be difficult to reach agreement among the different branches of government on trade policy, particularly when Congress and the Presidency are controlled by different political parties.

In the European Union, the EU and its Member States share different aspects of jurisdiction over trade and investment policy and international agreements.[82] The EU has exclusive jurisdiction to formulate and ensure the implementation of the Common Commercial Policy (CCP), which covers trade in all goods and most services. Since the Treaty of Nice entered into force on 1 February 2003, this jurisdiction covers the negotiation and conclusion of agreements on all aspects of trade in services and commercial aspects of intellectual property.[83]

The trade commissioner in Brussels conducts trade negotiations for the EU. However, the European Commission requires prior authorization from the European Council to negotiate trade agreements. The negotiations are conducted under directives from the European Council, and in consultation with a special committee appointed by the Council in accordance with Article 133(3) of the Treaty establishing the European Community. The assent of the European Parliament is

---

[79] See ibid. [80] Author interview with trade consultant, Yvonne Stinson Ortiz.
[81] Panel Report and Appellate Body Report, *Mexico–Taxes on Soft Drinks*.
[82] See Ramírez Robles, *Solución de controversias*, above note 68, at pp. 74–5.
[83] See Trade Policy Review: European Communities, Report by the Secretariat, 23 June 2004, WTO Doc WT/TPR/S/136, pp. 17–18, available at www.wto.org/english/tratop_e/tpr_e/tp_rep_e.htm#bycountry.

required for the conclusion of certain agreements going beyond the scope of the common commercial policy (CCP), as was the case with the MEUFTA. Agreements that go beyond the Community's internal powers conferred on it by the Treaty of Nice (which entered into force post-MEUFTA), or that go beyond what is necessary for the achievement of one of the Community objectives, also require the approval of Member States.[84]

III. Analysis of noteworthy substantive obligations

The structure of MEUFTA is as follows. It consists of the document entitled Free Trade Agreement between the European Communities and Mexico, which is Decision No. 2/2000 of the EC–Mexico Joint Council of 23 March 2000. This document, which is referred to as the Decision, is the main document of MEUFTA. In addition, there are seventeen annexes and fifteen joint declarations, which also form part of the agreement. This case study refers to the Decision as MEUFTA, a term also used to refer to the collection of documents as a whole.[85]

MEUFTA provisions address the following subjects (in some cases by incorporating WTO rules): tariff elimination; rules of origin; technical barriers to trade; sanitary and phytosanitary measures; safeguards; investment; trade in services; government procurement; competition policy; intellectual property; and dispute settlement. A limited list of sensitive products was excluded from tariff elimination; in the case of Mexico, the list includes cereal, meat and milk products. Domestic agricultural subsidies are not addressed, and subsidized exports were excluded from preferential market access. The agreement also established tariff quotas for certain agricultural and fisheries products.[86]

A. Provisions relating to goods

Prior to the entry into force of MEUFTA, the average Mexican tariff on EU industrial products was 8.6%, with a maximum of 35%. MEUFTA eliminated tariffs on industrial products in two stages, ending on 1 January 2003 (for the EU), and in four stages, ending on 1 January 2007 (for Mexico). In MEUFTA, the term 'industrial products' covers all but agricultural and fisheries products (defined as Harmonized System (HS) chapters 1–24, plus Annex I of the WTO Agreement on Agriculture).[87] Automobiles in Annex I (Tariff elimination schedule of the EC) are category B, meaning the tariffs were eliminated 1 January 2003. Most automobiles in Annex II (Tariff elimination schedule of Mexico) are also category B, with tariffs

---

[84] Trade Policy Review, above note 83, at pp. 17–18.
[85] For greater detail, see Ramírez Robles, *Solución de controversias*, above note 68, at pp. 96–7.
[86] Trade Policy Review: Mexico, Report by the Secretariat, 15 March 2002, WTO Doc WT/TPR/S/97, p. 25, available at www.wto.org/english/tratop_e/tpr_e/tp_rep_e.htm#bycountry.
[87] MEUFTA, Articles 4–7.

eliminated 1 January 2003, but some (such as electric golf carts) are category C, meaning the tariffs were eliminated 1 January 2007.

EU tariffs on Mexican agricultural and fisheries products are eliminated gradually over periods ranging from three to ten years from the entry into force of the agreement (i.e. 2003–2010).[88] However, special rules in Annex I (Tariff elimination schedule of the EC) of the MEUFTA apply to Mexican processed agricultural products ('category 7' products).[89] Moreover, these tariff eliminations do not affect duties applicable under the EU entry price systems.[90] Nor do they apply to products protected by denominations in the EU (category 'O' products).[91] Tariff quotas and duty-free quotas apply to some products during the tariff phase-out period. The rules for Mexico's tariff elimination mirror those of the EU, with processed agricultural products subject to a special rule in Annex II (Tariff elimination schedule of Mexico). However, two key differences are that Mexico does not apply entry price systems and only applies tariff quotas, not duty free quotas. The result is that MEUFTA does little to liberalize trade in agricultural products. Article 10 provided for a review of tariff elimination after three years.

For both Mexico and the EU, tariff elimination obligations apply to originating goods, which are defined according to the rules of origin in Annex III of the MEUFTA. Annex III incorporates the WTO Agreement on Customs Valuation by reference to define the term 'customs value'.[92] To qualify as originating goods, products must be:

(1) 'wholly obtained' in Mexico or the EU; or
(2) obtained in Mexico or the EU and incorporate materials that have undergone 'sufficient working or processing . . . within the meaning of Article 5'; or
(3) obtained in Mexico or the EU and incorporate materials from the other MEUFTA member (referred to as 'bilateral cumulation of origin').[93]

Article 5 incorporates further provisions contained in Appendix II of Annex III. It is beyond the scope of this case study to go into these rules in detail. Proof of origin can be based on a certificate of origin (document EUR.1), the exporter's declaration on the invoice (for shipments worth less than 6,000 euros or made by approved exporters: Article 20.1) or no documentation at all (for small packages sent by post and personal luggage: Article 25).[94]

With respect to non-tariff measures, Article 12 sets out a general prohibition against quantitative restrictions, while Annex IV sets out a positive list of permissible quantitative restrictions. Article 12 is subject to exceptions in Article 16, which resemble the exceptions of Article XI:2 of the GATT. Article 13 basically reproduces the national treatment provisions of Article III, paragraphs 2, 4 and 8, of the GATT

---

[88] Ibid., Article 8.   [89] Ibid., Article 8.8.   [90] Ibid., Article 8.9.   [91] Ibid., Article 8.10.
[92] Ibid., Annex III, Article 1(f).   [93] Ibid., Articles 2 and 3.   [94] Ibid., Article 15.

but provides a temporary exemption for measures listed in Annex V of the MEUFTA. Anti-dumping and countervailing measures are governed by the relevant WTO agreements (Article 14). Article 15 establishes specific safeguard rules for MEUFTA but, unlike NAFTA safeguard rules, Article 15 does not provide exemptions from WTO safeguards measures for members of the FTA. In this regard, Article 15 of the MEUFTA may be more consistent with the WTO Safeguards Agreement than the equivalent NAFTA provision, which requires NAFTA members to exclude each other from the application of safeguards taken under the WTO Safeguards Agreement.[95]

Article 17 establishes a framework for cooperation in customs procedures. Article 18 requires customs valuation to provide no less favourable treatment than that provided for any other country, including those with which Mexico or the EU have an agreement notified under Article XXIV of the GATT. Standards and technical regulations are governed by the WTO TBT Agreement, which is supplemented by a framework for bilateral cooperation set out in Article 19 of the MEUFTA. Similarly, sanitary and phytosanitary measures are governed by the WTO SPS Agreement, but the framework for cooperation set out in Article 20 of the MEUFTA is far less detailed than that of Article 19. Article 21 requires close cooperation where one of the parties invokes the GATT exception for balance of payments difficulties, including a schedule for the elimination of any restrictive measures that might be taken as a result.

Article 22 of the MEUFTA sets out a significantly modified version of the Article XX general exceptions of the GATT. The Article XX chapeau is moved to the end of Article 22 (perhaps to reflect the order of analysis that has been established in WTO jurisprudence) and its language has been shortened, but without any obvious changes in meaning. Four paragraphs contained in Article XX have been eliminated in Article 22: XX(e), relating to the products of prison labour; XX(h), for measures undertaken in pursuance of obligations under any intergovernmental commodity agreement; XX(i), involving restrictions on exports of domestic materials necessary to ensure essential quantities (under certain circumstances); and XX(j), essential to the acquisition or distribution of products in general or short supply.

In addition, Article 22 uses only two terms to introduce the six remaining paragraphs: 'are necessary', for the provisions that are equivalent to Article XX paragraphs a, b, and d; and 'relate to', for the provisions that are equivalent to Article XX, paragraphs c, f and g. This is consistent with the usage in Article XX, with two exceptions: Article XX, paragraph f, uses the term 'imposed for' to refer to the protection of national treasures, whereas Article 22 uses the term 'relate to'; and Article XX uses the term 'relating to', rather than 'relate to' in referring to the matters in paragraphs c (gold and silver) and g (conservation of exhaustible natural

---

[95] See NAFTA, Article 802; WTO Safeguards Agreement, Article 2.2; and Appellate Body Report, *US–Steel Safeguards*, paras. 443–4.

resources). The order in Article 22 has been changed from that of Article XX in order to group together paragraphs that begin with the same term (i.e. 'are necessary' or 'relate to'). Finally, paragraph d of Article XX has been shortened and the term 'intellectual property rights' used in place of the phrase 'protection of patents, trade marks and copyrights'.

While it is beyond the scope of this case study to delve into the significance of all of these changes, it is important to note a few points. First, since the list of measures in Article XX(d) is merely illustrative of the types of laws and regulations that are covered by that paragraph, it is not clear that the Article 22 modifications expand the scope of Article XX(d). Second, the elimination of the Article XX(e) paragraph 'relating to the products of prison labor' may affect the interpretation of Article 22(f), for measures that relate to the conservation of exhaustible natural resources, by changing the interpretative context from that of Article XX(g). The most likely effect is to introduce a more restrictive jurisdictional nexus requirement in the Article 22 version.[96] Third, the use of the term 'relate to' in reference to national treasures indicates an intention to apply the same standard to trade restrictions relating to national treasures as to those relating to the conservation of exhaustible natural resource. Finally, the changes Article 22 has made to the interpretative context of Article XX may result in divergent interpretations of these two provisions and the general exceptions they contain.[97]

Following Title II rules on trade in goods, Title III sets out detailed rules on government procurement. The next two titles are very brief. Title IV establishes a cooperation mechanism on competition, with the details set out in Annex XV. However, there are no substantive obligations regarding competition law. Title V establishes a special committee on intellectual property matters, but without modifying or adding to substantive WTO obligations.

Title VI sets out the dispute settlement mechanism, with fairly standard provisions regarding consultations, the establishment of panels, the selection of arbitrators, time limits for panel reports and rules regarding implementation. Panel reports are binding on the parties (Article 46). Parties must choose between the WTO and the MEUFTA dispute settlement mechanisms, cannot address WTO issues in the MEUFTA process, and must refrain from seeking recourse to one until proceedings are complete in the other forum (Article 47). This latter rule solves a problem that has arisen under NAFTA and the WTO, where different aspects of the same case have been pursued simultaneously in both fora, for example in the Canada–US dispute over anti-dumping and countervailing duties on softwood

---

[96] For a more detailed discussion on the interpretation of GATT Article XX, see Bradly Condon, *Environmental Sovereignty and the WTO: Trade Sanctions and International Law* (New York: Transnational Publishers, 2006).

[97] See Vienna Convention on the Law of Treaties, Article 31, particularly paras. 31(1) and 31(3)(c).

lumber and in the Mexico–US dispute over anti-dumping duties on high fructose corn syrup.

Edna Ramírez Robles notes that there are some key differences between the NAFTA and WTO dispute settlement mechanisms and the MEUFTA dispute settlement system.[98] Unlike NAFTA Chapter 20, it is not possible to block the formation of a panel under the MEUFTA. Unlike the WTO, MEUFTA does not restrict the range of permissible countermeasures, does not provide for compulsory jurisdiction and makes panel reports directly binding, rather than requiring adoption by negative consensus. There have been no disputes under MEUFTA (not even at the consultations stage).[99]

B. Services and investment

As a general rule, rather than set out lists of reservations, as NAFTA does for services, MEUFTA instead commits the parties not to enact legislation that is more restrictive than that in force. However, with respect to financial services, MEUFTA provides the same treatment as NAFTA and lists activities that are excluded from general rules on services (regarding market access, national treatment and MFN). Rather than negotiate a comprehensive agreement on investment as with NAFTA, investment was addressed on a bilateral basis between Mexico and each Member State of the EU.[100] This method of addressing services and investment reflects the structure of EU/Member State jurisdiction over these issues at the time of the MEUFTA negotiations.

IV. Impact and prospects for future application

MEUFTA appears to have helped EU exporters to recover some of the ground that they lost to the Americans with NAFTA. The percentage of EU imports and exports that make up Mexico's merchandise trade has recovered from pre-NAFTA levels. Automotive trade is the most significant sector for merchandise trade. While FDI in Mexico remains dominated by the US, European FDI in the Mexican financial services industry has expanded considerably under MEUFTA.

The developed world has begun to realize the importance of emerging markets to its economic future, although the focus is on China and India at the moment. With respect to trade with China and India, the European Commission has calculated that

---

[98] Edna Ramírez Robles, 'Political and Quasi-Adjudicative Dispute Settlement Models in European Union Free Trade Agreements', Seminar, WTO, 18 October 2006. See also Ramírez Robles, above note 1.

[99] Robles, Seminar, above note 98.

[100] As of September 2006, Mexico had bilateral investment treaties in force with sixteen of the EU(25) members, including the treaty with the UK, for which ratification was still pending: Germany, Austria, Denmark, Spain, Finland, France, Greece, Iceland, Italy, Netherlands, Portugal, Czech Republic, Sweden, Belgium, Luxembourg, UK: see www.economia.gob.mx/?P=1210.

the EU's per capita GDP could be 8% higher by 2050 with open economic policies, but 5% lower with protectionist policies.[101] As noted at the beginning of this case study, Mexico has the potential to become one of the largest economies in the world in the coming years. While these economic realities might not have been at the forefront of EU negotiators' minds when the MEUFTA negotiations took place, exports to Mexico have helped the euro area's exports to emerging economies grow by an annual average of 14% since 2000.[102]

Mexico is a major Latin American economy where the EU has largely been overtaken by the US in trade and FDI, unlike South America (where the EU has a more substantial percentage of trade and FDI). From Mexico's perspective, NAFTA has been its bread and butter. However, while that is good news when the US economy is growing, it is bad news when the US economy goes into recession. Thus, it is in Mexico's interest to diversify its economic ties and the EU is an obvious choice, due to its global ranking in both trade and FDI.

The potential for future trade disputes between Mexico and the EU, as with many WTO Members, depends in large part on the outcome of the Doha Round of multilateral trade negotiations, particularly with respect to agriculture. A lack of progress in finding negotiated solutions may motivate countries to seek progress through litigation, particularly with respect to agricultural trade. Failure to make progress in the Doha Round would increase the risk that WTO Members will challenge the preferential trade arrangements under agreements such as MEUFTA and seek their extension on a MFN basis through litigation under Article XXIV of the GATT. Thus, the failure of Doha could not just increase trade disputes between Mexico and the EU, but also increase disputes with countries such as China, India and Brazil over Mexico–EU trade arrangements. Countries that do not enjoy preferential access might seek through litigation what they have been unable to get through Doha or regional trade negotiations. Of course, in the case of MEUFTA, the limited liberalization of agricultural trade means that such challenges would likely be limited to industrial products.

The interpretation of Article XXIV of the GATT by the WTO Appellate Body, in *Turkey–Textiles*, has, in effect, introduced a least-trade restrictive test for preferential trade measures that could be difficult to pass. While the Appellate Body never used the term 'least-trade restrictive', it interpreted Article XXIV of the GATT as allowing trade measures without which the formation of a customs union would be impossible.[103] The same logic applies to free trade areas, as well as to the provisions of Article V of the GATS regarding regional trade agreements that cover services trade.

Accession of new members to MEUFTA has occurred, and likely will continue to occur, on the EU side, with EU enlargement.[104] However, it seems unlikely that

---

[101] 'The New Titans', above note 3, at p. 34.   [102] Ibid.   [103] Appellate Body Report, *Turkey–Textiles*.
[104] See Decision 4/2004 of the Mexico–EU Joint Council, Diario Oficial de la Federación, 30 April 2004, available at www.economia.gob.mx/work/snci/negociaciones/tlcuem/pdfs/1-1-46-DOF_UE300404.pdf.

other Latin American countries would accede to the MEUFTA; rather, they would negotiate directly with the EU to avoid the complication of Mexico seeking to preserve its advantages in areas where the Latin American countries would be competitors. Looking into the future, Turkey's accession might be difficult for Mexico to swallow, and might motivate Mexico to seek special arrangements.

Future negotiations on major issues or deeper integration seem unlikely in the MEUFTA context. Agricultural trade is the obvious area where more negotiations are required to liberalize trade in goods further and this must be addressed in the multilateral context. Deeper integration seems unlikely; the EU enlargement process has a geographic focus that would exclude Mexico and Mexican political sensitivities would rule out this possibility as well.

5

European Free Trade Association–Southern African Customs Union Free Trade Agreement

PETER DRAPER AND NKULULEKO KHUMALO*

I. Introduction

The Free Trade Agreement (FTA) negotiations between the European Free Trade Association (EFTA) (comprising Iceland, Liechtenstein, Norway and Switzerland) and the Southern African Customs Union (SACU) (comprising South Africa, Botswana, Lesotho, Namibia and Swaziland) were launched in May 2003 and successfully concluded in August 2005 after seven negotiating rounds. By 7 August 2006,[1] all countries had signed the agreement, which enters into force on the first day of the second month following the date on which the last Party has deposited its instrument of ratification, acceptance or approval or notified provisional application.[2]

SACU and EFTA are significant trading partners. In 2005, the EFTA States exported goods worth US$609 million to the SACU States and imported goods worth US$1.3 billion from the SACU States.[3] South Africa, in particular, has always enjoyed very good relations with both Switzerland and Norway and those relationships made it relatively easy for the parties to initiate and successfully conclude FTA negotiations. This agreement is therefore expected to enhance trade flows between EFTA States and their SACU counterparts and provide additional incentives for foreign direct investments with the net effect of boosting economic growth and development.

---

* The authors would like to thank the EFTA secretariat; Mr Markus N.P. Dutly (Deputy Head of Mission at the Swiss Embassy in Pretoria); Mr Danie Jordaan (Business representative in the South African National Economic Development and Labour Council); Dr Laurraine Lotter (Business Unity South Africa); Mr Wilhelm Smalberger (South African Department of Trade and Industry); and the staff in the economic and trade sections of Pretoria-based Embassies of Norway and Switzerland for offering assistance on information regarding the EFTA–SACU FTA which in some cases included face-to-face interviews and electronic questionnaire responses.

[1] The EFTA States were the first to sign the agreement on 26 June 2006 while Lesotho was the last to sign on 7 August 2006 (for more on the chronology of events see Annex 1 to this chapter).

[2] See http://secretariat.efta.int/Web/ExternalRelations/PartnerCountries/SACU/SouthernACU/SACU_FTA_Introduction.DOC.

[3] For recent statistics see http://secretariat.efta.int/Web/ExternalRelations/TradeStats/trade_statistics/SACU/SACU-5_Merchandise%20Trade.pdf.

Based on official documents, press releases, face-to-face interviews with some key players and questionnaire responses, this chapter seeks to give an overview of the EFTA–SACU FTA. Starting with the motivations of both parties, the chapter covers the actual negotiating process (who was involved, and how the negotiations were conducted); outlines the scope of the agreement and analyses the substantive obligations that the parties assumed. It concludes by giving a perspective on whether the original objectives of the parties are adequately covered in the final text of the agreement.

II. Motivations for the FTA and the negotiating process

A. Motivations

The European Union–South Africa Trade, Development and Cooperation Agreement (EU–SA TDCA) is a comprehensive agreement covering trade, aid and political cooperation which came into force in 2000. Real market access commitments are focused entirely on trade in goods, with new generation issues like services subject to future review and potential incorporation. This agreement covers about 90 per cent of trade between the two parties and is asymmetric in nature – the EU will fully liberalize 95 per cent of imports from South Africa over 10 years while South Africa will fully liberalize 86 per cent of its imports from the EU over 12 years.[4]

From SACU's side the push for the negotiations came mainly from the South African Department of Trade and Industry (DTI) which sought to use the FTA with EFTA to complement the EU–SA TDCA.[5] In particular, SACU wished to harmonize its trade relations with all countries in Western Europe so as to enlarge the market for its products. The South African business community did not push for the agreement, and only responded to a government decision to negotiate, as most of their exports enter this market duty free through the Generalized System of Preferences (GSP) offered by Switzerland and Norway.[6] Eventually, however, they recognized the importance of having a contractual agreement to replace unilateral schemes, since the latter are not guaranteed and can be theoretically withdrawn at any time. Further, SACU saw the FTA as an important starting point in advancing general development goals in the region through increased cooperation with EFTA countries.

SACU also aimed to use the FTA negotiation process to help deepen its own integration agenda by strengthening its structures and negotiating capacity. This is

---

[4] See Talitha Bertelsmann-Scott, Greg Mills and Elizabeth Sidiropoulos (eds.), *The EU–SA Agreement: South Africa, Southern Africa and the European Union* (Johannesburg: South African Institute of International Affairs, 2000).

[5] See ibid.

[6] This information is derived from an interview with Danie Jordaan and questionnaire responses from Laurraine Lotter, from the Business Unity South Africa, who holds the same view.

an important imperative for this region as it tallies with the clearly stated objectives of the new SACU agreement of 2002. This agreement[7] establishes new democratic institutional structures for SACU.[8] In particular Article 31 thereof requires SACU member countries to conduct all trade relations and negotiations with third parties as a single entity. The negotiations with EFTA offered South Africa and BLNS (Botswana, Lesotho, Namibia and Swaziland) countries an opportunity to galvanize their positions and approach things as a collective despite their differing interests and levels of development. As such the agreement with EFTA carries much significance as the first FTA to be successfully negotiated and signed by SACU as a group.

Motivation for the EFTA States mainly stemmed from a sober realization that they are 'all small countries dependent on international trade'.[9] This being the case, they have pragmatically endeavoured to avoid discrimination against their economic operators in foreign markets. According to Smalberger,[10] these countries have a simple trade policy whereby they wait for the EU to open up market access in third countries and then seek to match it.[11] In particular the FTA negotiations with SACU were motivated by the conclusion of the EU–SA TDCA and the potential discrimination for EFTA companies inherent in that Agreement.[12] Other factors besides trade were development cooperation and the willingness to contribute to the process of beneficially integrating the Sub-Saharan countries into the world economy.[13]

B. Negotiating process

Before we delve into the details of the actual talks, it is important to note that SACU and EFTA are two groups of countries with different legal standings. EFTA was established in 1960 following the signing of the EFTA Convention in Stockholm in the same year.[14] The Stockholm Convention was subsequently replaced by the Vaduz Convention which provides for the liberalization of trade among the Member States. EFTA does not have treaty-making powers and negotiations are done on behalf of individual Member States. Therefore, agreements with third countries

---

[7] The agreement came into force in July 2004.
[8] For more on SACU and its institutional structure, see www.sacu.int.
[9] Response from the EFTA secretariat to the authors' structured questionnaire.
[10] Wilhelm Smalberger is a senior trade negotiator from the DTI who was involved in the talks.
[11] According to EFTA sources EFTA has other motives for concluding free trade agreements. As a matter of fact EFTA has concluded several free trade agreements with countries that do not have agreements with the EU.
[12] See Bertelsmann-Scott et al., above note 4.
[13] According to the EFTA secretariat these factors are reflected in the asymmetrical treatment in favour of SACU, in the special and differential treatment granted to SACU as such and in particular the BLNS States.
[14] EFTA was meant to provide an alternative for those countries that could not or did not want to be members of the EU.

apply to trade relations between the individual EFTA State and the third party concerned.

On the other hand, SACU theoretically represents a deeper form of integration – a customs union. It was established by the Customs Union Agreement of 1910, and was later replaced with the SACU Agreement of 1969 and, more recently, with the SACU Agreement of 2002.[15] The customs union is meant to assure free movement of goods between member countries, as well as provide for a common external tariff and a common excise tariff to the customs union. However SACU countries are at very different levels of development, with South Africa dominating the group economically and otherwise. This also means that South Africa's interests are not necessarily the same as those of its counterparts which sometimes lead to difficulties when negotiating as a group.

The differences in the type of regional integration group as well as internal development asymmetries among members of the same group inevitably posed some challenges in the EFTA–SACU FTA negotiations. In the actual talks, the Departments of Foreign Affairs, Agriculture and the South African Revenue Services were involved in the negotiations under the general leadership of the DTI on the South Africa/SACU side. In EFTA, the Ministries of Foreign Affairs, the Ministries of Trade/Economic Affairs, the Ministries of Agriculture/Fisheries, Customs Authorities, the offices dealing with Intellectual Property Rights (IPR) and the EFTA secretariat were all part of the negotiations.

The preliminary or exploratory talks on the potential FTA took place in Geneva on 28–29 June 2001 between South Africa and the EFTA States. The parties exchanged views and shared information on each other's trade policies and levels of economic development, trade agreements entered into with third parties as well as the possible scope and coverage of the potential FTA. At the time, South Africa and its BLNS counterparts were still involved in negotiations for a new SACU agreement and the former was keen to bring the latter on board for the actual talks with the EFTA States.

The negotiations between the EFTA States and South Africa had a smooth beginning. After the BLNS countries joined the process, negotiations became more contentious until the EFTA countries scaled down their ambitions. According to the EFTA secretariat, the EFTA States and South Africa first aimed at a comprehensive agreement with high standards in areas such as investment, services and intellectual property rights but had to accommodate the concerns and interests of BLNS.[16] Negotiations henceforth concentrated on the liberalization of trade in goods. The

---

[15] See www.tralac.org/scripts/content.php?id=1593.
[16] However, according to some reports on the exploratory talks between the parties, even South Africa itself was not really keen to negotiate these so-called 'second generation' issues, preferring a traditional FTA as the starting point. One of the reasons proffered for such a position is the parties' experience in negotiating binding second generation issues. They had however indicated a willingness to go beyond the WTO's TRIPS Agreement on some intellectual property rights issues.

greatest challenge then became the drafting of rules providing for some special treatment for BLNS States without hollowing out basic rules of the agreement.

Though both parties agree that the negotiating atmosphere was generally characterized by a spirit of cooperation, complex legal and institutional issues were bound to arise since the talks involved two groups of countries with different needs and expectations. Additional challenges were posed by the fact that the 'talks took place against the backdrop of the World Trade Organization (WTO) Doha Development Agenda negotiations, where many of the same issues relating to trade and development were under consideration'.[17]

III. Analysis of noteworthy substantive obligations

A. Goods

During the negotiations EFTA's interest was mainly in industrial goods while SACU's focus was on agricultural goods.[18] The EFTA States offered SACU full duty and quota free access for most industrial goods, including fish and other marine products, as of entry into force of the agreement, coupled with rules of origin that are equivalent to or better[19] than those which the EU applies to South Africa in terms of the TDCA. However, this apparent 'generosity' is tempered by the fact that these countries are less liberal on agriculture; and the SACU States are not an industrial threat to them.

For its part SACU offered the EFTA countries concessions that are equivalent to those which South Africa gave the EU under the TDCA, with some adjustments that take into account BLNS sensitivities and technical errors that were made in that agreement. In particular, customs duties for goods imported into SACU are to be eliminated after transitional periods of different duration or a joint review by the Parties depending on which products are at stake.[20]

Such asymmetrical treatment is informed by the heterogeneity in the levels of development of the parties. In addition, Article 25 of the agreement provides for special and differential treatment for BLNS as follows:

1. Botswana, Lesotho, Namibia and Swaziland may, in accordance with Article 26 of the SACU Agreement 2002, temporarily levy duties on imports to protect infant

---

[17] See Lars E. Nordgaard, 'Trade and Development – The EFTA-SACU Agreement', in EFTA Bulletin: EFTA Free Trade Relations (Geneva: EFTA Secretariat, July–August 2006), pp. 27–9.
[18] This information is drawn from the EFTA secretariat's response to the authors' questions.
[19] This agreement provides for liberal rules of origin and allows for the use of up to 60 per cent of non-originating input in the production of certain products. The relaxed rules of origin will enable SACU garment manufacturers, for instance, to use imported fabric and still be eligible for duty free and quota free access to EFTA markets.
[20] See http://secretariat.efta.int/Web/ExternalRelations/PartnerCountries/SACU/SouthernACU/SACU_FTA_Introduction.DOC.

industries. Such duties shall be equally levied on goods originating in other SACU States and in countries outside SACU.
2. Botswana, Lesotho, Namibia and Swaziland may temporarily restrict the importation or exportation of goods for purposes of rural development, food security and poverty alleviation in a manner not inconsistent with the WTO Agreement. Such measures shall also be taken in respect of all other countries.

This level of flexibility on EFTA's side must have made it relatively easy for BLNS countries to sign the agreement as it appears that their sensitivities have been fairly if not fully addressed.

B. Agricultural products

Agriculture was another important area in the talks and the final agreement covers fisheries as well. SACU had insisted that improved and predictable market access for agricultural goods was a *sine qua non* for concluding an FTA. The negotiations on agricultural products distinguished between basic agricultural products (i.e. wheat) and processed agricultural products (i.e. bread). Agricultural goods originating from SACU will in some cases be granted more favourable treatment than under the GSP applicable in the EFTA States. On processed agricultural products the SACU States are granted the same market access conditions as the EFTA States grant the EU.[21]

For their part, the EFTA countries generally did not have an offensive agenda in agriculture and were mainly inward looking in approach. Switzerland, however, requested market access for high value added processed agricultural products like chocolate and specialty cheeses, but could not get any preferences due to industry sensitivities in South Africa.[22]

Unlike the EU, the EFTA countries do not have a common agricultural policy. In order to avoid convergence on the lowest common denominator or using a 'one size fits all' approach when negotiating trade agreements with third parties, basic agricultural products are dealt with in separate bilateral agreements between each EFTA State and the partner country in question. This allows each EFTA State sufficient flexibility to grant more favourable treatment on individual products to the benefit of the third party. In line with this approach, trade in basic agricultural products is covered by arrangements concluded bilaterally between each EFTA State and SACU. These agreements form part of the instruments establishing the free trade area and are also asymmetrical in favour of SACU (see Annex 2 to this chapter for some insights into the bilateral agreements).

---

[21] See http://secretariat.efta.int/Web/ExternalRelations/PartnerCountries/SouthernACU/SACU_RUAP/annexes/SACU-FTA-Annex_III.pdf.
[22] See www.nda.agric.za/docs/EFTA_May_2006.pdf.

IV. Intellectual property, services, and new generation issues

The FTA does not provide for additional obligations on any of these issues but reaffirms the obligations the parties have under the WTO. Additionally, the FTA exhorts parties to consider extending the current commitments in future. This outcome is clearly a compromise position since EFTA had wanted the FTA to include new binding obligations on new generation issues. Even though South Africa is not opposed to including these issues as a matter of principle, it is cautious and believes that it does not have much experience to commit to obligations that go beyond what has been agreed in the WTO. In addition, South Africa was negotiating as SACU and had to take into account BLNS sensitivities and sticking to WTO commitments may have been the only viable option at this stage. We discuss each of these issues below.

A. Intellectual property

The EFTA States normally aim at higher standards on intellectual property than provided for in the WTO Agreement on Trade-Related Aspects of Intellectual Property Rights (TRIPS Agreement). For reasons mentioned above, the FTA with SACU, however, does not introduce new obligations but confirms the multilateral standards provided for in the TRIPS Agreement.

Article 26(2) of the FTA does, however, require the Parties to grant and ensure adequate, effective and non-discriminatory protection of intellectual property rights based on existing international agreements. In addition, the EFTA States and their SACU partners have committed to review the intellectual property provisions of this FTA not later than five years after the entry into force of the agreement with the objective of progressively harmonizing their legal frameworks on these issues.

B. Services

Article 27 of the FTA commits the parties to 'underline the importance of strict observance of the General Agreement on Trade in Services (GATS)' in recognition of the vital role which services play in the development of their economies. Again, no new obligations are introduced. Parties will simply 'endeavour to extend the scope of this Agreement with a view to further liberalizing trade in services'. A Joint Committee (established by Article 33 of the FTA) is required to make the necessary recommendations for the inclusion of GATS-plus obligations in this area not later than five years after the entry into force of this agreement.

Further, Article 27(3) provides that if a party enters into a regional trade agreement to liberalize trade in services in accordance with Article V of GATS, it shall 'upon request from the other Parties afford adequate opportunity to them to seek to obtain, including through possible negotiations, comparable conditions, on a mutually beneficial basis'. This is an important clause in that should either EFTA or SACU enter into a services trade liberalization agreement, for instance with the United States or the EU, then the other party should be afforded the chance to seek to match such concessions. In other words liberalizing trade in services with any other party may mean new negotiations to cover services within the EFTA–SACU context.

C. Investment

The provisions on investment are generally hortatory, best-endeavour clauses that are non-binding. Parties are encouraged to create and maintain a stable and transparent investment framework and commit not to 'impair by unreasonable or discriminatory measures the management, maintenance, use, enjoyment or disposal of investments by investors of the other Party'.[23] Yet, parties will continue to admit investments by each other's investors in accordance with their laws and regulations.

Through cooperation mechanisms the parties will seek to facilitate cross-border investment and technology flows as a means for economic growth and development. Moreover, Article 28(4) provides for a review of investment issues by a Joint Committee within five years after the entry into force of the agreement. Further, a party that offers a more favourable investment framework to a third party after the entry into force of this agreement shall, upon request, provide the other parties with the opportunity to agree on comparable conditions on a mutually beneficial basis.

It is unlikely that South Africa/SACU will agree to binding FTA provisions on investment in the near future. Apart from South Africa's general lack of enthusiasm for making commitments on new generation issues, its recent challenges with bilateral investment treaties may exacerbate the situation. Post apartheid South Africa entered into a range of bilateral investment treaties (BITs), mainly with Western countries, perhaps as a way of inspiring confidence in foreign investors that it does not intend to expropriate their assets and that they are free to repatriate any profits made. Barring a few recent ones, 'most of these BITs are cast in a manner which is most favourable to investors, with little consideration given to the need for governments to regulate such foreign investment. Perhaps most remarkable, many of South Africa's earliest investment treaties do not contain a provision which expressly shelters those government measures which are designed to promote the achievement of equality or to advance the interests of the previously disadvantaged.'[24] As a result, the South African government has already lost an 'expropriation' case and is currently being challenged by a number of foreign investors for

---

[23] See Article 28(1) of the Agreement.
[24] Luke E. Peterson, *South Africa's Bilateral Investment Treaties: Implications for Development and Human Rights*. Briefing Paper prepared for the South African Institute for International Affairs (Geneva: Friedrich-Ebert-Stiftung, November 2006), available at www.fes-globalization.org/publications/FES_OCP26_Peterson_SA_BITs.pdf.

adopting policies that are alleged to be in breach of BITs especially in the mining sector.[25] This state of affairs certainly has an impact on how South Africa approaches negotiations that include investment.

D. Government procurement

The provisions on government procurement are hortatory in nature and generally emphasize cooperation between the parties in order to enhance the mutual understanding of their respective laws and regulations. Article 29 requires parties to publish, or otherwise make publicly available, their laws, regulations and administrative rulings of general application. They also undertake to 'hold consultations in the Joint Committee to consider possible steps to be taken with a view to mutually liberalizing their procurement markets' within five years after the entry into force of the agreement.

Further, as in services and investment, a party that enters into preferential agreements with a third country after this agreement comes into force shall, upon request, provide the other parties with the opportunity to agree on comparable conditions on a mutually beneficial basis.

The hortatory nature of the EFTA–SACU FTA provisions is perfectly understandable when one considers the sensitivities surrounding this issue in South Africa/SACU.[26] South Africa in particular has a policy of black economic empowerment (BEE) which aims to redress the discriminatory effects of the apartheid era. This involves preferential treatment in State-related tendering for companies fulfilling the criteria of black ownership and empowerment. BEE seeks to redress South Africa's historical imbalances and integrate previously excluded sections of the population into the wider economy and to level the playing fields in the arena of economic development and wealth creation – pivotal to South Africa's economic future. Not surprisingly there are concerns that making commitments on government procurement may have a negative impact on the BEE policy and ultimately lead to domestic political instability in South Africa. As such, South Africa and by extension SACU are currently not in a position to negotiate commitments on this issue because of its sensitivity.

E. Competition

Under Article 15 of the agreement parties undertake to cooperate and exchange information so as to prevent anti-competitive business practices and abuses of

---

[25] For more on South Africa's legal challenges, see Brendan Ryan, 'Left Behind', *Financial Mail* (SA), 26 January 2007.

[26] Besides, government procurement is one of the issues that were struck out of the WTO's Doha Agenda mainly due to intense opposition from developing countries.

dominant positions that adversely affect the operation of this agreement in each other's territories. If cooperation between the parties does not resolve the issue, then the aggrieved party 'may request consultations in the Joint Committee with the aim of reaching a mutually satisfactory solution'.

V. Other important provisions

This agreement contains some important provisions on economic cooperation and technical assistance, institutional provisions, and dispute settlement procedures that are meant to support its implementation.

A. Economic cooperation and technical assistance

One of the important objectives outlined in the preamble of the agreement is to further economic and social development within the SACU States with the support of the EFTA countries. In pursuit of this goal, the agreement contains extensive provisions on economic cooperation and technical assistance whereby the EFTA States agree to assist the SACU States in implementing their obligations under the agreement.[27]

The focus of EFTA support embraces the crucial issue of post liberalization adjustment assistance which is clearly development friendly. In particular Article 30(3) provides as follows:

> Assistance by the EFTA States shall focus on sectors affected by the process of liberalization and restructuring of the economy of the SACU States as well as on sectors likely to bring the economies of the EFTA States and the SACU States closer together, particularly those generating growth and employment.

The parties will cooperate in trying to find the best means of providing such assistance and are willing to coordinate efforts with relevant international organizations. Fields of cooperation between the parties include: trade policy, trade facilitation and trade promotion; customs and origin matters; technical regulations, standards and conformity assessment as well as sanitary and phytosanitary measures; local enterprise development; and regulatory assistance and implementation of laws in areas such as services, investment, intellectual property and public procurement.

B. Institutional provisions and dispute settlement

To support and ensure the proper implementation of the provisions of this agreement, Article 33 establishes a Joint Committee composed of representatives of the

---

[27] See Articles 30–2 of the Agreement.

EFTA States and the SACU States. Article 33(2) enjoins the parties to exchange information and to hold consultations within the Joint Committee on any matter concerning the interpretation or application of this agreement at the request of a party. If the issue is not resolved within 90 days, the aggrieved party is allowed to apply provisional remedial measures and the matter can be taken to arbitration.[28] A dispute on the same matter arising under both this agreement and the WTO rules can be settled in either forum at the discretion of the aggrieved party and the chosen forum shall be used to the exclusion of the other.

C. Future negotiations and deeper integration

Article 38(1) formally provides for the possibility of extending the scope of the agreement to cover other areas in future. According to this 'evolutionary clause':

> The Parties undertake to review this Agreement in light of further developments in international economic relations, inter alia in the framework of the WTO, and to examine the possibility of further developing and deepening the cooperation under this Agreement and to extend it to areas not covered therein. The Parties may instruct the Joint Committee to examine this possibility and, where appropriate, to make recommendations to them, particularly with a view to opening up negotiations.

This is clearly a hortatory provision but is important in that it lays a legal basis upon which future calls to 'update' the agreement to align with a fast changing international trading environment could be legitimately made by any or all of the parties to the agreement.

VI. Conclusion

Though the EFTA–SACU FTA has not yet entered into force and no lessons have been learnt from the practical implementation of its provisions, its provisions seem to reflect adequately the original negotiating motivations of the parties. Unsurprisingly all those who were interviewed or who responded to our structured questionnaire expressed satisfaction with the results.

Through this FTA SACU has, among other things, managed to secure a predictable contractual framework to guarantee the preferential market access for their goods that replaces the unilateral GSPs. In addition, SACU has managed to gain market access equivalent to that which the EFTA countries offer the EU and has established an important platform to enhance broader development cooperation with EFTA.

For its part, EFTA has managed to level the playing field vis-à-vis EU economic operators who had been enjoying better market access to South Africa because of the

---

[28] See Articles 35–7 of the Agreement.

TDCA. Though the FTA does not include WTO-plus binding obligations on, inter alia, services, intellectual property and new generation issues, the evolutionary clause and review clauses are an important starting point for future engagement.

Annex 1: EFTA–SACU negotiations: chronology of events[29]

6 Nov 2000	High-level talks in Pretoria
28–29 June 2001	Exploratory exchange of information with South Africa in Geneva
27–28 Nov 2002	Exploratory exchange of information with South Africa in Geneva
19–23 May 2003	Formal launch of negotiations on the EFTA–SACU FTA in Pretoria
29 Sept–2 Oct 2003	Second round of negotiations on the EFTA–SACU FTA in Geneva
15–18 Mar 2004	Third round of negotiations on the EFTA–SACU FTA in Pretoria
13–17 Sept 2004	Fourth round of negotiations on the EFTA–SACU FTA in Geneva
2–7 Dec 2004	Fifth round of negotiations on the EFTA–SACU FTA in Pretoria
12–16 April 2005	Sixth round of negotiations on the EFTA–SACU FTA in Geneva
24–26 Aug 2005	Seventh round of negotiations on the EFTA– SACU FTA in Pretoria
26 Jun 2006	Free trade agreement with SACU signed by Iceland, Norway and Liechtenstein in Höfn
1 Jul 2006	Free trade agreement signed by Switzerland, South Africa and Swaziland in Geneva
14 Jul 2006	Free trade agreement signed by Botswana and Namibia in Gaborone
7 Aug 2006	Free trade agreement signed by Lesotho in Pretoria.

Annex 2: bilateral agricultural offers[30]

Specific areas of interest for the BLNS are beef and mutton, sugar, citrus, table grapes and certain agro-processing products, as well as specialty products like

---

[29] See http://secretariat.efta.int/Web/ExternalRelations/PartnerCountries/Chronology.pdf.
[30] The information is almost entirely taken from an update by the South African National Department of Agriculture as is, save for slight modifications. The original document is available online at www.nda.agric.za/docs/EFTA_May_2006.pdf.

game or ostrich meat. No preferences were offered to Norway on basic agricultural products due to support given to its farmers. Iceland was granted market access for meat of horses, asses, mules or hinnies, fresh, chilled or frozen. In the case of Switzerland, preferential access into SACU markets has been granted for live animals, feed supplements and tobacco. The following paragraphs provide a summary of some of the preferences SACU managed to secure under this agreement.

A. SACU–Switzerland (covers Liechtenstein)[31]

The SACU–Switzerland FTA provides that most canned fruit enter duty free at most favoured nation (MFN) levels, except canned apples, where full MFN duties will have to be paid by South African exporters. In terms of the EFTA–SACU agreement, reduced rates will apply for canned oranges, mandarins and apricots, with zero duty for peaches, grapefruit and lemons.

Fresh table grapes are free at an MFN basis from 15 July to 14 September. Under the agreement, a further 1,000 tons will be free for the period 1 January to 30 June. All dried grapes are duty free regardless of the period. Cider apples and apples for distilling will be free within the limits of Switzerland's WTO minimum market access quota. For other apples, MFN duties will be payable, except for apples in open packages (free). Most fruit juices are offered duty free except apple juice, which will attract normal MFN duties.

Sparkling wine and sweet wine are offered at a reduced rate of 71 per cent and 27 per cent of MFN respectively. Oranges and mandarins will enjoy reduced tariff rates (40 per cent of MFN), while the other products will be able to enter Switzerland free of duty.

B. SACU–Norway[32]

The SACU–Norway FTA provides for duty free access for canned fruit: pineapple (2009.20), pears (2008.40), apricots (2008.50), peaches (2008.50) and mixtures entirely containing fruits of heading 0803–0810 (2008.92.01) and except for those classified under 'other' (2008.92.09) at 20 per cent MFN.

Apples are duty free from 1 December to 30 April and 15 per cent duty from 1 May to 30 November while citrus are, respectively, duty free and 10 per cent MFN duty. Only table grapes are duty free from 1 August to 28/29 February and for others from 1 March to 31 July, with fruit juices mostly duty free. Sparkling wine is duty free.

---

[31] http://secretariat.efta.int/Web/ExternalRelations/PartnerCountries/SACU/SouthernACU/CH_Ag.pdf.
[32] http://secretariat.efta.int/Web/ExternalRelations/PartnerCountries/SACU/SouthernACU/NO_Ag.pdf.

C. SACU–Iceland[33]

The SACU–Iceland FTA offers duty free access to all canned fruit, fruit juices and wine, wine, grapes, citrus and apples and, contrary to the TDCA, all preferences offered by EFTA are fixed. However, SACU requested further concessions from EFTA on a range of products, including some other preserved (including canned) fruit. Switzerland offered a full reduction of duties on preserved citrus, pulp and other, peaches and apricots, but so far preferences are not extended on preserved pears, as well as apple juice. With the negotiations finalized between SACU and EFTA, it was agreed that a review clause be included in the text of the bilateral agreements with the list of priority products of interest where preferences were not granted at this stage. This review will take place no later than three years after implementing the agreements.

---

[33] http://secretariat.efta.int/Web/ExternalRelations/PartnerCountries/SACU/SouthernACU/IS_Ag.pdf.

6

Japan–Mexico Economic Partnership Agreement

BRYAN MERCURIO*

I. Introduction

Following the collapse of the World Trade Organization (WTO) Cancún Ministerial Conference, the corresponding lack of progress on the Doha Agenda and the relative explosion of bilateral free trade agreements (FTAs) being negotiated globally, Japan reviewed its trade strategies and policy and, for the first time,[1] expressed its intention to pursue both bilateral and multilateral trade agreements.[2] Consequently, and with the stated aim of pursuing bilateral FTAs in order to strengthen and progress the multilateral agenda, Japan began investigating the possibilities of FTAs with Singapore, Mexico, Malaysia, Korea, Thailand and the Association of Southeast Asian Nations (ASEAN).

Japan quickly concluded its first FTA (termed an Economic Partnership Agreement (EPA)) with Singapore in January 2002.[3] Negotiations with Mexico progressed more slowly, and for a time it appeared that they would collapse entirely over the issue of agricultural liberalization.[4] Finally, on 17 September 2004, Prime Minister Junichiro Koizumi of Japan and President Vicente Fox Quesada of Mexico signed the Agreement between Japan and the United Mexican States for the Strengthening

---

* This chapter is based on, but significantly expands upon, Bryan Mercurio, 'Japan–Mexico Economic Partnership Agreement: Completing The Matrix' in Leon Trakman, Nick Ranieri, Marlon Lopez (eds.), *Doing Business in México* (New York: Transnational Publishing, 2005).

[1] It must be noted that Japan and South Korea did half-heartedly begin negotiating an FTA in 1998, but these efforts failed to result in an agreement and were quickly abandoned.

[2] See, e.g., Japan External Trade Organization (JETRO), 'White Paper on International Trade' (2000), available at www.jetro.go.jp/en/stats/white_paper/trade2000.pdf. For a more complete account of Japan's shift in trade policy, see Noboru Hatakeyama, 'Japan's New Regional Trade Policy – Which Country Comes Next after Singapore?', second annual Whitman International Lecture, Washington, DC, 13 March 2002, available at www.iie.com/publications/papers/paper.cfm?researchid=453.

[3] See Japan–Singapore Economic Partnership Agreement, signed 13 January 2002, in force 30 November 2002, available at www.mofa.go.jp/region/asia-paci/singapore/jsepa.html. On the bilateral activities of Japan, see generally Japan Ministry of Foreign Affairs webpage, 'Free Trade Agreement (FTA) and Economic Partnership Agreement (EPA)', at www.mofa.go.jp/policy/economy/fta. For more on the recent history of Japan's trade ambitions, see Hatakeyama, above note 2.

[4] It was widely expected to conclude when the Mexican President, Fox visited Japan in October 2003; however, an agreement was not in fact reached until sometime later.

of the Economic Partnership (JMEPA or 'the Agreement') in Mexico City,[5] thus ending nearly two years of tough negotiations in which both sides were forced to compromise and overcome some substantial and divisive issues.[6]

The stated purposes and effects of the Agreement are to:

> [P]romote a liberalization of trade and investments as well as a freer flow of persons for business purposes between Japan and México. The Agreement also aims to promote a comprehensive economic partnership, which includes competition policy, improvement of business environment and bilateral cooperation in such fields as vocational education and training, and support for small and medium enterprises. The Agreement contributes to making the most of the economic complementarity between Japan and México and thus to strengthening the bilateral economic relations.[7]

In a joint statement, Prime Minister Koizumi and President Fox expressed the view that 'enhanced economic ties between Japan and Mexico will promote Japan's economic relationship with Latin America, and Mexico's economic relationship with Asia, thereby giving a fresh impetus to trade and investment flows across the Pacific'.[8] In this regard, the JMEPA is significant for a number of reasons: first, the Agreement increases Japanese market access in the Mexican market, and vice versa. Importantly, the pact is the first such agreement to cover and open the politically sensitive and highly protected agricultural sector in Japan. Second, the Agreement eliminates the competitive disadvantages Japan has faced in Mexico and now allows Japanese companies to enjoy equal treatment with companies of the United States (US), Canada and the European Union (EU), in areas such as custom duties, services, investment and government procurement. Third, the Agreement facilitates Japanese entry into the North and South American as well as the European markets via Mexico. This is particularly

---

[5] See Agreement between Japan and the United Mexican States for the Strengthening of the Economic Partnership, signed 17 September 2004, in force 1 April 2005; Protocol amending the Agreement signed 20 September 2006, in force 1 April 2007. The JMEPA can be viewed and downloaded at: www.mofa.go.jp/region/latin/mexico/agreement/.

[6] Formally, governmental negotiations began in November 2002 after the Japan Federation of Economic Organizations released its final report entitled the 'Japan–Mexico Joint Study Group on the Strengthening of Bilateral Economic Relations' (the report was commissioned in September 2001) [hereinafter 'Joint Study Group']. The findings of the Group can be found at: www.mofa.go.jp/region/latin/mexico/relation0207/.

[7] See Ministry of Foreign Affairs of Japan, 'Agreement between Japan and the United Mexican States for the Strengthening of the Economic Partnership (Overview)', September 2004, at www.mofa.go.jp/region/latin/mexico/agreement/overview.html. In a joint statement, Prime Minister Koizumi and President Fox expressed hope that the Agreement would allow the two countries 'to make the most of their economic complementarity and to further promote the development of their respective economies, through creating a large-scale harmonized market for both countries and accelerating the structural reforms'. See Ministry of Foreign Affairs of Japan, 'Joint Statement on the occasion of the Signing of the Agreement between Japan and the United Mexican States for the Strengthening of the Economic Partnership', 17 September 2004, para. 3, available at www.mofa.go.jp/region/latin/mexico/agreement/joint.html.

[8] See Ministry of Foreign Affairs of Japan, 'Joint Statement', above note 7, at para. 13.

advantageous as Mexico has concluded twelve comprehensive free trade agreements with forty-five countries, including the US, Canada, twenty-five countries in the EU and many countries in Latin America, as well as five partial or preferential economic cooperation agreements encompassing nine additional countries.[9]

While the JMEPA is simply one piece in a complex matrix of bilateral and regional agreements which Mexico has been negotiating in earnest since its inclusion in the North American Free Trade Agreement[10] (NAFTA), the Agreement signalled a significant shift in Japanese trade policy. Previously, Japan had focused its energies entirely at the multilateral level, with its only FTA being the less than comprehensive FTA with Singapore mentioned above; however, with the implementation of the JMEPA, which covers over 1,200 goods and 300 agricultural products, as well as providing significant coverage on issues such as custom duties, services, investment and government procurement, Japan signalled its intentions to pursue seriously a bilateral agenda in parallel to the multilateral framework.[11] In this regard, the JMEPA provided momentum to the effort and Japan has since concluded agreements with Chile,[12] Brunei,[13] Indonesia,[14] Malaysia,[15] the Philippines[16] and Thailand.[17] Additionally, Japan is in negotiations or completing a scoping study with ASEAN, the Gulf Cooperation Council, Vietnam, India, Switzerland and Australia.[18]

While the volume of bilateral trade has always been relatively low, and stood at approximately US$7.3 billion when the Agreement was signed in 2004, the JMEPA is designed to increase the level of bilateral trade by gradually liberalizing trade and investment between the two countries over a number of years.[19] Moreover, JMEPA

---

[9] See the WTO webpage, 'Regional Trade Agreements', at www.wto.org/english/tratop_e/region_e/region_e.htm; WorldTradeLaw.net webpage, 'Bilateral and Regional Trade Agreements Notified to the WTO', at www.worldtradelaw.net/fta/ftadatabase/ftas.asp; and SICE webpage, at www.sice.oas.org/Trade/mex_e.ASP.

[10] Signed 17 December 1992, in force 1 January 1994.

[11] Japan also saw the deal with Mexico as a practice round for further FTAs it is looking to reach into Asia. According to Japanese Foreign Minister, Yoriko Kawaguchi, 'Japan learned a lot from the negotiations with Mexico and that will be useful for our negotiations with other Asian countries': see 'Japan, México Reach Free Trade Agreement', *Bridges Weekly Trade News Digest*, vol. 8(10), 18 March 2004. In fact, several powerful lobby groups in Japan have also recently proposed the creation of a strategy panel to promote bilateral FTAs: see 'Key Business Lobby Floats FTA Panel', *The Japan Times*, 13 March 2004, available at www.japantimes.co.jp/cgi-bin/getarticle.pl5?nb20040313a2.htm.

[12] Japan–Chile Economic Partnership Agreement, signed 27 March 2007, in force 3 September 2007.

[13] Japan–Brunei Economic Partnership Agreement, signed 18 June 2007, not yet in force.

[14] Japan–Indonesia Economic Partnership Agreement, signed 20 August 2007, not yet in force.

[15] Japan–Malaysia Economic Partnership Agreement, signed 13 December 2005, in force 13 July 2006.

[16] Japan–Philippines Economic Partnership Agreement, signed 8 September 2006, not yet in force.

[17] Japan–Thailand Economic Partnership Agreement, signed 3 April 2007, in force 1 November 2007.

[18] See Japan Ministry of Foreign Affairs webpage, above note 3; and Bryan Mercurio, 'Should Australia Continue Negotiating Bilateral Free Trade Agreements?: A Practical Analysis' (2004) 27(3) *University of New South Wales Law Journal* 667–702 at 691.

[19] In fact, using 1999 statistics, Mexico's share of Japanese trade represented 1.1% of exports and 0.5% of imports while Japan's share accounted for 0.6% of exports and 3.6% of imports. Japan's exports to Mexico consisted mainly of electronics and appliances, auto parts and industrial machinery, while oil,

provisions relating to labour, environment and other social issues could prove noteworthy for a number of bilateral, regional and multilateral reasons. Overall, the Japan–Mexico Joint Study Group found that an FTA between the nations would increase Mexican exports to Japan by 1.68 per cent and, while the Mexican gross domestic product (GDP) would only increase in real terms by 1.08 per cent and Japanese exports to Mexico will increase by only 0.13 per cent, the gains to be made in certain sectors are substantial.[20]

While the JMEPA has already resulted in an increase of bilateral trade of more than 30 per cent in its first year of operation, more importantly, Japan viewed the Agreement as providing a level playing field against economic competitors who already have an FTA with Mexico (notably the US, Canada and the EU). In fact, Japan's Ministry of Economy, Trade and Industry (METI) estimated that the nation has suffered economic damage of almost 400 billion yen (approximately US$3.3 billion) annually due to its disadvantage in tariff rates, service, investment and government procurement without a free trade pact.[21]

This chapter reviews and evaluates the effects of the JMEPA. Section II provides an overview of the negotiating process, highlighting the products, services and legal issues and the governmental actors involved in the negotiations. Section III provides an overview of the Agreement by examining its key provisions. Section IV discusses the potential gains for both Japan and Mexico and briefly notes the issues which led to the negotiations and eventual agreement: namely, the NAFTA, the Free Trade Area of the Americas[22] (FTAA), European Union–Mexico Economic Partnership, Political Coordination and Cooperation Agreement[23] (EU–Mexico FTA), the Mexican business climate, market access for Mexican agricultural products and the perceived need to diversify the Mexican economy. Section V concludes.

II. The negotiating process

In 2001 Prime Minister, Junichiro Koizumi and Mexican President, Vincente Fox Quesada agreed to the importance of strengthening bilateral relations between

---

foodstuffs and industrial products captured a significant share of Mexico's exports to Japan. See JETRO, 'JETRO and SECOFI Announce Strategies for Japan-México Trade', Report on Closer Economic Relations between Japan and Mexico (April 2000), available at www.jetro.go.jp/en/stats/survey/epa/fta_mexico/.

[20] Joint Study Group, above note 6, at p. 48 (citing a study conducted by the Research Institute of Economy, Trade and Industry). Another finding which the Joint Study Group cited was that Mexico's real GDP and national income would increase by 4.20% and 5.36%, respectively, while Japan's real GDP and national income would increase by 0.10% and 0.21% (citing the Japan Centre for Economic Research).

[21] See Joint Study Group, above note 6, at p. 14 note 1; and 'Japan and México sign free-trade agreement', *The Japan Times*, 19 September 2004, available at http://search.japantimes.co.jp/print/news/nn09-2004/nn20040919a1.htm.

[22] Ministerial Declaration of Miami, 8th Ministerial Meeting, adopted 20 November 2003.

[23] Signed 8 December 1997, in force 1 October 2000.

Japan and Mexico and established the Japan–Mexico Joint Study Group on the Strengthening of Economic Relations (comprised of government officials, leading academics and business representatives from both nations). In July 2002 the Joint Group published a report restating the need to strengthen bilateral relations and increase trade between the two nations. The Joint Study Group Ministerial Negotiations on the JMEPA began in Tokyo in November 2002.[24] While the Parties both intended to negotiate the JMEPA within one year, Mexico's early demands in the agriculture industry proved to be a major sticking point throughout the course of the negotiations.[25]

At the outset, Japan's negotiations were led by Ryuichiro Yamazaki, Ambassador for International Trade and Economy of the Ministry of Foreign Affairs (MOFA), and conducted by MOFA and METI. Also represented were the relevant Ministers from the Ministry of Foreign Affairs, the Ministry of Finance, the Ministry of Agriculture, Forestry and Fisheries and the Ministry of Economy, Trade and Industry. Mexico was represented by the Mexican Deputy Minister of the Economy, Angel Villalobos and relevant Ministers.[26]

The second round of negotiations took place in February 2003 (the parties considered the first round to be the Meeting of the Joint Study in November 2002).[27] The highlight of the round was consensus on the timing and structure of negotiations, in that there would be three levels of meetings: heads level (to be held every three months), plenary meetings and working level meetings. The other major breakthrough of the round occurred after the third day of the ambassadorial level of negotiations, when Japan agreed to reduce the tariff rate on Mexican avocados. While the Japanese Minister of Economy, Trade and Industry heralded that an agreement could be reached as early as October of 2003, in reality the concession was only the start of the tough agricultural negotiations.[28]

In March 2003, the Parties held a working level meeting in Mexico City where a broad range of topics were discussed, including: agriculture, manufacturing, rules of origin, safeguards, anti-dumping procedures, government procurement, dispute resolution and compensation.[29] Following the meetings, the Parties exchanged lists of the industrial and agricultural products for which they sought to gain preferential

---

[24] See www.mofa.go.jp/policy/economy/apec/2002/joint_me.html.
[25] 'México wants Japan to open farm market wider', *Jiji Press Service*, 19 November 2002.
[26] See www.mofa.go.jp/announce/press/2002/11/1115.html#2; and www.mofa.go.jp/region/latin/mexico/nego0302.html.
[27] The Japanese delegation was again headed by the Ambassador for International Trade and Economy of the MOFA, and other participants included representatives from the Ministry of Foreign Affairs, Ministry of Finance, the Ministry of Agriculture, Forestry and Fisheries, Ministry of Economy, Trade and Industry and other related ministries and agencies. The Mexican delegation included the Under Secretary of International Trade Negotiation of the Ministry of Economy and other relevant agencies. See www.mofa.go.jp/region/latin/mexico/nego0302.html.
[28] 'Free Trade Agreement expected with Japan this Fall', *Corporato México*, 17 February 2003.
[29] 'México, Japan end round four of Free Trade Talks', *Reuters*, 15 March 2003.

treatment under the agreement.[30] In April, another working level meeting discussed similar issues and agriculture – more specifically Mexico's displeasure with Japan's agricultural offer – emerged as the most contentious issue.

In May 2003, the third heads level negotiations took place in Mexico City.[31] At this meeting, the October deadline for the completion of the negotiations became unrealistic due to the lack of consensus on the agricultural sector. It has been reported that Japanese negotiators refused to agree to meaningful liberalization of its agriculture market and the Mexican Minister of Finance even stated that the Japanese stance was forestalling progress.[32] Apart from agriculture, other areas discussed included proposals for human resources development and education, support industry, small and medium-sized enterprises, science and technology, trade and investment promotion, fishing, environmental issues and energy.

In June 2003, the sixth round of negotiations was held, with a working party discussing the issues surrounding agriculture. In the meetings, Mexico sought a lesser quarantine period and process under the FTA, while Japan rejected the request on the grounds of public health and for other reasons including the safety of indigenous animal and plant life. Mexico also again called for a reduction in tariffs on its agricultural exports to Japan. Japan also requested Mexico to allow Japanese firms to tender on an equal footing with Mexican bids as part of the revamping of Mexico's state owned oil company's (PEMEX) facilities in Mexico.

In July 2003, the working party was still attempting to conclude the negotiations by October. Significantly, Mexico agreed to the above request for permission for the Japanese to participate in tenders and auctions. Another interesting aspect to this meeting was that it came in the wake of several prominent Japanese businessmen and associations expressing support for the Agreement, including the Japan Business Federation (Nippon Keidanren), the Japan Chamber of Commerce and Industry, the Japan Association of Corporate Executives and the Japan Foreign Trade Council.[33]

The fourth heads level meeting, held in August 2003, again centred on agricultural protection and concessions. Japan had always strongly resisted reducing tariffs on all agricultural products and at this meeting made it clear it could not meet such demands. In addition, Japan stated its intention to remove certain industrial sectors and especially the pork industry from the scope of the JMEPA. In contrast, Mexico

---

[30] 'México and Japan enter 4th round of FTA Accord talks', *Dow Jones International News*, 13 March 2003.
[31] This Round was headed by Japan's Ambassador for International Trade and Economy, Ryuichiro Yamazaki and the Mexican Under Secretary of International Trade Negotiation, Angel Villalobos. See www.mofa.go.jp/region/latin/mexico/nego0305.html.
[32] 'Japan, México agree to speed up Free Trade Agreement', *BBC Monitoring*, 16 May 2003.
[33] See 'Japan Govt to Conclude FTA with México', *Jiji Press Service*, 5 August 2005; and 'Japan Trade Group Calls for FTA with México', *Jiji Press Service*, 15 July 2003 (Council chairman, Kenji Miyahara stated that Japanese businesses were disadvantaged because of the current lack of an FTA and business would benefit by being able to compete for Mexican projects.).

demanded that pork (as well as leather) be included in the Agreement, but did propose a compromise whereby it would agree to a transitory ten-year period for Japan to open its market totally.[34] Additionally, Japan faced pressure by its own industrialists, who argued that the liberalization of the pork industry would be a price worth paying in order to match Mexico's preferential treatment schemes with the EU and the US.[35] By the end of the meetings, Japan had agreed to many agricultural concessions; however Mexico was still disappointed with the Japanese offers. The Parties did agree, though, to redouble efforts to conclude the negotiations by the October deadline.

The September 2003 working party meeting revealed even deeper and widening cracks between the Parties in the agricultural offers, with pork again becoming the main issue. Finally, in March 2004, following a total of seven heads level negotiations and fourteen rounds of negotiation at the working level, both parties agreed in substance on the Agreement. The Agreement was signed on 17 September 2004 and went into effect on 1 April 2005.

It must be noted that throughout the negotiations, political events in both countries further delayed the completion of the negotiations. For instance, in July 2003 Mexican President Fox's National Action Party lost seats in its lower-house Congressional election, public support for the President declined amid a struggling domestic economy and industry groups began successfully pressuring the government for inclusion in (or at least to accompany) the Mexican negotiating delegation.[36] At the same time, Japan was preparing for its own lower-house election in November 2003 and an upper-house election the following summer. These elections undoubtedly impacted upon Japan's willingness to make concessions or be seen as possibly hurting domestic farmers, a strong base of support for Prime Minister Koizumi's Liberal Democratic Party.

III. Analysis of noteworthy substantive obligations

A. Trade in goods

The level of protection via tariffs in Mexico differs widely from that in Japan. For example, Mexico maintains relatively high tariff protection; its simple average bound tariff is 36.24 per cent, while the simple average applied tariff is 16.23 per cent.[37] On the other hand, Japan's simple average bound tariff is 8.7 per cent, while

---

[34] 'Japan, México start trade pact talks', *The Jakarta Post*, 12 August 2003.
[35] 'México and Japan started talks about a FTA on 11 August', *Latin America Mexico and NAFTA Report* (19 August 2003).
[36] Hussain Khan, 'México Free Trade Founders on Japan's Farmers', *Asia Times*, 23 October 2003.
[37] Joint Study Group, above note 6, at p. 13. Japan also pointed out that Mexico frequently changes its applied tariff rates and claimed the Mexican system needs to be more transparent, predictable and stable. See ibid., at p. 14.

the simple average applied tariff is 8.1 per cent.[38] Both nations, however, maintain significant tariff peaks on 'sensitive' products.

The JMEPA reduces or eliminates customs duties on an extensive range of goods, including agricultural and industrial products. The Agreement immediately removes tariffs on 95 per cent of Mexican products to Japan and 44 per cent of Japanese products to Mexico. In addition, the Agreement phases out tariffs on 90 per cent of goods within ten years, by which time 98 per cent of Japanese exports and 87 per cent of Mexican exports will receive duty free market access in the other's market.[39] Prior to the JMEPA, only 16 per cent of Japanese exports received duty free treatment from Mexico, while 70 per cent of Mexican exports entered Japan duty free.[40]

Agricultural products

Without question, the biggest obstacle to the Agreement was the liberalization of the agricultural sector.[41] Japan heavily subsidizes, protects and supports its agricultural sector – support accounts for 58 per cent of gross producer receipts (almost twice the OECD average),[42] with rice, wheat, other grains, meat, sugar and dairy being the most heavily supported commodities. Despite several papers by the Ministry of Agriculture, Forestry and Fisheries raising the idea of decreasing support and importing more cheaply, producer lobbying interests have prevailed and price controls, subsidies and tariffs remain.

Additionally, the JMEPA negotiations were threatened by Japan's insistence that 'sensitive' agricultural products should be protected or excluded entirely from the Agreement. From Mexico's standpoint, an agreement excluding certain agricultural products would not have been worth completing due to the fact that an FTA which merely reduced industrial tariffs would, in all likelihood, fail to stimulate the exportation of Mexican industrial products to Japan since Japanese import tariffs on industrial products are already low (average approximately 4.9 per cent). On the other hand, Japan maintains high agricultural tariff protection (average approximately

---

[38] Ibid.
[39] By contrast, in the Japan–Singapore EPA, 100% of Japanese goods enter Singapore duty free while 93.8% of Singaporean goods enter Japan duty free. Moreover, in the NAFTA, over 99% of American, Canadian and Mexican goods enter the other markets duty free, while in the EU–Mexico FTA, 97.6% of Mexican goods and 96.8% of European goods enter the other market with duty free access. See ibid., at p. 49.
[40] 'FTA with México Paves Way for Talks with Asian Nations', *The Nikkei Weekly*, 15 March 2004.
[41] Talks broke down in October 2003 over a request for a non-tariff quota on Mexican orange juice. See, e.g., Khan, above note 36; and Kenichi Kawasaki, Research Institute of Economy, Trade and Industry, 'Toward the Conclusion of a Japan–México FTA', 11 November 2003, available at: www.rieti.go.jp/en/columns/a01_0105.html. The nations debated whether Mexican agricultural exports would threaten, compete against, or complement the Japanese agricultural industry. See Joint Study Group, above note 6, at pp. 16–17.
[42] OECD, 2002–2004 statistics, available at www.oecd.org. It should be noted that the percentage is down from 61 per cent in 1986–1988.

26 per cent) and Mexico, with less than 1 per cent of the total Japanese farm-import sector, felt it needed substantial concessions in order to stimulate its agricultural exports to Japan. Therefore, the inclusion of agriculture was, from Mexico's standpoint, 'indispensable' to an agreement and a deal that did not substantially open the Japanese market to Mexican agricultural products would not be a deal which would assist Mexico's economic growth.[43]

It has also been posed that, as a result of NAFTA, food importation from the US has increased to the point of damaging Mexican farmers and that the Mexican government looked to build electoral, political and economic stability by diversifying its exports of agricultural products (and thereby stimulating the sector) to other nations, including Japan.

In October 2003, Mexico expressed its desire for Japan substantially to liberalize imports of numerous agricultural products from Mexico, including pork, oranges and orange juice, chicken and beef. Unsurprisingly, Japan found the request unacceptable and negotiations stalled. By January 2004, Mexico reportedly lowered its demands and requested a tariff exemption on 120,000 tons of pork, 30,000 tons of chicken, 40,000 tons of beef and 10,000 tons of oranges.[44]

The two sides eventually restarted the negotiations and finally reached a compromise on this important sector whereby Japanese import tariffs on most Mexican produce will be lowered over three to ten years (interestingly, several agricultural tariff rates are to be ultimately finalized following the first two years of the Agreement).[45] Overall, the Agreement opens the Japanese market to over 300 kinds of agricultural and marine products from Mexico.[46] Importantly, the Agreement increases quotas and reduces tariffs for a number of key agricultural products, including all of the previously mentioned 'sensitive' products. For instance, Japan will establish an import quota of 4,000 tons for orange juice on which tariffs will be halved for the first year.[47] The quota will be expanded to up to 6,500 tons from the fifth year. Japan will also halve tariff rates on 38,000 tons of high-quality pork from Mexico in the first year, and expand the quota to 80,000 tons from the fifth year.[48] For both oranges and beef, Japan will introduce duty free import quotas of ten tons for the initial two years.[49] It will set ten tons in a duty free quota for chickens in the first year. Thereafter Japan will raise the duty free import quotas to up to 4,000 tons for oranges, 6,000 tons for beef and 8,500 tons for chicken in the fifth year.[50]

In total, the JMEPA classifies products in a variety of segments for the treatment of custom duties:[51]

---

[43] Joint Study Group, above note 6, at p. 20.
[44] See Yamamoto Junichi, FTA Watch, 'Japan Stumbles over the Japan–México Free Trade Agreement (FTA)', unpublished comment, July 2004, available at www.parcjp.org/parc_e/Other_articles/fta07_04.html (last accessed 10 October 2006).
[45] For specific information, see JMEPA, Annex 1 referred to in Chapter 3: Schedules in relation to Article 5.
[46] Ibid. [47] Ibid. [48] Ibid. [49] Ibid. [50] Ibid. [51] Ibid.

- immediate elimination of custom duties (i.e. grapes (previously 17 per cent)),
- gradual elimination of custom duties over a period of three (i.e. pineapples and pineapple juice, wheat and pasta) to ten years (bananas),
- establishment of a non-taxable quota (with amounts increasing each year),
- reduction of custom duties (from four to eleven equal instalments),
- consultation (i.e. certain fish and fish products), or
- exclusion from the regulation of the Agreement (i.e. several meat products).

Thus, in the end, Japan agreed to eliminate or substantially reduce tariffs on almost all agricultural products; however, it refused to liberalize substantially certain sectors, including rice and meats. The reason for this unbending stance is to prevent Japan – a country where multifunctionality is apparently taken seriously and food security (i.e. self-reliance) is rapidly decreasing (Japan currently imports approximately 60 per cent of its food)[52] – from further relying on imports to the consternation of domestic producers. In other words, the ruling Liberal Democratic Party needed to maintain import protection to placate its strong rural support base. Nevertheless, Mexican officials believe the Agreement will substantially increase agricultural exports to Japan. In fact, Mexican Agriculture Minister, Javier Usabiaga estimated that Mexico's exports to Japan could increase by as much as 10.6 per cent annually over the next ten years and create 277,000 new jobs in the same period.[53] In addition, Minister Usabiaga stated that Mexico was positioning itself to become a principal player in Japan's US$35 billion food-import industry.[54]

Mining, manufacturing and other products

The JMEPA liberalizes the mining and manufacturing sectors through the gradual elimination of custom duties. Under the terms of the Agreement, customs duties will be eliminated on almost all products within ten years.

Notably, and in exchange for the Japanese agricultural concessions, Mexico has undertaken to liberalize the steel and automobile sectors. The Japanese automotive industry lobbied hard for an FTA with Mexico not only due to Mexico's expanding market but perhaps more importantly due to Mexico's potential for becoming a strategic base in accessing the North American market. While still having to navigate through NAFTA local content rules in order to access the US and Canada, the finished car market in Mexico and the spare parts market are both large. More specifically, the JMEPA obligates Mexico to create additional duty free import quotas for Japanese automobiles, including passenger cars, small buses and trucks, equivalent to 5 per cent of the Mexican auto market in the previous year (compared with the current 3 per cent), on top of the current duty free import quotas.[55]

---

[52] See Joint Study Group, above note 6, at p. 16.
[53] See 'Japan, México Reach Free Trade Agreement', above note 11.   [54] Ibid.
[55] For specific information, see JMEPA, Annex 1 referred to in Chapter 3: Schedules in relation to Article 5.

Overall, tariffs on automobile imports from Japan will be gradually eliminated over six years and thus will enter without a tariff in the seventh year of the Agreement.[56] Even with tariffs being gradually liberalized, Japan has already seen significant export gains in this area. For instance, prior to the JMEPA, Mexico allowed the duty free importation of only 58,000 cars, but the FTA more than doubled this quota to 120,000, which not only influenced automobile manufacturers directly but also aided the exportation of 'other' transport equipment to increase 47.8 per cent to over US$2 billion.[57]

In addition, Mexico will abolish tariffs on all types of steel products from Japan within ten years. Moreover, duties on products used in specified industries (electronics, home appliances, capital goods, automobiles) have been immediately eliminated.[58]

While the Mexican tariff rate on Japanese goods stood at between 20 and 30 per cent prior to the JMEPA, imports from NAFTA countries were only subject to 3.3 per cent duty. Therefore, other Japanese industries, particularly the electronic and electrical equipment industries, also felt their competitiveness was being undermined and lobbied hard for the gains created by the JMEPA.

For Mexico, in what may prove to be a significant change, the Agreement immediately eliminated the 25.2 yen-per-litre tariff on tequila imports from Mexico.[59] According to Eduardo Orendain, president of the National Chamber of the Tequila Industry, this liberalization 'will immediately increase to 30 per cent more than we export now and will be double in three years'.[60] The reason behind the optimism is twofold. First, Japanese imports of tequila rose from 380 million yen in 2002 to 680 million yen in 2003 and have continued to rise. Second, tequila immediately becomes cheaper in Japan, which should increase sales. Empirical evidence substantiates this assertion, as tequila exports to the EU following the 1997 EU–Mexico FTA have increased by 50 per cent.[61]

The immediate tariff elimination on beer and other alcoholic beverages also allows both Mexican and Japanese producers to compete more effectively in the other's market.[62]

B. Trade in services

Mexico maintains an upper limit of 49 per cent on the ratio of foreign capital in many services fields, requires governmental approval on certain services, and

---

[56] Ibid.
[57] JETRO Economic Research Department, *Japanese Trade in 2005* (June 2006), at p. 9, available at www.jetro.go.jp/jpn/stats/data/pdf/trade2005.pdf.
[58] Ibid.   [59] Ibid.
[60] See, e.g., Nozomi Kobayashi, 'Tariff-free tequila flow from México to Japan under FTA', *The Japan Times*, 16 September 2004, available at http://search.japantimes.co.jp/cgi-bin/nb20040916a2.html.
[61] Ibid.   [62] See JMEPA, Annex 1 referred to in Chapter 3: Schedules in relation to Article 5.

maintains nationality requirements and other restrictions on foreign service providers. As Mexico has offered national treatment to many of its FTA partners, Japanese business opportunities were disadvantaged.[63] The JMEPA uses the 'negative list' approach to trade in services and commits both Parties to provide national treatment and most favoured nation (MFN) treatment in the cross-border trade in services, subject to certain exceptions.[64]

Chapter 8 applies to a number of 'measures adopted or maintained by a Party affecting cross-border trade in services by service suppliers of the other Party', and Article 97(1) specifically lists the following to which the Agreement applies:

(a) the supply of a service (note: the measures respecting the supply of a service include those respecting the provision of any financial security as a condition for the supply of a service);
(b) the purchase or use of, or payment for, a service;
(c) the access to services offered to the public generally and the use of them, in connection with the supply of a service; and
(d) the presence in its Area of a service supplier of the other Party.

On the other hand, Article 97(2) explicitly excludes the following from Chapter 8:

(a) financial services, as defined in Chapter 9;
(b) cabotage in maritime transport services, including navigation in inland waters;
(c) with respect to air transport services, measures affecting traffic rights, however granted; or measures affecting services directly related to the exercise of traffic rights, other than measures affecting:
　(i) aircraft repair and maintenance services;
　(ii) the selling and marketing of air transport services; and
　(iii) computer reservation system (CRS) services;[65]
(d) procurement by a Party or a state enterprise;
(e) subsidies provided by a Party or a state enterprise thereof, including grants, government supported loans, guarantees and insurance;
(f) measures pursuant to immigration laws and regulations;

---

[63] See Joint Study Group, above note 6, at pp. 25–6.

[64] The Parties initially disagreed on the format for services commitments, with Japan favouring a 'positive list' approach (such as that of the Japan–Singapore EPA) in which only the service sectors listed are covered, while Mexico favoured the 'negative list' approach (such as that of the NAFTA) in which all services sectors are included in the agreement and each party maintains a list of reservations for sensitive sectors. In Mexico's opinion, this approach provides more certainty and transparency over the positive list approach. See ibid., at p. 26.

[65] Note in Original JMEPA: The term 'traffic rights' means the rights for scheduled and non-scheduled services to operate and/or to carry passengers, cargo and mail for remuneration or hire from, to, within, or over a Party, including points to be served, routes to be operated, types of traffic to be carried, capacity to be provided, tariffs to be charged and their conditions, and criteria for designation of air lines, including such criteria as number, ownership, and control.

(g) services supplied in the exercise of governmental authority;[66] and
(h) measures of a Party with respect to a national of the other Party seeking access to its employment market, or employed on a permanent basis in that Party.

Article 98 provides for national treatment, specifically stating that 'treatment no less favourable' shall be accorded to services and service suppliers of the other Party than that it accords, in like circumstances, to its own services and service suppliers. A note to Article 98 clarifies the provision by adding that nothing in Article 98 shall be construed to require either Party to 'compensate for any inherent competitive disadvantages which result from the foreign character of the relevant services or service suppliers'.

Article 99 is the complementary provision applying MFN status to each Party, meaning that 'treatment no less favourable' shall be accorded to services and service suppliers of the other Party than that it accords, in like circumstances, to services and service suppliers of any non-Party. A note to Article 99 then adds that each Party is to 'accord to services and service suppliers of the other Party the better of the treatment required by Articles 98 and 99'.

With a view to ensuring that any measure adopted or maintained by a Party relating to the licensing, certification, or technical standards of service suppliers of the other Party does not constitute an unnecessary barrier to cross-border trade in services, Article 104 provides that each Party 'shall endeavour' to ensure that its licensing and certification measures are based on objective and transparent criteria (such as competence and ability), are not more burdensome than necessary to ensure the quality of the services and do not constitute a disguised restriction on the cross-border supply of the services.[67]

Importantly, the Agreement specifically prohibits either Party from requiring a service supplier of the other Party to establish or maintain a representative office or any form of enterprise, or to be resident, in its Area as a condition for the cross-border supply of a service.[68]

However, the Chapter does contain several important reservations, such as that Articles 98–100 do not apply to 'any existing non-conforming measure that is maintained by a Party at the federal or central government level' (as set out in its Schedule to Annex 6).[69] Thus, the JMEPA contains so-called 'grandfather' clauses in this regard. In addition, Article 105 contains several illustrations of when a Party may deny the benefits of Chapter 8 to a service supplier of the other Party where the

---

[66] Note in Original JMEPA: For the purposes of this Chapter, services supplied in the exercise of governmental authority means any service which is supplied neither on a commercial basis nor in competition with one or more service suppliers.
[67] Article 104(2) qualifies this provision by stating that, where a Party recognizes education, experience, licences or certifications obtained in a non-Party, nothing in Article 99 shall be construed to require the Party to accord such recognition to education, experience, licences or certifications obtained in the other Party.
[68] JMEPA, Article 100.   [69] Ibid., Article 101(1)(a).

Party establishes that the service is being supplied by an enterprise that is owned or controlled by persons of a non-party. Therefore, comprehensive understanding of the Chapter can only be gained from studying the reservations and denial of benefit regulations and appreciating how they relate to current operations.

Article 103 establishes a Sub-Committee on Cross-Border Trade in Services to (a) review the implementation and operation of this Chapter; (b) discuss any issues related to this Chapter; (c) report the findings of the Sub-Committee and make recommendations to the Joint Committee; (d) report their findings to the Joint Committee; and (e) to carry out other functions which may be delegated by the Joint Committee pursuant to Article 165.

C. Investment

Mexico maintains an upper limit of 49 per cent on the ratio of foreign capital in many fields; requires governmental approval on certain services; maintains nationality requirements and other restrictions on foreign providers; and is liable to sudden regulatory changes.[70] Furthermore, as Mexico offered national treatment, MFN status and other preferential terms to many foreign investors, Japanese business opportunities were disadvantaged.[71]

The JMEPA uses the 'negative list' approach to investment but, in doing so, provides for extensive regulation. With some exceptions, the JMEPA commits both nations to providing national treatment and MFN treatment to the other Party; thus improving both legal certainty and legal security in the area of investment. Following the conclusion of the Agreement, METI claimed the improvement in the Mexican investment climate would (1) slow the 'growing trend for Japanese firms to pull out of Mexico'; (2) increase Mexico's attractiveness as a base not only for exporting to North America but also, due to Mexico's extensive FTA network, to numerous Latin American countries; and (3) increase inward investment from Japan (estimated at US$12 billion over ten years leading to the direct employment of nearly 277,000 persons) and, correspondingly, increased diversification of inward investment.[72]

In terms of national treatment, Article 58 states that each Party 'shall accord to investors of the other Party and to their investments treatment no less favourable than the treatment it accords, in like circumstances, to its own investors and to their investments with respect to the establishment, acquisition, expansion, management, conduct, operation, maintenance, use, enjoyment and sale or other disposition of investments [investment activities]'.

Article 59 provides for MFN by stating that '[e]ach Party shall accord to investors of the other Party and to their investments, treatment no less favourable than the

---

[70] See ibid., Chapter 7. [71] See ibid.
[72] METI, 'Japan's Policy on FTAs/EPAs' (March 2005), at p. 13, available at www.meti.go.jp/english/policy/index_externaleconomicpolicy.html.

treatment it accords, in like circumstances, to investors of a non-Party and to their investments with respect to investment activities'. Note 2 to the Article confirms that in the application of Articles 58 and 59 a Party (a) may not impose on an investor of the other Party a requirement that a minimum level of equity in an enterprise in the Area of the former Party be held by its nationals; or (b) may not require an investor of the other Party, by reason of its nationality, to sell or otherwise dispose of an investment in the Area of the former Party.

Note 3 also provides that no less favourable treatment, in like circumstances, shall be granted to its own investors or investors of a non-Party with respect to access to the courts of justice and administrative tribunals and agencies in all degrees of jurisdiction, both in pursuit and in defence of such investors' rights.

Article 60 contains the standard clause on 'General Treatment', that each Party shall accord treatment 'in accordance with international law, including fair and equitable treatment and full protection and security' to investments of investors of the other Party.

In a note, the Article also:

> prescribes the customary international law minimum standard of treatment of aliens as the minimum standard of treatment to be afforded to investments of investors of the other Party. The concepts of 'fair and equitable treatment' and 'full protection and security' do not require treatment in addition to or beyond that which is required by the customary international law minimum standard of treatment of aliens. A determination that there has been a breach of another provision of this Agreement, or of a separate international agreement, does not establish that there has been a breach of this Article.

The addition of the above note is significant and is a direct response to a controversial dispute involving Mexico and the US in the NAFTA.[73] A similar provision is included in other agreements, such as the Australia–United States Free Trade Agreement (AUSFTA).[74]

Article 61 prohibits both direct and indirect expropriation or nationalization of an investment of an investor of the other Party except: (a) for a public purpose; (b) on a non-discriminatory basis; (c) in accordance with due process of law and Article 60; and (d) on payment without delay and to be fully realizable and made in a freely usable currency[75] (and including interest at a commercially reasonable rate for that

---

[73] For the problem, see NAFTA Ch. 11 Arbitral Tribunal, *Metalclad Corporation v. United Mexican States*, ICSID Case No. ARB(AF)/97/1 (Award of 30 August 2000), 40 ILM 36 (2001), specifically at p. 46. For further discussion, see William S. Dodge, 'International Decisions: *Metalclad Corp. v. México* and *México v. Metalclad Corp*' (2001) 95(4) *American Journal of International Law* 910–18.

[74] Signed 18 May 2004, in force 1 January 2005. See Chapter 11, para. 5. More information and the text of the agreement can be found at the Australian Department of Foreign Affairs and Trade (DFAT) webpage, 'Australia-United States Free Trade Agreement', at www.dfat.gov.au/trade/negotiations/us.html.

[75] See JMEPA, Article 61(4), which provides for circumstances of payment in a non-freely convertible currency.

currency from the date of expropriation until the date of actual payment) equivalent to the fair market value of the expropriated investment immediately before the expropriation occurred.[76]

Article 62 protects the Parties from 'civil strife', mandating that each Party accord to investors of the other Party and to their investments treatment no less favourable than treatment it accords to its own investors or investors of a non-Party and to their investments (whichever is more favourable), with respect to 'measures, such as restitution, indemnification, compensation or any other settlement, it adopts or maintains relating to losses suffered by investments in its Area owing to armed conflict, civil strife or any other similar event'.

Importantly, Article 63 provides that all transfers (with limited exceptions, i.e. bankruptcy or criminal offences)[77] relating to an investment in either nation of an investor of the other Party be 'made freely and without delay ... in a freely usable currency at the market rate of exchange prevailing on the date of the transfer with respect to spot transactions in the currency to be transferred'.[78] The Article then lists a non-exhaustive illustrative list, which includes:

(a) the initial capital and additional amounts to maintain or increase the investment;
(b) profits, dividends, interest, capital gains, royalty payments, management fees, technical assistance fees and other fees;
(c) proceeds from the sale or liquidation of all or any part of the investment;
(d) payments made under a contract including payments made pursuant to a loan agreement;
(e) payments made in accordance with Article 61; and
(f) payments arising out of the settlement of a dispute under Section 2.[79]

The Agreement also prohibits a Party from requiring that an enterprise of an investor of the other Party appoint to senior management positions individuals of any particular nationality.[80] However, a Party may require that a majority of the board of directors, or any committee thereof, or enterprise of an investor of the other Party, be of a particular nationality, or resident of the Party, provided that the requirement does not materially impair the ability of the investor to exercise control over its investment.[81]

The Agreement also prohibits performance requirements, such as measures requiring the following:

(a) to export a given level or percentage of goods or services;
(b) to achieve a given level or percentage of domestic content;

---

[76] The fair market value shall not reflect any change in value occurring because the expropriatory action had become known earlier. Valuation criteria to determine the fair market value may include declared tax value of tangible property (Article 61(2)).
[77] See JMEPA, Article 63(3), for the full list of exceptions.   [78] Ibid., Article 63(1) and (2).
[79] Ibid., Article 63(1).   [80] Ibid., Article 64(1).   [81] Ibid., Article 64(2).

(c) to purchase, use or accord a preference to goods produced or services provided in its Area, or to purchase goods or services from persons in its Area;
(d) to relate in any way the volume or value of imports to the volume or value of exports or to the amount of foreign exchange inflows associated with such investment;
(e) to restrict sales of goods or services in its Area that such investment produces or provides by relating such sales in any way to the volume or value of its exports or foreign exchange earnings;
(f) to transfer technology, a production process or other proprietary knowledge to a person in its Area, except when the requirement is imposed or the commitment or undertaking is enforced by a court, administrative tribunal or competition authority to remedy an alleged violation of competition laws or to act in a manner not inconsistent with multilateral agreements in respect of protection of intellectual property rights. A measure that requires an investment to use a technology to meet generally applicable health, safety or environmental requirements shall not be construed to be inconsistent with this paragraph. For greater certainty, Articles 58 and 59 shall apply to the measure; or
(g) to act as the exclusive supplier of the goods it produces or services it provides to a specific region or world market.[82]

Furthermore, Article 65(2) prohibits the Parties from conditioning the receipt or continued receipt of an advantage, in connection with an investment in its Area of an investor of a Party or of a non-Party, on compliance with any of the following requirements:

(a) to achieve a given level or percentage of domestic content;
(b) to purchase, use or accord a preference to goods produced in its Area, or to purchase goods from producers in its Area;
(c) to relate in any way the volume or value of imports to the volume or value of exports or to the amount of foreign exchange inflows associated with such investment; or
(d) to restrict sales of goods or services in its Area that such investment produces or provides by relating such sales in any way to the volume or value of its exports or foreign exchange earnings.[83]

Article 65(5) provides exceptions to subparagraph 1(b) and (c) and 2(a) and (b). It states that, provided such measures are not applied in an arbitrary or unjustifiable

---

[82] Ibid., Article 65(1).
[83] However, paragraph 2 is not to be construed to prevent a Party from conditioning the receipt or continued receipt of an advantage, in connection with an investment in its Area of an investor of a Party or of a non-Party, on compliance with a requirement to: (a) locate production; (b) provide a service; (c) train or employ workers; (d) construct or expand particular facilities; or (e) carry out research and development in its Area: JMEPA, Article 65(3).

manner, or do not constitute a disguised restriction on international trade or investment activities, the agreement shall not be construed to prevent any Party from adopting or maintaining measures: (a) necessary to secure compliance with laws and regulations that are not inconsistent with the provisions of this Agreement; (b) necessary to protect human, animal or plant life or health; or (c) necessary for the conservation of living or non-living exhaustible natural resources.

In addition, Articles 66 and beyond provide a lengthy list of exceptions and reservations, including certain existing non-conforming measures. One notable exception is the 'grandfathering' of previous inconsistencies within each country, meaning that the investment guarantees provided in the JMEPA do not apply to existing investments.[84] Another exception is contained in Article 72, which allows temporary safeguards to be maintained. Specifically, under this Article, a Party may adopt or maintain measures not conforming with its obligations under Article 58 relating to cross-border capital transactions and Article 63:

1. (a) in the event of serious balance-of-payments and external financial difficulties or imminent threat thereof; or
   (b) in cases where, in exceptional circumstances, movements of capital cause or threaten to cause serious difficulties for macroeconomic management, in particular, monetary and exchange rate policies.
2. Measures referred to in paragraph 1 above:
   (a) shall be consistent with the Articles of Agreement of the International Monetary Fund, as may be amended;
   (b) shall not exceed those necessary to deal with the circumstances set out in paragraph 1 above;
   (c) shall be temporary and shall be eliminated as soon as conditions permit; and
   (d) shall be promptly notified to the other Party.

Articles 76–95 provide for a detailed model of investor-state dispute settlement provisions and extensive procedural rules for investment disputes. It is closely modelled on the investor-state model of dispute settlement set out in the NAFTA.

D. Intellectual property

Given Japan's interests in promoting and strengthening intellectual property rights and protection, it is somewhat surprising that the JMEPA does not include a chapter on intellectual property. The Agreement does, however, mention intellectual property in a number of locations.

For instance, intellectual property features in Chapter 15 (Bilateral Cooperation). More specifically, in Article 144 (Cooperation in the Field of Intellectual Property),

---

[84] See JMEPA, Article 66(1)(a). For specific information on existing measures, see Annex 6 referred to in Chapters 7 and 8: Reservations for Existing Measures.

both parties 'recogniz[ing] the growing importance of intellectual property as a factor of economic competitiveness in the knowledge-based economy, and of IP protection in this new environment, shall develop their cooperation in the field of IP'. The article then elaborates upon the prior sentence by providing what appears to be a non-exhaustive list of potential informational exchange cooperation, including:

(a) public awareness activities of the importance of IP protection and the function of IP protection systems to their respective nationals;
(b) improvement of IP protection systems and their operation;
(c) policy measures conducive to ensuring adequate enforcement of IP rights; and
(d) automation of administrative processes of IP authority in order to enhance its efficiency.

Interestingly, a note to Article 144 states that information provided pursuant to the Article shall not include information regarding individual cases of infringement of intellectual property rights so as not to be used by the receiving party in criminal proceedings carried out by a court or a judge.

Furthermore, included in the chapter on Trade in Goods is Article 8, 'Protection of Geographical Indications for Spirits'. This Article refers to Article 22(1) of the WTO Agreement on Trade Related Aspects of Intellectual Property (TRIPS) in Annex 1C and as may be amended. It is a binding Article based on the relevant provisions of the WTO with respect to the protection of geographical indications and shall take measures to prohibit the use of geographical indications seen in Annex 3, for spirits that do not originate in the place indicated by the respective geographical indication.

Another example of Intellectual Property rights within the Agreement is contained in Article 65(f) in Chapter 7 (Investment) in relation to performance requirements. Both parties agree to neither Party imposing nor enforcing the 'transfer of technology, a production process or other proprietary knowledge to a person in its Area, except when the requirement imposed on the commitment or undertaking is enforced by a court, administrative tribunal or competition authority to remedy an alleged violation of competition laws or to act in a manner not inconsistent with multilateral agreements in respect of protection of intellectual property rights'. The Article then continues with an exception, stating an investment would not be considered inconsistent with the Article when the technology is used to meet the generally applicable health, safety or environmental requirements.

Further in Chapter 7 Article 73, we again see a reference to intellectual property rights. Article 73(1) expresses a positive obligation in which it reiterates the premise that 'Nothing in this chapter shall be construed so as to derogate from the rights and obligations under multilateral agreements in respect of protection of intellectual property rights to which the Parties are parties'. Paragraph 2 further emphasizes that nothing in the Chapter 'shall be construed so as to oblige either party to extend to investors of the other Party and their investments treatment accorded to investors of a non-Party and their investments by virtue of multilateral agreements in respect of intellectual property rights...'.

There is also reference to intellectual property rights in Chapter 11 (Government Procurement), in the exceptions provided in Article 126(2)(c). This Article denotes the following exception in relation to Government Procurement: 'Nothing in this chapter shall be construed to prevent a Party from taking any action or not disclosing any information which it considers necessary for the protection of its essential security interests...'. The Article does provide a caveat, however, with paragraph 2 limiting the use of the exception in Article 126(1) where it states '... such measures shall not be applied in a manner that would constitute a means of arbitrary or unjustifiable discrimination'. It limits the Parties' ability to disguise the exceptions as de facto trade restriction and furthermore states that nothing in the Chapter shall be construed to prevent a Party from imposing, enforcing or maintaining measures:

(a) necessary to protect public morals, order or safety;
(b) necessary to protect human, animal or plant life or health;
(c) necessary to protect intellectual property; or
(d) relating to goods or services of handicapped persons, of philanthropic institutions or of prison labour.

Article 142, entitled 'Cooperation in the Field of Science and Technology', and contained in Chapter 14 on Bilateral Cooperation, seemingly provides an express duty to ensure that the Parties protect intellectual property rights. Article 142(4) states that, in accordance with the applicable laws and regulations of the Parties and with the relevant international agreements to which the Parties are parties, the Parties shall ensure the adequate and effective protection, and give due consideration to the distribution, of intellectual property rights or other rights of a proprietary nature resulting from the cooperative activities under this Article.

E. Rules of origin

Chapter 5 sets out the general rules of origin for goods under the JMEPA. Under the terms of the Agreement, these rules are applied to determine whether a good produced in the territory of one or both Parties using some materials produced elsewhere is an 'originating good' and therefore eligible for preferential treatment under the JMEPA.[85] Similarly to many North American FTAs, the JMEPA uses (for the most part) a simple 'change in tariff classification' to determine eligibility under the Agreement,[86] subject to the detailed product-specific rules contained in Annex 4 to the Agreement. Therefore, in order to receive preferential treatment under the

---

[85] Article 22(1). [86] Article 22(2).

JMEPA, non-originating goods must have gone through a sufficient change within the territory of a Party to alter the tariff classification according to which they are imported and exported. Importantly, more stringent requirements apply for certain key Mexican exports, such as footwear and natural resources (e.g. copper and zinc).[87]

However, a good may still be deemed an 'originating good' even if it fails to undergo a change in classification if the value of non-originating materials used in its production is *de minimis* (defined as 'not more than 10 per cent of the transaction value of the good'), if the good satisfies any applicable regional value content, based on certain methods specified in Article 23, and satisfies all other applicable requirements of the Chapter.[88]

F. Labour, environment, and other social issues

Unlike some FTAs (such as the NAFTA), the JMEPA has relatively little to say about social issues. As a starting point, Article 168 of the JMEPA incorporates Article XX of the General Agreement on Tariffs and Trade (GATT) 1994 and Article XIV of the General Agreement on Trade in Services (GATS) into the Agreement.

However, the Agreement does not contain any provisions relating to labour policy or standards. In terms of the environment, the Agreement contains a clause on 'Environmental Measures' in the Investment Chapter (Chapter 7) which states that 'it is inappropriate to encourage investment by relaxing domestic health, safety or environmental measures'.[89] The provision continues:

> a Party should not waive or otherwise derogate from, or offer to waive or otherwise derogate from, such measures as an encouragement for the establishment, acquisition, expansion or retention in its Area of an investment of an investor. If a Party considers that the other Party has offered such an encouragement, it may request consultations with the other Party and the Parties shall consult with a view to avoiding any such encouragement.

Moreover, in Article 147, entitled 'Cooperation in the Field of the Environment', the Parties 'recogni[ze] the need for environmental preservation and improvement to promote sound and sustainable development' and agree to cooperate in the field of environment in ways which may include:

(a) exchange of information on policies, laws, regulations and technology related to the preservation and improvement of the environment, and the implementation of sustainable development;
(b) promotion of capacity and institutional building to foster activities related with the Clean Development Mechanism under the Kyoto Protocol to the United Nations Framework Convention on Climate Change, as may be amended, by

---

[87] For these exports, classification heading or subheading changes are required with a further requirement of at least 50–55 per cent regional contents.
[88] Article 25(1). [89] Article 74.

means of workshops and dispatch of experts, and exploration of appropriate ways to encourage the implementation of the Clean Development Mechanism projects;

(c) encouragement of trade and dissemination of environmentally sound goods and services; and

(d) encouraging the exchange of information for the identification of investment opportunities and the promotion and development of business alliances in the field of environment.[90]

Interestingly, while many of Mexico's FTAs with Latin American nations at least mention human rights, the term is not directly or indirectly mentioned in the JMEPA.

G. Government procurement

Chapter 11 regulates the subject of government procurement. Importantly, in the procurement of services and goods by government organizations or government-related companies, both countries committed to provide national treatment. Specifically, according to Article 120(1), 'each Party shall provide immediately and unconditionally to the goods, services and suppliers of the other Party offering goods or services of the other Party, treatment no less favourable than that accorded to domestic goods, services and suppliers'.

Article 121 provides guidelines on 'rules of origin' determinations while Article 124 requires Parties to publish and provide relevant information regarding, inter alia, laws, regulations, determinations and reviews.

Additionally, Article 125 provides for a transparent challenge procedure in the event of a complaint by a supplier alleging a breach of this Chapter. In such circumstances, Article 125(1) states that each Party shall 'encourage the supplier to seek resolution of its complaint in consultation with the procuring entity' and, in such instances, 'the procuring entity shall accord impartial and timely consideration to any such complaint, in a manner that is not prejudicial to obtaining corrective measures under the challenge system'. Moreover, Article 125(2) requires each Party to provide 'non-discriminatory, timely, transparent and effective procedures enabling suppliers to challenge alleged breaches of this Chapter arising in the context of government procurements in which they have, or have had, an interest'.

Article 125(7) further requires that challenges be heard:

> [B]y an impartial and independent reviewing authority with no interest in the outcome of the government procurement and the members of which are secure from external influence during the term of appointment. A reviewing

---

[90] Article 148 specifically excludes Chapter 14 from Chapter 15 dispute settlement procedures.

authority which is not a court shall either be subject to judicial review or shall have procedures which provide that:

(a) participants can be heard before an opinion is given or a decision is reached;
(b) participants can be represented and accompanied;
(c) participants shall have access to all proceedings;
(d) proceedings can take place in public;
(e) opinions or decisions are given in writing with a statement describing the basis for the opinions or decisions;
(f) witnesses can be presented; and
(g) documents are disclosed to the reviewing authority.

Furthermore, under limited circumstances, Article 125(8) provides for interim relief.

Article 126 provides the list of exceptions to the Chapter. The Article provides:

1. Nothing in this Chapter shall be construed to prevent a Party from taking any action or not disclosing any information which it considers necessary for the protection of its essential security interests relating to the procurement of arms, ammunition or war materials, or to procurement indispensable for national security or for national defence purposes.
2. Provided that such measures are not applied in a manner that would constitute a means of arbitrary or unjustifiable discrimination between the Parties where the same conditions prevail, or a disguised restriction on trade between the Parties, nothing in this Chapter shall be construed to prevent a Party from imposing, enforcing or maintaining measures:

(a) necessary to protect public morals, order or safety;
(b) necessary to protect human, animal or plant life or health;
(c) necessary to protect intellectual property; or
(d) relating to goods or services of handicapped persons, of philanthropic institutions or of prison labour.

Article 127 establishes a Sub-Committee on Government Procurement to (a) analyse available information on each Party's government procurement market including the statistical information; (b) evaluate the effective access of suppliers of a Party to the government procurement market of the other Party covered by this Chapter; (c) monitor the application of the provisions of this Chapter and provide a forum to identify and address any problems or other issues that may arise; (d) report their findings to the Joint Committee; and to (e) carry out other functions which may be delegated by the Joint Committee pursuant to Article 165.

The Parties also agreed to cooperate, on mutually agreed terms, to increase their respective understanding of the other Party's respective government procurement systems, 'with a view to maximizing for the suppliers of both Parties the access to their respective government procurement market'. In furtherance of this goal, each Party agreed to develop and implement, within one year after the entry into force of this Agreement, 'concrete measures for the cooperation', which, Article 127 notes, may include 'training and orientation programmes for government personnel or interested suppliers regarding such aspects as how to identify government procurement opportunities and how to participate in the respective government procurement markets'. The Article also states that, in developing the above measures, 'special attention should be given to small businesses in each Party'.

Importantly, Annexes 12–18 limit the scope of coverage in the goods, services and construction services sectors, as well as provide for minimum threshold limits under the Agreement and provide for procurement procedures (applicable to Japan) in accordance with select Articles of the WTO Government Procurement Agreement. Therefore, knowledge of the annexes is required in order to gain a comprehensive understanding of the Agreement.

H. Competition policy

Chapter 12 of the Agreement sets out limited obligations in the area of regulation for anticompetitive activities. More specifically, Article 131 states that:

> Each Party shall, in accordance with its applicable laws and regulations, take measures which it considers appropriate against anticompetitive activities, in order to facilitate trade and investment flows between the Parties and the efficient functioning of its market.

The Agreement also requires the Parties to 'cooperate in the field of controlling anticompetitive activities', but provides no further guidance as to how such cooperation is to be accomplished.[91] However, Article 133 does provide a national treatment requirement, stating that '[e]ach Party shall apply its competition laws and regulations in a manner which does not discriminate between persons in like circumstances on the basis of their nationality', and Article 134 states that '[e]ach Party shall implement administrative and judicial procedures in a fair manner to control anticompetitive activities, pursuant to its relevant laws and regulations'. Notably, however, Article 164 and the dispute settlement procedures provided for in Chapter 15 do not apply to Chapter 12.[92]

I. Improvement of the business environment

Chapter 13 of the Agreement establishes a Committee for the Improvement of the Business Environment composed of representatives from the public sector, who 'may invite' relevant private sector personnel of both countries to attend or sit on the Committee.[93]

---

[91] See JMEPA, Article 132. [92] Ibid., Article 135. [93] Ibid., Article 137(3).

The reason for this Committee, as enunciated in Article 136, is to create a 'more favourable business environment with a view to promoting trade and investment activities by their private enterprises' and to 'address issues concerning the improvement of the business environment in the Parties'. More specifically, according to Article 137(2), the Committee:

(a) shall discuss ways and means to improve the business environment in the Parties;
(b) may, as needed, make recommendations on appropriate measures to be taken by the Parties. Such recommendations should be taken into consideration by the Parties;
(c) shall be provided with information on the implementation of such recommendations;
(d) may make public such recommendations in an appropriate manner; and
(e) may give the Joint Committee advisory opinions, where appropriate.

The rules and procedures of the Committee are to be established by the Committee and the dispute settlement procedures detailed in Chapter 15 of the Agreement do not apply to Chapter 13.

J. Bilateral cooperation

The Parties agreed in Chapter 14 of the Agreement to cooperate in nine areas: trade and investment promotion, supporting industries, small and medium-sized enterprises, science and technology, technical and vocational education and training, intellectual property, agriculture, tourism and the environment.

Cooperation includes such activities as the formation of relevant sub-committees, exchanging information, experts, scholars, teachers and trainees, encouraging the organization of seminars, fairs and exhibitions, implementing joint programmes and projects, supporting industries, promoting entrepreneurial networks, improving protection of certain rights (i.e. intellectual property) and improving efficiencies in the bilateral relationship.

The dispute settlement procedures provided for in Chapter 15 do not apply to Chapter 14.

K. Dispute settlement

A state to state dispute settlement mechanism is included in this Agreement as Chapter 15, and operates as follows. First, in normal circumstances, the complaining Party requests consultations with the other Member. Consultations shall be entered into within 30 days of receipt of the request. If the consultations are unsuccessful at resolving the dispute within 60 days, the complaining Party is then given the option of presenting its grievance to an arbitral tribunal to rule on the matter. Recourse to and the decision of the panel is binding on the Parties. In addition, the language of the FTA requires compliance with the recommendations or rulings of the panel within a reasonable period of time and failure to comply with the recommendations and rulings of the panel may result in retaliatory measures in the form of a suspension of the application of concessions or other obligations under the Agreement.

Like a large percentage of the dispute settlement processes included in FTAs, this Agreement's dispute settlement mechanism is very closely modelled on the World Trade Organization Understanding on Rules and Procedures Governing the Settlement of Disputes (DSU). Notably, the JMEPA follows the DSU model in terms of its 'closed' nature. For instance, according to Article 154, '[t]he arbitral tribunal shall meet in closed session' and '[t]he deliberations of the arbitral tribunal, the documents submitted to it and the draft award ... shall be kept confidential'.[94] However, again modelling itself on the WTO, Article 154(3) does not prohibit a Party 'from disclosing statements of its own position to the public'. In addition, at the request of the other Party, a Party 'shall ... provide a non-confidential summary of the information contained in its written submissions that could be disclosed to the public'. Such a system has not been successful in the WTO context at keeping interested outsiders informed for a number of reasons, most notably no timetable for compliance or sanction for failure to comply. It is not anticipated that the system will produce differing results in this context.[95]

While Chapter 15 outlines the general rules regarding dispute settlement, more specific 'details and procedures for the arbitral tribunal provided for in this Chapter shall be in accordance with the Rules of Procedure to be adopted by the Joint Committee within the first year of the date of entry into force of this Agreement'.[96]

IV. Impact and prospects for future application

The economies of Japan and Mexico make for perfect trading partners, or in the words of the Joint Study, the economies are 'endowed to complement each other'.[97] What is meant by this statement is that each country can make use of its economic strengths to increase trade and investment between the countries. For instance, Mexico is a large developing country rich in natural resources with a market of 100 million people and a GDP of US$617.7 billion and a large supply of young, inexpensive and relatively skilled workers.[98] Japan, on the other hand, is a developed country with the second largest economy in the world, a population of 126 million people and a large amount of capital and technology.[99] In such a situation, the circumstances are ripe for both nations to contribute to and prosper from increased economic ties.

---

[94] See ibid., Article 154(1) and (2).
[95] For more detailed analysis of this issue, see Bryan Mercurio, 'Improving Dispute Settlement in the WTO: The DSU Review – Making It Work?' (2004) 38(5) *Journal of World Trade* 795–854 at 807–8.
[96] JMEPA, Article 159.   [97] Joint Study Group, above note 6, at p. 9.   [98] Ibid.   [99] Ibid.

Until this point, the economic relationship between Japan and Mexico has been strong, but the relationship has the potential to grow. At the time of the negotiations, Japan was Mexico's third largest supplier of imports (worth US$7.62 billion in 2003) and the seventh largest export market (worth US$605.8 million in 2003).[100] However, while the volume of trade and investment has in absolute terms increased in recent years, the relative weight of the trading relationship has declined. Moreover, while Mexico's share of Japanese trade has remained relatively constant, Japan's importance in trading terms to Mexico has declined. This decline in due to the existence of the NAFTA and the EU–Mexico FTA, which has caused a sharp increase in the percentage of trade which Mexico conducts with those trading partners. Thus, Japan's percentage of total Mexican imports has fallen from 6.1% in 1994 to 4.8% in 2001, while at the same time the percentage of Mexico's total exports to Japan fell from 1.6% to 0.3%.[101] By contrast, the US takes up 68% of Mexico's imports and 88.5% of its exports and the EU has a 9.6% share in Mexico's imports and 3.4% of its exports (in value terms).[102] In terms of investment, Japan's share in terms of FDI in Mexico accounted for only 3.3% for the years 1994–2001, while the US accounted for 67.3% and the EU 18.6%.[103]

Therefore both countries believed that the trading relationship could be improved and the 'complementarities' better exploited through an FTA. The JMEPA has thus far unquestionably increased bilateral trade between the parties. For instance, Japanese exports to Mexico have increased substantially from pre-JMEPA levels; Japan exported US$3.6 billion worth of goods to Mexico (representing 0.8% of Mexican imports) in 2003 and more than US$6.9 billion in 2005 (representing 1.2% of Mexican imports).[104] Moreover, while Japan experienced negative export growth rates to Mexico of −8.5% in 2002 and −3.5% in 2003 (while at the same time experiencing total growth of 2.6% in 2002 and 13% in 2003), its exports to Mexico grew by 43% in 2004 and another 33.5% in 2005 (compared with total growth rates of 20.3% in 2004 and 5.9% in 2005).[105] Mexican exports to Japan have also increased at a small, but steady rate (dipping from US$1,785 million in 2002 to US$1,770 million in 2003 before

---

[100] See Japan Ministry of Foreign Affairs, 'Japan-México Relations', April 2005, at: http://infojapan.org/region/latin/mexico/index.html (last accessed 27 March 2006). Mexico has a substantial trade deficit with Japan. According to figures from the Ministry of Economy, Mexico exported US$605 million to Japan in 2003 while it imported US$7,622 million worth of goods. See Alcantara Francisco, 'The Free Trade Agreement between Japan and México', *Wakayama International Newsletter*, April 2005, available at www.wakayama-info.net/intl/archives/2005_04_001372.php. The Annex to the Joint Study Group quotes slightly different figures. See Joint Study Group, above note 6, at pp. 59–66.

[101] Joint Study Group, above note 6, at pp. 59–66. Although it must be noted in terms of overall trade, trade has grown between 30–60 per cent since 1993. See ibid. at p. 51. For a complete listing of bilateral trade between Japan and Mexico between 1993–2000, see ibid. at pp. 59–66.

[102] Ibid.   [103] Ibid.

[104] JETRO Economic Research Department, above note 57, at pp. 17 and 200. Total Mexican imports rose from US$469,862 million in 2003 to US$598,215 million in 2005.

[105] Ibid., at p. 18. Importantly, growth rates to Mexico outpaced Japanese export growth to Central and South America, which increased by 16.1 per cent in 2005.

rising to US$2,170 million in 2004 and US$2,552 million in 2005). Mexico's share of the Japanese import market remains at approximately 0.5%,[106] but its import growth rate to the Japanese market increased relative to the total Japanese import growth over the same period. Again, the JMEPA appears to have had a role in this result. For instance, while Japanese imports declined by 4.1% in 2002, imports from Mexico declined by 11.4%; furthermore, while Japanese total imports increased by 13.3% in 2003, imports from Mexico declined another 0.9%.[107] However, while Japanese imports rose by 19.2% in 2004 and 14.1% in 2005, imports from Mexico increased by 22.6% in 2004 and 17.6% in 2005.[108]

The remaining part of this section analyses the predicted gains for both countries in greater detail.

A. Japan

Prior to the Agreement, the Japanese business community repeatedly expressed its anxiety over the fact that, as a result of NAFTA (1994) and the EU–Mexico FTA (2000), Japan has been disadvantaged compared with its Western competitors.[109] In addition, steady progress in the FTAA negotiations involving the entire American continent (except for Cuba) to create the largest ever free trade area further added to Japanese concern that it would not be competitive in the Western hemisphere (this progress has since halted).

The situation led one prominent Japanese official to conclude that, 'actual damage has started being felt by Japanese companies due to the FTAs of the other economies'.[110] To illustrate, while American companies have been exporting most goods to Mexico free of tariffs as a result of NAFTA and EU companies can do the same; as a result of the EU–Mexico FTA, Japanese companies have been charged on average a 16.2 per cent tariff when exporting goods to Mexico.[111]

In addition, while Japan paid import duties ranging from 10 to 15 per cent for automotive engines and turbine generators, its American and EU competitors entered Mexico with duty free access. To further illustrate, import tariffs for most European steel, plastic, cables (including optical fibre) and other sizable industrial products were initially reduced, via the EU–Mexico FTA, by 10–29 per cent and completely eliminated in 2007. All of the above products directly compete with Japanese products and gained a large economic advantage over their Japanese competitors by virtue of the preferential trade agreement.

The fear of the Japanese business community was empirically substantiated when METI estimated that the loss caused by the unequal terms of business totalled

---

[106] Ibid., at p. 19. Total Japanese imports increased from US$336,832 million in 2002 to US$518,638 million in 2005.
[107] Ibid., at p. 20.   [108] Ibid.
[109] The Joint Study asserted that Japanese enterprises are placed at a 'seriously disadvantaged position' compared with NAFTA and EU companies: Joint Study Group, above note 6, at p. 13.
[110] Hatakeyama, above note 2.   [111] Ibid.

400 billion yen annually, which METI stated could lead to a decrease of GDP by about 620 billion yen and increase unemployment by 32,000.[112] These circumstances led Japanese Economy, Trade and Industry minister, Shoichi Nakagawa to insist that the JMEPA would assist Japanese firms in regaining competitiveness in Mexico.[113]

Thus, Japan felt that, in order to secure access to this enormous economic area, it had to conclude an FTA with a nation that already had established an extensive FTA network with most major trading nations. Mexico fitted the bill and was chosen as the target market for a number of reasons. First, Mexico has already successfully concluded FTAs with a number of diverse countries. It has, therefore, proven it has the ability to negotiate FTAs and, in doing so, has shown that it can accommodate the 'sensitive' issues of other nations. Second, with its extensive network of FTAs, Mexico is viewed as the gateway to North and Latin America as well as Europe and, with an FTA network covering 60 per cent of the world's GDP,[114] an agreement with Mexico was seen as the only one that would allow Japanese companies to enjoy equal treatment with companies from these regions, in areas such as custom duties, services, investment and government procurement. In addition to viewing Mexico as an important gateway to the American and European market, Japan also saw the Agreement as significant for its economic competition with China. Importantly, the Agreement will also allow Japanese companies to increase their investment in Mexico and export products within the Americas and to Europe at a preferential rate. This change is expected to be most rewarding to the manufacturing sector.

Through the JMEPA, Japan also gains expanded access to Mexico, a growing and dynamic market with the ninth largest economy in the world (equivalent to the combined economic scale of ASEAN). By concluding the JMEPA, which will see, among other things, Japan increasing Mexican imports of pork, oranges and other agricultural products, while increasing Japanese exports of steel, automobiles and other industrial products. Japan has also used the JMEPA to level the playing field with its competitors with Mexican tariffs, ranging between 18 per cent and 30 per cent on Japanese games, motorcycles, computer peripherals, photocopiers, telecommunications equipment, CD players and musical instruments, lifted as is the duty free export quota for cars.[115] Negotiating this agreement was difficult for Japan,

---

[112] Joint Study Group, above note 6, at p. 14 note 1.
[113] 'Japan, México Reach Free Trade Agreement', above note 11.
[114] See Joint Study Group, above note 6, at p. 2 para. 2.
[115] Mayumi Negishi, 'With México FTA set, Japan turns toward Asia', *The Japan Times*, 12 March 2004, available at http://search.japantimes.co.jp/cgi-bin/nb20040312a2.html. Japan also anticipates that the cost of food products (Japan pays an estimated 3.8 trillion yen to import 60 per cent of its total food consumption) will decrease. Mexico claims the FTA will encourage Japanese investment worth an average US$1.3 billion a year, or US$12.7 billion over ten years. Mexico currently receives only 1.3 per cent of Japan's foreign direct investment: ibid. See also, Joint Study Group, above note 6, at p. 5. See generally, 'Japan, México reach broad agreement on FTA', *The Japan Times*, 11 March 2004, available at www.japantimes.com/cgi-bin/getarticle.pl5?nn20040311a2.htm.

as the powerful Japanese agriculture lobby worried about cheap agricultural imports flooding the Japanese market.[116] But Japan realized that its lack of bilateral activity was disadvantaging its exports and thus rendering its industries non-competitive in the marketplace.[117]

For some time, the exact level of disadvantage was not fully seen, as many Japanese corporations operating in Mexico had been taking advantage of the Maquiradora system introduced by the Mexican government as one of the initiatives for inviting foreign capital and direct investments into Mexico. However, the advantages enjoyed by manufacturers under the Maquiradora system essentially ended in 2001 (for the re-exportation of goods into NAFTA), and the subsequent introduction did little to stabilize the situation as the Programme of Sectoral Promotion (PROSEC) only covers limited products and is subject to revisions.[118] With the end of duty free importation of the parts and components for re-exporting, Japanese-owned manufacturing in Mexico has been much less competitive than those countries which had concluded FTAs with Mexico.

Such unfavourable business circumstances has led to some Japanese companies pulling out of the Mexican market, even though Mexico took emergency rescue measures temporarily for Maquiradora corporations by introducing Sectoral Promotion Programmes (SPP) to lessen the burdens of import duties for specific goods, parts and products.[119]

But with the signing of the JMEPA, Mexico not only locked in equal status for Japan with its other FTA partners but also strengthened investment-protection rules, thus easing concerns from some Japanese investors about a less than stable governmental, judicial and federal system in Mexico.

Finally, the Agreement also allows Japanese companies access to the Mexican government procurement market. While Japan is a signatory to the WTO Agreement on Government Procurement, Mexico has thus far refused to sign this plurilateral agreement.[120] Throughout negotiations, Japan claimed that it had been deprived of business opportunities by Mexico's 'unclear and ... complicated' bidding procedures and that, in essence, the rules and procedures were an 'obstruction

---

[116] See 'Japan, México reach broad agreement on FTA', above note 115; and Negishi, above note 115. Japan already imports almost all its avocados, tequila and salsa from Mexico, as well as limited volumes of pork, poultry, meat, tuna, juice and pumpkins (the FTA increases the quotas for the restricted products).
[117] See JETRO, above note 2; and 'Editorial: Free trade with México. Bilateral pact doesn't mean giving up on WTO', *The Asahi Shimbun*, 12 March 2004, available at www.bilaterals.org/article.php3?id_article=334.
[118] See Joint Study Group, above note 6, at pp. 14–15.
[119] Industrial tariffs and unfavourable business conditions were very detrimental to Japanese manufacturers, a point illustrated by Canon Inc., NEC Corp. and Sanyo Electric Co., who all withdrew from Mexico due in part to the high price of machine parts imported from Japan. See Joint Study Group, above note 6, at pp. 14–15.
[120] Interestingly, Mexico has signed FTAs which include national treatment and favourable conditions to all but three signatory countries (Republic of Korea, Singapore and Hong Kong). See Joint Study Group, above note 6, at p. 23.

to investment' from Japan.[121] In addition, as Mexico's FTA partners received national treatment and more favourable conditions, Japan was disadvantaged against its trading competitors. The JMEPA levels the playing field and should improve Japan's competitiveness in this lucrative market.

B. Mexico

Recent Mexican trade policy has attempted to build relationships with a diverse range of countries in an attempt to enhance its investment profile and distinguish it from other developing economies. To that end, Mexico has signed twelve free trade agreements with a total of forty-two countries. However, Mexico still relies on the US for much of its trade and investment opportunities.

For example, of the US$165.4 billion worth of goods Mexico exported in 2003, US$149.6 billion were exported to the US (approximately 70 per cent of Mexican exports).[122] In contrast, only US$605.8 million exported to Japan.[123] In addition, US investment capital accounted for 67 per cent of the US$91 billion in foreign direct investment (FDI) that entered Mexico from 1994 until the end of September 2001. Japan, by contrast, contributed only 3.4 per cent of the total FDI in that same period.[124]

It can be stated with absolute certainty that a good portion of Mexico's interests in an FTA with Japan stemmed from the fact that it would like to become less reliant on the US for both its exports and its inward investment. This goal was confirmed by Mexican President, Vicente Fox, who, while stating the desire for increased Japanese investment in Mexico, stated that 'Mexico's commercial and investment efforts are very concentrated to the north, with the United States . . . But part of what we want is to diversify, open new markets to look for new opportunities.'[125] Moreover, while stressing that opening factories in Mexico will provide Japanese investors tariff free access to Mexico's forty-two free trade partners, Fox alluded to Mexico's desire for

---

[121] Ibid., at p. 22.
[122] 'México, Japan to Sign Free Trade Agreement', *The New York Times*, 17 September 2004, available at www.manattjones.com/newsletters/newsbrief/20040922.html.
[123] Ibid. Between 1994 and 2001 there were 444 Japanese enterprises with FDI in Mexico. By contrast, in the same period, there were 13,715 American and 5,216 European enterprises with FDI in Mexico: see Joint Study Group, above note 6, at p. 50.
[124] The figure accounts for only 0.3 per cent of total Japanese FDI and is in line with similar numbers from Finland, Denmark, the United Kingdom and the Cayman Islands. However, if Japanese companies operating in the US are included in that total, then Japan is responsible for up to 20 per cent of the Mexican FDI for the period. Other factors also weighed on Japanese–Mexican commerce besides the global slowdown and brisker Asia competition, according to comments from Shigetoshi Ikeyama, trade attaché at the Japanese Embassy in Mexico. Ikeyama pointed to protracted domestic recession as having a continuing effect on investment flows. See Robert Donnelly, 'Dealing with the Rising sun, México eyes a Japanese trade deal', *México Connect*, 1 May 2002, available at www.mexconnect.com/mex_/travel/bzm/bzmjapan.html.
[125] 'México, Japan to Sign Free Trade Agreement', above note 122.

increased ties with Asia, stating that '[w]ithout a doubt, Japan is becoming a bridge for us, a bridge that connects us to other countries in Asia, and that is the (agreement's) strategic importance to us'.[126]

Mexico expects the Agreement to increase direct investment, financing and technology transfers from Japan as well as diversifying its exports. Indeed, Minister Usabiaga of Mexico stated that, as a result of the Agreement, he expects foreign direct investment from Japan to rise to US$12.7 billion over the next ten years.[127]

As the peso strengthens and China's manufacturing base expands, it is also believed that Mexico saw an FTA with Japan as a means to attract firms but also to avoid firms moving operations to locations where labour is cheaper. In other words, Mexico believed that a trade agreement with Japan could provide an inducement to stay.[128]

In addition to greater direct investment from Japan, Mexico expects that the increased market access provisions provided for by the JMEPA will increase its exports to Japan by more than 10 per cent annually.[129] The majority of that increase will come from agricultural exports, giving a needed boost to producers who have struggled to compete in a global economy.[130] This is welcome news to many Mexican farmers.

This agreement also has ramifications for competitors, such as Australia, as food products make up a large amount of Australian exports to Japan, many of which are directly competitive with food products from Mexico. As a result, Australian exports to Japan are now disadvantaged vis-à-vis Mexican products. Thus, Australian agriculture and food exports to Japan are likely to see slower than expected or even negative growth in the coming years.[131] This may, in the long run, cause Australia and other competitors to seek their own agreements with Japan in the future.

V. Conclusion

The JMEPA is a comprehensive agreement with key provisions covering a wide range of trade in goods, services and investment; in this regard, it is expected to improve the trading relationship between the two nations substantially.

---

[126] Ibid. [127] See 'Japan, México Reach Free Trade Agreement', above note 11.
[128] Japanese companies have recently abandoned Mexico as a manufacturing base. For instance, Canon Inc., Japan's largest office equipment maker, shut down its Tijuana inkjet printer plant and shifted 450 jobs to Thailand and Vietnam. Following the Canon shutdown, the Japanese Maquiladora Association warned that more moves are in the offing. The lobbying group attributed the Canon move to an unclear regulatory framework and the strong peso.
[129] See 'Japan, México Reach Free Trade Agreement', above note 11.
[130] The Agreement will also bring added certainty to Mexican producers who, as a result of the Japanese Generalized System of Preferences (GSP) Scheme, were never quite certain of their level of access to the Japanese market. See Joint Study Group, above note 6, at p. 16.
[131] See Mercurio, above note 18, at pp. 688–9. While all Australian businesses are disadvantaged, the negative consequences disproportionately affect small and medium-sized businesses. For that reason, these businesses strongly support Australian involvement in FTAs. See Mark Fenton-Jones, 'Asian Opportunities Beckon', *Australian Financial Review*, 29 June 2004, p. 49.

In terms of trade in goods, the JMEPA takes a cautious, gradual approach to liberalization and excludes many goods from any liberalization whatsoever (particularly in agriculture).[132] In this regard, the Agreement fails to promote 'free' trade, instead only promoting a liberalized form of current protection. That said, an Agreement promoting full free trade was not possible, as both sides, and Japan in particular, were not ready to open up their markets fully in exchange for liberalized access into the other market. Thus, the JMEPA will have less of an economic impact than would a more complete 'free trade agreement'.

In terms of investment, although the JMEPA 'grandfathers' existing restrictive investment measures (they are not covered by the Agreement and can remain in place),[133] the Agreement basically adopts and, in certain instances, exceeds the NAFTA model. Specifically, the Agreement provides for financial transfers free of controls. The Agreement also prohibits investment requirements such as export and local content requirements, preferences for local procurement, trade balancing and technology transfer requirements. It also prohibits conditionality in benefits or advantages, such as tax breaks, on the investor meeting certain other performance requirements. In addition, while national rules can require that a majority of the board of directors be of a specific nationality, a Party cannot limit senior management posts to local nationals. Thus, the JMEPA provides substantial protection for investors and, in the case of Mexico, significantly strengthens and protects Japanese investors from arbitrary, unfair or unpredictable treatment.

The increased investment protection provided in the Agreement may be the key – it will encourage more investment into Mexico, thus providing economic gains and jobs, as well as provide preferential access to Mexico's forty-plus FTA partners for Japanese investors. For this reason, as well as increased industrial market access and the elimination of input duties, Japan felt the benefits of the Agreement outweighed the negatives stemming from increased competition to its agricultural industries. For its part, Mexico believed the increase in market access for its agricultural products was worth providing Japan with increased manufacturing and industrial access and improved investment security.

Now that Japan and Mexico have forged ahead with the JMEPA, Mexico appears to be in a holding pattern with FTA negotiations. On the other hand, the JMEPA signified Japan's shifting agenda with FTAs becoming the focal point of Japan's trade policy strategy (it soon reached agreements with Malaysia and the Philippines and is currently negotiating at least nine FTAs with at least fifteen nations). It appears once again that agriculture is already playing a crucial role in these negotiations.

---

[132] For specific information on the rules of origin used in the Agreement, see JMEPA, Annex 4 referred to in Chapter 4: Specific Rules of Origin.
[133] The same can be said for services.

7

United States–Morocco Free Trade Agreement

JASON KEARNS*

I. Introduction

Even though it is not one of the most commercially significant agreements among trading partners, the United States–Morocco Free Trade Agreement ('the Agreement') is noteworthy in several respects. First, the Agreement is likely to strengthen the longstanding ties between the two important allies. The relationship between the United States (US) and Morocco is important and, following the events of 11 September 2001, the importance of that relationship may be growing. Second, the Agreement is also significant in that it eliminates many considerable barriers to trade and investment – in everything from agriculture to government procurement – in a developing country that only recently became interested in opening its markets. Finally, it is also noteworthy as an agreement between the US and a country that is a neighbour of the European Union (EU).

A. The impetus for a free trade agreement

The Agreement illustrates that the impetus for a trade agreement can have more to do with broad foreign policy concerns than with narrow commercial interests. From the purely commercial perspective of Morocco, the US was a relatively insignificant trading partner before the Parties negotiated the Agreement. The US represented just 4.7% of Moroccan foreign trade in 2000, compared with 56.9% for the five largest trading partners among the EU Member States (France – 27.7%; Spain – 11.1%; Great Britain – 7.5%; Italy – 5.7%; Germany – 4.9%).[1] From the perspective of the US, Morocco is its seventy-fourth largest goods trading partner with US$1.04 billion in total (two-way) goods trade in 2004.[2]

Nevertheless, the US had a broad foreign policy interest in strengthening its commercial ties with Morocco. At the signing of the Agreement, Congressman

---

* Any views expressed in this study, as well as any errors or omissions, are solely those of the author.
[1] American Chamber of Commerce in Morocco, 'Written Comments to the Office of the United States Trade Representative on the Proposed US–Morocco Free Trade Agreement', 22 November 2002, p. 3, available at www.amcham-morocco.com.
[2] See www.moroccousafta.com/tradedata.htm (visited 12 June 2006).

Lincoln Diaz-Balart reflected on the long and close relationship between the two countries:

> In December of 1777 when war raged between the American colonies and Britain, Sultan Sidi Muhammad boldly recognized our young and not yet free republic. That magnanimous act of recognition was cemented in a treaty of peace and friendship between our countries, ratified in July of 1787. That enduring document remains the oldest unbroken treaty in the history of the foreign relations of the United States. Quite simply the kingdom of Morocco is our most permanent and enduring friend.[3]

Indeed, the then-US Trade Representative, Ambassador Robert B. Zoellick, also recognized that Morocco 'was the very first nation to recognize the sovereignty of a newly independent United States'.[4]

While this long history between the two nations provides the beginning of an explanation for their decision to negotiate a free trade agreement (FTA), events in recent history played an even more important role. Morocco and the US agreed to negotiate an agreement just eight months after the terrorist attacks of 11 September 2001. The US was looking to strengthen its relationship with a reform-minded Muslim nation in the Middle East – and to provide economic opportunities in that region as a way to counter terrorism.

For instance, US Trade Representative Zoellick hoped in particular that an agreement with Morocco would lead to agreements with other countries in Northern Africa, notably Tunisia and Algeria.[5] When he announced his plan to negotiate an agreement with Morocco, he suggested that an FTA would help Morocco 'accelerate its embrace of the modern world'. He also noted that the Administration's commitment to free trade with a leading moderate Arab State 'sends a signal throughout a tempestuous region: of America's support of tolerant, open, and more prosperous Muslim societies'.[6]

Other prominent US trade policy-makers shared this view. Former US Trade Representative Charlene Barshefsky argued that the US should develop an integrated, long-term strategy for returning the Middle East to the world economy (noting that the region controlled 13 per cent of world exports in 1980 but only 3 per cent in 2003) and expressed support for the Bush Administration's negotiations with Morocco. She asserted that, like world trade negotiations immediately after World War II, trade negotiations with countries in the Middle East would help 'secure a more stable peace' in these Muslim countries.[7]

---

[3] US–Morocco Free Trade Agreement Signing Ceremony, 15 June 2004. Text available on USTR website: www.ustr.gov.
[4] Ibid.
[5] 'US Officials See FTA with Morocco as Potential Link to Tunisia, Algeria', *Inside US Trade*, 1 August 2003.
[6] 'Zoellick Announces Official Notification To Congress on Launching Free Trade Talks', *BNA Daily Report for Executives*, 2 October 2002, No. 191 at A-20.
[7] Charlene Barshefsky, 'The Middle East Belongs in the World Economy', *New York Times*, 22 February 2003.

In May 2003, while negotiations with Morocco were ongoing, President Bush announced the goal of working toward a Middle East Free Trade Area (MEFTA) by 2013. The MEFTA initiative would employ a 'building block' approach: first ensuring that countries accede to the WTO,[8] then negotiating trade and investment agreements with individual countries in the region (such as the Agreement with Morocco), and finally reaching a comprehensive United States–Middle East Free Trade Area. The US had already concluded a free trade agreement with Israel[9] (its first FTA trading partner) in 1985, and an agreement with Jordan[10] (its fourth FTA trading partner, after concluding the NAFTA with Canada and Mexico) in 2000. The US signed the Agreement with Morocco (and another FTA with Bahrain) in 2004. It also signed a free trade agreement with Oman in 2006 and is currently negotiating a free trade agreement with the United Arab Emirates.

In its Final Report, the National Commission on Terrorist Attacks Upon the United States (better known as the '9/11 Commission') noted that '[e]conomic openness is essential' to counter terrorism and recommended that the US adopt 'economic policies that encourage development, more open societies, and opportunities for people to improve the lives of their families and to enhance prospects for their children's future'. The Commission referred specifically to the Agreement with Morocco – and the MEFTA more generally – as an initiative that would help to achieve those goals.[11]

This emphasis on broader foreign policy considerations was not well received by all members of Congress or the US business community. For instance, in February 2003, Willard Workman, senior vice president for international affairs at the US Chamber of Commerce, criticized the decision to negotiate an FTA with Morocco as commercially insignificant.[12] And, in June 2003, the Senate Finance Committee ranking Democrat Max Baucus and three House Democrats with influence on trade issues (Representatives Cal Dooley, John Tanner and William Jefferson) urged Ambassador Zoellick to give the size of a potential FTA partner's market 'significant weight' in deciding which FTA candidates to pursue.[13]

While the commercial relationship between Morocco and the US was not particularly significant, there was no question that an agreement could reduce

---

[8] A February 2003 study by a US think tank (the Progressive Policy Institute) noted that Muslim regions of the Middle East and Central Asia have proportionally fewer WTO Members than any other world region.
[9] United States–Israel Free Trade Agreement, signed 22 April 1985, in force 1 September 1985.
[10] United States–Jordan Free Trade Agreement, signed 24 October 2000, in force 17 December 2001.
[11] National Commission on Terrorist Attacks upon the United States, *The 9/11 Commission Report: Final Report of the National Commission on Terrorist Attacks Upon the United States* (1st edn, New York: W.W. Norton & Company, 2004), pp. 378–9. The 9/11 Commission was created by an Act of Congress (Public Law 107–306, 27 November 2002) to investigate the terrorist attacks that occurred on 11 September 2001, and to offer advice as to how the US could avoid a similar attack in the future.
[12] 'Business Coalition Counters Criticism of Morocco FTA', *Inside US Trade*, 21 February 2003.
[13] 'Pro-Trade Democrats Urge Zoellick To Weigh Market Size in FTA Choices', *BNA Daily Report for Executives*, 12 June 2003, No. 113 at A-10.

Table 7.1 *US goods trade with Morocco (in millions of US dollars)*[20]

Select Years	1980	1990	2000	2001	2002	2003	2004
Trade Balance	309	386	82	−152	173	83	9
US Exports	344	395	523	282	565	468	524
US Imports	35	109	441	435	392	385	515

significant barriers to trade and investment between the two countries. For example, Ambassador Zoellick noted that Morocco's average applied import tariff exceeded 20 per cent, compared with less than 2 per cent in the US.[14] Morocco's ambassador to the US, Aziz Mekouar, also noted that the competitive advantages lost to US businesses as a result of the European Union–Morocco Association Agreement[15] would be restored by an FTA with the US.[16]

For these reasons, and perhaps recognizing that an ambitious agreement with Morocco would serve as a precedent for future agreements with more commercially significant countries, several influential US business groups, including the National Foreign Trade Council (NFTC) and the Business Council for International Understanding, supported an FTA with Morocco early in the process.[17] These two groups founded the US–Morocco FTA Coalition, a 42-member organization co-chaired by AOL Time Warner and CMS Energy, a Michigan-based energy firm and the largest US investor in Morocco.[18]

B. Trade and investment relations between the countries

In 2004 (the year the Agreement was signed), Morocco's exports of goods to the US totalled US$515 million, while US exports to Morocco totalled US$524 million.[19] The US enjoyed a trade surplus with Morocco for many years before the conclusion of the Agreement, but that trade surplus was narrowing over time, as Table 7.1 illustrates.

Morocco's five largest categories of exports to the US in 2004 were mineral fuel (US$118 million), electrical machinery (US$109 million), minerals (US$79 million), woven apparel (US$47 million) and olives and other preserved foods (US$30 million). More generally, exports of agriculture products – including olives

---

[14] 'ITC to Conduct Study into Impact on US of Concluding Free Trade Pact with Morocco', *BNA Daily Report for Executives*, 20 September 2002, No. 183 at A-20.
[15] Signed 26 February 1996, in force 1 March 2000.
[16] 'US and Morocco to Hold Talks Nov. 26 To Set Framework for Free Trade Negotiations', *BNA Daily Report for Executives*, 22 November 2002, No. 226 at A-19.
[17] Ibid. [18] 'Business Coalition Counters Criticism of Morocco FTA', above note 12.
[19] See www.moroccousafta.com/tradedata.htm (trade overview) (visited 12 June 2006).
[20] Ibid.

and mandarin oranges – from Morocco totalled US$90 million in 2004. The top categories of exports from the US to Morocco were: aircraft (US$141 million), cereals (US$115 million), machinery (US$53 million), miscellaneous grain, seed, and fruit (US$32 million), electrical machinery (US$29 million) and mineral fuel (US$22 million).[21]

An increase in agricultural exports was expected to be one of the more significant benefits which the US would gain from an agreement with Morocco. This benefit is due in large part to the fact that US producers would gain an advantage over EU producers due to the fact that the trade pact between Morocco and the EU has limited commitments concerning agriculture.[22] US agriculture exports to Morocco totalled US$169 million in 2004, accounting for almost one-third of US exports of goods to Morocco. The leading categories included corn (US$82 million), wheat (US$33 million), soybeans (US$29 million) and soybean oil (US$12 million).[23] Of course, not everyone in the US agricultural community supported an agreement with Morocco; in particular, olive growers and processors and producers of dehydrated onion and garlic opposed the Agreement, expressing concern over the likely increase in low-priced imports that would result from lower tariffs. While Florida citrus growers did not oppose an agreement, they demanded that the agreement provide for long tariff phase-out periods and include strong sanitary and phytosanitary rules.[24]

The US and Morocco also had a healthy investment relationship before negotiating the Agreement. In 2002, approximately 120 US companies and franchises had production facilities, distribution facilities or a representation office in Morocco. These firms, representing more than US$630 million in investment, operate in a variety of sectors, from telecommunications (3Com and AT&T) to consumer products (Coca Cola, Colgate, Palmolive, and Gillette), pharmaceuticals (Eli-Lilly, Pfizer, Bristol Myers Squibb), textiles and apparel (Jordache, Fruit of the Loom, Gap) and fast food (McDonalds, Pizza Hut).[25] These companies were among the primary proponents in the US of an agreement with Morocco.

II The negotiations

The negotiations relating to the Agreement reflect the comprehensive nature, and the ambitious objectives, of the Parties. The organization of the year-long

---

[21] Ibid.
[22] 'US–Morocco Negotiations To Be Based Solely On US Proposals', *Inside US Trade*, 28 February 2003.
[23] See above note 19.
[24] United States International Trade Commission (USITC), 'US–Morocco Free Trade Agreement: Potential Economywide and Selected Sectoral Effects', Investigation No. TA-2104–14, USITC Publication 3704 (June 2004) (hereinafter 'ITC Study'), at pp. 111–15; and 'Zoellick Highlights Importance of Trade, Investment with Morocco', *Inside US Trade*, 1 February 2002.
[25] American Chamber of Commerce in Morocco, above note 1, at p. 2.

negotiations is itself impressive, with twelve different negotiating groups, eight rounds of negotiations on three different continents and more than one hundred negotiators from dozens of government agencies.

A. The players

On the US side, staff from the Office of the United States Trade Representative (USTR), an entity within the Executive Office of the President, served as the lead negotiators, and lead lawyers, for the various chapters of the Agreement.[26] A variety of other agencies also played important supporting roles in the negotiations.

As required by statute,[27] the President has established an interagency organization to advise the President and the USTR in trade negotiations (the 'Trade Policy Committee', with the subordinate coordinating groups, the Trade Policy Review Group (TPRG) and the Trade Policy Staff Committee (TPSC)). The US Trade Representative chairs this interagency organization, with the Secretary of Commerce, Secretary of State, Secretary of Treasury, Secretary of Agriculture, and Secretary of Labour participating. The USTR also invites other agencies, such as the Environmental Protection Agency, to participate. Most, if not all, of these agencies attended some or all of the negotiations, at least with respect to those chapters in which they have special concerns.

The lead negotiators of the Agreement were Minister Taib Fassi-Fihri for Morocco and Ms Cathy Novelli for the US. Minister Fassi-Fihri, Morocco's Minister-Delegate of Foreign Affairs and Cooperation, an urbane senior diplomat in the Moroccan government, was known to have the respect of King Muhammad VI and to have considerable influence within his government. US Trade Representative Zoellick described him as 'very gentlemanly, and at least to an American, [having] a somewhat reserved style'.[28]

Ms Novelli was the Assistant US Trade Representative for Europe and the Mediterranean – a region covering at least sixty-five countries and including key trading partners such as the EU, Russia and the other former Soviet republics and

---

[26] Until the 1960s, the US Department of State was responsible for negotiating US international trade agreements. A special office for trade negotiations (now known as the USTR), with a more direct link to the White House, was created in 1962, after many critics – including key members of Congress – complained that the State Department 'had been trading away our economic advantages for political advantages'. According to Rep. Henry Reuss, a Wisconsin Democrat, what was needed in a US Trade Representative was a 'good trial lawyer who's had to represent insurance companies in personal injury cases for a decade or two ... somebody who smokes a cigar without lighting it and doesn't smile very often'. Steve Dryden, *Trade Warriors: USTR and the American Crusade for Free Trade* (New York: Oxford University Press, 1995), p. 52.

[27] 19 USC 1872; Public Law 87–794, as amended by Public Law 93–618, Public Law 96–39, Reorganization Plan No. 3 of 1979, and Public Law 100–418.

[28] Press Conference, US Trade Representative, Robert B. Zoellick and Moroccan Minister-delegate of Foreign Affairs and Cooperation, Taib Fassi-Fihri, Washington, DC, 2 March 2004, available at USTR website www.ustr.gov.

countries in the Middle East and Northern Africa. She was a lawyer and a twelve-year veteran of USTR who had previously served as the lead negotiator of the United States–Jordan Free Trade Agreement. Despite her friendly and unassuming demeanour and her quick smile, she had a reputation as a 'no-nonsense' negotiator who could quickly unravel a trade issue and get to its core and who was always willing to call the bluff of a counterpart across the table.

The negotiating groups were divided into agriculture, customs rules, electronic commerce, environment, government procurement, intellectual property, investment, market access, labour, services and textiles. A twelfth group, primarily negotiated by the lead lawyers of the Agreement, discussed the structural and general provisions of the Agreement. These provisions included the general definitions and general exceptions in the Agreement, the dispute settlement provisions and the general transparency provisions in the Agreement.

B. The process

Morocco and the US began strengthening their economic relationship long before FTA negotiations began. In 1985, the Parties signed a bilateral investment treaty which entered into force in 1991. And, in 1995, the Parties signed a 'Trade and Investment Framework Agreement', designed to facilitate discussions involving international trade between the two governments.

Seven years later, in April 2002, President Bush and King Mohammed VI agreed to negotiate an FTA.[29] Ambassador Zoellick formally notified Congress of the Administration's intent to initiate negotiations six months later, on 1 October.[30] The Parties held informal talks in November to set the framework for negotiations, including establishing a calendar and modalities for the negotiations.[31]

Shortly before the Parties began negotiations (the week of 20 January 2003, in Washington, DC), the Foreign Trade Minister of France, Francois Loos, reportedly told Morocco it must choose between a free trade agreement with the US or the EU (an FTA between the EU and Morocco entered into force in 2000). According to reports, on a visit to Rabat on 14 January, Minister Loos stated, 'You cannot say you want a closer partnership with the EU and at the same time sign a free trade agreement with the US. You have to decide to choose.'

Ambassador Zoellick responded immediately that the Minister was spreading a view 'left over from the age of colonialism and mercantilism . . . It's good for Africa

---

[29] 'US and Morocco to Hold Talks', above note 16.
[30] 'Zoellick Announces Official Notification To Congress', above note 6. Under the Trade Act of 2002, the Administration is required to provide that notice at least 90 days before beginning negotiations, if it intends to gain Congressional approval for the deal under 'fast track' procedures. Fast track allows the administration to present trade agreements to Congress for a straight 'up or down' vote with no opportunity to offer amendments to the legislation implementing the agreement.
[31] 'US and Morocco to Hold Talks', above note 16.

to have trade relations with Europe, the United States, India, and China. We want to offer more opportunity here, not try to constrict it.'[32] After Morocco asked the French government to 'clarify' the French position, the French government informed Morocco and the US that there had been a 'misunderstanding' and that there was no 'incompatibility' with the two agreements.[33]

From the start of the negotiations, the Parties recognized that agriculture was likely to be the most difficult issue to resolve, due in large part to Morocco's high tariffs, especially on wheat and beef.[34] The US recognized that roughly 40 per cent of Morocco's population lived in rural areas, but Assistant US Trade Representative Novelli stated that she hoped the FTA would 'complement' agricultural reforms being carried out by the Moroccan government.[35]

More specifically, the US hoped Morocco would agree that its subsidy programme for wheat farmers and its high import duties on agricultural products should be reformed. Morocco protected almost 500,000 small wheat farmers through subsidies and high tariffs.[36] The government also subsidized one million tons of wheat flour each year. As part of that system, a Moroccan cereals office sets a threshold price for wheat flour and generally purchased wheat from domestic producers to use for the subsidized flour programme.[37] Morocco also imposed a 21 per cent import duty on durum wheat, a 33.33 per cent duty on other wheat, a 30 per cent duty on barley and a 17.5 per cent duty on corn.[38]

While agriculture was expected to be the most difficult issue in the negotiations, the Parties also expected services and investment negotiations, especially in the financial services sector, to have great potential but also to raise some of the most sensitive issues. Assistant US Trade Representative Novelli explained: 'A lot of the benefit for Morocco is putting itself on the map as a good place for US companies to do business.' Moroccan officials agreed, noting that increased US investment in liberalized services sectors would be a primary benefit of an agreement for both the US and Morocco.[39] In January 2003, Ambassador Zoellick pointed to Morocco's tourism, telecommunications and insurance industries as sectors representing great potential for US investors.[40]

---

[32] 'US Says France "Colonialist" to Make Morocco Pick Between FTA with US or EU', *BNA Daily Report for Executives*, 17 January 2003, No. 12 at A-8.
[33] 'US, Morocco Launch Free Trade Talks, With Agriculture Likely to be Toughest Issue', *BNA Daily Report for Executives*, 22 January 2003, No. 14 at A-21.
[34] Ibid.
[35] 'US, Morocco End First Week of FTA Talks "On Target" to Finish Negotiations This Year', *BNA Daily Report for Executives*, 27 January 2003, No. 17 at A-20.
[36] See 'US, Morocco Fail to Wrap Up FTA Negotiations, to Resume Early Next Year', *Inside US Trade*, 12 December 2003.
[37] 'US to Focus on Procurement, Customs for Next Morocco FTA Round', *Inside US Trade*, 31 January 2003.
[38] Ibid. [39] Ibid.
[40] 'US, Morocco Launch FTA Talks, Aim for 2003 Completion', *Inside US Trade*, 24 January 2003.

Labour issues generally were not expected to be a major problem in the negotiations. Morocco's Parliament was already considering a new labour code when the negotiations began, and its officials expected that code would address 'most issues' covered in the FTA.[41] Nevertheless, before the first round began, US labour groups identified child labour in the Moroccan rug making industry as a potential problem for the signing of a FTA with Morocco. The Moroccan ambassador to the US conceded that there were child labour issues in that industry, but stated that Morocco was committed to International Labour Organization standards and was working to solve the problem.[42]

Textiles and apparel trade was also not expected to be a sensitive subject. While textiles and apparel products are import-sensitive in the US, imports from Morocco were relatively small in the past, even though Morocco was not subject to US import quotas (unlike many other textile and apparel exporting countries).[43] American textiles and apparel associations generally took the same approach to Morocco that they had taken to agreements dating back to the NAFTA: they generally wanted a 'yarn-forward' rule of origin that would require an apparel item to be made of regional fabric, regional yarn and sewn in the region (where the region is generally defined as the territories of the FTA parties). And they opposed the inclusion of provisions – called 'tariff preference levels' (TPLs) – that would allow a specified number of apparel items that do not meet rules of origin requirements to enter duty free.[44] These demands were based on the fact that US producers of yarns and fabrics (i.e. textiles) are relatively competitive, compared with US producers of apparel. As a result, the strategy of the US industry has been to condition duty free treatment for apparel imports from countries with relatively inexpensive labour on the use of regional yarns and fabrics.

Prior to the second round, the US tabled negotiating proposals for all of the negotiating groups. Those proposals served as the basis for the negotiations, with Morocco proposing changes to those documents, rather than tabling competing texts.

The war in Iraq impacted the second round, the week of 24 March 2003. The lead negotiators did not participate in person in the negotiations, which were moved from Rabat, Morocco, to Geneva, Switzerland, for security reasons.[45] During the second round, the negotiators focused on some of the more technical aspects of the Agreement and on understanding key segments of the Moroccan system that were unfamiliar to the US negotiators. One area that the US negotiators closely examined was government procurement. Because Morocco is not a party to the

---

[41] 'US to Offer Initial Negotiating Text for FTA with Morocco Week of March 24', *BNA Daily Report for Executives*, 10 March 2003, No. 46 at A-9.
[42] 'House Members Say US Investment Benefits from FTA with Morocco', *Inside US Trade*, 25 October 2002.
[43] 'US, Morocco Launch Free Trade Talks', above note 33.
[44] 'Business Seeks Support for Morocco FTA as ITC Cancels Hearing', *Inside US Trade*, 11 October 2002.
[45] 'War in Iraq Impacts US–Morocco FTA Negotiations', *Inside US Trade*, 28 March 2003.

plurilateral WTO Agreement on Government Procurement, each side needed to do a good deal of homework to determine the consistencies and inconsistencies between Morocco's laws and practices and the standard international procurement commitments.[46]

In June 2003, the Parties resumed negotiations and began dealing with the difficult issues: agriculture, services and investment. On services, Morocco was unwilling to open its markets in sectors where it had not yet developed its own industry, such as insurance.[47] In agriculture, Morocco generally sought longer transition periods to tariff phase-outs, with a disproportionate level of the phase-out coming toward the end of the process.[48]

In the fourth round of negotiations, which began in Washington on 21 July 2003, Minister Fassi Fihri proposed a transition period of between twelve and fifteen years for imports of sensitive agricultural products, 'like wheat or like meat'.[49] He also proposed that, during this transition period, the two sides 'evaluate' the effects of liberalization in these markets annually or bi-annually and consider adjustments.[50] Assistant US Trade Representative Novelli countered that the US–Morocco agreement was likely to mirror past US agreements, which had phase-in periods of up to ten years with some exceptions.[51] Minister Fassi Fihri also proposed extended periods to implement obligations on the protection of intellectual property rights, services and labour reforms.[52]

The Parties continued to make steady progress in the fifth and sixth rounds of negotiations, in Rabat in October and in Washington in November 2003. Those rounds were largely uneventful. The Parties' positions on key issues had already been established clearly, and many purely technical issues (i.e. the 'underbrush') still needed to be resolved before final compromises could be made.

The Parties had hoped to wrap up negotiations during the seventh round, from 5 December to 8 December, in Washington, but differences over agriculture caused a delay. Specifically, Moroccan negotiators reportedly sought to protect Morocco's local market from imports of wheat, red meat, chicken parts and legumes by resisting tariff reductions in those areas.[53] US producers reportedly requested a tariff-rate quota (TRQ) that would phase out over time or, at a minimum, a permanent TRQ that would provide for stable and significant access that would increase to reflect market growth. While these producers recognized Morocco's small market size, their concerns were largely based on the precedential value which the agreement would set for future agreements. As a result, these producers lobbied

---

[46] 'US to Focus on Procurement', above note 37.
[47] 'US Officials See FTA with Morocco as Potential Link', above note 5.   [48] Ibid.   [49] Ibid.
[50] 'Morocco Seeks Transition to Freer Farm Trade in Agreement with US', *BNA Daily Report for Executives*, 22 July 2003, No. 140 at A-21.
[51] 'US Officials See FTA with Morocco as Potential Link', above note 5.   [52] Ibid.
[53] See 'US, Morocco Fail to Wrap Up FTA Negotiations', above note 36.

the USTR to ensure that all tariffs would be phased out by a certain date.[54] They also wanted access equal to that enjoyed by European producers.[55]

The Parties held the eighth round of negotiations in January 2004. At this point, many of the chapters had been 'closed out', and the focus was now squarely on agriculture. The Chief US Agriculture Negotiator, Allen Johnson, travelled to Morocco in advance of the official start of the round, while Ambassador Zoellick met Moroccan Prime Minister, Driss Jettou at the same time.

During the final phase of negotiations, which began the week of 23 February 2004, Senate Finance Committee Chairman, Charles Grassley, urged Ambassador Zoellick to seek the immediate elimination of tariffs on US exports to Morocco of soybeans and corn and corn products. Senator Grassley asserted that immediate duty elimination would benefit Morocco's poultry producers who, 'due in large part to high duties on imports of corn and soybeans, have among the world's most expensive production costs'.[56]

On 2 March 2004, the US and Morocco announced the conclusion of negotiations.[57] Ambassador Zoellick called it 'the best market opening package of any US Free Trade Agreement with any developing country'. He noted that the provisions on agriculture would 'help US farmers and ranchers get a new tool to compete against Canada and the EU in Morocco's markets'. For his part, Minister Fassi Fihri noted that it was the first agreement which Morocco had negotiated that included provisions in the areas of services, including financial services, intellectual property rights, electronic commerce, labour and the environment.[58]

President Bush notified Congress on 8 March 2004, of the Administration's intention to sign the Agreement. Ambassador Zoellick and Minister Fassi Fihri signed the Agreement in Washington on 15 June 2004, in the grand Benjamin Franklin room of the US Department of State. At the signing ceremony, Ambassador Zoellick noted the room was 'fitting', given that Franklin had urged the US Congress to pursue a treaty of peace and friendship with Morocco more than two centuries earlier.

President Bush transmitted the Agreement to Congress on 15 July 2004. Implementing legislation passed the US House of Representatives by a vote of 323 to 99, and passed the US Senate by a vote of 85 to 13 on 22 July 2004. The President signed the legislation into law in August and Morocco completed its implementation process by the end of 2005. The Agreement entered into force on 1 January 2006.

---

[54] See ibid.   [55] Ibid.
[56] 'Grassley Urges Immediate Tariff Elimination on Corn Products, Soybeans in Morocco FTA', *BNA Daily Report for Executives*, 27 February 2004, No. 38 at A-10.
[57] 'US, Morocco Conclude Free Trade Pact with Most Ag Tariffs Scrapped Over 15 Years', *BNA Daily Report for Executives*, 3 March 2004, No. 41 at A-25.
[58] Transcript of Press Conference with Ambassador Zoellick and Minister Fassi Fihri, Washington, DC, 2 March 2004, available at www.ustr.gov.

III. Analysis of substantive obligations

A quick review of the FTAs around the globe demonstrates that there is no single model for a free trade agreement: generally speaking, the text of a US trade agreement is structured very differently from the text of an EU agreement, or a Japan agreement. The US–Morocco FTA is fairly similar to other agreements which the US has negotiated since it negotiated the North American Free Trade Agreement (NAFTA) in the early 1990s. This section describes the provisions of the Agreement in detail.

A. Chapter 1: Establishment and Definitions

Chapter 1 formally establishes a free trade area 'consistent with Article XXIV of GATT 1994 and Article V of GATS' and clarifies the relationship between the Agreement and other bilateral or multilateral agreements to which the Parties are party. The Parties generally affirm existing rights and obligations under any other agreement, but provide that the dispute settlement provisions of their bilateral investment treaty generally are suspended on the date of entry into force of the Agreement.

B. Chapter 2: National Treatment and Market Access

Each Party agrees to accord national treatment to the goods of the other Party 'in accordance with Article III of GATT 1994', with a short list of exceptions (e.g. for the suspension of tariff concessions or other obligations (commonly called 'retaliation') where authorized by the Dispute Settlement Body of the WTO).[59] They also agree to grant duty free treatment with respect to the temporary admission of goods, goods re-entered after repair or alteration and for commercial samples and printed advertising materials of negligible value.[60] In addition, neither Party may prohibit or restrict imports of the other Party, or exports to the other Party, except in accordance with Article XI of GATT 1994[61] and each Party shall ensure that all fees and charges are applied in a manner consistent with Article VIII of GATT 1994.[62] The Parties also agree not to adopt or maintain any tax or other charge on the export of any goods to the territory of the other Party, unless the charge also applies to goods destined for domestic consumption.[63]

Of course, the central commitment in Chapter 2 is that each Party is required to eliminate its customs duties on originating goods in accordance with its Schedule to Annex IV (Tariff Elimination). The FTA will eliminate tariffs on virtually all trade between the two countries within ten years. More than 95 per cent of trade between the US and Morocco in consumer and industrial products would become tariff free

[59] Article 2.2 and Annex 2-A.   [60] Articles 2.5–2.7.   [61] Article 2.8.   [62] Article 2.9.   [63] Article 2.10.

immediately upon the entry into force of the Agreement, with all the remaining tariffs targeted for elimination within nine years.

The following are some of the key tariff concessions (outside of agriculture, which will be discussed separately below) that result from the Agreement:

- *Sardines.* Morocco is the world's largest canned sardine producer and exporter in quantity terms, accounting for 15 per cent of world production. In 2001, it produced US$58.9 million, or 10 per cent of the world total. US production during this period was estimated to be US$27 million. Morocco is the second leading supplier to the US market, after Canada.[64]

  While most Moroccan canned sardine exports to the US entered duty free under the GSP programme before the Agreement entered into force, the Agreement provided that the 20 per cent duty applied to Moroccan exports of skinned or boned canned sardines, packed in oil, not smoked (HTS 1604.13.30) would be eliminated immediately. Similarly, the 15 per cent duty applied to Moroccan exports of canned sardines, packed in oil, not smoked, neither skinned nor boned (HTS 1604.13.20) would be eliminated over nine equal annual stages. Morocco also agreed to eliminate its 50 per cent duty on US canned sardines immediately, but this action was unlikely to have a significant impact on US exports.

- *Textiles and Apparel.* Tariffs will be eliminated over six years for the majority of textile products. For more information on textiles and apparel imports, see section IIID below.

- *Information Technology.* As a result of the Agreement, Morocco will join the WTO Information Technology Agreement (ITA) to provide immediate duty free access for IT products.

- *Machinery, Construction Equipment and Chemicals.* Other key US export sectors that will gain duty free access immediately are machinery, construction equipment and chemicals. However, not all of the products in these sectors will be subject to immediate duty free access.[65]

C. Chapter 3: Agriculture and Sanitary and Phytosanitary Measures

US market access commitments

The US agreed to provide preferential market access on all agricultural products according to specific schedules negotiated on a product-specific basis. Those schedules provide for tariff phase-outs immediately, in five years, eight years, ten

---

[64] ITC Study, above note 24, at pp. 35–6.
[65] For example, after the negotiations were complete, an advisory committee for the chemicals sector stated: 'it is truly unfortunate that there are so many "F's" (9-year staging) in our sector, especially since in many instances the base tariff rate is 50%'. The report of the advisory committee is available on the USTR website at www.ustr.gov.

years, twelve years, fifteen years, and eighteen years. The Agreement also establishes preferential TRQs for imports from Morocco for beef, dairy products, peanuts, cotton, tobacco, sugar and sugar-containing products, tomato products and sauces, dried onion and garlic. Under these TRQs, the Moroccan product receives a zero duty for a specific quantity that expands over the implementation period. Volumes imported over the specific amounts have higher tariffs, but the higher tariffs are gradually eliminated over fifteen years (except for sugar and sugar-containing products, which have an eighteen-year phase-out period).

Olives Before the Agreement, US tariffs on processed olives ranged from 4.3 cents to 10.1 cents per kilogram, with the bulk of imports from Morocco subject to the high end of the range. Under the Agreement, certain preserved olives (the most important item included relative to those olives produced domestically) would have the existing duty eliminated in equal annual instalments over ten years. Duties on Moroccan processed olives will receive immediate duty free entry.[66]

Citrus fruit and juice Before the Agreement, US citrus juice tariffs ranged from 30 to 40 per cent. Under the Agreement, US duties on many processed citrus products, such as orange juice, would be phased out over eighteen years, but with no decrease during the first six years. US citrus fruit tariffs were relatively low before the Agreement was signed, generally less than 3 per cent, but US phytosanitary restrictions with respect to the Mediterranean fruit fly had posed a significant obstacle to Moroccan exports of clementines (virtually all US imports of citrus fruit from Morocco consist of clementines, imports of which fluctuated dramatically from US$2.8 million in 1999 to just US$235,000 in 2001, to US$13 million in 2003).[67] Under the Agreement, US duties on most fresh citrus will be immediately removed, but it is unclear what effect US phytosanitary restrictions will have on imports from Morocco in the future.

Sugar Unless it is a net exporter of sugar, Morocco cannot export sugar to the US under the Agreement. Based on recent data, it is unlikely that Morocco will be a net exporter of sugar in the near future. In 2002, Morocco was a net importer of more than 573,000 metric tons.

Morocco's market access commitments

Morocco agreed to provide preferential market access on all agricultural products according to schedules negotiated on a product-specific basis. Tariffs will be phased out on most products over the following periods: immediate, five years, eight years, ten years, twelve years, fifteen years and eighteen years. Tariffs on other products will

---

[66] ITC Study, above note 24, at pp. 32–3.   [67] See ITC Study, above note 24, at p. 39.

be phased out, using special, non-linear formulas, over six years, eighteen years, nineteen years and twenty-five years.

Durum and common wheat Before the Agreement, Morocco imposed tariffs as high as 75 per cent for durum wheat and 135 per cent for common wheat. For imports of durum wheat, Morocco agreed to establish an initial TRQ in-quota quantity of 250,000 metric tons that will increase by 10,000 metric tons each year. The in-quota tariff will be set at 25 per cent below the applied MFN rate (75 per cent when the Agreement was signed) during the first five years of the Agreement, and thereafter will be eliminated in equal annual instalments by the tenth year after the Agreement enters into force.

The market access commitments for common wheat are more complicated, in part because Morocco frequently adjusts its applied MFN tariff rate on this product. In essence, if Morocco's MFN tariff is equal to 135 per cent, imports from the US will be subject to an in-quota duty of 83.7 per cent. If the MFN tariff is lower, the in-quota duty for imports from the US is lowered as well. The TRQ in-quota quantities in years two to ten inclusive will range from 400,000 metric tons to 1,060,000 metric tons, depending on domestic production.

Corn and corn products Before the Agreement, Morocco imposed a tariff on US corn of 35 per cent and a tariff on corn products (e.g. flour, meal and starch) as high as 60 per cent. Morocco agreed to reduce these tariffs by 50 per cent in year one and will eliminate tariffs over the following five years in equal annual instalments.

Beef Before the Agreement, Morocco's tariffs on beef were as high as 275 per cent. Under the Agreement, the in-quota tariff on high-quality beef will be phased out over five years, while over-quota tariffs will be eliminated in eighteen years in equal annual instalments. The in-quota tariff on standard-quality beef will be phased out over ten years, while over-quota tariffs will remain in place unless Morocco negotiates a reduction with another trading partner. Morocco also agreed to accept export certificates from the US Department of Agriculture's Food Safety and Inspection Service as the means for certifying compliance with standards on hormones and antibiotics.

Poultry and poultry products Before the Agreement, Morocco's tariffs on most poultry were 124 per cent. Under the Agreement, Morocco will immediately eliminate its tariffs on mechanically deboned chicken and chicken nuggets and patties. Over-quota tariffs on chicken leg quarters and wings will be phased out by year twenty-five using a non-linear formula. Over-quota tariffs on whole chickens will be phased out by year nineteen, again using a non-linear formula. Over-quota tariffs on frozen chicken thigh meat will be phased out over ten years, while over-quota tariffs on other frozen poultry meat will be phased out by year nineteen using a non-linear formula.

Other commitments

The Parties agree that any procedures to administer agricultural TRQs under the Agreement are to be non-discriminatory, transparent, minimally burdensome, responsive to market forces and available to the public. In-quota quantities under its TRQs are to be allocated in commercially viable shipping quantities and are generally not to be allocated to producer groups or other non-governmental organizations. Food aid and other non-commercial shipments are not to be counted against any applicable TRQ.

The Parties agree that neither Party may maintain any export subsidy on any agricultural goods. If an exporting Party considers that a non-Party is exporting with the benefit of export subsidies, the Parties will consult with a view to agreeing on specific measures that an importing Party will take to counter any effect that subsidized imports from a non-Party have on the exporting Party.[68]

The Agreement also contains an elaborate and detailed set of rules for applying an agricultural safeguard. An agricultural safeguard measure may only be applied to imports of a short list of agricultural products. The US may only apply such a measure on imports of certain products (onion, garlic, tomato, asparagus, olives, pears, apricots, nectarines, peaches and orange juice). Morocco may only apply a measure on imports of certain products (whole birds, poultry leg quarters and wings, chickpeas, almonds and dried prunes). In addition, the US may only apply a safeguard measure if one of the goods specified enters the US at a unit import price below the 'trigger price' specified for that good; Morocco may only apply an agricultural safeguard measure if in a calendar year the volume of imports of one of those goods exceeds the volume specified in an Annex to the Chapter. The Parties also specify what the additional duty shall be which depends, in the case of US imports, on how far below the trigger price the import price is and, in the case of Moroccan imports, on how many years the agreement has been in force (i.e. the additional duty that may be applied drops after seven years and then again after thirteen years).

D. Chapter 4: Textiles

The textile and apparel sector accounted for 14 per cent of industrial output in Morocco, 42 per cent of industrial employment (about 200,000 workers) and 34 per cent of total exports in 2001. Morocco, however, was a relatively high-cost producer of textile and apparel products. Although labour productivity in Morocco is comparable with that in China and India, labour costs are much higher. For example, the

[68] Article 3.3.

hourly wage rate for workers in spinning and weaving in 2002 averaged US$1.89 in Morocco, compared with US$0.41 in China.[69] Under the WTO Agreement on Textiles and Clothing, US import quotas were to be eliminated at the beginning of 2005, and almost all observers predicted (correctly) that exports from China would displace exports from many other countries. Thus, the elimination of duties under the Agreement was expected to do no more than help the Moroccan industry retain its existing share of the US market.

Under Article 4.1, tariffs on textile and apparel products are to be eliminated according to four staging categories: (1) immediate duty-free entry; (2) a 50 per cent reduction in year 1, then five equal annual stages; (3) nine equal annual stages; and (4) 3 per cent per year reductions for four years, then six stages (i.e. ten years to duty free). Most textile and apparel goods are covered under the second category (i.e. duties will be eliminated within five years).

The Parties also created a hybrid tariff staging category: some apparel goods – including Morocco's leading exports to the US, such as men's and women's trousers, underwear and sweaters – are subject to immediate duty free treatment up to an annual quantity specified in an annex to the Chapter (i.e. a tariff-rate quota). Duties on goods above those quantities will be eliminated within five years. The annual quantities grow over time: from 270 million 'square metres equivalent' (SMEs) in the first year to 542 million SMEs by the fifth year. Given that US apparel imports from Morocco totalled just 15.9 million SMEs in 2003,[70] these annual quantities provide for considerable growth in imports from Morocco entering duty free.

Article 4.2 provides a textile-specific safeguard, separate from the general safeguard in the Agreement. Under the textile-specific safeguard, a Party could increase the duty rate on originating goods to the MFN rate in effect at the time the action is taken or the MFN rate at the date of entry into force of the FTA, whichever is lower. A safeguard can be maintained for no more than three years, with a two-year extension, and no action may be taken more than once against the same good, or more than ten years after the elimination of customs duties for that good. The Party imposing the safeguard is required to provide trade-liberalizing compensation to the exporting Party.

Article 4.3 establishes the rules of origin that apply to textiles and apparel. These rules require that imports of most textile and apparel articles from an FTA party be assembled from inputs made either in the US or Morocco, generally from the yarn stage forward ('yarn forward rule', which means that only the fibres used to make the yarns may be from third countries). A fibre-forward origin rule applies to a limited number of products (mainly yarns and knit fabrics), which must be made in Morocco or the US from the fibre stage forward.

---

[69] ITC Study, above note 24, at pp. 40–4.
[70] See ITC Study, above note 24, at p. 43 note 121.

The yarn forward rule can be difficult for many apparel manufacturers to satisfy, especially in countries such as Morocco that specialize in labour-intensive apparel production, rather than capital-intensive textile production. As a result, the Agreement also contains TPLs that provide duty preferences for specified quantities of certain 'non-originating goods' (goods that do not meet the FTA origin rules because they are made of yarns or fabrics from countries other than the US and Morocco). The TPL grants duty preferences for ten years to non-originating knit and woven fabrics and apparel of cotton, man made fibres and wool that total 30 million SMEs per year during the first four years. The TPL will be reduced in roughly equal increments over the following six years, reaching zero after ten years. The TPL is almost double the level of US imports of textile and apparel from Morocco in 2003, which totalled 16.5 million SMEs.[71]

The Agreement also includes a special and permanent TPL of more than 1 million kilograms for textile and apparel articles of cotton grown in a least-developed Sub-Saharan African country, provided the cotton fibres are carded or combed there.[72] This provision is based on a preference programme under Moroccan law that is designed to help some of the poorest countries in Africa.

The Parties also agreed to consider whether the rules of origin applicable to a particular textile or apparel good should be revised to address issues of availability of supply of fibres, yarns or fabrics in the territories of the Parties.[73] A similar provision under the NAFTA has resulted in changes to the textile and apparel rules of origin over time.

Finally, the Parties agreed, in Article 4.4, to cooperate in enforcing measures affecting trade in textile and apparel goods, verifying the accuracy of claims of origin, enforcing measures implementing international agreements affecting trade in textiles and apparel, and preventing circumvention of international agreements affecting trade in textiles and apparel. These customs cooperation provisions provide the customs authorities with ample authority to ensure the accuracy of claims of origin. The customs authorities of the importing Party have the right to assist in verifying a claim of origin, including by conducting visits in the territory of the exporting Party to the premises of an exporter or producer.[74] The importing Party has the right to suspend the application of preferential tariff treatment while a verification is being conducted, where a reasonable suspicion of unlawful activity relates to that good.[75]

E. Chapters 5 and 6: Rules of Origin and Customs Cooperation

In the Customs Cooperation Chapter, the Parties agree to cooperate with each other in administering customs laws[76] and to release goods quickly ('to the extent

---

[71] Ibid. [72] Article 4.3.15. [73] Article 4.3, paras. 3–6. [74] Article 4.4.4. [75] Article 4.4.6(b).
[76] Article 6.5.

possible, within 48 hours of arrival') and before customs duties are finally determined.[77] They also agree to adopt or maintain expedited procedures for express shipments (e.g. to allow a shipper to submit information before the shipment arrives, and to allow the release of the express shipment no later than six hours after the necessary information has been submitted).[78] They also agree to issue 'advance rulings', prior to the importation of a good and within 150 days of a request, concerning tariff classification, customs valuation and origin and duty treatment determinations.[79]

F. Chapter 7: Technical Barriers to Trade

In the Chapter on Technical Barriers to Trade, the Parties affirm their rights and obligations under the WTO Agreement on Technical Barriers to Trade and agree to several additional commitments. Most of those additional commitments are only to 'intensify' their cooperation in areas like the development of standards and technical regulations, and the exchange of information regarding conformity assessment procedures. But each Party also generally agrees to recognize conformity assessment bodies in the other Party's territory on terms no less favourable than those it accords to its own bodies.[80] The Parties also agree to enhance the opportunity for persons to provide comments on proposed technical regulations and conformity assessment procedures by, for example, requiring each Party to include in a notice of a proposed regulation or procedure a statement describing the objective of the proposal, and to publish its response to 'significant' comments it receives on the proposal.[81]

G. Chapter 8: Safeguards

The Agreement provides a safeguard mechanism in Chapter 8. If, 'as a result of the reduction or elimination of a customs duty under this Agreement', a good is being imported in such increased quantities and under such conditions that the imports of the good from the other Party constitute a 'substantial cause' or 'serious injury', or threat thereof, to a domestic industry, the Party may increase the rate of duty to the MFN rate. A safeguard measure generally is not to be applied for a period exceeding three years, and is not to be applied beyond five years after duties on that good have been eliminated.

The Parties also agreed to provide compensation for a safeguard measure. The Party applying the safeguard measure 'shall endeavour to provide' tariff concessions equivalent to the trade effect of the measure or to the value of the additional duties. If the Parties cannot agree on compensation within 30 days, the other Party may

---

[77] Article 6.2.   [78] Article 6.7.
[79] Article 6.10. This Article did not apply to Morocco until two years after the Agreement entered into force.
[80] Article 7.5.3.   [81] Article 7.6.3.

suspend its tariff concessions with an effect on trade 'substantially equivalent' to the effect of the safeguard measure.

H. Chapter 9: Government Procurement

Government procurement is one of the few areas of the Agreement in which the Parties were starting essentially from scratch. The WTO Agreement on Government Procurement (GPA) is a 'plurilateral' agreement: only a fraction of WTO Members are parties to it, and almost every GPA party is a developed country. Morocco is not a party to the GPA and, as a result, was free to discriminate against US suppliers before the Agreement entered into force. And, because US federal government agencies are generally prohibited under US laws from purchasing goods and services from countries that do not offer reciprocal access to their procurement markets for US goods and services, Moroccan goods and services were generally excluded from the government procurement market in the US as well.[82]

Thus, the inclusion of government procurement obligations in the Agreement is a significant improvement in trade liberalization over the status quo ante. Moreover, given that the Agreement includes several transparency[83] and anti-corruption[84] provisions – and that corruption is frequently linked to government procurement in many countries – the inclusion of procurement in the Agreement should contribute to good governance and the rule of law in Morocco and the US.

Overview of obligations

The structure of the Government Procurement Chapter, and the commitments in it, are similar to those found in the GPA. Each Party agrees:

- to provide national and most favoured nation treatment to the goods, services, and suppliers of the other Party;[85]
- to ensure that technical specifications are not applied with the purpose or the effect of creating 'unnecessary obstacles to trade';[86]
- to publish various notices and tender documentation to give prospective suppliers sufficient time and information to prepare and submit responsive tenders;[87]

---

[82] See Section 302(a) of the Trade Agreements Act of 1979, as amended (19 USC section 2512(a)).
[83] See, e.g., Article 9.3 (Publication of Procurement Measures); Article 9.4 (Publication of Notice of Intended Procurement and Notice of Planned Procurement); and Article 9.10.5 (Publication of Award Information).
[84] See Article 9.11 (Ensuring Integrity in Procurement Practices). [85] Article 9.2 (General Principles).
[86] Article 9.7 (Technical Specifications).
[87] See Article 9.4 (Publication of Notice of Intended Procurement and Notice of Planned Procurement); Article 9.5 (Time Limits for Tendering Process); and Article 9.6 (Information on Intended Procurement). As a general rule, a procuring entity shall provide no less than 40 days from the date of publication of a notice of intended procurement to the deadline for submission of tenders for a supplier to submit a tender. See Article 9.5.1.

- to limit any conditions for participation that a supplier must satisfy to those that are essential to ensure that the supplier has the legal, technical, and financial abilities to fulfil the requirements and technical specifications of the procurement;[88]
- to award contracts by means of open competition, absent exceptional circumstances;[89] and
- to provide suppliers the right to challenge a procurement measure or decision in a domestic judicial court or before an impartial administrative authority.[90]

The Procurement Chapter does not rely on the general exceptions of the Agreement.[91] Instead, it contains its own exceptions, which are similar to those found in the GPA.

One of the few obligations in the Chapter that has no equivalent in the GPA is found in Article 9.11 (Ensuring Integrity in Procurement Practices). That Article provides that each Party shall adopt and maintain procedures to declare ineligible for participation in the Party's procurements suppliers that the Party has determined to have engaged in fraudulent or illegal action in relation to procurement. It also provides that Morocco and the US shall exchange information, where appropriate, regarding those suppliers.

Scope and coverage of the obligations

The obligations described above apply to 'government procurement'[92] by certain procuring entities, of certain goods and services, above certain monetary thresholds, that are not otherwise excluded from coverage.[93] Like the parties to the GPA, Morocco and the US provide that the Chapter covers procurement 'by any contractual means'.[94] Unlike the GPA, however, the Parties clarify that those 'contractual means' would include public works concession contracts and build-operate-transfer contracts, which are often quite commercially significant.

---

[88] Article 9.8 (Conditions for Participation). [89] Article 9.9 (Limited Tendering).
[90] Article 9.12 (Domestic Review of Supplier Challenges).
[91] The Chapter does rely, however, on the essential security exception that applies to the entire Agreement.
[92] While the FTA defines 'government procurement' as 'the process by which a government obtains the use of or acquires goods or services, or any combination thereof, for governmental purposes and not with a view to commercial sale or resale, or use in the production or supply of goods or services for commercial sale or resale', it is not always clear what is included in that definition and what is not.
[93] Like the GPA, the Procurement Chapter includes an Article that enables each party to 'modify', and make 'rectifications' to, its coverage. See Article 9.13, compare with GPA Article XXIV:6. A modification may require the party to offer 'compensatory adjustments' to 'maintain a level of coverage comparable to that existing before the modification' (e.g., replacing one procuring entity on the list of coverage with another). Under the GPA, these modifications have often involved situations in which the party asserts that 'government control or influence has been effectively eliminated', in which case a compensatory adjustment is not necessary. This is an area of some friction between the GPA parties, as they have not always agreed that government control or influence has been eliminated.
[94] See Article 9.1.2(a) and GPA Article I:2.

Procuring entities Annexes to the Procurement Chapter include 'positive lists'[95] of the procuring entities covered by the Chapter. The coverage includes entities at the central and sub-central levels of government, as well as 'other' entities that do not fit within those two categories (e.g. quasi-governmental authorities or corporations that are controlled by the government and that serve public purposes, such as electricity or water authorities).

The vast majority of procuring entities in Morocco and the US are covered by the obligations, although it is not clear what percentage of government procurement is covered by the Chapter. At the central level of government, both Parties cover their Ministries of Defence, Justice, Energy, Transportation, Health, Education, Environment, Labour and Employment, Foreign Affairs and Foreign Trade, Finance, Interior and Housing, along with a long list of more specialized offices and agencies. At the sub-central level of government, Morocco lists seventy-seven provinces and municipalities that are covered, while the US lists twenty-three states.[96] Morocco also lists 137 'other' entities, including many schools, institutes, universities, hospitals, electricity, water and other public utility offices. The US lists seven 'other' entities, mostly public utility authorities.

Coverage of goods and services Almost all goods and services are covered by the procurement chapter. The Parties take a 'negative list' approach to the coverage of goods and services, and very few goods and services are on that negative list. The Chapter applies to all goods except goods directly relating to drought and natural disaster relief programmes.[97] In the case of services (other than construction services), Morocco covers everything except certain testing services, geological prospecting services and utilities management services; the US covers everything except certain basic telecommunications services, research and development, maintenance services, ship repair, operation of government-owned facilities, utilities, transportation services and services in support of military forces outside the US. In the case of construction services, Morocco covers everything except port and river dredging and construction of landmark and religious buildings; the US covers everything except dredging services.

Monetary thresholds The chapter only applies to procurements of goods, services and construction services above certain monetary 'thresholds'. These thresholds are the same as the thresholds that apply to US procurements under the GPA. The procurement chapter applies to procurements of goods and services at or above

---

[95] A 'positive list' lays out a list of entities (or goods or services) that are covered by an obligation. A 'negative list' provides that an entity is covered by an obligation, unless it is included on a list of entities that are *not* covered by the obligation.

[96] Due to the federal system of government in the United States, the USTR takes the position that it will only cover those US states that agree to be bound by the procurement obligations in the Agreement.

[97] See Annex 9-B.

US$175,000 at the central level of government and US$477,000 at the sub-central level of government. Procurements of goods and services for 'other' entities are generally subject to a monetary threshold of US$250,000. Procurements of construction services are subject to a monetary threshold of US$6,725,000 for all entities, regardless of the level of government. The Parties will adjust the thresholds (other than the US$250,000 threshold for most 'other' entities) every two years to account for inflation.

Procurements otherwise excluded from coverage The Parties have included a handful of general exclusions from coverage. For example, in the case of the US, the Chapter does not apply to 'set asides on behalf of small or minority-owned businesses'.[98] The Parties have also carved out procurements funded by international grants and loans and the acquisition of services related to fiscal agencies and government debt.[99]

I. Chapter 10: Investment

While Morocco and the US signed a bilateral investment treaty in 1985 (which entered into force in 1991), the FTA negotiations provided an opportunity for the Parties to strengthen and clarify their obligations with respect to one another's investors. In actual fact, the US developed a 'Model Bilateral Investment Treaty' in 2004, and the Chapter is similar, in all material respects, to the 2004 Model.[100]

The scope and coverage of the Chapter is broad. The Parties agree to an open-ended (and fairly circular) definition of investment. Investment means:

> [E]very asset that an investor owns or controls, directly or indirectly, that has the characteristics of an investment, including such characteristics as the commitment of capital or other resources, the expectation of gain or profit, or the assumption of risk.

The definition provides some examples of forms that an investment may take, such as stock and bonds, futures, concession contracts, intellectual property rights, certain forms of licences and permits and 'other tangible or intangible, movable or immovable property, and related property rights such as leases, mortgages, liens, and pledges'.[101] In addition, the Parties take a 'negative list' approach to the sectors that are covered by the Chapter: each Party lists the specific measures, sectors and activities that are excluded from certain obligations in the Chapter.[102] All other measures, sectors, and activities are covered.

---

[98] See Annex 9-F.   [99] See Article 9.1.3.
[100] See www.ustr.gov/Trade_Sectors/Investment/Model_ BIT/Section_Index.html (visited 13 January 2007).
[101] See Article 10.27.   [102] See Article 10.12 (Non-Conforming Measures) and Annexes I and II.

Section A of the Chapter contains all substantive obligations. Under Articles 10.3 and 10.4, each Party commits to provide national and most favoured nation treatment to the investors of the other Party and to their investments. While some investment treaties do not apply to 'pre-establishment' phases of an investment, Morocco and the US agree to provide national and MFN treatment at all phases, from the 'establishment' and 'acquisition' of an investment, to the 'expansion, management, conduct' and 'operation' of the investment, to the 'sale or other disposition of investments'.[103]

The Parties agree to accord to covered investments 'treatment in accordance with customary international law, including fair and equitable treatment and full protection and security'. Because this obligation was the subject of controversy in several disputes under the NAFTA, this Article clarifies that the 'customary international law' commitment prescribes the 'minimum standard of treatment' to be afforded to covered investments. The Parties also describe what 'fair and equitable treatment' and 'full protection and security' mean. They also include an annex (Annex A) that defines 'customary international law'. The basic idea behind these clarifications and definitions is to make clear that a tribunal is to judge the treatment a Party provides to an investment against 'a general and consistent practice of States that they follow from a sense of legal obligation'. A tribunal is not to determine whether it subjectively considers a particular treatment to be 'unfair' or otherwise substandard, without reference to the practice of States.

Under Article 10.6, neither Party may expropriate or nationalize a covered investment either directly or 'indirectly through measures equivalent to expropriation or nationalization' except '(a) for a public purpose; (b) in a non-discriminatory manner; (c) on payment of prompt, adequate, and effective compensation; and (d) in accordance with due process of law'. The Parties also describe in some detail what constitutes 'payment of prompt, adequate, and effective compensation'.[104] Once again because this obligation was the subject of controversy in several disputes under the NAFTA, the Parties adopted an annex that clarifies the scope of this obligation.[105] The annex provides that Article 10.6 is intended to reflect customary international law with respect to expropriation. It also provides that 'indirect expropriation' – a controversial area where it is difficult to draw bright lines – occurs where an action or series of actions by a Party has an effect equivalent to direct expropriation without formal transfer of title or outright seizure. The Parties included the following two subparagraphs to clarify what would constitute an indirect expropriation:

> (a) The determination of whether an action or series of actions by a Party, in a specific fact situation, constitutes an indirect expropriation, requires a case-by-case, fact-based inquiry that considers, among other factors:

---

[103] See Article 10.3, paras. 1 and 2; and Article 10.4, paras. 1 and 2.   [104] See Article 10.6, paras. 2–4.
[105] Chapter 10, Annex B.

(i) the economic impact of the government action, although the fact that an action or series of actions by a Party has an adverse effect on the economic value of an investment, standing alone, does not establish that an indirect expropriation has occurred;
(ii) the extent to which the government action interferes with distinct, reasonable investment-backed expectations; and
(iii) the character of the government action.
(b) Except in rare circumstances, non-discriminatory regulatory actions by a Party that are designed and applied to protect legitimate public welfare objectives, such as public health, safety, and the environment, do not constitute indirect expropriations.

The factors listed in subparagraph (a) are similar to the factors which international tribunals have considered in previous disputes and to the factors enunciated in US Supreme Court jurisprudence under the somewhat parallel Takings Clause of the US Constitution. Obviously, these subparagraphs do not provide governments with complete certainty as to the scope of the obligations under Article 10.6 and arguably raise as many questions as they answer. Still, the annex is likely to provide governments with a greater degree of clarity than would exist in its absence.

Article 10.7 of the Agreement requires each Party to permit all transfers relating to a covered investment to be made freely and without delay into and out of its territory. The Parties recognize a handful of circumstances in which a Party may prevent a transfer (e.g. in connection with the protection of the rights of creditors and ensuring compliance with judgments in judicial proceedings).[106] Unlike some other investment agreements, however, the text does not include a 'balance of payments' exception to address an international financial crisis.

Article 10.8 limits the 'performance requirements' which a Party may impose on an investment in its territory. Neither Party may impose or enforce a requirement, or condition the receipt of an advantage on compliance with any requirement: to achieve a given level or percentage of domestic content; to purchase goods produced in its territory; to relate the volume of imports to the volume of exports or to the amount of foreign exchange inflows associated with an investment; or to restrict sales by relating such sales to the volume of the exports or foreign exchange earnings of the investment. In addition, a Party may not impose a requirement (but may condition the receipt of an advantage on compliance with a requirement): to export a given level or percentage of goods or services; to transfer proprietary knowledge to a person in its territory; or to supply a good or service exclusively from its territory to a specific regional market or to the world market. While these commitments are often compared with similar provisions in the WTO Agreement on Trade-Related Investment Measures (TRIMS Agreement), it is important to recognize that, unlike the Article 10.8 requirements, the TRIMS Agreement commitments must have some

---

[106] See Article 10.7.4.

effect on *trade* and necessarily relate back to Articles III and XI of the GATT.[107] It is also worth noting that the obligations in Article 10.8 apply to measures relating to *all* investments in the territory of the Party, not only to measures applied to investors of the other Party.[108] In other words, a Moroccan investor in the US may object if the US provides a tax exemption to a Mexican investor in the US who agrees to use only US inputs to produce its final product.

Article 10.9 provides that a Party may not require that an enterprise appoint to senior management positions natural persons of any particular nationality, but may require that a majority of the board of directors be of a particular nationality, or resident in the territory of the Party, 'provided that the requirement does not materially impair the ability of the investor to exercise control over its investment'.

Articles 10.10 and 10.11 are designed to ensure transparency in the regulatory process. Article 10 requires a Party to publish all investment-related laws and adjudicatory decisions. Article 11 provides, among other things, that a Party shall provide interested persons with an opportunity to comment on proposed investment-related laws and shall ensure that its administrative proceedings comply with basic principles of due process.

Under Articles 10.12 and 10.13, each Party 'shall strive to ensure' that it does not waive or otherwise derogate from environmental and labour laws[109] 'as an encouragement for the establishment, acquisition, expansion, or retention of an investment in its territory'.

The only exception that applies to all of these obligations is the essential security exception. The other exceptions arguably are not necessary because the investment obligations are written in such a way that there is no need to rely on the general exceptions that apply to most of the other Chapters of the Agreement. For example, if a Party takes a plot of land as a measure 'necessary to protect human, animal, or plant life or health', the Party nevertheless is expected to compensate the investor for that expropriation.

Section B of the Chapter contains the investor-State dispute settlement provisions. While a full description of Section B is beyond the scope of this study (the text covers roughly 13 pages), several provisions are worth noting.

---

[107] See Annex to the TRIMS Agreement. [108] See Article 10.2.1(c); and Article 10.8, paras. 1 and 2.
[109] In the case of labour laws, the waiver or derogation must occur in a manner that weakens or reduces adherence to certain 'internationally recognized labor rights'. Article 10.13.2 refers to the labour rights that have long been recognized under the US generalized system of preferences: (1) the right of association; (2) the right to organize and bargain collectively; (3) a prohibition on the use of any form of forced or compulsory labour; (4) labour protections for children and young people, including a minimum age for the employment of children and the prohibition and elimination of the worst forms of child labour; and (5) the right to 'acceptable conditions of work with respect to minimum wages, hours of work, and occupational safety and health'. The first four of these rights are also recognized in the Declaration on Fundamental Principles and Rights at Work and its Follow-Up (1998) of the International Labour Organization. The fifth and final right recognized in the 1998 Declaration – regarding discrimination in the workplace – is absent from the list.

An investor may submit to arbitration a claim that the responding Party has breached an obligation under Section A and has incurred loss or damage by reason of, or arising out of, that breach. But the scope of investor-State dispute settlement under Section B is not limited to the obligations under Section A. An investor may also claim that the responding Party has breached 'an investment authorization' or 'an investment agreement'. An 'investment authorization' is an authorization that 'the foreign investment authority of a Party' grants to a covered investment or an investor of the other Party.

An 'investment agreement' has a very specific definition: the agreement must grant rights to the covered investment or investor (a) with respect to natural resources that a national authority controls; (b) to supply services to the public on behalf of the Party; or (c) to undertake infrastructure projects that are not for the exclusive or predominant use and benefit of the government. Thus, while 'umbrella clauses' in investment treaties have created some ambiguity as to whether an investor may seek damages in investor-State arbitration for any breach of contract by a State, the Parties here have attempted to establish a narrower range of contracts that may be covered by arbitration.

Section B also provides that no more than three years may have elapsed from the date on which the claimant first acquired, or should have first acquired, knowledge of the alleged breach and knowledge that the claimant has incurred loss or damage.[110] It also provides that the claimant must waive any right 'to initiate or continue before any administrative tribunal or court under the law of either Party, or other dispute settlement procedures, any proceeding with respect to any measure' that is the subject of the investor-State arbitration. In other words, while some investment treaties provide a 'fork' (i.e. an investor cannot initiate investor-State arbitration if he or she has previously filed a complaint in the respondent Party's domestic courts), Morocco and the US have agreed to a 'no U-turn' provision.

Section B also provides the 'non-disputing Party' (i.e. the Party of the investor-claimant) with a right to make oral and written submissions to the tribunal regarding the interpretation of the Treaty.[111] (While trading partners are often reluctant to allow the US a right to make a submission in a dispute involving a US investor, the fact is that, in past disputes under the NAFTA, the US submission has almost always favoured the position of the disputing Party, *not* the position of its own investor.[112]) It also grants the tribunal the authority to accept and consider *amicus curiae* submissions from a person or entity that is not a disputing party[113] and requires the respondent to make available to the public the chief documents in the arbitration (e.g. the pleadings, briefs, minutes of transcripts of hearings and orders and awards of the tribunal).[114]

---

[110] Article 10.26.1. [111] See Article 10.28.2.
[112] These submissions are available on the website of the US Department of State: see www.state.gov/s/l/c3439.htm.
[113] See Article 10.28.3. [114] See Article 10.29.1.

Section B also includes a mechanism that allows the Parties to agree to issue a joint declaration interpreting a provision of the Chapter and requires a tribunal to follow that declaration.[115] The text would appear to allow the Parties to issue such a declaration even after an investor requests arbitration. As a result, this mechanism may serve as a safeguard against exceedingly novel arguments by investors in the course of investment disputes.

The final section of the Chapter provides a list of 'non-conforming measures'. In Annex I, a Party may carve out of the national treatment obligation, most favoured nation obligation, performance requirement obligation, or 'senior management and board of directors' obligation any *existing* non-conforming measure. The Party is free to amend any non-conforming measure listed in Annex I, but only 'to the extent that the amendment does not decrease the conformity of the measure, as it existed immediately before the amendment'.[116] In other words, if the Party *increases* the conformity of its measure after the Agreement enters into force, it may not subsequently *decrease* the level of conformity even back to the original level: this is known as the 'ratchet' effect. All existing non-conforming measures by a Party at a local level of government are excluded from these four obligations, without any notation in the Annex.[117]

In Annex II, a Party may carve any existing or future measure, with respect to a particular sector, subsector, or activity, out of these four obligations. In other words, Annex II provides a greater degree of flexibility: a Party may reserve the right to adopt a measure in the future that is inconsistent with one of the four obligations listed above, even if at the time the agreement is negotiated the Party fully complies with those four obligations with respect to a particular sector.

In Annex I, Morocco has taken 29 reservations with respect to investment. The reservations cover tourism, mining, the hydrocarbon sector, architectural services, education, professional legal services, health care services and pharmaceuticals, accounting services, audiovisual film production services, news services, agriculture, fishing and transportation services. Two reservations apply to all sectors (so-called 'horizontal' reservations). Under one reservation, enterprises (other than banks or financing companies) that are not organized under Moroccan law are not permitted to issue negotiable debt securities with a maturity of less than one year in Morocco. Under the other, an enterprise whose headquarters are not in Morocco or a natural person who is not a Moroccan resident may effect a public issue of debt or equity securities only after securing the prior approval of the Moroccan Finance Minister.

---

[115] Articles 10.30.3 and 10.31.
[116] Article 10.14.1(c). It is not clear how an amendment can 'decrease the conformity' of a measure. Normally, the question is *whether* a measure conforms to an obligation, not *to what extent* the measure conforms. There may be situations in which it is difficult to judge the degree of conformity with an absolute obligation.
[117] See Article 10.14.1(a)(iii).

The US has taken a handful of reservations with respect to investment in Annex I. The reservations cover atomic energy, mining, air transportation, customs brokers and radio communications. Horizontal reservations taken by the US address the programmes of the Overseas Private Investment Corporation; the registration of public offerings of securities; and all existing non-conforming measures (without identification of any specific measures) at the State level.

In Annex II, Morocco has taken just three reservations. One relates to professional paramedical services. The second addresses communications (radio and television services). Third, it has also taken a horizontal reservation for measures that accord preferential treatment to countries under bilateral or multilateral international agreements signed prior to the entry into force of the Agreement.

The US has taken six reservations with respect to investment in Annex II. The reservations cover communications, social services (e.g. law enforcement and correctional services, social security insurance and child care), minority affairs (e.g. measures according preferences to disadvantaged minorities) and maritime transportation. The US has also taken a horizontal reservation for measures that accord preferential treatment to countries under bilateral or multilateral international agreements that have been signed prior to the entry into force of the Agreement.

J. Chapter 11: Cross-Border Trade in Services

The central commitments in the Cross-Border Trade in Services Chapter are similar to those found in the WTO General Agreement on Trade in Services (GATS). The Chapter contains national treatment, most favoured nation treatment, market access, and mutual recognition obligations that are like those obligations in the GATS. Like the GATS, it also provides that each Party generally shall permit transfers and payments relating to the cross-border supply of services to be made freely and without delay into and out of its territory.[118] The difference is in the exceptions to this general rule: the GATS recognizes restrictions to safeguard the balance of payments,[119] but the Agreement's Services Chapter does not. It does, however, recognize other exceptions, such as the need to prevent a transfer for reasons of bankruptcy, or to ensure compliance with orders in judicial proceedings.[120] Finally, the Chapter provides that neither Party may require a service supplier to establish or maintain any form of enterprise, or to be resident, in its territory as a condition for the cross-border supply of a service (the 'local presence' obligation).[121]

While the commitments in the Chapter are roughly similar to those in the GATS, the scope of services coverage goes well beyond the coverage of the GATS. In

---

[118] Article 11.10.1, compare with GATS, Article XI. [119] GATS, Article XII. [120] Article 11.10.3.
[121] Article 11.5.

contrast to the GATS, the Agreement adopted a 'negative list' approach to describe the services covered by the agreement (i.e. a service is covered unless a Party explicitly carves that service out of its list of coverage). After concluding the Agreement, the US noted that its banks, insurance companies, telecommunications firms, audiovisual services companies, computer and related services companies, express delivery companies, distribution services companies and construction and engineering services would gain from new market access opportunities.[122]

The negative list takes the form of two annexes of 'non-conforming measures' (NCMs). Annex I includes all existing NCMs that are excluded from certain obligations in the Chapter, while in Annex II each of the Parties reserves the right to take measures, including measures adopted in the future, that are inconsistent with certain obligations.

In Annex I, the US carved out of its national treatment obligation certain export-related business services, transportation services and patent-related professional services. It also carved out all existing NCMs of all US states. It carved out of its MFN obligation certain air transportation services, patent-related professional services and all existing NCMs of all US states. It carved out of its 'local presence' obligation certain export-related business services, transportation services, patent-related professional services and all existing NCMs of all US states.

In Annex II, the US carved out of its national treatment obligation certain social services, measures related to the protection of minorities and maritime transport services. It carved out of its MFN obligation certain communications services, social services and maritime transport services. It carved out of its market access obligation certain social services and any measure that may otherwise be inconsistent with the market access obligation, but that is not inconsistent with the market access obligation in the GATS. Finally, it carved out of its local presence obligation certain social services, measures relating to the protection of minorities and maritime transport services.

For its part, in Annex I Morocco carved out of its national treatment obligation certain tourism services, architectural services, private higher education services, legal services, health care, accounting and maritime transport services. It carved out of its MFN obligation certain legal services, health care, accounting and maritime transport services. It carved out of its market access commitments services related to its food markets, the distribution of ethyl alcohol, electricity and potable water distribution services, the exploration of certain ores, architectural services, legal services, health care, audiovisual services, communications, tobacco distribution, transportation services, postal services and port operations. From its local presence commitments, it carved out private higher education, legal services, health care and pharmaceuticals, accounting and waste disposal services.

---

[122] ITC Study, above note 24, at pp. 44–9.

In Annex II, Morocco carved out of its national treatment obligation certain private education services, social services and health care. It carved out of its MFN obligation social services, health care and 'culture-related industries and services'. It carved out of its market access commitments certain social services, polling services and communications services. From the local presence obligation it carved out private education, social services, communications and hazardous waste management.

Both countries also reserved the right, notwithstanding the MFN obligation, to adopt or maintain any measure that accords differential treatment to countries under any international agreement in force or signed prior to the date of entry into force of this Agreement. The rationale for this NCM is that each Party can review the commitments which the other Party has made under existing international agreements and, if it wants treatment no less favourable than the treatment a third country received under that other international agreement, it can request that in the course of the negotiations.

K. Chapter 12: Financial Services

The Financial Services Chapter applies to measures relating to financial institutions of the other Party, investors of the other Party in financial institutions in a Party's territory and cross-border trade in financial services. Each Party must accord national treatment and MFN treatment to investors of the other Party and provide market access for financial services without limitations on the number of financial institutions, value of transactions, number of service operations or number of persons employed.

Each Party must allow cross-border trade in certain financial services (listed in an annex) and must permit a financial institution of the other Party to provide new financial services that it would permit its own institutions to provide without additional legislative action.

Pursuant to Article 12.8, a Party may not require financial institutions of the other Party to hire individuals of a particular nationality or require more than a simple majority of the board of directors to be nationals or residents of the Party. Where a Party requires membership in a self-regulatory organization, the Chapter provides that such organizations are also subject to the national treatment and MFN obligations of the Chapter.

The Financial Services Chapter also incorporates from the Investment Chapter the commitments regarding expropriation, transfers, investment and environment, denial of benefits and special formalities. It also clarifies that the investor-State dispute settlement mechanism in Section B of the Investment Chapter is incorporated into the Financial Services Chapter, but only for claims that a Party has breached one of the commitments incorporated from the Investment Chapter.

The Chapter also includes its own set of stand-alone exceptions, rather than relying on the general exceptions in the Agreement as a whole. The Parties reserve their rights to adopt measures for 'prudential reasons' and to take non-discriminatory measures of general application in pursuit of 'monetary and related credit polices or exchange rate policies'. They also provide that each Party may prevent transfers 'through the equitable, non-discriminatory, and good faith application of measures relating to maintenance of the safety, soundness, integrity, or financial responsibility of financial institutions'.[123]

One of the most significant limitations to the provision of financial services *in* Morocco is its law prohibiting individuals and organizations, including foreign investors, from investing or maintaining accounts *outside* Morocco. Because financial services investors like to diversify their investments – including by investing abroad – the attractiveness of investing in Morocco is diminished if a financial services investor in Morocco cannot also invest outside Morocco. For example, according to a study of the Agreement by the US International Trade Commission, '[i]nsurance firms routinely invest their premium proceeds widely in order to hedge the risks of medium- and long-term insurance policies. As Morocco is a small market with limited investment opportunities, a prohibition on outside investment makes it "commercially infeasible" for many US financial firms to locate in Morocco.'[124] In the Agreement, Morocco agreed to eliminate this restriction with respect to US investors four years after the date of entry into force of the Agreement.[125]

L. Chapter 13: Telecommunications

The Telecommunications Chapter is designed to ensure that the telecommunications market in the territory of each Party is competitive and that telecommunications service suppliers of one Party will, in fact, be able to access the market of the other Party. Unlike in most other Chapters of the Agreement, the Chapter requires the Parties to take positive steps to provide a competitive market – not merely to refrain from adopting measures that could serve as a barrier to trade or investment. Thus, many of the commitments in the Chapter are similar to commitments in the GATS Telecommunications Reference Paper, which is also focused on ensuring competition in the telecommunications sector.

Each Party is required to ensure that service suppliers of the other Party have access to and use of any public telecommunications service 'on reasonable and non-discriminatory terms and conditions'. Among other things, this means that a service supplier must be permitted to purchase or lease and attach equipment that

---

[123] Article 12.10.
[124] ITC Study, above note 24, at p. 53 (describing the report on the Agreement of the Industry Sector Advisory Committee on Services).
[125] See Annex III-Morocco-15.

interfaces with a public telecommunications network and to provide services to end-users over leased circuits.[126]

Each Party is also required to ensure that public telecommunications service suppliers: (1) provide interconnection with suppliers of the other Party; (2) do not impose unreasonable or discriminatory conditions or limitations on the resale of public telecommunications services; (3) provide 'number portability' (i.e. ability to retain at the same location existing telephone numbers when switching between the same category of suppliers) to the extent technically feasible and on reasonable terms and conditions; and (4) provide 'dialling parity' (i.e. ability of an end-user to use an equal number of digits to access a like public telecommunications service) to suppliers of the other Party.[127]

The Chapter also includes a long list of 'additional obligations relating to major suppliers' of telecommunications services.[128] Each Party shall ensure, inter alia, that major suppliers: (1) accord suppliers of the other Party treatment no less favourable than such major suppliers accord to their subsidiaries, affiliates, or non-affiliated service suppliers regarding, for example, the availability of telecommunication services and technical interfaces necessary for interconnection; (2) do not engage in anticompetitive practices;[129] (3) provide reasonable interconnection for the facilities and equipment of suppliers of the other Party (e.g. at any technically feasible point in the major supplier's network, under non-discriminatory terms and in a timely fashion);[130] (4) make publicly available interconnection offers and file all interconnection agreements with the Party's telecommunications regulatory body; (5) provide enterprises of the other Party leased circuits services on terms and conditions, and at rates, that are reasonable and non-discriminatory; and (6) generally provide suppliers of the other Party physical co-location of equipment necessary for interconnection on terms and conditions, and at cost-oriented rates, that are reasonable, non-discriminatory, and transparent.

Each Party is also required to provide its telecommunications regulatory body the authority to require major suppliers in its territory to offer access to network elements on an unbundled basis on terms and conditions, and at cost-oriented rates, that are reasonable, non-discriminatory and transparent for the supply of telecommunications services. Each Party shall also 'endeavour to ensure' that major suppliers afford access to poles, ducts, conduits and rights

---

[126] Articles 13.2.1 and 13.2.2.   [127] Article 13.3.
[128] A 'major supplier' is a supplier that can materially affect the terms of participation (having regard to price and supply) in the relevant market as a result of control over essential facilities or use of its position in the market.
[129] The provisions relating to 'competitive safeguards' are nearly identical to Article 1 of the GATS Telecommunications Reference Paper.
[130] The provisions relating to interconnection are nearly identical to Article 2 of the GATS Telecommunications Reference Paper.

of way on terms and conditions, and at rates, that are reasonable and non-discriminatory.[131]

The Chapter also includes obligations regarding the supply of value-added services that are quite different from the kinds of obligations described above regarding public telecommunications services. For example, neither Party may require a value-added services supplier that supplies those services over facilities it does not own, to interconnect its networks with any particular customer for the supply of those services or cost-justify its rates for those services.[132]

The Parties have also agreed to ensure that their telecommunications regulatory bodies are separate from all telecommunications suppliers and that the decisions and procedures of those bodies are impartial. They also agree to 'maintain the absence of or eliminate as soon as feasible national government ownership in any supplier of public telecommunications services'.[133]

The Chapter also includes Articles regarding 'universal service' obligations, the licensing process, and the 'allocation and use of scarce resources' that are similar to provisions in the GATS Telecommunications Reference Paper.

Finally, the Parties also agree that each Party shall ensure that enterprises of the other Party may seek review by a telecommunications regulatory body to resolve disputes regarding: (1) the Party's measures relating to the obligations contained in the Telecommunications Chapter; and (2) the terms, conditions, and rates for interconnection offered by a major supplier. It also provides that any enterprise that is aggrieved, or whose interests are adversely affected by a determination or decision of its telecommunications regulatory body, may petition the body to reconsider the determination or decision and may obtain judicial review.[134]

M. Chapter 14: Electronic Commerce

The Agreement also includes a short Chapter addressing electronic commerce. The Parties affirm that measures affecting the supply of a service using electronic means are subject to the obligations contained in the relevant provisions of the Investment, Services and Financial Services Chapters. The most commercially significant provisions in the Electronic Commerce Chapter may be those relating to 'digital products'.

In this regard, the Parties agree not to apply customs duties in connection with the importation or exportation of 'digital products by electronic transmission'.[135] This is significant not only because it means that a product that otherwise would have been subject to a duty will enter duty free if transmitted electronically; it is also significant because the Parties apparently agree, implicitly, that 'computer programs, text, video, images, sound recordings, and other products that are digitally

[131] Article 13.4. [132] Article 13.6. [133] Article 13.7. [134] Article 13.12(b) and (c).
[135] Article 14.3.1.

encoded' are 'digital products', not services.[136] This is an open debate in the WTO, where some Members consider such products to be services, not goods. Many WTO disciplines (e.g. the WTO Agreement on Subsidies and Countervailing Measures) apply only to goods, not services.

Under Article 14.3.2, each Party shall determine the customs value of an imported carrier medium bearing a digital product (e.g. a compact disc of *The Beatles* White album) 'based on the cost or value of the carrier medium alone, without regard to the cost of the digital product stored on the carrier medium'. Given that, in almost all cases, the cost of the carrier medium is a very small fraction of the cost of the content on that carrier medium, this provision effectively reduces tariffs considerably and may set a precedent for the treatment of such products under WTO rules in the future.

The Parties also provide anti-discrimination rules that take into account the special circumstances surrounding the production of digital products. In particular, the Parties recognize that less favourable treatment could be based either on the *place* where the digital product is 'created, produced, published, stored, transmitted, contracted for, commissioned, or first made available on commercial terms' or on the identity of the *person* who is the 'author, performer, producer, developer, or distributor' of the digital product.[137]

N. Chapter 15: Intellectual Property Rights

Chapter 15 (Intellectual Property Rights) incorporates many of the obligations found in the WTO Agreement on Trade-Related Aspects of Intellectual Property Rights (TRIPS Agreement), but it goes beyond those obligations in many important respects. The following description will focus on just some of the 'TRIPS-Plus' aspects of the chapter.

Each of the Parties is required to ratify or accede to eight international agreements concerning intellectual property[138] and to make 'all reasonable efforts' to ratify or accede to two others.[139]

---

[136] See Article 14.4: '**digital products** means computer programs, text, video, images, sound recordings, and other products that are digitally encoded, regardless of whether they are fixed on a carrier medium or transmitted electronically'.

[137] See Article 14.3, paras. 3 and 4.

[138] The international agreements are: the Patent Cooperation Treaty (1970), as amended in 1979; the Convention Relating to the Distribution of Programme-Carrying Signals Transmitted by Satellite (1974); the Protocol Relating to the Madrid Agreement Concerning the International Registration of Marks (1989); the Budapest Treaty on the International Recognition of the Deposit of Microorganisms for the Purpose of Patent Procedure (1977), as amended in 1980; the International Convention for the Protection of New Varieties of Plants (1991); the Trademark Law Treaty (1994); the WIPO Copyright Treaty (1996); and the WIPO Performances and Phonograms Treaty (1996).

[139] These agreements are the Patent Law Treaty (2000) and the Hague Agreement Concerning the International Registration of Industrial Designs (1999).

Trademarks

The Agreement requires each Party to accede to the Trademark Law Treaty (1994),[140] and to provide a system for the registration of all trademarks.[141] It also ensures that licensees will no longer have to register their trademark licences to assert their rights in a trademark.[142]

Whereas the TRIPS Agreement provides that Members 'may require, as a condition of registration, that signs be visually perceptible',[143] Article 15.2.1 of the Agreement provides the opposite: 'Neither Party may require, as a condition of registration, that signs be visually perceptible, nor may a Party deny registration of a trademark solely on the ground that the sign of which it is composed is a sound or a scent'. In addition, whereas the TRIPS Agreement provides that the initial registration, and each renewal of registration,[144] of a trademark shall be for a term of no less than seven years, Article 15.2.10 provides for a term of no less than ten years. And, whereas the TRIPS Agreement provides that Members may make registrability depend on use, the Agreement is silent on this issue.

The Agreement also ensures 'an appropriate procedure' for the settlement of domain name disputes, based on the principles established in the Uniform Domain-Name Dispute Resolution Policy.[145] This is intended to prevent 'cyber-squatting' of trademarked domain names.

Article 15.3.1 includes procedural requirements that must be followed if a Party provides the means to apply for protection for geographical indications. Article 15.3.2 provides that a geographical indication must be refused protection or recognition if it is likely to be confusingly similar to a pre-existing trademark. Thus, the Agreement includes commitments with respect to geographical indications that go beyond what may be found in the TRIPS Agreement.

Copyright and related rights

The TRIPS Agreement provides that, whenever the term of protection of a work is calculated on a basis other than the life of a natural person, the term shall be no less than fifty years from the end of the calendar year of authorized publication. By contrast, Article 15.5.5 provides for a term of no less than seventy years.

The Chapter includes several provisions that address Internet and other digital piracy of copyrighted materials, such as music recordings, movie videos and business software. For example, Article 15.5.8 requires each Party to apply criminal penalties to any person who circumvents any technological measure that controls access to a protected work, or who traffics in devices primarily designed for the purpose of enabling the circumvention of any effective technological measure. Similarly, Article 15.5.9 requires each Party to apply criminal penalties to any person

---

[140] Article 15.2(f).   [141] Article 15.2.7.   [142] Article 15.2.11.   [143] TRIPS Agreement, Article 15.1.
[144] TRIPS Agreement, Article 18.   [145] Article 15.4.1.

who knowingly removes or alters any information that identifies a work, the author of the work or the owner of any right in the work (so-called 'rights management information').

The Chapter also provides that only copyright holders have the right to make their works available online.[146] Copyright holders maintain all rights to their works on computers and networks, thereby protecting copyrighted material from unauthorized sharing on the Internet. Also, protection for encrypted programme-carrying satellite signals is extended to both the signals and the programming, in order to deter piracy of satellite television programming.[147]

Finally, the Chapter recognizes that, in the procurement of software, governments themselves often infringe on copyrights. It provides that each Party must adopt measures mandating that its agencies use computer software only as authorized by the right holder. These measures 'shall actively regulate the acquisition and management of software for government use'.[148]

Patents

Article 15.9.4 of the Agreement generally prohibits the practice of 'parallel importation' (i.e. the situation in which a patent holder sells a product to a buyer who exports the product to a second buyer in another country). Parallel importation can undermine a patent holder's attempt to engage in international price discrimination, and thus can affect profitability and strategic planning. Parallel importation is not in and of itself a breach of any provision of the TRIPS Agreement.

Article 15.9.6 links 'marketing approval' to the patent status of a product. This provision relates most directly to the approval of pharmaceutical products. It provides, in essence, that a drug regulatory authority of a Party may not register a generic version of a drug that is under patent, without the consent of the patent holder (in the vast majority of countries, the regulatory approval process used to determine the safety and efficacy of a drug operates independently of the patent process). By contrast, the TRIPS Agreement contains no such obligation.

Article 15.10.1 provides for what is commonly known as 'data exclusivity'. Typically, a drug regulatory authority conditions marketing approval of a new drug on the submission of information regarding clinical trials and other 'safety and efficacy data'. Generic drug manufacturers often rely on data submitted by the patent holder to gain approval for the generic version of the same product for the same use. But Article 15.10.1 provides that the Party may not permit the generic manufacturer to market the generic product on the basis of the approval granted to the patent holder for at least five years from the date on which the patented product was approved in the territory of that Party, without the consent of the patent holder. The TRIPS Agreement contains no such provision.

---

[146] Article 15.5.1.   [147] Article 15.8.   [148] Article 15.5.10.

Another set of patent obligations with special application to pharmaceutical products is to be found in Article 15.9.7 and Article 15.10.3. Pharmaceutical producers typically secure a patent many years before the drug regulatory authorities grant authority to market the drug to the public. As a result, the term of the patent is significantly eroded. Under Article 15.9.7, each Party is required to extend the term of a patent to 'compensate for unreasonable delays that occur in granting the patent'. A delay is 'unreasonable' if the patent is issued more than four years from the date of filing of the application, or two years after a request for examination of the application, whichever is later. Similarly, Article 15.10.3 provides that each Party shall make available an extension of a patent term covering a pharmaceutical product to compensate for 'unreasonable curtailment of the effective patent term as a result of the marketing approval process'.

Enforcement

While many of the enforcement-related obligations in Chapter 15 are similar to the enforcement-related obligations in the TRIPS Agreement, Chapter 15 devotes almost six pages of text to the treatment of Internet service providers.[149] The basic purpose of these provisions is to limit liability for these providers (e.g. by precluding monetary relief and restricting court-ordered relief to compel certain actions), subject to a variety of conditions and exceptions.

O. Chapter 16: Labor

Chapter 16 (Labor) provides that each Party 'shall strive to ensure' that its law recognizes and protects the principles in the ILO Declaration on Fundamental Principles and Rights at Work and its Follow-up (1998) (ILO Declaration) and the following internationally recognized labour rights:

(a) the right of association;
(b) the right to organize and bargain effectively;
(c) a prohibition on the use of any form of forced or compulsory labour;
(d) labour protections for children and young people, including a minimum age for the employment of children and the prohibition and elimination of the worst forms of child labour; and
(e) acceptable conditions of work with respect to minimum wages, hours of work, and occupational safety and health.[150]

---

[149] See Article 15.11.28.
[150] The fundamental principles in the ILO Declaration are: freedom of association and the effective recognition of the right to collective bargaining, elimination of all forms of forced or compulsory labour, the effective abolition of child labour and the elimination of discrimination in respect of employment and occupation. Thus, these principles are essentially identical to the 'internationally recognized labor rights' listed in the Labor Chapter, with the exception of the last. Whereas the Labor Chapter includes

Similarly, each Party 'shall strive to ensure' that it does not waive or otherwise derogate from its labour laws in a manner that weakens or reduces adherence to these internationally recognized labour rights 'as an encouragement for trade with the other Party' or as an encouragement for investment in its territory.[151]

Article 16.2.1(a) contains one of the few fully-fledged substantive commitments (i.e. beyond 'striving to') and the only commitment that can be the subject of dispute settlement between the Parties.[152] It provides that neither Party shall 'fail to effectively enforce its labor laws, through a sustained or recurring course of action or inaction, in a manner affecting trade between the Parties'. However, in subparagraph (b), the Parties recognize that 'each Party retains the right to exercise discretion with respect to investigatory, prosecutorial, regulatory, and compliance matters and to make decisions regarding the allocation of resources to enforcement with respect to other labor matters determined to have higher priorities'. Therefore, 'a Party is in compliance with subparagraph (a) where a course of action or inaction reflects a reasonable exercise of such discretion, or results from a *bona fide* decision regarding the allocation of resources'.

Article 16.2.1(a) has been the source of controversy for some time in the US. Many policy-makers (in particular, a large group of Democratic Members of Congress), stakeholders and trade observers believe that the parties to an FTA should agree to enforce internationally recognized core labour rights, such as the rights identified in the ILO Declaration, and that an agreement merely to enforce one's own domestic laws – regardless of whether those laws recognize those core labour rights – is insufficient.

In the case of the US–Morocco FTA, however, this was not a significant issue because Morocco adopted labour laws that gave meaning to the internationally recognized core labour rights. According to USTR, '[t]he prospect of a free trade agreement (FTA) with the United States helped to forge a domestic consensus for labor law reform in Morocco, spurring reform efforts that had been stymied for more than 20 years'. A comprehensive new labour law went into effect on 8 June 2004. The new law raises the minimum employment age (from twelve to fifteen), guarantees rights of association and collective bargaining, prohibits employers from taking actions against workers because they are union members, reduces the working week from forty-eight to forty-four hours and improves worker health and safety regulations.[153]

While a Party does have recourse to dispute settlement in connection with a matter arising under Article 16.2.1(a), the Dispute Settlement Chapter limits the

---

'acceptable conditions of work' – a term with a long history in US trade law, including in the US Generalized System of Preferences – the ILO Declaration includes 'the elimination of discrimination'.
[151] Article 16.2.2. [152] See Article 16.6.5.
[153] See USTR fact sheet 'Morocco FTA Leads to Progress on Labor Reform', 23 June 2004, at www.ustr.gov/Document_Library/Fact_Sheets/2004/Morocco_FTA_Leads_to_Progress_on_Labor_Reform.html.

remedies available to that Party in the event of a breach of that commitment. Normally, where a dispute settlement panel determines that a Party has breached an obligation in the Agreement, and that Party fails to eliminate the non-conformity and fails to compensate the complaining Party, the complaining Party ultimately has the right to 'suspend the application to the other Party of benefits of equivalent effect' (this is sometimes called 'retaliation', for lack of a better term). But there is no right to suspend benefits of equivalent effect in connection with a breach of Article 16.2.1(a), even though by definition such a breach 'affect[s] trade between the Parties'. Instead, the complaining Party is entitled to collect from the Party complained against a 'monetary assessment', never to exceed US$15 million.

Article 16.3 requires each Party to provide interested persons with access to impartial administrative or judicial tribunals for the enforcement of its labour laws. The proceedings of those tribunals generally must be open to the public and must comply with due process of law.

The Parties also agree to establish a 'Labor Cooperation Mechanism' relating to 'labor matters of common interest, such as: promoting fundamental rights and their effective application; eliminating the worst forms of child labor; enhancing labor-management relations; improving working conditions; developing unemployment assistance programs and other social safety net programs; encouraging human-resource development and life-long learning; and utilizing labor statistics'.[154] Under the Mechanism, the Parties foresee that they will arrange for study visits between government delegations, exchange information on standards and regulations, and undertake joint research projects, among other things.[155]

P. Chapter 17: Environment

The structure and some of the basic obligations of the Environment Chapter are similar to the structure of the Labor Chapter. For example, each Party 'shall strive to continue to improve [its environmental] laws and policies' and 'shall strive to ensure that it does not waive or otherwise derogate from . . . such laws in a manner that weakens or reduces the protections afforded in those laws as an encouragement for trade with the other Party, or as an encouragement for the establishment, acquisition, expansion, or retention of an investment in its territory'.[156]

In addition, Article 17.2.1 is quite similar to Article 16.2.1. Subparagraph (a) provides that neither Party shall 'fail to effectively enforce its environmental laws, through a sustained or recurring course of action or inaction, in a manner affecting trade between the Parties'. However, subparagraph (b) provides that a Party is in compliance with subparagraph (a) where a course of action or inaction reflects a reasonable exercise of [its discretion with respect to investigatory, prosecutorial,

---

[154] Article 16.5. [155] See Annex 16-A, para. 5. [156] Articles 17.1 and 17.2.2.

regulatory and compliance matters and regarding the allocation of resources], or results from a *bona fide* decision regarding the allocation of resources. Moreover, as with the Labor Chapter, neither Party may have recourse to dispute settlement under the Agreement for any matter arising under any provision of the Environmental Chapter other than Article 17.2(a),[157] and a 'monetary assessment' generally replaces the right to retaliate in the case of 'non-implementation'.[158]

The Parties are also required to make available to interested persons fair and transparent judicial or administrative proceedings with a view to providing an effective sanction or remedy for violations of its environmental laws.[159] They are also required to 'ensure that procedures exist for dialogue with its public concerning the implementation' of the Environment Chapter. And they 'are committed to expanding their cooperative relationship', pursuant to a 'United States–Morocco Joint Statement on Environmental Cooperation',[160] a mechanism not unlike the Labor Cooperation Mechanism created under the Labor Chapter.

While all of the foregoing obligations have analogies in the Labor Chapter, two Articles in the Environment Chapter are unique. Under Article 17.5, each Party is required to encourage the development of 'mechanisms that facilitate voluntary action to protect or enhance the environment' (such as 'voluntary guidelines for environmental performance') and 'incentives, including market-based incentives where appropriate, to encourage conservation, restoration, enhancement, and protection of natural resources and the environment'. Under Article 17.8, the Parties agree to 'seek means to enhance the mutual supportiveness of multilateral environmental agreements to which they are both party and trade agreements to which they are both party'.

Q. Chapter 18: Transparency

Chapter 18 contains general obligations regarding transparency. Each Party agrees to publish promptly any law or administrative ruling of general application respecting any matter covered by the Agreement and, to the extent possible, to provide interested persons and the other Party with an opportunity to comment on proposed measures.[161] They also agree to provide persons of the other Party who are directly affected by an administrative proceeding with an opportunity to present facts and arguments in support of their positions during those proceedings.[162] Any final administrative action is subject to review by an impartial judicial, quasi-judicial or administrative tribunal.[163] Finally, each Party agrees to establish that bribery is a criminal offence under its law, in matters affecting international trade or investment.[164]

---

[157] Article 17.7.5. [158] Article 20.12. [159] Article 17.4. [160] Article 17.3. [161] Article 18.1.
[162] Article 18.3. [163] Article 18.4. [164] Article 18.5.

R. Chapter 19: Administration of the Agreement

In Chapter 19 (Administration of the Agreement), the Parties establish a 'Joint Committee', chaired by officials of the Office of the US Trade Representative and of Morocco's Ministry of Foreign Affairs and Cooperation, to supervise the implementation of the Agreement. The Committee may, among other things, facilitate the settlement of disputes arising under the Agreement and adopt amendments and issue interpretations of the Agreement. The Committee is to convene in a regular session every year and in special session within thirty days of a request of a Party.

S. Chapter 20: Dispute Settlement

Article 20.2 provides that the Dispute Settlement Chapter generally applies with respect to the avoidance or settlement of all disputes between the Parties regarding the interpretation or application of the Agreement or wherever a Party considers that:

(a) a measure of the other Party is inconsistent with its obligations under the Agreement;
(b) the other Party has otherwise failed to carry out its obligations under the Agreement; or
(c) a benefit which the Party could reasonably have expected to accrue to it under Chapter 2 (Market Access for Goods), Chapter 5 (Rules of Origin), Chapter 9 (Government Procurement), Chapter 11 (Cross-Border Trade in Services), or Chapter 15 (Intellectual Property Rights) is being nullified or impaired as a result of a measure that is not inconsistent with the Agreement.

In other words, 'non-violation nullification or impairment' disputes are not possible under those Chapters not listed in Article 20.2(c).

The Parties also agree that a complaining party may 'forum shop' between the WTO and the Agreement where a dispute arises under both the Agreement and the WTO Agreement, but once a forum is selected, 'the forum selected shall be used to the exclusion of other possible fora'.[165]

As the first step in the dispute settlement process, a Party may request consultations with the other Party.[166] During those consultations each Party is required to 'solicit and consider the views of interested non-governmental entities on the matter in order to draw on a broad range of perspectives'.[167] If the consultations fail to resolve the matter, either Party may refer the matter to a 'Joint Committee' comprised of representatives from each Party.

If the Committee is unable to resolve the matter, the complaining Party may refer the matter to a panel, which normally consists of three members. Each Party has the

---

[165] Article 20.4.3.   [166] Article 20.5.1.   [167] Articles 20.5.3(a) and 20.5.4.

right to appoint one panellist, and the Parties shall endeavour to agree on a third panellist who serves as the chair. If the Parties fail to agree on the chair, the chair is selected by lot from a 'reserve list' of panellists, which is to be agreed upon by the Parties.

While the Parties agree to establish model rules of procedure after the Agreement is signed, the Chapter provides a basic outline of those procedures (e.g. a right to at least one hearing, an opportunity to provide initial and rebuttal submissions). The model rules of procedure are also to provide that each Party's written submissions and oral statement are made available to the public and that the panel will consider requests from non-governmental entities to provide written views.[168]

A panel generally is required to present its initial report to the Parties within 180 days after the chair is appointed, and its final report within 45 days of presentation of the initial report.[169] On receipt of the final report, the Parties shall agree on the resolution of the dispute; thus there is no option to appeal the panel report. If the panel has determined that a Party 'has not conformed with its obligations' or that its measure is causing nullification or impairment, the resolution, 'whenever possible, shall be to eliminate the non-conformity or the nullification or impairment'.[170]

If the Parties are unable to reach agreement on a resolution, they must negotiate with a view to developing 'mutually acceptable compensation'.[171] If they are unable to agree on compensation, the complaining Party shall notify the other Party that it intends 'to suspend the application to the other Party of benefits of equivalent effect'.[172] If the Party complained against considers that the level of benefits to be suspended is 'manifestly excessive' or that it has eliminated the non-conformity or the nullification or impairment, it may request that the panel be reconvened to consider the matter.[173]

Even after a panel determines the level of benefits it considers to be of equivalent effect, the Party complained against has one more opportunity to avoid the suspension of benefits. A complaining Party may not suspend benefits if, within thirty days after the panel provides its determination, the Party complained against provides written notice to the other Party that it will pay an 'annual monetary assessment'. If the Parties are unable to agree on the amount of the assessment within thirty days, the amount of the assessment shall be set at a level 'equal to 50 per cent of the level of the benefits the panel has determined ... to be of equivalent effect'.[174] There is nothing comparable to this provision in the WTO Understanding on Rules and Procedures Governing the Settlement of Disputes (DSU).

The Parties also agreed to a mechanism that would resolve disputes as to whether the suspension of benefits should continue. Article 20.13 provides that, if the Party complained against considers that it has eliminated the non-conformity or the nullification or impairment that the panel has found, it may refer the matter to the

---

[168] Article 20.8.1(c) and (d).   [169] Articles 20.9, paras. 1–4.   [170] Article 20.10.   [171] Article 20.11.1.
[172] Article 20.11.2.   [173] Article 20.11.3.   [174] Article 20.11.5.

original panel. If the panel agrees with that Party, the complaining Party shall promptly reinstate any benefits it has suspended, and the Party complained against shall no longer be required to pay any monetary assessment. Again, there is nothing quite comparable to this provision in the WTO DSU.

T. Chapter 21: Exceptions

Chapter 21 contains exceptions to the obligations contained in the Agreement. The Parties provide an 'Essential Security' exception that applies to the whole of the Agreement.[175] In addition, Article XX of GATT 1994 applies to the obligations contained in Chapters 2 to 7 (National Treatment and Market Access for Goods, Agriculture, Textiles and Apparel, Rules of Origin, Customs Administration and Technical Barriers to Trade), and Article XIV of GATS applies to the obligations contained in Chapters 11, 13 and 14 (Cross-Border Trade in Services, Telecommunications and Electronic Commerce). Thus, Article XX of the GATT 1994 and Article XIV of GATS do not apply to the obligations in Chapters 9 (Government Procurement), 10 (Investment), 12 (Financial Services), and 15 (Intellectual Property Rights). Those Chapters include their own exceptions, or the commitments are drafted in such a way that an exception is not necessary.[176]

The Agreement also includes a lengthy Article regarding taxation. As a general rule, nothing in the Agreement applies to taxation measures or affects the rights and obligations of either Party under any tax convention. However, the national treatment obligations in the Market Access, Cross-Border Trade in Services, Investment and Financial Services Chapters generally apply to certain taxation measures, as do the performance requirement obligations in the Investment Chapter. The Parties also include a 'tax filter' for investor claims of expropriation: an investor that seeks to invoke the expropriation Article in an investor-State arbitration with respect to a taxation measure must first refer to the 'competent authorities' of the two Parties the issue of whether the measure involves an expropriation. The investor may not submit its claim to arbitration if the competent authorities determine that the measure is not an expropriation.

---

[175] Article 21.2 provides that nothing in the Agreement shall be construed to preclude a Party from applying measures that it considers necessary for the fulfilment of its obligations with respect to the maintenance or restoration of international peace or security or the protection of its own essential security interests. These measures 'may include, *inter alia*', measures relating to the production of or traffic in arms, ammunition and implements of war and to such traffic and transactions in other goods, materials, services and technology undertaken directly or indirectly for the purpose of supplying a military or other security establishment. Thus, the exception appears to be broader than the scope of the security exception in Article XXI of the GATT 1994 and Article XIV*bis* of the GATS.

[176] For example, in the Investment Chapter, the Parties agree not to expropriate property without providing compensation. Even if a Party expropriates property to, for example, conserve an exhaustible natural resource, the Parties intend that Party to compensate the property holder.

Finally, the Parties agree that a measure may be imposed for 'balance of payments purposes' only if that measure is in accordance with the GATT 1994. In adopting such measures, the Party 'shall not impair the relative advantages accorded to the goods of the other Party under this Agreement'.

U. Chapter 22: Final Provisions

Chapter 22 contains the 'final provisions' of the Agreement. Among other things, the Parties agree that any country may accede to the Agreement subject to terms and conditions agreed between such country and the Parties. The Parties also agree that the Agreement will enter into force three months after the Parties certify that they have completed their respective legal procedures and that either Party may terminate the Agreement on 180 days, written notice.

IV. Impact and prospects for future application

A. The economic impact of the agreement

It would be premature to reach any conclusions about how the Agreement – which entered into force on 1 January 2006 – has impacted trade or investment between Morocco and the US. Still, preliminary data on trade in goods suggest the Agreement may be beginning to achieve its objective of stimulating trade between the two countries.[177]

Exports from Morocco to the US grew 6.5 per cent (from US$401 million to US$427 million) in the first ten months of 2006, compared with the same period in 2005[178] (the rate of growth would have doubled if petroleum exports had not declined from US$45 million to US$18 million during this period). During this period, exports of olives and other prepared or preserved vegetables grew from US$17 million to US$27 million; exports of olive oil grew from US$5 million to US$14 million; and exports of semiconductor devices grew from US$40 million to US$48 million.

But the most impressive area of growth in Moroccan exports was in the apparel sector. The US eliminated import quotas on apparel at the beginning of 2005, as required by the WTO Agreement on Textiles and Clothing. Most observers expected that the elimination of quotas would lead to a major increase of market share in the US apparel market for countries with low labour costs, like China, India and Pakistan. By contrast, they expected that countries like Morocco, with relatively higher labour costs, would suffer. The predictions about countries like China have proven accurate, and a number of other apparel exporting countries have suffered.

---

[177] Data on trade in services in 2006 were not available before the publication of this case study.
[178] Data available on US International Trade Commission website: http://dataweb.usitc.gov.

Table 7.2 *Total apparel exports*

	2004	2005	Year-to-Date Through October 2005	Year-to-Date Through October 2006
Total Apparel Exports to US	$74.3 million	$55.9 million	$46.6 million	$81.5 million

But Morocco appears to be an exception. The Agreement may provide at least one of the reasons why Morocco has not lost market share.

In fact, Morocco's exports of apparel *grew* considerably over this period. In particular, exports of women's and girls' apparel (including jackets, blazers, dresses, trousers and skirts) grew from US$16 million to US$27 million in the first ten months of 2006, compared with the same period in 2005. The growth in exports of total apparel items during this period was 75 per cent. But, as Table 7.2 illustrates, what is most impressive is that total apparel exports in the first ten months of 2006 exceeded total apparel exports in 2004, before the US eliminated the import quotas.[179]

Exports from the US to Morocco grew 61.3 per cent (from US$465 million to US$750 million) during this same period. While this rate of growth is remarkable, much of it can be attributed to an increase in aircraft exports, the single largest category of exports, which grew from US$137 million in the first ten months of 2005 to US$223 million during the same period in 2006. But exports of corn also grew considerably, from US$67 million to US$106 million over the same period. Other areas of significant growth include soybeans (from US$45 million to US$50 million), petroleum products (from US$9 million to US$18 million) and data processing machines (from US$6 million to US$14 million).

B. *Potential for future negotiations, deeper integration, and accession*

As part of the Agreement, the Parties established a 'Joint Committee' that will convene at least once each year.[180] Among other things, the Joint Committee is to 'consider ways to further enhance trade relations between the Parties and to promote the objectives of this Agreement, including through cooperation and assistance'. The Joint Committee may also consider and adopt any amendment or other modification to the Agreement. They also agreed to 'consider strategies and policies

---

[179] Data on trade in textiles and apparel are available on the US Department of Commerce website: http://otexa.ita.doc.gov.
[180] Article 19.2.

for developing and promoting new economic activities in [each other's] territory that would contribute to realizing the objectives of this Agreement'.[181]

The Agreement also includes a number of issue-specific provisions that contemplate future negotiations and deeper integration. For example, the Textiles and Apparel Chapter provides that, on the request of either Party, the Parties shall consult to consider accelerating the elimination of customs duties on textile and apparel products, and to consider whether the rules of origin applicable to a particular textile or apparel good should be revised to address issues of availability of supply of fibres, yarns or fabrics in the territories of the Parties.[182]

Finally, the Agreement provides that '[a]ny country or group of countries may accede to this Agreement subject to such terms and conditions as may be agreed between such country or countries and the Parties'.[183] Indeed, given that the Agreement is part of a larger US initiative to create a Middle East Free Trade Area by 2013, accession (or some other mechanism to 'dock' the Agreement to other FTAs) may be more than a theoretical possibility.

C. Potential for disputes between the parties and WTO consistency

While disputes over the interpretation and application of a comprehensive free trade agreement may be inevitable, there are good reasons to doubt that any formal dispute between Morocco and the US will arise in the near future. As explained in Section I above, the Agreement is more of an outgrowth of a close political and diplomatic relationship than a commercially significant one. The same could be said with respect to the FTAs which the US has concluded with other countries in the Middle East, including Israel and Jordan, and no panel has had to resolve any dispute between the parties under either of those two agreements.

More specifically, by the end of 2006, there did not appear to be any areas of serious disagreement between Morocco and the US over the terms of the Agreement. While there may be bumps in the road in the future, especially as deadlines approach for Morocco to implement some of the obligations of the Agreement under negotiated 'transition periods', it is unlikely that the Parties will need to resort to formal dispute settlement to settle any differences.

While the WTO Committee on Regional Trade Agreements had not started even its factual examination of the Agreement as of September 2006, there do not appear to be any provisions in the Agreement that are inconsistent with Article XXIV of the GATT or Article V of the GATS. The Agreement appears to cover 'substantially all trade' in goods between the Parties. As explained above, more than 95 per cent of trade in consumer and industrial products would become tariff free immediately upon entry into force of the Agreement, with all the remaining tariffs on those products targeted for elimination within nine years. In addition, the Agreement

[181] Article 22.4.   [182] Article 4.1.9 and 4.3.3.   [183] Article 22.5.

covers all agricultural products. It provides immediate bilateral tariff elimination on many agricultural products, and the US agreed to phase out all agricultural tariffs within fifteen years.

Moreover, the Agreement does not require either Party to apply import duties or other regulations of commerce 'higher or more restrictive than' the corresponding duties and other regulations of commerce existing prior to the formation of the Agreement.[184] This requirement was the focus of the successful challenge in *Turkey–Textiles*,[185] but it would not appear to create an issue under the Agreement.

On the services side, the Agreement appears to have 'substantial sectoral coverage' and to provide for the absence or elimination of 'substantially all discrimination' between the parties in those sectors. One of the few likely issues regarding the WTO consistency of the Agreement may relate to 'Mode 4': the supply of a service 'by a service supplier of one Member, through presence of natural persons of a Member in the territory of any other Member'.[186] Article V of the GATS provides that the 'substantial sectoral coverage' condition 'is understood in terms of number of sectors, volume of trade affected and modes of supply. In order to meet this condition, agreements should not provide for the *a priori* exclusion of any mode of supply'.[187]

While Mode 4 is a sensitive issue in the US, there does not appear to be any '*a priori* exclusion' of this mode in the Agreement. While concerns have arisen regarding the fact that some US FTAs carve out immigration from the scope of the services commitments,[188] the Agreement apparently does not include an explicit carve-out. And, more importantly, it is not clear that carving out immigration measures is tantamount to carving out all of Mode 4 in its entirety.

---

[184] See GATT, Article XXIV:5(b).   [185] See Appellate Body Report, *Turkey–Textiles*.
[186] See GATS, Article I:2(d).   [187] GATS, Article V:1, note 1.
[188] See, e.g., side letter between the US and the Kingdom of Bahrain, which provides that, in the course of negotiations regarding the services commitments, the parties reached an understanding that '[n]o provision of this Agreement shall be construed as imposing any obligations on a Party regarding its measures concerning immigration (including with respect to visas) or, except as provided in Chapter Fifteen (Labor), the right to secure employment in the territory of a Party'. Letter dated 14 September 2004, available through the USTR website at www.ustr.gov. See also US–Colombia Trade Promotion Agreement (signed 22 November 2006, not yet in force), Article 11.1.7.

8

Association of Southeast Asian Nations–China Free Trade Agreement

JIANGYU WANG

I. Introduction

There have been, arguably, too many regional free trade agreements (hereinafter 'FTAs' or 'RTAs') in Asia.[1] The Association of Southeast Asian Nations (ASEAN)–China Free Trade Agreement (ACFTA), albeit only half-materialized, is certainly one of these many that have caught most of the attention. Starting with a Framework Agreement signed in November 2002, it aims to create, by 2010, the third largest free trade area in the world after the EU and NAFTA. The parties have completed negotiations on trade in goods and services as well as on dispute resolution, and are now working on how to implement the FTA fully and tackle certain sensitive issues. There is already a growing body of literature on the economic and geopolitical dimensions of ACFTA even though discussions on its legal aspects are still in the nascent stage. This chapter is an attempt to explore the various legal issues concerning the ACFTA, including mainly:

(a) the tariff reduction arrangement under ACFTA;
(b) the investment;
(c) the services;
(d) some contentious trade law issues in ACFTA, including rules of origin and contingency protection policies;
(e) dispute settlement under ACFTA; and
(f) the legal nature of ACFTA and its impact on the legal relations concerning the rights and obligations of the parties under ACFTA.

Why are these issues important? The chapter starts with an introduction to the negotiations and conclusion of the relevant ACFTA instruments. It proceeds to address the legal aspects of some essential – and, to some extent, contentious – issues

---

[1] By early 2006, fifteen FTAs had been signed in Asia since 1998, with twenty more being negotiated and at least sixteen proposed. See David Pilling, 'ADB chief hits out at "noodle bowl" trade', *Financial Times* (Asia), 9 February 2006, p. 1.

in the free trade agreement, including the tariff arrangement, rules of origin, and trade remedy measures, followed by an examination of the dispute settlement regime of ACFTA. Based on the examination of the specific institutions of ACFTA, the chapter then begins to discuss the international legal nature of the Agreement with regard to its legal status as an instrument under international law. At first glance, ACFTA appears to be simply a bilateral agreement between China and the Association of Southeast Asian Nations. However, in reality, it is a multi-party agreement concluded by eleven sovereign nations, as ASEAN does not have capacity to act as an independent party. Such construction of this legal instrument will have profound implications on ACFTA's legal status and its dispute settlement mechanism, as well as its future negotiations. Finally, the World Trade Organization (WTO) consistency of ACFTA is analysed. Given that most signatories to ACFTA are WTO members and the rest are striving to join the WTO, it is important for ACFTA to comply with WTO disciplines. From the above analyses and examinations, the chapter draws some policy implications and recommendations with a view to making this free trade agreement mutually beneficial for both China and WTO, and a building block for the multilateral trading system.

II. Background: the emergence of ACFTA

Almost coming as a surprise to his counterparts in the ASEAN countries, Chinese Premier Zhu Rongji proposed at the China–ASEAN Summit of November 2000 to form a 'free trade agreement' between China and ASEAN. A China–ASEAN Experts' Group on Economic Cooperation was established to study the feasibility of the proposed FTA, which issued its report in October 2001, recommending that China and ASEAN should adopt a comprehensive and forward-looking framework for economic cooperation, so as to forge closer economic relations in the twenty-first century. One year later, formal negotiations were launched. In November 2002, Chinese and ASEAN leaders signed the Framework Agreement on Comprehensive Economic Cooperation (hereinafter the Framework Agreement), which lays the groundwork for the eventual formation of a free trade agreement (ACFTA) by the year 2010 for China and the six older members of ASEAN ('ASEAN 6', comprising Brunei Darussalam, Indonesia, Malaysia, the Philippines, Singapore and Thailand), and by 2015 for the newer ASEAN member states (the 'CLMV' countries, comprising Cambodia, Laos, Myanmar and Vietnam).[2] The Framework Agreement was

---

[2] Jiangyu Wang, 'China's Regional Trade Agreements: The Law, Geopolitics, and Impact on the Multilateral Trading System' (2004) 8 *Singapore Year Book of International Law* 119–47 at 124. The text of the Framework Agreement is available at the ASEAN secretariat's official website at www.aseansec.org/13196.htm (last visited 31 March 2006).

amended by a Protocol on 6 October 2003 by the contracting parties at their annual summit in Bali (hereinafter 'the Protocol').[3]

The Framework Agreement establishes only preliminary measures for trade liberalization between China and ASEAN countries as well as agendas for further negotiations. Through it, the eleven countries have committed to strengthen cooperation and to 'progressively liberalise and promote trade in goods and services as well as create a transparent, liberal and facilitative investment regime'.[4] This suggests that the proposed ACFTA will cover trade in goods and services, as well as trade and investment facilitation. Specifically, the contracting parties have undertaken to liberalize trade and investment among them in the following manner:[5]

(a) progressive elimination of tariffs and non-tariff barriers in substantially all trade in goods;
(b) progressive liberalization of trade in services with substantial sectoral coverage;
(c) establishment of an open and competitive investment regime that facilitates and promotes investment within the ASEAN–China FTA;
(d) provision of special and differential treatment and flexibility to the newer ASEAN member states;
(e) provision of flexibility to the Parties in the ASEAN-China FTA negotiations to address their sensitive areas in the goods, services and investment sectors with such flexibility to be negotiated and mutually agreed based on the principle of reciprocity and mutual benefits;
(f) establishment of effective trade and investment facilitation measures, including, but not limited to, simplification of customs procedures and development of mutual recognition arrangements;
(g) expansion of economic cooperation in areas as may be mutually agreed between the Parties that will complement the deepening of trade and investment links between the Parties and formulation of action plans and programmes in order to implement the agreed sectors/areas of cooperation; and
(h) establishment of appropriate mechanisms for the purposes of effective implementation of this Agreement.

The Framework Agreement also establishes an Early Harvest Programme ('EHP') which aims to reach the immediate concessions offered by the parties, mainly China. The EHP will be further discussed in section IIIB.

In the areas of trade in goods and dispute settlement, the negotiations on the modalities for tariff reduction/elimination schedules for goods trade and dispute resolution were concluded in October 2004. On 29 November 2004, at the ASEAN + China summit in Vientiane, two historical agreements to implement the Framework

---

[3] The text of the Protocol is available at the ASEAN secretariat's official website at www.aseansec.org/15157.htm (last visited 31 March 2006).
[4] Framework Agreement, Article 1(b).   [5] Framework Agreement, Article 2.

Agreement were signed by ASEAN and Chinese leaders, namely the Agreement on Trade in Goods of the Framework Agreement on Comprehensive Economic Cooperation (the 'Trade in Goods Agreement' or 'TIG Agreement'),[6] and the Agreement on Dispute Settlement Mechanism of the Framework Agreement on Comprehensive Economic Cooperation (the 'Dispute Settlement Mechanism Agreement' or 'DSM Agreement').[7]

The TIG Agreement represents the important, second, phase of the strategy to form the ACFTA. From July 2005, China and the ASEAN 6 have begun to reduce tariffs of commodities trade. On 20 July 2005, tariffs on more than 7,000 items, accounting for over 90 per cent of all goods traded between China and the ASEAN 6, were slashed to 5 per cent or less.

The DSM Agreement represents another landmark achievement in China–ASEAN bilateral trade relations. It provides, first of all, a formal, institutional design for solving trade and investment disputes between China and an ASEAN member state. The significance of this Agreement lies in its establishment of a rule-based setting for the resolution of economic disputes between the nations concerned, without which the governments are likely to resort to unilateral and retaliatory measures if they feel – sometimes rightly – that the multilateral trading system like the WTO does not provide for efficient and fair dispute settlement methods.

III. Tariff arrangements of ACFTA

A. Tariff reduction and elimination programme

The Framework Agreement and the TIG Agreement set up a 'tariff reduction or elimination programme' for the contracting parties, requiring 'the applied MFN tariff rates on listed tariff lines to be gradually reduced and where applicable, eliminated, in accordance with [Article 3 of the TIG Agreement]'.[8]

Obviously, in conducting liberalization in trade in goods, the eleven contracting parties have adopted a mixed approach which includes both negative listing and positive listing of products. With this, there are two levels of tariff arrangements. One is the normal arrangement which follows the negative listing approach, aiming to slash gradually tariffs on goods, eventually reaching zero tariff rates by 2010 and 2015 respectively. The other is the positive listing based EHP, which has targeted to cut tariffs on agricultural goods ahead of the planned establishment of ACFTA in 2010. The two different arrangements are discussed in the following.

---

[6] The text of the TIG Agreement is available at the ASEAN secretariat's official website at www.aseansec.org/16646.htm (last visited 31 March 2006).
[7] The text of the DSM Agreement is available at the ASEAN secretariat's official website at www.aseansec.org/16635.htm (last visited 31 March 2006).
[8] TIG Agreement, Article 3.

B. Early Harvest Programme (EHP)

The Framework Agreement establishes an Early Harvest Programme which was implemented as of 1 January 2004. The EHP aims to reap the immediate concessions offered by the parties, mainly by China. The EHP allows the reduction of tariffs on certain products before the onset of ACFTA. Initially, it aimed to implement tariff reduction on these products over three years: to 10 per cent before 2004, to 5 per cent before 2005, and to zero tariffs no later than 1 January 2006.[9] A key element of the EHP is that China has also given unilateral concessions to ASEAN members who feel they would not benefit as much from the EHP.[10] This is because, for ASEAN's exports to China, all the products in Chapters 1–8 of the Harmonized System (HS) are covered for preferential tariff rates, while for exports to ASEAN countries, not all of the products in Chapters 1–8 are covered. ASEAN countries are allowed to come up with exclusion lists indicating the items for which they would not grant tariff concessions to Chinese goods. In essence, the EHP 'allows ASEAN products to be exported to China at significant concessionary rates so that ASEAN countries can actually benefit from the benefits of a free trade agreement even before the agreement itself is finalized'.[11] In total, the EHP has targeted a host of some 600 products listed in Chapters 1–8 of the HS, mostly agricultural products which are to be unilaterally liberalized by China.[12] Under the EHP, China has also agreed to grant tariff concessions to dozens of specific manufactured products to ASEAN countries, which are listed in Annex 2, Appendix 3 of the Protocol.[13] In addition, China agrees to grant WTO benefits (mainly most favoured nation (MFN) treatment) to those ASEAN members which are not yet official WTO members.[14]

Initially the Framework Agreement took a multilateral approach to tariff reduction. Namely, that the tariff concessions under the HS approach were to be multilateralized to all parties (i.e. all ASEAN members and China) provided that the same products were included in their EHPs. But, because the Philippines and China failed to establish an EHP scheme, other countries in the region subsequently considered that this would therefore allow the Philippines to 'free ride'. In addition, the fear that some ASEAN countries, such as Thailand, had more efficient farm sectors that could suppress the growth of the agricultural sector in others also deterred ASEAN members from implementing a multilateral approach under the

---

[9] Framework Agreement, Annex 3, Part B. A slightly different schedule is used for the newer ASEAN members.
[10] Framework Agreement, Annex 2.
[11] 'ASEAN, China Launch First Stage of Free-Trade Plan', *AFP*, 7 October 2003.
[12] China, however, has excluded from the EHP some agricultural products such as rice and palm oil, which are said to be major exports from ASEAN countries. These products are to be negotiated in the coming years.
[13] For instance, Singaporean exporters are entitled to enjoy tariff reduction for an additional 75 industrial goods, and Malaysia for 87 industrial goods.
[14] Framework Agreement, Article 9. Currently Vietnam and Laos are not WTO members.

EHP. Malaysia was amongst the first that negotiated a clause in 2003 allowing it to offer lower agriculture tariffs *only* to China in return for the latter's concessions under the EHP.[15] This practice has since been consolidated in the 2003 Protocol, which replaces the original Article 6(3)(b)(i) of the Framework Agreement with a new provision. The new provision recognizes that a party may accelerate its tariff reduction and/or elimination under the EHP to the rest of the parties 'on a unilateral basis'.[16] Meanwhile, one or more ASEAN members are still allowed to conduct negotiations and enter into acceleration arrangements with China to fast-track their tariff reduction or elimination, which will be done, however, only on a 'bilateral or plurilateral' basis. In other words, no conditional or unconditional MFN status is granted under the EHP except to Brunei and Singapore.[17]

C. The normal liberalization arrangement

The TIG Agreement provides a tariff reduction and elimination programme for goods not covered by the EHP. Those tariff lines are categorized into two tracks. According to the tariff liberalization modality for the ASEAN 6 and China, tariff lines placed by each party in the Normal Track on its own accord shall have tariff rates gradually reduced in four phases beginning July 2005 and eventually eliminated by 2010. For Vietnam, Cambodia, Laos and Myanmar, there will be eight phases of tariff reduction, with tariff rates slashed to zero only in 2015. Furthermore, for the ASEAN 6 and China, each party to the TIG Agreement shall reduce tariffs to 0–5 per cent not later than 1 July 2005 for at least 40 per cent of their products placed in the Normal Track by 2005 and 60 per cent by 1 January 2007. In so far as the parties should eliminate all tariffs placed on the Normal Track, extended time frames for tariff elimination up to 2012 will be given to each party for not more than 150 tariff lines. Newer ASEAN Members are given a longer time up to 2018.[18] The launch of the first batch of liberalization was postponed to 20 July 2005, from the original 1 July, because of administrative difficulties including ironing out new tariff structure and procedures cited by the parties.[19]

It is worth noting that the TIG Agreement generally adopts the negative listing approach. In Annex 1 of the TIG Agreement which prescribes the modality for Normal Track tariff concessions, the long list of products might confuse the readers

---

[15] 'Malaysia Early Harvest Clause a Way out for RP', *The Manila Times*, 7 April 2003, available at www.manilatimes.net/national/2003/apr/07/business/20030407bus4.html.
[16] The Protocol, Article 2.
[17] Ibid. Only Brunei and Singapore will, subject to conformity with specified requirements, automatically become parties to any arrangements that have been agreed on or will be agreed to between China and any other ASEAN State under the EHP. See ibid., Annex 2. Singapore has already become a party to the China–Thailand EHP arrangement.
[18] TIG Agreement, Annex 1.
[19] Anna Maria Samsudin, 'China, ASEAN to lower tariffs from July 20', *New Straits Times* (Malaysia), 3 July 2005, p. 21.

by creating the impression that only those items on the list will be liberalized. In fact, those products which are not listed in Annex 1 and Annex 2 (which prescribes the Sensitive Track) are automatically covered, meaning that they are subject to the tariff reduction and elimination modality of the Normal Track. The tariff lines listed by the parties in Annex 1–Appendix 1 of the TIG Agreement are permitted exceptions, indicating that the listed products are to have their tariffs eliminated by 1 January 2012 (instead of 2010) for the ASEAN 6 and China, and by 1 January 2018 (instead of 2015) for the newer ASEAN members (CLMV countries).[20]

The Sensitive Track provides a mechanism for the participating countries to protect a limited amount of traded goods which, according to their own perception, are sensitive for their economies. The number of sensitive tariff lines must not exceed 400 (or 10 per cent of the total import value based on 2001 trade statistics) for the ASEAN 6 and China, and 500 for the CLMV countries.[21] Tariff lines placed by each party in the Sensitive Track are further divided into a Sensitive List (SL) and a Highly Sensitive List (HSL). The ASEAN 6 and China can put no more than 40 per cent of the total goods or 100 tariff lines, whichever is lower, on the HSL. For Vietnam, Cambodia, Laos and Myanmar, the number of tariff lines placed on the HSL can be 150. Tariffs on products on the SL for the ASEAN 6 and China will be reduced to 20 per cent by 2012 and subsequently to 0–5 per cent by 2018. Vietnam, Cambodia, Laos and Myanmar are, however, allowed to reach the 20 per cent level by 2015 and 0–5 per cent by 2020.[22]

D. Assessing the tariff liberalization arrangements in the global context

The modality on tariff reduction and elimination, including the EHP especially, is thus far undoubtedly the jewel in the crown of the ACFTA. The EHP has given ASEAN exporters significant advantage over other WTO members in the trade of agricultural goods with China. In the first half year after the EHP was implemented, ASEAN exports of fruits and vegetables increased by 30 per cent.[23] According to the statistics released by the government of Malaysia, Malaysia's exports to China under the EHP reached RM514 million and RM540 million in 2004 and 2005 respectively. During the same period, it imported only RM14 million from China.[24] Overall, China–ASEAN trade reached US$100 billion in 2004 and US$130 billion in 2005. The average annual growth of bilateral trade has been over 25 per cent in recent years. Having a surplus of US$19.6 billion, ASEAN is one of China's largest suppliers

---

[20] Ibid. See also the explanatory notes of the Singapore government in its official website on FTAs at http://app.fta.gov.sg/asp/faqs/acfta_tradeingoods.asp (last visited 5 April 2006).
[21] TIG Agreement, Annex 2.   [22] Ibid.
[23] Gary Clyde Hufbauer and Yee Wong, 'Prospects for Regional Free Trade in Asia', Working Paper 05–12, Institute for International Economics, Washington, DC (2005), at p. 7, available at www.iie.com.
[24] See information on the website of the Ministry of International Trade and Industry of Malaysia at www.miti.gov.my (last visited 5 April 2006).

of commodities goods.[25] Needless to say, tariff concessions have played a significant role in expanding the trade volume between China and ASEAN.

In the global context, tariff reduction is still an unfinished business. Given the substantial tariff concessions (especially for industrial goods) during the past rounds of multilateral trade talks, an impression could easily be created that tariffs are no longer a major barrier to international trade. But as noted in a WTO discussion paper, 'However, notwithstanding the achievements of the [Uruguay Round] and previous rounds of negotiations, especially the increase in the proportion of tariff lines that are subject to bindings together with negotiated cuts in bound rates, tariffs remain an important obstacle to international trade and consequently a distortion to competition and thus economic development.'[26]

In this context, the WTO-plus tariff reduction in ACFTA is commendable. The modality of tariff reduction and elimination in ACFTA will lead to a tariff-free trade area for most goods by 2012. From the perspective of the multilateral trading system, there remains a concern that this preferential arrangement might erode the scope of application of MFN tariffs of the WTO.[27] There is, however, little evidence that the tariff liberalization under ACFTA has had any trade-diverting effect. Further, as both ASEAN countries and China have benefited tremendously from this liberalization, they are unlikely to be persuaded to stop this liberalization movement on the grounds of protecting the integrity of the MFN principle.

The negative listing approach of ACFTA, whereby all tariff lines are generally reduced and exceptions are spelled out on an annexed list, is preferable as it can bring broader liberalization of trade in goods and deeper integration. In contrast, other regional trade arrangements in Asia, such as the ASEAN–India, Japan–Singapore and some other RTAs, follow a positive listing approach, whereby tariffs are reduced only for those goods stipulated on a list by each contracting party.

IV. Quantitative restrictions and non-tariff trade barriers

Article 8 of the TIG Agreement prohibits the parties from using quantitative restrictions and other non-tariff measures to retard the cross-border free flow of goods. It reads:

1. Each Party undertakes not to maintain any quantitative restrictions at any time unless otherwise permitted under the WTO disciplines.[28]

---

[25] See statistics on the website of the Ministry of Commerce of China at www.mofcom.gov.cn (last visited 5 April 2006).
[26] Rohini Acharya and Michael Daly, 'Selected Issues Concerning the Multilateral Trading System', WTO Discussion Paper No. 7 (2004), at p. 5.
[27] Ibid., at p. 12.
[28] The TIG Agreement requires that non-WTO members of ASEAN shall phase out their quantitative restrictions three years [Vietnam: four years] from the date of entry into force of this Agreement or in accordance with their accession commitments to the WTO, whichever is earlier. See footnote 2 of the TIG Agreement.

2. The Parties shall identify non-tariff barriers (other than quantitative restrictions) for elimination as soon as possible after the entry into force of this Agreement. The time frame for elimination of these non-tariff barriers shall be mutually agreed upon by all Parties.
3. The Parties shall make information on their respective quantitative restrictions available and accessible upon implementation of this Agreement.

In so far as quantitative restrictions are concerned, this provision is similar to Article XI of the General Agreement on Tariffs and Trade (GATT), paragraph 1 of which stipulates:

> No prohibitions or restrictions other than duties, taxes or other charges, whether made effective through quotas, import or export licences or other measures, shall be instituted or maintained by any contracting party on the importation of any product of the territory of any other contracting party or on the exportation or sale for export of any product destined for the territory of any other contracting party.

Given that most of the contracting parties to ACFTA are WTO members, and the rest are likely to join the WTO soon, it is a curious question as to why such a special provision is made in the ACFTA. A possible explanation is that the extra obligation of non-maintenance of quota measures and the elimination of non-tariff barriers undertaken by ACFTA signatories in addition to their similar WTO commitments can provide a second safety net for them. The trade regulatory regimes of most parties to ACFTA are still plagued by non-transparency and administrative arbitrariness, which are likely to cause trade frictions between China and the individual ASEAN countries. Under ACFTA, such a dispute can be settled – probably more efficiently and amicably – under the DSM Agreement.

V. The rules of origin issue

Rules of origin (ROO), understood as the criteria used to define where a product was made, have become a key source of problems in the RTAs. ROO exist because there is considerable differentiation of treatment of imports of different origins. Currently under the WTO there are no established ROO to govern trade between WTO members. In the world of RTAs, ROO can be a potential trade barrier because each RTA has its own ROO regime. This phenomenon has led to the so-called 'spaghetti bowl' phenomenon, a term first coined by economist Jagdish Bhagwati in the 1990s, which indicates the complex trade barriers caused by protection-accommodating ROO.[29] For example, as reported in a Singapore newspaper, a United Nations study has concluded that there are few possible negative consequences from Singapore's bilateral trade agreements, one of them being the 'spaghetti bowl effect'. As the report notes, this opens the door for bilateral trade frictions: 'Apart from higher costs of administering multiple agreements, it makes Singapore more vulnerable to trade disputes based on rules-of-origin violations, given the entrepot nature of Singapore's foreign trade structure.'[30]

Annex 3 of the TIG Agreement prescribes the ROO for ACFTA. Under Annex 3, products which are wholly obtained or produced in the exporting country shall be, of course, deemed to be originating and eligible for preferential concessions. If a product is not wholly produced or obtained in the exporting country, a 40 per cent value-added rule applies. From the ASEAN perspective, this means that the ASEAN content is at least 40 per cent either on the 'Single Country Content' test or the 'Cumulative Content' test.

The TIG Agreement also endorses the universally recognized 'substantial transformation rule'. Rule 6 of Annex 3 stipulates 'product specific criteria', pursuant to which the parties are to negotiate a list of products which, if recorded in Attachment B to Annex 3, will be considered as 'goods to which sufficient transformation has been carried out in a Party'. Currently, the list includes 424 items of textile and textiles products, 2 items of preserved fish, 6 items of wool, 22 items of leather goods, 14 items of firkins and 4 items of footwear.

A survey of several RTAs in Asia demonstrates that the 'spaghetti bowl' effect is apparent. For example, under the Singapore–Australia Free Trade Agreement,[31] the general rule of a specified threshold of local value content is either 30 per cent or 50 per cent. According to the Japan–Singapore Economic Partnership Agreement,[32] each product has one corresponding specific rule of origin, although a significant portion of the rules require 60 per cent of local content. Such a world of complex clauses governing ROO, as criticized by the President of the Asian Development Bank, 'could create a bureaucratic tangle that might put individual companies off trading together'.[33]

VI. The Services Agreement under ACFTA

On 14 January 2007, China and the ten ASEAN countries signed the historical Agreement on Trade in Services of the Framework Agreement on Comprehensive Economic Cooperation (hereinafter the TIS Agreement) in Cebu, the Philippines,

---

[29] Jagdish Bhagwati and Arvind Panagariya, 'Preferential Trading Areas and Multilateralism – Strangers, Friends, or Foes?' in Jagdish Bhagwati, Pravin Krishna and Arvind Panagariya (eds.), *Trading Blocs: Alternative Approaches to Analyzing Preferential Trade Agreements* (Cambridge, MA: The MIT Press, 1999), Chapter 2 at p. 77.
[30] Daniel Buenas, 'Downside of FTAs Highlighted', *The Business Times*, 31 March 2006, p. 12.
[31] Signed 17 February 2003, in force 28 July 2003.   [32] Signed 13 January 2002, in force 30 November 2002.
[33] Pilling, above note 1.

which entered into force on 1 July 2007. The TIG aims to be a WTO-plus agreement on services by providing preferential market access for Chinese and ASEAN services suppliers in each other's market and establishing an institutional framework for China–ASEAN services trade. This is also China's first services trade agreement with its trading partners. Seen from the content of the liberalization, it is an agreement with shallow integration.

A. Positive-listing and WTO-plus market access

The preamble of the TIS Agreement states that a goal of the Agreement is to 'expand the depth and scope of [trade in services] with substantial sectoral coverage beyond those undertaken by China and the ASEAN Member Countries under the [WTO's] General Agreement on Trade in Services'. In this spirit, China and ASEAN have made substantial WTO-plus liberalization commitments under the TIS Agreement.

The TIS Agreement follows the positive-listing approach of GATS, under which a party liberalizes only those sectors or subsectors listed in its TIS schedule, subject to all the terms, limitations and conditions agreed and specified in the schedule.[34]

On China's part, China offers to ASEAN services suppliers market access commitments additional to its general commitments under GATS in five sectors including business services; construction and related services; environmental services; recreational, cultural and sporting services; and transport services, covering twenty-six subsectors. For example, China would allow ASEAN services suppliers to establish joint ventures with foreign majority ownership or even wholly foreign-owned enterprises (WFOE) in environmental services relating to sewage, solid waste disposal, cleaning of exhaust gases, noise abatement, nature and landscape protection and sanitation. WFOE are also permitted for road transport services and maintenance and repair services of motor vehicles. None of these has been committed by China at the multilateral front.

China also receives WTO-plus concessions from each ASEAN member individually which, aggregately, cover sixty-seven subsectors in twelve sectors. For example, several ASEAN nations permit Chinese nationals to establish joint ventures to offer restaurant and hotel services. Singapore and Brunei both open the international maritime transport services (freight and passengers) to Chinese services providers.

B. Non-discrimination

The TIS Agreement's National Treatment provision simply copies that of GATS. Namely, within the boundary of its commitments, each party to the TIS Agreement is required to grant national treatment to services and services suppliers of any

---

[34] The TIS Agreement, Article 18, para. 1.

other party in respect of all measures regarding the supply of services. The Agreement however does not include a most favoured nation (MFN) principle, nor does it incorporate the MFN clause of GATS Article II. That is, unlike the North American Free Trade Agreement (NAFTA) or some other FTAs (such as the US–Singapore Free Trade Agreement), the parties to the TIS Agreement are not required to grant ACFTA parties the same preferential treatments they give to non-parties.

C. Development dimension

The TIS Agreement recognizes the need to give special and differential treatment and flexibility for newer – and less developed – ASEAN countries, including Cambodia, Laos, Myanmar and Vietnam. They are permitted to grant fewer concessions. Further, Article 17 of the Agreement attempts to lay down a general policy for increasing participation of the CLMV countries, which reads:

> The increasing participation of Cambodia, Lao PDR, Myanmar and Viet Nam in this Agreement shall be facilitated through negotiated specific commitments, relating to:
>
> (a) the strengthening of their domestic services capacity and its efficiency and competitiveness, inter alia through access to technology on a commercial basis;
> (b) the improvement of their access to distribution channels and information networks;
> (c) the liberalization of market access in sectors and modes of supply of export interest to them; and
> (d) appropriate flexibility for Cambodia, Lao PDR, Myanmar, and Viet Nam for opening fewer sectors, liberalizing fewer types of transactions and progressively extending market access in line with their respective development situation.

D. Progressive liberalization

At the signing of the TIS Agreement, the parties were able to furnish the first package of specific commitments which were annexed to the Agreement. The Agreement requires the parties, 'with the aim of substantially improving the first package of specific commitments, [to] conclude the second package of specific commitments within a year from the date of entry into force of this Agreement'.[35] Further, the ASEAN Economic Ministers and the Chinese Minister of Commerce (or their designated representatives) are mandated to meet within a year from the date of entry into force of the Agreement and then to review the Agreement for the purpose

---

[35] Ibid., Article 23.

of considering further measures to liberalize trade in services as well as to develop disciplines and negotiate agreements on relevant services trade matters.[36] On this basis, the parties shall enter into further rounds to negotiations to offer more packages of specific commitments.

E. Modification of schedules

A very interesting part of the TIS Agreement is that it permits a party to modify or withdraw any commitment in its schedule, at any time after three years from the date on which that commitment becomes effective, provided that it gives a three-month notification to all the other parties as well as the ASEAN secretariat and that it enters into negotiations with any affected party to agree to the necessary compensation adjustment. If a compensation agreement cannot be reached, the concerned parties shall resolve the matter pursuant to the Agreement on Dispute Settlement Mechanism discussed in section VIII below.

VII. Contingency protection

A. The use of contingency measures under ACFTA

Contingency measures in the area of foreign trade law refer to regulatory rules used by governments to restrict imports of foreign goods, such as anti-dumping duties, countervailing duties or safeguard measures. In the trade of goods, anti-dumping can be applied when dumping, defined as a private commercial activity 'by which products of one country are introduced into the commerce of another country at less than the normal value of the products', occurs and causes or threatens material injury to an established industry of the importing country or materially retards the establishment of a domestic industry.[37] Anti-subsidies or countervailing duties may be applied against exports that have benefited from a subsidy granted by the government of the exporting country that is injurious to a domestic industry of the importing country.[38] Safeguards are temporary emergency measures permitted to counter a sudden surge of imports that cause or threaten serious injury to a domestic industry.

It is unfortunate that ACFTA still retains these trade remedy measures, given the strong body of economic theory and evidence suggesting that there is no economic justification for maintaining trade restrictions through contingency policies and safeguards.[39] While ACFTA does not have special rules regarding anti-dumping

---

[36] Ibid. [37] GATT, Article VI:1.
[38] WTO Agreement on Subsidies and Countervailing Duties.
[39] Michael J. Trebilcock and Thomas M. Boddez, 'The Case for Liberalizing North American Trade Remedy Laws' (1995) 4(1) *Minnesota Journal of Global Trade* 1–41.

and countervailing duties, relying instead on existing WTO disciplines,[40] it does however have a relatively lengthy clause on safeguard measures.[41]

ACFTA has borrowed the basic logic of safeguards from the WTO disciplines. According to Article 9.3 of the TIG Agreement, safeguard measures can be applied by a party under the following conditions:

- If, as an effect of the obligation incurred by that Party, including tariff concessions under the EHP, or as a result of unforeseen developments and of the effects of the obligations incurred by that Party, including tariff concessions under the EHP,
- imports of any particular product from the other Parties increase in such quantities, absolute or relative to domestic production,
- and under such conditions so as to cause or threaten to cause serious injury to the domestic industry of the importing Party that produces like or directly competitive products.

Apparently, Article 9.3 of the TIG Agreement combines the rules on the conditions for initiating safeguard measures contained in Article XIX of GATT and Article 2 of the Agreement on Safeguards. However, the safeguard disciplines under ACFTA are remarkably less restrictive than the corresponding rules in the WTO Agreements in respect of the application and duration of safeguard measures.

First, an ACFTA safeguard measure can only be initiated on a product within the 'transition period' of that product. Under ACFTA, 'the transition period for a product shall begin from the date of entry into force of [the TIG Agreement] and end five years from the date of completion of tariff elimination/reduction for that product'.[42] After the five years have elapsed, trade in the liberalized goods can no longer be subject to investigation and the imposition of safeguard measures. On the other hand, under the WTO rules, safeguard measures can be initiated and applied at any time. Clearly, while the WTO only disciplines safeguard measures, ACFTA aims at eliminating this form of protection completely after a short transition period.

Second, the use of quantitative restrictions in ACFTA is prohibited. Under the WTO, the importing nation can use tariff measures or quantitative restrictions such as quotas. If a quantitative restriction is used, the level of quota applied is not to be lower than the actual import level of the most recent three representative years, unless there is clear justification for setting a different lower level.[43] The TIG Agreement, in contrast, does not allow the contracting parties to use quantitative restriction measures set out in Article 5 of the WTO Agreement on Safeguards.[44]

---

[40] Article 7 of the TIG Agreement provides that, 'the parties hereby agree and reaffirm their commitments to abide by the provisions of the WTO disciplines on, among others ... subsidies and countervailing measures, anti-dumping measures ...'. It further states that 'the provisions of the WTO Multilateral Agreements on Trade in Goods, which are not specifically mentioned in or modified by this Agreement, shall apply, *mutatis mutandis*, to this Agreement unless the context otherwise requires'.
[41] TIG Agreement, Article 8.   [42] Ibid., Article 9.2.   [43] WTO Safeguards Agreement, Article 5.
[44] TIG Agreement, Article 9.6.

Third, not only are tariff measures the only form of safeguard protection under ACFTA, but there is furthermore a maximum limit on the level to which a tariff can be increased. Namely, the tariff can only be increased from the ACFTA preferential tariff rate to the importing country's WTO MFN tariff rate applicable to the product. So, even in the worst case scenario, the exporting country is still guaranteed treatment as a WTO partner of the importing country.

Fourth, the duration of any applied safeguard measure is considerably shorter under ACFTA than under the WTO rules. Under the WTO rules, the duration of any safeguard measure is four years, unless it is extended according to the Safeguards Agreement provisions. However, the initial period of application and any extension cannot exceed eight years.[45] The ACFTA, on the other hand, shortens the duration of safeguard measures quite substantially. Under paragraph 5 of Article 9 of the TIG Agreement, 'Any ACFTA safeguard measure may be maintained for an initial period of up to 3 years and may be extended for a period not exceeding 1 year.' Further, 'Notwithstanding the duration of an ACFTA safeguard measure on a product, such measure shall terminate at the end of the transition period for that product.' Put simply, within the transition period, the total period allowed under ACFTA is four years, which is only half of the maximum period allowed by the WTO rules.

In terms of the duration and extension of safeguard measures, ACFTA excludes the application of Article 9 of the WTO Safeguards Agreement, which prescribes special treatment for developing members. Although, literally speaking, all signatories to ACFTA are developing countries, they have undertaken not to invoke the more flexible rules reserved for them under the WTO when initiating an ACFTA safeguard measure. More specifically, they would lose the privilege to apply a safeguard measure again to an import which has previously been subject to such a measure.[46]

B. Substituting safeguard actions for anti-dumping and countervailing measures?

It is lamentable that ACFTA still retains the use of contingency policies. As previously noted, there is little evidence that justifies the economic efficiency of trade remedy measures. Take anti-dumping as an example. Anti-dumping is purported to defend against 'predatory pricing', which refers to the practice of a foreign company using temporary low prices to drive its competitors out of a market, after which it will then raise its prices.[47] As pointed out by Trebilcock and Boddez, '[t]here are strong theoretical reasons and empirical evidence suggesting that predatory pricing, and in particular, international predation, will be a very improbable occurrence. In any market and particularly international markets, sustainable market power

---

[45] WTO Safeguards Agreement, Articles 7.1 and 7.2.   [46] Ibid., Article 9.2.
[47] Trebilcock and Boddez, above note 39, at pp. 13–14; and N. Gregory Mankiw and Phillip L. Swagel, 'Antidumping: The Third Rail of Trade Policy' (2005, December) *Foreign Affairs* – WTO Special Edition.

is extremely difficult to achieve through predatory pricing'.[48] In the increasingly globalized and connected world markets, the predator, in order to achieve its objective, must eliminate not only domestic competition in the domestic market, but also worldwide competition as well. Eventually, the predator must raise the prices to a supra-competitive level in order to recoup its loss as a result of dumping, but doing so also then invites both domestic and foreign entrants into the domestic market. It is unlikely that the predator can sustain these seemingly endless rounds of competition.

Apart from the 'predatory pricing' argument, another justification of anti-dumping actions is the prevention of market destabilization caused by transitory or intermittent dumping. In this situation, 'foreign exporters sell in the domestic market at low prices in order to maintain capacity utilization and a high home market price during a period of low demand in the home market. By doing so, the exporters may successfully avoid the costs of temporary adjustment in plant utilization and maintain current employment levels.'[49] Trebilcock and Boddez note that an anti-dumping duty, however, can only make domestic inefficient production economically viable.[50] It is observed that:

> In summary, there are no economic justifications for ADD law. In reality, what is called dumping in the international context is usually healthy competition, generally welcomed in the domestic context. Foreign firms with legitimate comparative advantage are branded unfair traders for performing in a manner which would be commendable had they been domestic producers.[51]

In reality, anti-dumping has become a pure tool for protectionist purposes. Mankiw and Swagel remark that, although the ostensible purpose of anti-dumping law is to help ensure competition, '[i]n practice, however, anti-dumping has strayed far from this purpose, becoming little more than an excuse for special interests to shield themselves from competition at the expense of both American consumers and other American companies'.[52] The situation in other countries is no better.

As for countervailing or anti-subsidies duties, it is, first of all, still very difficult to evaluate whether subsidies contribute to or derogate from efficient resource allocation. A study shows that the evaluation exercise is highly indeterminate because of three factors: (1) the pervasiveness of externalities which subsidies may help internalize; (2) potential private–public intersectoral economies; and (c) the possibility that the subsidization of a firm by government is used to offset some burden that has been imposed by the government.[53]

But even assuming that subsides distort international trade, it is questionable that imposing laws regarding countervailing duties is the appropriate policy instrument

---

[48] Trebilcock and Boddez, above note 39, at p. 14.   [49] Ibid., at p. 16.   [50] Ibid.
[51] Ibid., at p. 17.   [52] Mankiw and Swagel, above note 47.
[53] Michael J. Trebilcock and Robert Howse, *Regulation of International Trade* (London: Routledge, 2005), p. 282.

to reduce the distortions. Trebilcock and Howse observe it as unlikely that anti-subsidies action can improve resource allocation:

> [I]t has now been convincingly demonstrated that in almost every conceivable set of circumstances, countervailing duties reduce domestic social welfare in the importing country, where social welfare is defined as the maximization of producer, consumer and government surplus. Gains to domestic producers from the higher prices induced by the duties are offset by losses to consumers who remain in the market and pay the higher prices, while some consumers who would have purchased the product are priced out of the market and suffer deadweight welfare losses. Even accounting for the increase in government surplus in terms of increased revenue from duties, consumer losses outweigh all gains, leaving total welfare lower. Thus, however ambiguous the welfare effects of a subsidy either in the country providing it or globally, there is nothing ambiguous about the welfare effects of the subsidy in the importing country. This analysis suggests that rather than condemning foreign subsidies, importing countries should send expressions of gratitude to the subsidizing country, noting only their regret that the subsidies are not larger and timeless.[54]

It is important to note that, apart from economic justifications, there are other justifications which are probably sufficient to support the maintenance of some form of trade remedy measures at this stage of international trade. One powerful argument is that trade remedy measures can lead to a higher quantum of market access at any given point in time than would be the case without them.[55] The logic behind this is that governments 'may be willing to go further in opening markets if they know they are protected against unforeseen circumstances'.[56] This 'buying votes' approach, as so termed by John Jackson, can pragmatically address a few concerns, including, inter alia, allocating the market adjustment costs, providing a safety valve for protectionist pressures and giving a sense of security for those sceptical of free trade. In the end, having such an 'escape' can help earn domestic support for trade liberalization.[57]

Given both the domestic and international political economy of foreign trade, it is not realistic to eliminate trade remedy measures entirely from the regional trade agreements of Asia, although they are more trade-distorting than the actions against which they are set up. However, it is highly advisable that, if some form of contingency protection must remain, it would be a much better idea, from both domestic and regional perspectives, to keep only the safeguard measures and abandon the use of anti-dumping and countervailing measures.

There are several strong advantages for substituting safeguard measures for anti-dumping and anti-subsidies measures. First, safeguard actions are much more

---

[54] Ibid., at p. 283.
[55] WTO, *World Trade Report 2003* (Geneva: WTO Publications, 2003), p. 179. [56] Ibid.
[57] Ibid. See also John H. Jackson, *The World Trading System*, (2nd edn, Cambridge, MA: The MIT Press, 1997), p. 176.

flexible. The foreign trade authority of the importing country can tailor a contingency protection package to match individual situations, ideally by balancing the major different needs (including the overall national welfare and the need for efficient allocation of resources) of the economy. Second, the domestic producers petitioning for safeguard protection must put together a plan to revive and increase their competitiveness. As such, pressure is placed on the domestic industry to run efficiently, which is the original objective of the trade remedy policies.[58] Third, a safeguard measure is less protectionist because its duration lasts, even under the WTO, no more than eight years. The maximum period of a safeguard action taken under the ACFTA is four years. This stands in huge contrast to anti-dumping and countervailing duties which may be imposed and extended indefinitely. Finally, safeguard actions, while indeed manifest protection measures, are at least neither 'hypocritical' nor predicated on any notion of 'unfair trade', but rather on an economic and political choice. In the words of Barfield, 'increased use of safeguard actions would reduce the inflammatory and often-spurious comparisons made between fair and unfair trade practices'.[59]

VIII. Dispute settlement under ACFTA

A. Overview of the dispute settlement procedures under ACFTA

As an international treaty, ACFTA is a legal system of rights and obligations for the contracting parties. The enforcement of a trade agreement, which translates provisions on paper into economically meaningful results, lies in the implementation of the obligations and resolution of disputes arising from the implementation.

The Dispute Settlement Mechanism Agreement under ACFTA is a landmark document in China's economic relations with ASEAN countries. The ACFTA dispute settlement procedures comprise three stages. First, Article 4 of the DSM Agreement provides a mechanism for consultations. A party complained against is required to 'accord due consideration and adequate opportunity' for consultations requested by a complaining party with respect to any matter concerning the implementation or application of the ACFTA. Paragraphs 2 and 4 emphasize the importance of full exchange of information. The complaint should include not only the specific measures at issue, but also the factual and legal basis. The parties are required to 'provide sufficient information to enable a full examination of how the measure might affect the operation' of ACFTA, as well as keep confidential the information exchanged during the consultations which have been designated as confidential.[60] Paragraph 3 mandates prompt response to any request for

---

[58] Claude E. Barfield, 'Anti-dumping Reform: Time to Go Back to Basics' (2005) 28(5) *The World Economy* 719–37 at 731.
[59] Ibid., at 731.
[60] DSM Agreement, Article 4.4(a) and 4.4(b).

consultations: the respondent is to reply to the request within seven days and enter into good faith consultations within a period of not more than thirty days after the date of receiving the request, otherwise the complaining party is entitled to proceed directly to request the appointment of an arbitral tribunal.[61] In cases of urgency, the parties shall enter into consultations within ten days.[62]

Another stage of dispute resolution under ACFTA is conciliation or mediation. This, however, is not a stage following consultations, as the parties to a dispute may at any time agree to commence conciliation or mediation, and may continue conciliation or mediation even during the arbitration proceedings of the case.[63]

The formal and last stage is arbitration, used if the parties cannot settle a dispute within sixty days after the date of request for consultations or within twenty days in cases of urgency. An arbitral tribunal, composed of three arbitrators, shall be established to solve a dispute.[64] Each of the two parties concerned shall, respectively, appoint one arbitrator. The two shall then endeavour to agree on an additional arbitrator who shall serve as chair. If they are unable to reach such an agreement, they should request the Director-General of the WTO to appoint a chair. In the event that one of the parties to the dispute is a non-WTO member, the President of the International Court of Justice shall be entrusted with such a task.

Unlike the North American Free Trade Agreement[65] (NAFTA), ACFTA does not provide for a roster of arbitrators. The requirements on the qualifications of the arbitrators include that they shall have expertise or experience in law, international trade, other matters covered by ACFTA, or resolution of disputes arising under (other) international trade agreements. In addition, the chair must not be a national of any party nor have his or her usual place of residence in the territory of, nor may be employed by, any party to a dispute.[66]

The terms of reference of the arbitral tribunal are specified in Article 8, paragraph 2, as: 'To examine, in the light of the relevant provisions in the Framework Agreement, the matter referred to this arbitral tribunal by (name of party) . . . and to make finding, determinations and recommendations provided for in the Framework Agreement'. With this, the tribunal is granted the power to recommend that the party complained against is to bring measures inconsistent with ACFTA into conformity with provisions of the Agreement.[67]

After deliberations on the case, the arbitral tribunal shall draft its report on the case, which is of course its judgment. A draft report should be released to the parties concerned for them to comment. The final report should be released to the parties to the dispute by the arbitral tribunal within 120 days from the date of its composition. In cases of urgency, the report should be released within sixty days. Although the

---

[61] Ibid., Article 4.3. [62] Ibid., Article 4.7.
[63] Ibid., Article 5. [64] Ibid., Article 7. [65] Signed 17 December 1992, in force 1 January 1994.
[66] ACFTA, Article 7.6. [67] Ibid., Article 8.1.

deadlines can be extended, in no case should the period from the composition of an arbitral tribunal to the release of the final report exceed 180 days.[68]

The litmus test of the efficacy of any trade dispute resolution system is, of course, the implementation and enforcement of the decisions of the tribunal. Under ACFTA, if it is impractical to comply immediately with the recommendations and rulings of the arbitral tribunal, the respondent shall be accorded a reasonable period of time to adjust its policies. The reasonable period of time should be mutually determined by the parties to the dispute, otherwise they should refer the matter to the original arbitration tribunal.[69]

If the recommendations and rulings of the tribunal are eventually not implemented within a reasonable period of time, the proceedings on compensation and suspension of concessions or benefits will be triggered. If the responding party fails to bring illegal measures into compliance with the recommendations of the arbitral tribunal, it shall enter into negotiations with the complaining party with a view to concluding a mutually satisfactory agreement on any compensatory adjustment. Absent such an agreement, which should be reached within twenty days after receiving the request for negotiation, the complaining party may request the original arbitral tribunal to determine the appropriate level of any suspension of concessions or benefits conferred on the responding party. Although it is required by the DSM Agreement that the complaining party should first seek to suspend concessions or benefits in the same sector or sectors affected by the illegal measures of the responding party, cross-sector retaliation is allowed under the Agreement. Namely, 'the complaining party may suspend concessions or benefits in other sectors if it considers that it is not practicable or effective to suspend concessions or benefits in the same sector'.[70]

B. Relationship to other dispute settlement mechanisms

A trade dispute arising under ACFTA is also likely to be covered by the WTO Agreements including the GATT, given that most signatories of ACFTA are WTO members, and by the ASEAN Free Trade Agreement (AFTA), to which only China is not a party. With the signing of ACFTA, none of the contracting parties renounced their rights under the WTO and/or AFTA, both of which have their own dispute settlement procedures. Obviously, uncertainty will arise if the parties to a dispute cannot reach agreement as to which forum to select for resolving the dispute between them.

The DSM Agreement under ACFTA does not exclude the right of the parties to have recourse to dispute resolution mechanisms of any other treaty to which they are parties.[71] It, however, has a 'rule of exclusion'. Presumably in order to avoid

---

[68] DSM Agreement, Article 9.8. [69] Ibid., Article 12.2. [70] Ibid., Article 13.
[71] Ibid., Article 2.5.

parallel proceedings, and above all, contradictory decisions, the DSM Agreement mandates that, once dispute settlement proceedings have been initiated under ACFTA or any other treaty to which the parties concerned are signatories, the forum chosen by the complaining party shall be used to the exclusion of any other for such a dispute.[72]

Interestingly, the DSM Agreement does not have a 'single forum' requirement. Article 2, paragraph 7, of the Agreement implies that the parties to a dispute may expressly agree to the use of more than one dispute settlement forum in respect of a particular dispute. In contrast, under Chapter 20 of NAFTA, the parties should choose one forum to solve the dispute between them, be it the WTO or NAFTA.[73] Allowing the parties to choose multiple fora may lead to a great deal of uncertainty, especially when the different tribunals render contradictory rulings regarding one dispute.

Apart from the institutional aspect of the relationship to the WTO, it is more than likely that an ACFTA tribunal might have to borrow extensively from the jurisprudence of GATT/WTO dispute settlement. This is because, first of all, with respect to dispute in international trade, the GATT/WTO has the richest body of jurisprudence. The norms, principles and methods established by the dispute settlement system through the course of its over fifty-year history, including even the reasoning and analytical approaches, can be applied, in many instances, to a dispute arising under ACFTA.

C. Implication of the DSM Agreement

Jackson observes that there are two techniques of modern diplomacy in trade relations:

> In broad perspective one can roughly divide the various techniques for the peaceful settlement of international disputes into two types: settlement by negotiation and agreement with reference (explicitly or implicitly) to relative power status of the parties, or settlement by negotiation or decision with reference to norms or rules to which both parties have previously agreed.[74]

Although all diplomacy is featured with a mixture of these two types of techniques, it can be argued that, to a large degree, 'the history of civilization may be described as a gradual evolution from a power-oriented approach, in the state of nature, towards a rule-oriented approach'.[75] Jackson further notes that, in addition to the generally perceived advantages of the rule-oriented approach, including 'less reliance on power, and the temptation to exercise it or flex one's muscles, which gets out of hand', 'a fairer break for the smaller countries, or at least a perception of

---

[72] Ibid., Article 2.6.   [73] NAFTA, Chapter 20, Article 2005.
[74] Jackson, above note 57, at p. 109.   [75] Ibid., at p. 110.

greater fairness', and 'the development of agreed procedures to achieve the necessary compromise', there are special reasons for relying more on this approach in economic affairs.[76] As the world becomes more economically interdependent, private citizens, realizing that their welfare is tremendously affected by government policies, would assert for participation and representation in the processes of international economic policy. Jackson remarks:

> This makes international negotiations and bargaining increasingly difficult. However, if citizens are going to make their demands heard and influential, a 'power-oriented' negotiating process (often requiring secrecy, and executive discretion so as to be able to formulate and implement the necessary compromises) becomes more difficult, if not impossible. Consequently, the only appropriate way to turn seems to be toward a rule-oriented system, whereby the various citizens, parliaments, executives and international organizations will all have their inputs, arriving tortuously to a rule – which, however, when established will enable business and other decentralized decision makers to rely upon the stability and predictability of governmental activity in relation to the rule.[77]

Traditional Chinese perception of world order in East Asia, which was the 'cultural jurisdiction' of the Chinese concept of '*Tianxia*', was based on Sinocentrism and cultural supremacy.[78] With the military, economic and cultural invasion of Western powers in the second half of the nineteenth century, the concepts of nation-state and national sovereignty took root in China. The People's Republic of China, since its establishment in 1949, has been extremely sensitive about its sovereignty. In the settlement of bilateral disputes, China, preferring informal over formal mechanisms, has been very cautious of utilizing international arbitration or judicial institutions. For instance, China has never agreed to the jurisdiction of the International Court of Justice. As for arbitration, China was vigorously against any type of arbitration before the mid-1980s.[79]

The significance of ACFTA lies in the fact that it is China's first foreign trade agreement in which it agrees to resolve bilateral and regional trade disputes through formal mechanisms. This represents a shift toward a rule-oriented approach (or legalism), from the assertion of absolute sovereignty and, to some extent, Sinocentrism in China's foreign trade relations.

Smith observes that bilateral dispute settlement mechanisms present institutional options as a standard set that ranges from direct negotiation on one extreme to

---

[76] Ibid., at p. 111. [77] Ibid.
[78] Zhaojie (James) Li, 'Traditional Chinese World Order' (2002) 1(1) *Chinese Journal of International Law* 20–58 at 25.
[79] In contrast, China is now a very active participant in international arbitration and is the host to one of the largest arbitration centres in the world, China International Economic and Trade Arbitration Commission (CIETAC).

third-party adjudication on the other.[80] Specifically, the level of legalism is determined by several features. The first is the existence of an explicit right to third-party review of complaints regarding the implementation of treaty obligations. Many trade agreements provide only for consultations and perhaps mediation or conciliation. The second issue is the legally binding effect under international law of the rulings that result from the dispute settlement process. Although many agreements impose an international law obligation on the disputants to comply with rulings, such as panel reports or arbitral awards, others provide that the rulings have legal effect only after they have been officially adopted, 'and perhaps substantially revised, by political representatives of the member governments acting through one of the pact's governing institutions'.[81] The third issue is about how the panel or arbitral tribunal is composed. In particular, in the event that the parties to the dispute cannot agree on the composition of the tribunal, whether a third, impartial party can be designated to appoint the remaining members. In the most legalist way, a standing tribunal of justices is established to rule collectively on disputes during extended terms of service. The next question concerns the standing of the parties to file complaints and obtain rulings. Most trade agreements allow only member states to initiate disputes, but many others grant *locus standi* to treaty organizations (such as a secretariat or commission), or even private individuals or firms, to file complaints. Finally, what remedies are available in case of treaty violation is also a factor affecting the level of legalism. Ideally, a legalist solution entails a direct enforcement effect of the rulings in domestic law, such as that of the judgment of the European Court of Justice. In most trade pacts, a less legalistic solution is adopted, in which permission is given to the complaining parties to impose sanctions or take retaliatory measures against the responding party.

Measured against the above measures, it is fair to characterize ACFTA as a trade agreement which has reached a certain degree – probably only a low level – of legalism. ACFTA provides independent third-party review of complaints. The members of the tribunal, if not agreed by the disputants, can be appointed by an independent third-party which is the Director-General of the WTO in the case of ACFTA. It, however, does not have a standing body for dispute resolution. There is no permanent secretariat or central commission for ACFTA, and private individuals and enterprises are not allowed to file complaints. Further, in case of treaty violation, in the most radical scenario, ACFTA allows for retaliatory sanctions, but does not grant domestic enforcement effect to rulings made by the dispute settlement process.

---

[80] James McCall Smith, 'The Politics of Dispute Settlement Design: Explaining Legalism in Regional Trade Pacts' (2000) 54(1) *International Organization* 137–80 at 139–42.
[81] Ibid., at p. 140.

IX. The legal nature of ACFTA

A. ACFTA as an international treaty

If signed, ACFTA will be a treaty as a matter of international law. Article 2 of the Vienna Convention on the Law of Treaties of 1969[82] defines a 'treaty' as 'an international agreement concluded between states in written form and governed by international law, whether embodied in a single instrument or in two or more related instruments and whatever its particular designation'. Thus, to be a treaty, an agreement has also to be 'an international agreement' which is 'concluded between states', 'in written form', and 'governed by international law'. The phrase 'governed by international law' entails an 'intention to create obligations under international law' according to the International Law Commission's Commentary.[83] The Vienna Convention on the Law of Treaties between States and International Organizations or between International Organizations[84] of 1986, in its Article 2:1(a), modifies this definition by recognizing a treaty that is 'between one or more States and one or more international organizations; or between international organizations'. As such, both states and international organizations can conclude treaties or agreements and thus create binding international legal obligations.

B. Treaty-making power of international organizations

The treaty-making power of an international organization is closely associated with whether it possesses objective international legal personality. As a leading text on international law observes:

> Whether an organization possesses personality in international law will hinge upon its constitutional status, its actual powers and practice. Significant factors in this context will include *the capacity to enter into relations with states and other organizations and conclude treaties with them*, and the status it has been given under municipal law. Such elements are known in international law as the indicia of personality. (emphasis supplied)[85]

States, as the original and major subjects of international law, derive their personality from the very nature and structure of the international system which recognizes independence (or sovereignty) and equality as the fundamental characteristics of states.[86] For international organizations, their role in the world order centres on their possession of international legal personality as well as the scope of powers

---

[82] Signed at Vienna on 23 May 1969; in force 27 January 1980.
[83] See Fourth Report on the Law of Treaties, United Nations International Law Commission, *Yearbook of the International Law Commission* (New York: UN, 1965), vol. II, p. 12.
[84] Done at Vienna on 21 March 1986; not yet in force.
[85] Malcolm N. Shaw, *International Law* (5th edn, Cambridge: Cambridge University Press, 2003), p. 241.
[86] Ibid., at pp. 242 and 189–93.

derived from this personality. The acquisition of personality of international organizations in the first instance depends primarily on the terms of the instrument establishing the organization, as has been observed: 'If states wish the organization to be endowed specifically with international personality, this will appear in the constituent treaty and will be determinative of the issue'.[87]

C. The international legal personality of ASEAN

Popular view has it that ACFTA, or at least its Framework Agreement, is a bilateral agreement between ASEAN and China. This view however has to be called into question after a serious examination based on international law and ASEAN's own legal and policy instruments.

The assertion that ASEAN cannot be a party to an international agreement such as the ACFTA is caused by ASEAN's loose institutional structure and the unsettled question of ASEAN's legal personality, as well as the institutional powers that exist thereunder. Since ASEAN is an inter-governmental organization, it is largely up to its constituent instruments to determine its legal personality and powers. ASEAN was established by the ASEAN Declaration that was reached by the five original member states on 8 August 1967.[88] Also known as the Bangkok Declaration, the ASEAN Declaration 1967 is actually the founding instrument establishing ASEAN as a regional international organization. The Declaration contains five major clauses, laying down some very general principles of cooperation. It has been argued that, although lacking in detail, the Declaration 'goes beyond "a mere statement of intent for cooperation", to enumerate the aims and purposes of the Association and to establish a machinery to carry out the aims set forth in the Declaration'.[89] Arguably, the parties' subsequent conduct, including the conclusion of a number of political accords for the gradual strengthening of ASEAN's institutional character, is indicative that ASEAN is an international institution with some power.[90] However,

---

[87] Ibid., at pp. 1187–8. It is however important to note that, although the constituent document is without doubt the most important source of treaty-making power of an international organization, as a principle of international law, the absence of explicit provisions conferring legal personalities and treaty-making power does not necessarily lead to a lack of capacity in this regard. In many cases, the legal personality of an international organization may be inferred from the powers or purposes of the organization and its practice. See *Reparation for Injuries Suffered in the Services of the United Nations* – Advisory Opinion, ICJ Reports 1949.

[88] The legal text of the ASEAN Declaration 1967 is available online at www.aseansec.org/1629.htm. The five States are, respectively, Indonesia, Malaysia, Philippines, Singapore and Thailand.

[89] Paul J. Davidson, *The Evolving Legal Framework for Economic Cooperation* (Singapore: Times Academic Press, 2002), p. 34.

[90] Major political accords after the ASEAN Declaration 1967 include the Zone of Peace, Freedom and Neutrality Declaration, Kuala Lumpur, 27 November 1971; Declaration of ASEAN Accord, Bali, 24 February 1976; Treaty of Amity and Cooperation in Southeast Asia, Bali, 24 February 1976; ASEAN Declaration on the South China Sea, Manila, 22 July 1922; Treaty on the Southeast Asia Nuclear Weapon-Free Zone,

none of the instruments give explicit legal personality to ASEAN nor do they confer treaty-making power to the organization.

As analysed above (i.e., the International Court of Justice's analysis in *Reparation for Injuries Suffered in the Services of the United Nations*[91]), the legal personality and powers of an international institution do not necessarily have to come from its constituent instruments. Absent the relevant provision in the constituent instrument, these legal characteristics can also be evidenced by other agreements, established practices, direct or implicit intention of the members, or an understanding that they are indispensable for the fulfilment of the organization's purposes.

Rodolfo C. Severino, the formal Secretary-General of ASEAN, summarized the organization's mission as follows:

> ASEAN's founders in 1967 intended ASEAN to be an association of all the states of Southeast Asia cooperating voluntarily for the common good, with peace and economic, social and cultural development its primary purposes.[92]

However, he further noted that, to achieve these purposes, does not entail the need for a strong ASEAN institution:

> [ASEAN] is not and was not meant to be a supranational entity acting independently of its members. It has no regional parliament or council of ministers with law-making powers, no power of enforcement, no judicial system.[93]

Alagappa quite rightly observes the basic shortcomings suffered by the present ASEAN machinery and operandi:[94]

- It lacks an integrated decision-making structure. ASEAN basically serves as a forum for talks and there is virtually no central decision-making body in the organization.
- Application of the consensus method is applied to all issues and all levels, which has considerably reduced the effectiveness of intra-ASEAN cooperation.
- The principle of rotation, heavily emphasized in ASEAN, has had a debilitating effect on the role of the ASEAN secretariat, which is largely marginalized by the system of national secretariats.

Bangkok, 15 December 1997; ASEAN Vision 2020I, Kuala Lumpur, 15 December 1997; and Declaration of ASEAN Accord II, Bali, 7 October 2003.

[91] See above note 87.
[92] Rodolfo C. Severino, 'Asia Policy Lecture: What ASEAN is and What It Stands For', paper presented by Rodolfo C. Severino, Secretary-General of ASEAN, at the Research Institute for Asia and the Pacific, University of Sydney, Australia, 22 October 1998, transcript available online at www.aseansec.org/3399.htm (visited 10 November 2004).
[93] Ibid.
[94] Muthiah Alagappa, 'Institutional Framework: Recommendations for Change', in Sharon Siddique and Sree Kumar (eds.), *The 2nd ASEAN Reader* (Singapore: Institute of Southeast Asian Studies, 2004), pp. 22–7 at pp. 22–4.

- The ASEAN structure reflects the dominant emphasis on national interests and national representation; in contrast, there is no provision for representation of the ASEAN 'community interest'.
- ASEAN relies almost entirely on a policy regime and does not have a legal regime.

In short, ASEAN is deliberately designed to have a loose structure, which provides opportunities and room for behaviours that conform to the cultural environment in this particular part of the world, i.e., 'face saving' which is considered vital for regional solidarity and cohesion.[95] More significantly, ASEAN was designed not as a sovereign body, but as a regional grouping of sovereign nations. At this stage, ASEAN is more an instrument of cooperation than integration.[96] The common desire of the member states here is to promote regional and national peace, progress and security, and these goals are perceived to be better achieved by a social community than a legal community.[97] In conclusion, it is yet too early to decide on whether ASEAN has an independent, objective international legal personality and treaty-making power.

In so far as legal personality and powers of an international organization can also be acquired through practices and recognition, this cannot be applied to the ACFTA as it has already been rebuffed by ASEAN's external relations practices. In recent years, ASEAN has developed 'dialogue' relations with major nation-states and regions, including China, Japan, Korea, India and the European Union. Increasingly, foreign countries and regions have shown an interest in dealing with ASEAN as a collective whole.[98] ASEAN, however, has not taken this opportunity to make use of the 'recognition' principle in international law. Instead, it seems to be developing a 'selective exercise of legal personality' practice. In recent years, for important agreements with foreign countries, ASEAN's ten heads of state have affixed their signatures without representation of ASEAN as an organization. Examples in this regard include the three 'Framework' agreements on comprehensive economic cooperation/partnership with China, India and Japan, as well as the Instruments of Extension to the Treaty of Amity and Cooperation in Southeast Asia which admit the accession of China, Japan and India, respectively, to the Treaty of Amity and Cooperation in Southeast Asia. In contrast, agreements concerning issues in a special area – which is also probably considered less important – can be signed by the Secretary-General of ASEAN. For example, the Memorandum of Understanding between the Association of Southeast Asian Nations (ASEAN) Secretariat and the Ministry of Agriculture of the People's Republic of China, concluded on 2 November 2002, was signed by ASEAN's Secretary-General, Rodolfo C. Severino and the Vice Minister of Agriculture, Qi Jingfa. A more representative agreement is the Memorandum of Understanding between the Governments of the Member Countries of the Association of Southeast Asian Nations (ASEAN) and the Government of the People's Republic of China on Cooperation

---

[95] Ibid., at p. 22. [96] Davidson, above note 89, at p. 29. [97] Ibid. [98] Ibid., at p. 37.

in the Field of Non-Traditional Security Issues, which was signed by ASEAN's incumbent Secretary-General, Ong Keng Yong and the representative of China on 10 January 2004.

This 'selective personality' practice, as I call it, is not yet sufficient to establish that ASEAN as an institution has international legal personality and treaty-making powers. One can easily see from the title of the two Memorandums of Understanding mentioned above that the ASEAN Secretary-General's representation was more likely based on an ad hoc basis than a regular exercise of authority. Furthermore, assuming that 'selective personality' can be established through this practice, it actually strengthens the view that those 'important agreements' between ASEAN states and foreign countries, including the Framework Agreements with China, India and Japan, are definitely not agreements between those individual countries and ASEAN as a collective whole. In any case, the ACFTA Framework Agreement is not a bilateral agreement between China and ASEAN as an independent entity.

D. The legal nature of ACFTA

It is yet too early to tell the exact nature of this agreement as it is in the negotiating process. Its current form looks more like a multilateral agreement, with its parties being China and individual ASEAN countries. However, a more precise view would be that it is largely a collection or combination of bilateral agreements between China and individual ASEAN members.

With certain exceptions, this view is confirmed by the language and rights/obligation structure of the Framework Agreement. The provisions in the Framework Agreement and its various Annexes support this view: they show that China's obligations – e.g., those under the EHP – are towards individual countries, and vice versa, although sometimes the term 'ASEAN Member States' as a whole was used for convenience. This is first evidenced in the language of the Framework Agreement through the Preamble, in which the parties declared the Framework Agreement as being signed by:

> WE, the Heads of Government/State of Brunei Darussalam, the Kingdom of Cambodia, the Republic of Indonesia, the Lao People's Democratic Republic ('Lao PDR'), Malaysia, the Union of Myanmar, the Republic of the Philippines, the Republic of Singapore, the Kingdom of Thailand and the Socialist Republic of Viet Nam, Member States of the Association of South East Asian Nations (collectively, 'ASEAN' or 'ASEAN Member States', or individually, 'ASEAN Member State'), and the People's Republic of China ('China') ... [99]

---

[99] Framework Agreement, the Preamble, para. 1.

It is noted that all the names of the ten member states of ASEAN as well as the name of China appear in the Framework Agreement as the Contracting Parties. While it is also stated in the Preamble that the ten Southeast Asian states should be 'collectively' called 'ASEAN' or 'ASEAN Member States', or 'individually', 'ASEAN Member State', at the end of the Framework, only the heads of the eleven nation-states (ASEAN-10 and China) affixed their signatures to the agreement, while no ASEAN representative was called to sign the Framework Agreement.

Paragraph 3 of the Preamble, which states the parties' desire to adopt a Framework Agreement on Comprehensive Economic Cooperation *between ASEAN and China* (emphasis added), interprets the phrase 'ASEAN and China' to mean 'collectively, "the Parties", or individually referring to an ASEAN Member State or to China as a "Party"'.[100] All these expressions, with little doubt, explicate the contracting parties' intention to make the eleven sovereign nations parties to the Framework Agreement.

The core of the Framework Agreement is its Article 6 that prescribes the EHP. Unlike other provisions which aim at establishing a framework for conducting negotiations, Article 6 is a provision that involves substantive rights and obligations. Under international law, this is considered as imposing binding obligations upon the contracting parties. Article 6 allows ASEAN member states to export to China at preferential tariff rates on all the goods covered by Chapters 1–8 of the Harmonized System. China's unilateral concessions to the member states of ASEAN are embodied in the stipulation that ASEAN countries are allowed to 'carve out' those products for which they have difficulties in granting market access. In short, every ASEAN country can put forward an Exclusion List for agricultural products, denying market access to imports. In addition, China agreed to grant concessions on 130 categories of manufactured goods to individual ASEAN countries, provided that those countries put forward an 'inclusion' list of products. For goods included in the list, China will extend special and preferential tariff treatment to the ASEAN country. The ASEAN country concerned has to render some concessions to China which, however, will be offered on less than a full reciprocal basis.[101]

In terms of mutual grant of preferential benefits, the Framework Agreement initially followed a 'multilateralism' approach, which once made the Framework Agreement like a multilateral agreement. The essence was that, under the EHP, for agricultural products, except for those placed in the Exclusion List as prescribed in Article 6(a)(i) of the Framework Agreement, each ASEAN country should not only extend preferential treatment to China, but should also accord the same privilege to other ASEAN members. As the Philippines did not eventually put forward an exclusion list, Malaysia managed to secure a clause allowing it to offer EHP benefits

---

[100] Framework Agreement, the Preamble, para. 3.
[101] The lists of goods put forward by ASEAN countries are contained in Annex 2 of the Framework Agreement.

only to China. This practice was later on incorporated into the Framework Agreement through the 2003 Protocol, effectively changing the direction of ACFTA in terms of agricultural products from multilateralism to bilateralism. The 2003 Protocol to amend the Framework Agreement consolidated this practice by adding the following amendments, among others, to Article 6(3)(b)(i) of the Framework Agreement:

(1) A Party may accelerate its tariff reduction and/or elimination under this Article in relation to the rest of the parties on a unilateral basis;
(2) One or more ASEAN Member States may also conduct negotiations and enter into a bilateral or plurilateral acceleration arrangement with China to accelerate their tariff reduction and/or elimination under this Article.

Half-hearted multilateralism is also embodied in Article 6(a)(iii) of the Framework Agreement, which prescribes that:

> The specific products set out in Annex 2 of this Agreement shall be covered by the Early Harvest Programme and the tariff concessions shall apply only to the parties indicated in Annex 2. These parties must have extended the tariff concessions on these products to each other.

So far, only Indonesia, Malaysia and Thailand have submitted their 'inclusion list' under Article 6(a)(iii) of the Framework Agreement. These countries, plus Brunei and Singapore which are allowed to 'be parties to any arrangements that have been agreed on or will be agreed to between China and any other Party pursuant to Article 6(a)(iii)',[102] constitute only half of the ASEAN states who can participate in the EHP.

The Framework Agreement only sets up principles for conducting negotiations toward the final FTA, i.e. ACFTA. The nature of ACFTA itself is thus yet undisclosed. However, the essential question in this regard actually depends on the institutional characteristics of ASEAN. If ASEAN continues to be an organization without legal personality, which can be established either explicitly through legal provisions in the constituent instruments, or implicitly through practice, ACFTA cannot be a bilateral FTA deal between ASEAN as a group and China.

E. The implications of ACFTA being not a bilateral agreement between ASEAN as an entity and China

The recognition that ACFTA is not a bilateral agreement between China and ASEAN as an entity will impact on a number of significant issues, including the organization's and the member states' respective responsibility and liability to a third state (in this case China), especially when disputes arise out of the agreement.

---

[102] Framework Agreement, Annex 2.

International legal personality brings forth responsibility and liability. However, it is still an unsolved international law issue – whether a treaty concluded by an international organization has a binding effect upon the member states of the organization. In the negotiating process of the 1986 Vienna Convention on the Law of Treaties between States and International Organizations or between International Organizations, the International Law Commission put forward a draft clause on this issue, providing that member states of an international organization shall be bound by a treaty if: (1) the states members have agreed to be bound by virtue of the constituent instrument of the organization; and (2) the assent of the states members to be bound has been duly brought to the knowledge of the negotiating states and negotiating organizations.[103] Such an arrangement has particular value to international trade deals, for example, a tariff agreement concluded by a close regional organization, such as the European Community (EC), and another state/organization. As one commentator observes, 'such agreement would be of little value if they were not to be immediately binding on member states'.[104] However, despite the strong support from the EC, the draft clause was rejected at the Conference adopting the 1986 Convention, and was instead replaced by Article 74(3) of the Convention which stipulates:

> The provisions of the present Convention shall not prejudice any question that may arise in regard to the establishment of obligations and rights for states members of an international organization under a treaty to which that organization is a party.

It has now become a general principle of international law that the question of the legal effect of a treaty concluded by an international organization on its member states should be 'resolved on the basis of the consent of the states concerned in the specific circumstances and on a case-by-case basis'.[105]

As a comparison, the EC, apart from having objective personality and the ability to implement common policy in social, commercial and other areas, boasts a close organizational structure unlike any other major international institution in the world. On the international stage, the EC often acts as representative of its member states with explicit authorized powers from its constitutional instrument. The EC itself is an independent member of the WTO, the major international economic institution in the world. It has become a widely recognized state practice that, in the WTO's dispute settlement system, the EC acts as one party, bearing rights and obligations collectively on behalf of its constituent members.[106]

ASEAN, however, is not like the EC. It is an international organization with ambiguous legal personality and without a central decision-making structure or enforcement regime. It is rather more a forum for political dialogue. In all the

---

[103] Shaw, above note 85, at p. 859.   [104] Ibid.   [105] Ibid., at p. 860.
[106] See, e.g., Appellate Body Report, *EC–Bananas III*.

formal agreements made with outside countries, all the sovereign state members, instead of the organization itself representing them as a whole, must be present and provide their respective signatures. It follows accordingly that ASEAN appeals directly to its individual members to implement their treaty obligations. The language, rights and obligations structure of the ACFTA Framework Agreement further confirm this – that the rights and obligations of the treaty are directly borne by individual members; and that the rights and obligations directly apply between individual ASEAN members and China or, as the case may be, between individual ASEAN members. This in turn will have profound implications on the enforcement of obligations and the dispute settlement of the ACFTA. The parties, namely the eleven nation-states, are directly responsible to each other in terms of performing the obligations. In this sense, ACFTA more resembles the WTO which is a multilateral agreement but is in fact bilateral in nature. ACFTA, however, will, in all likelihood, mainly contain the bilateral rights and obligations between individual ASEAN members and China, together with some coverage on the ASEAN nations' rights and obligations to each other. Among the ASEAN countries, if the reciprocal benefits offered by ACFTA are no better than those contained in the ASEAN Free Trade Area (AFTA), ACFTA will be of little value to them in terms of their relationship with each other.

This bilateral nature of obligations is most reflected in the ACFTA dispute settlement mechanism. It will be fundamentally a mechanism for resolving disputes between China and the concerned individual ASEAN country, as well as disputes between two or more ASEAN nations, if obligations between them are breached. However, in no case can be there a dispute resolution system that adjudicates between China and ASEAN as a collective whole. For China, the difficulty will be that it will have to pursue every ASEAN member to enforce the trade privileges accorded to it. ASEAN as an organization will offer political, goodwill help but will not give legal assistance by commanding the individual countries to perform their obligations. Given its current structure, ASEAN does not have the legal position to call upon a responsible member to remedy its default. And neither will it, as an institution, bear any responsibility and liability towards China. The same is also true in the reverse – that ASEAN, as an organization which is not a party to ACFTA on its own part, does not have the right to pressure China to enforce any ACFTA obligation.

X. Concluding remarks

This chapter examines various legal issues concerning the forthcoming ACFTA, namely the tariff reduction and elimination arrangements; trade remedy measures including anti-dumping, countervailing duties and safeguards; the rules of origin; the dispute resolution mechanism; and the legal nature of ACFTA which has consequential impact on the understanding and implementation of ACFTA rights and obligations by the contracting parties.

The examination demonstrates that the Framework Agreement, and the several agreements concluded subsequently, represent a landmark achievement in the China–ASEAN economic relationship. The general theme of this relationship can be characterized as liberalization and legalization. The WTO-plus tariff concessions in the ACFTA, fixed by legal obligations, will tremendously increase the trade between China and ASEAN countries, and promote regional economic integration in East Asia.

Multilateralism and regionalism are both important for trade liberalization and growth. Further, both multilateral and bilateral agreements can be beneficial if designed appropriately. This chapter observes that special attention should be drawn to the rules of origin in ACFTA. Regional and bilateral trade agreements are proliferating in Asia, which might lead to the 'Asian noodle bowl effect' as highlighted by officials of the Asian Development Bank. It is important to harmonize the rules of origin in Asian FTAs. In this regard, ACFTA should endeavour to adopt identical or similar rules of origin with other FTAs. Further, in order to achieve substantial liberalization, it is recommended that the contracting parties of ACFTA should give up the use of anti-dumping and anti-subsidy actions, while retaining the use of safeguards as a means of escape. In the case of dispute resolution, it is advised that the ACFTA should move towards more legalism in its dispute settlement system.

The title of ACFTA connotes that it is a bilateral accord. This, however, is a misunderstanding of the legal nature of this agreement. Given the non-existence of an international legal personality in ASEAN, as well as participation in ACFTA by individual countries as sovereign states, ACFTA is actually a regional agreement with eleven parties. This legal nature will have profound implications on the implementation of ACFTA obligations.

Additional Sources

Agata Antkiewicz and John Whalley, 'China's New Regional Trade Agreements' (2005) 28(10) *Journal of World Trade* 1539–57.

Raul L. Cordenillo, 'The Economic Benefits to ASEAN of the ASEAN–China Free Trade Area (ACFTA)', Studies Unit of the Bureau for Economic Integration, ASEAN secretariat, 18 January 2005, at www.aseansec.org/17311.htm.

Hiro Lee, David Roland-Holst and Dominique van der Mensbrugghe, 'China's Emergence in East Asia under Alternative Trading Agreements' (2004) 15(4) *Journal of Asian Economics* 697–712.

Chalongphob Sussangkarn, 'The Emergence of China and ASEAN Revitalization', paper presented at the Annual World Bank Conference on Development Economics-Europe, Brussels, Belgium, 10–11 May 2004. Available at http://wbln0018.worldbank.org/eurvp/web.nsf/Pages/Paper+by+Sussangkarn/$File/SUSSANGKARN.PDF.

Jose L. Tongzon, 'ASEAN-China Free Trade Area: A Bane or Boon for ASEAN Countries?' (2005) 28(2) *World Economy* 191–210.

Jiangyu Wang, 'The International Legal Personality of ASEAN and the Legal Nature of the China–ASEAN FTA' in John Wong, Zou Keyuan and Zeng Huaqun (eds.), *China-ASEAN Relations: Economic and Legal Dimensions* (Singapore: World Scientific, 2006).

Tieya Wang, *Guojifa [International Law]* (Beijing: Falü Chuban [Law Press], 2004).

John Whalley, 'China in the World Trading System', paper presented at the CESifo Economic Studies Conference on Understanding the Chinese Economy, CESifo Conference Centre, Munich, 10–11 June 2005. Available at http://cesifo.de.

WTO, *World Trade Report 2003* (Geneva: WTO Publications, 2003).

INDEX

3Com, 148

Abbott, Tony, 18, 19
ACFTA
  assessment, 223–4
  dispute settlement, 209–14
    arbitration, 210–11
    choice of forum, 211–12
    consultations, 209–10
    DSM Agreement, 195, 209–11
    enforcement, 211
    legalism v diplomacy, 212–14
    mediation, 210
    WTO jurisprudence and, 212
  Framework Agreement, 193–5
    Early Harvest Programme, 194, 196–7, 220–1
    multilateral agreement, 219–21
    Protocol, 194, 221
  legal nature, 215–23
    definition of treaty, 215
    legal personality of ASEAN, 193–5, 216–19
    multilateral agreement, 193, 219–23
    treaty-making powers of International Organizations, 215–16
  negotiations, 194–5
    services, 203–4
  non-tariff barriers, 200
  origins, 193
  parties, 193–4, 220
  quotas, 199–200
  rules of origin, 200–1
  scope, 194
  services, 201
    developing countries, 203
    modification of schedules, 204
    non-discrimination, 202–3
    positive listing, 202
    progressive liberalization, 203–4
    WTO-plus, 202
  tariffs, 195–9
    assessment, 198–9
    Early Harvest Programme, 196–7
    liberalization, 197–9
    negative listing, 197–8, 199
    Sensitive Track, 198
    Trade in Goods Agreement, 195
  trade remedies, 204–9
    anti-dumping, 204, 206–7
    countervailing duties, 204, 207–8
    economic theory, 204, 206–9
    safeguards, 204–6, 209
Alagappa, Muthia, 217–18
Algeria, 145
anti-dumping measures, value, 206–7
AOL Time Warner, 147
Arias, Oscar, 57
ASEAN
  ASEAN 6 193
  ASEAN–China FTA. *See* ACFTA
  Australia–New Zealand FTA, 37
  establishment, 216–17
  India FTA, tariff listing, 199
  international dialogues, 218
  Japan FTA, 111, 113
  legal nature, 193–5, 216–19, 222–3
  mission, 217
AT&T, 148
AUSFTA
  agriculture, 15–17
    quotas, 15
    safeguard measures, 15
    subsidies, 15
    sugar, 16–17, 42
    tariffs, 15
  air services, 19, 36
  anti-dumping, 42

226

INDEX

assessment, 42
audiovisual services, 21
Australian implementing legislation, 11–12
Australian rationale, 7–8
bargaining imbalance, 8
copyright, 31
  anti-circumvention measures, 31
  sanctions, 31
  term, 31
dispute settlement, 37–40
  choice of forum, 38
  consultations, 38
  exclusions, 37
  exhaustion of local remedies, 28
  interpretation rules, 38
  investment, 27–9
  investor-state, 10, 28–9
  labour and environmental laws, 40
  non-violation complaints, 37–8
  power imbalance, 40
  public hearings, 38
  remedies, 39–40
economic effects, 35–7
  trade diversion, 36
education services, 36
electronic commerce, 24
environment, 34
financial services, 23
  market access, 23
  MFN treatment, 23
  national treatment, 23
goods, 13–19
government procurement, 19
implementation, 34–5
intellectual property, 26, 29–34
  copyright, 31
  patents, 31–3
  TRIPS-plus, 30
investment, 24–9
  dispute settlement, 27–9
  exceptions, 26–7
  existing non-conforming measures, 26–7
  expropriation, 26
  investor-state dispute settlement, 10, 28–9
  non-discrimination, 25
  performance requirements, 25
  scope, 25
MFN treatment
  electronic commerce, 24
  financial services, 23
  investment, 25, 26–7

national treatment
  electronic commerce, 24
  exemptions, 13–14
  financial services, 23
  GATT incorporations, 13
  goods, 13–14
  investment, 25, 26–7
  services, 20–1
negotiations, 9–12
  1st round, 9–10
  2nd round, 10
  3rd round, 10
  agreement, 10, 11
  consultation, 11, 12
  democratic deficit, 12
  rush, 42
  State involvement, 12
patents, 31–3
  compulsory licensing, 32–3
  parallel imports, 32
  pharmaceuticals, 31–3
  term, 32
  unfair commercial use, 32
pharmaceuticals
  Australian PBS, 17–19
  generic drugs, 32
  patents, 31–3
reviews, 36
rules of origin, 14
second-hand cars, 14
services, 19–24
  exemptions, 19–20
  existing non-conforming measures, 21
  local presence, 20–1
  market access, 20–1
  MFN treatment, 20–1
  national treatment, 20–1
  negative listing, 20
substantive obligations, 13–34
telecommunications, 23, 27
third wave FTA, 6
US rationale, 8
WTO, improvement on, 6
WTO PTA rules and, 40–2
Australia
audiovisual services, GATS and, 22
Constitution
  dispute resolution, 28
  expropriation, 26
  treaty powers, 11
Cultural Diversity Convention, 22

Australia (cont.)
  Foreign Investment Review Board, 27
  foreign policy, 8, 9
  FTAs
    ASEAN, 37
    China, 37
    Japan, 37, 113
    Korea, 37
    Malaysia, 37
    New Zealand, 14
    policy, 7
    Singapore, 14, 36, 201–4
    Thailand, 14, 36
    United States. *See* AUSFTA
  intellectual property rights, importance, 30
  Iraq War support, 8
  Pharmaceutical Benefits Pricing Authority, 17
  Pharmaceutical Benefits Scheme, 17–19
  trade
    Japan, 142
    United States, 6–7
  treaty-making process, 11
    democratic deficit, 12
  WTO disputes with US, 7
  WTO negotiations, sugar, 17

Bahrain–US FTA, 146, 191
Bambrick, Hilary, 19
Banamex, 82
Bangkok Declaration (1967), 216
Barshefsky, Charlene, 145
Baucus, Max, 146
Belize, 47
Bhagwati, Jagdish, 200
Blaine, James, 44
Bo Xilai, 63
Boddez, Thomas, 206–7
Botswana, 97, 101–2
Brazil, 17, 76, 81
Bristol Myers Squibb, 148
Brunei, 113, 193, 197
Budapest Convention, 53
Budapest Convention (1977), 53
Bush, George W., 46, 56, 146, 150, 154

CAFTA–DR–US
  agriculture
    ethanol, 50–1
    export subsidies, 50
    safeguards, 49
    sugar, 50
  Costa Rican commitments
    insurance, 51
    political reactions, 51, 52
    services, 51–2
    telecommunications, 51, 56
  distribution laws, 52
  effects, 58
  entry into force, 58
  environment, 55–6
    Cooperation Agreement, 55–6
  intellectual property, 53
    drug patents, 53
    TRIPS-plus, 53
  labour standards, 54
    union rights, 54
  market access, 49–50
  membership, 47
  multilateral agreement, 48
  negotiations, 48–9
    inclusion of Dominican Republic, 49
    migration, 48
    timeline, 48–9
  origins, 44–8
  quotas, 49
  ratifications, 56–8
  rules of origin, 51
  schedules of commitments, 48
  services, 51–2
  SPS measures, 50, 58
  substantive obligations, 49–56
  tariffs, 49
  textiles, 51
Cambodia and ACFTA, 193, 197, 203
Canada
  FDI in Mexico, 81, 82
  oil exports to US, 79
  trade with EU, 76
Canon, 142
Capling, Ann, 12
Cárdenas, Lázaro, 74
Caribbean Basin Initiative, 45–6, 51
Casas, Kevin, 57
Central America
  banana trade, 45
  CAFTA–DR–US. *See* CAFTA–DR–US
  Common Market, 45
  freedom of association, 54
  integration, 58
  Mexico FTAs, 76

migration to US, 48
NAFTA and, 46
regional trade, 47–8
textile industry, 46
union rights, 54
US influence, 44–6
WTO accessions, 46
Chile
  See also Chile–China FTA
  Japan FTA, 113
  relations with China, 59
  trade with China, 59–61
  UNSC membership, 59
  US FTA
    intellectual property, 30
    model PTA, 48
    sugar, 16
Chile–China FTA
  agricultural export subsidies, 64
  anti-dumping, 66
  Committee on Trade in Goods, 64–5
  cooperation, 71
    labour and social issues, 63, 71
    TBT, 68
  countervailing duties, 66
  dispute settlement, 69–70
    arbitration, 70
    choice of forum, 69
    Commission intervention, 69
    consultations, 69
    remedies, 70
  Free Trade Commission, 69
  GATT obligations and, 66
  market access, 63–5
    exclusions, 64
  negotiations, 61–3
    1st round, 62
    2nd round, 62–3
    3rd round, 63
    4th round, 63
    5th round, 63
    consultation, 62
    future, 62
    reviews, 72
  prospects, 71
  rules of origin, 65
  safeguards, 66
  SPS measures, 66–7
    Committee, 67
  substantive obligations, 63–71
  tariffs, 63–4

  technical barriers to trade, 68
    Committee, 68
    cooperation, 68
    mutual recognition, 68
  trade remedies, 66
China
  Chilean relations, 59
  Chilean trade, 59–61
  competition with Japan, 139
  EU trade, 94
  FTAs
    ASEAN. *See* ACFTA
    Australia, negotiations, 37
    Chile. *See* Chile–China FTA
    Mexico, 76
  relations with ASEAN, 218–19
  Sinocentrism, 213
  Tianxia, 213
  trade with EU, 76
Citigroup, 82
Clean Development Mechanism, 131
climate change, Framework Convention, 131
Clinton, Bill, 46
CMS Energy, 147
Coca Cola, 148
Colgate, 148
copyright, TRIPS, 179
Cortez, Hernán, 74
Costa Rica
  See also CAFTA–DR–US
  banana trade, 45
  CAFTA–DR–US and
    membership, 47
    ratification, 52, 56–8
    referendum, 57–8
    services, 51
  diversification, 47
countervailing duties, effectiveness, 207–8
Crump, Larry, 11, 15–16, 19, 31
Cultural Diversity Convention, 22

Davey, William, 40
Davis, Bette, 74
Dee, Philippa, 16, 35
dessert economies, 45
developing countries
  ACFTA and, 203
  safeguards, 206
Diaz-Balart, Lincoln, 144
Díaz, Porfirio, 74
Disney Corporation, 31

Dodge, William, 27
Doha Declaration on TRIPS and Health, 33
Dominican Republic, 56
    See also CAFTA–DR–US
Dooley, Cal, 146
DSU
    model, 136
    remedies, 39

EFTA
    See also EFTA–SACU FTA
    Generalized System of Preferences, 102
    legal nature, 99–100
    membership, 97
    Stockholm Convention (1960), 99
    Vaduz Convention, 99
EFTA–SACU FTA
    agriculture, 102
        bilateral offers, 108–10
        SACU–Iceland, 110
        SACU–Norway, 109
        SACU–Switzerland, 109
    assessment, 107–8
    competition, 105–6
    dispute settlement, 106–7
    entry into force, 97
    goods, 101–2
    government procurement, 105
    intellectual property, 103
    investment, 104–5
    Joint Committee, 106
    motivations, 98–9
    negotiations, 99–101
        chronology, 108
        future, 107
        rounds, 97
    services, 103–4
    substantive obligations, 101–6
    technical assistance, 106
    trade statistics, 97
El Salvador, 47, 56
    See also CAFTA–DR–US
Eli-Lilly, 148
emerging markets
    importance, 94
    Mexico and, 81, 83–4
European Union
    ASEAN, relations, 218
    automotive goods, 77
    EC – Sugar Subidies, Australian stance, 17
    Latin America and, 96
    legal nature, 222
    manufactures, 78
    Mexico FTA. See MEUFTA
    Morocco Association Agreement, 147
    office and telecom equipment, 77
    South Africa TDCA, 98, 99
    trade
        agriculture, 78–9
        chemicals, 79
        deficit, 75
        pharmaceuticals, 79
        policy-making, 89–90
        statistics, 76–80
        textiles, 78
        with India and China, 94
    WTO disputes, statistics, 80

Fassi-Fihri, Taib, 149, 153, 154
Faunce, Thomas, 19
Fox, Vicente, 111, 112, 114, 117, 141–2
France, 82, 144, 150–1
Franklin, Benjamin, 154

GATS
    exceptions
        JMEPA and, 131
        US–Morocco FTA and, 187
    market access, 84
    positive listing, 20
    PTA exception (Article V), 84
        AUSFTA and, 40–2
        EFTA–SACU FTA and, 103
        interpretation, 95
        US–Morocco FTA and, 191
GATT 1994
    conservation of natural resources, 34
    exceptions
        JMEPA and, 131
        US–Morocco FTA and, 187
    national treatment, AUSFTA and, 13
    prison labour, 34
    PTA exception (Article XXIV), 84
        AUSFTA and, 40–2
        conditions, 42
        MEUFTA and, 95
        Turkey – Textiles, 95
        US–Morocco FTA and, 190–1
    quotas, 200
Germany, 82, 144
Grassley, Charles, 154
Guatemala

See also CAFTA–DR–US
  CAFTA–DR–US membership, 47
  drug patents, 53
  ratification of CAFTA–DR–US, 56
Gulf Cooperation Council, 113

Hapsburg, Maximilian von, 74
Harrison, Benjamin, 44
Honduras
  See also CAFTA–DR–US
  banana trade, 45
  CAFTA–DR–US membership, 47
  ratification of CAFTA–DR–US, 56
  US FTA, intellectual property, 30
Howard, John, 9
Howse, Robert, 208
HSBC, 82, 85
Hu Jintao, 62

Iceland, 97, 110
Ikeyama, Shigetoshi, 141
India
  ASEAN FTA, tariff listing, 199
  EU trade, 76, 94
  Japan FTA, 113
  relations with ASEAN, 218
  trade with Mexico, 81
Indonesia, 113, 193, 221
ING, 82, 85
intellectual property
  FTAs and, 33
  treaties, 178
  TRIPS, 179
International Labour Organization
  CAFTA–DR–US and, 54
  Fundamental Principles, 181
  US–Morocco FTA and, 152, 181
International Law Commission, legal
    personality, 222
Iraq War, 8, 152
Israel–US FTA, 146, 190
Italy, trade with Morocco, 144

Jackson, John, 208, 212–13
Japan
  2003 elections, 117
  Australian trade, 142
  competition with China, 139
  economic effects of JMEPA, 138–41
  farming subsidies, 118
  FTAs

Australia, 37, 113
Brunei, 113
Malaysia, 111, 113
Mexico. *See* JMEPA
Singapore, 111, 199, 201
strategy, 111–13
Thailand, 111, 113
Mexican trade, 137
relations with ASEAN, 218
tariffs, 117
Jefferson, William, 146
Jettou, Driss, 154
JMEPA, 76
  agriculture, 118–20
    avocados, 115
    beef, 119
    chickens, 119
    negotiations, 115, 116, 117, 140
    orange juice, 119
    pork, 117, 119
  air transport, 122
  assessment, 142–3
  automobile sector, 120–1
  beverages, 121
    geographical indications, 129
    tequila, 121
  competition policy, 134–5
    dispute settlement, 134
    improving business environment, 134–5
    national treatment, 134
  cooperation, 135
    dispute settlement, 135
    government procurement, 133–4
    intellectual property and, 130
  dispute settlement, 135–6
    competition, 134
    consultations, 135–6
    cooperation, 135
    DSU model, 136
  economic effects, 82, 113–14, 136–42
    Japan, 138–41
    Mexico, 141–2
  electronic equipment, 121
  environment, 131–2
  financial services, 122
  goods, 117–21, 143
  government procurement, 132–4, 140–1
    challenges, 132–3
    cooperation, 133–4
    exceptions, 133
    intellectual property, 130

JMEPA, (cont.)
  rules of origin, 132
  scope, 134
  Sub-Committee, 133
 intellectual property, 128–30
  cooperation and, 130
  geographical indications, 129
  government procurement, 130
 investment, 124–8
  assessment, 143
  capital transfers, 126
  civil strife, 126
  dispute settlement, 128
  exceptions, 128
  existing non-conforming measures, 128
  expropriation, 125–6
  MFN treatment, 124–5
  national treatment, 124
  nationality requirements, 126
  negative listing, 124
  performance requirements, 126–8, 129
  standards of treatment, 125
  technology transfer and, 127, 129
 negotiations, 111–12, 114–17
  agriculture, 140
  political background, 117
 objectives, 112–13
 rules of origin, 130
  government procurement, 132
 services, 121–4
  exclusions, 122–3
  existing non-conforming measures, 123–4
  MFN treatment, 123
  national treatment, 123
  negative listing, 122
  residence requirements, 123
  Sub-Committee, 124
  technical regulation, 123
 significance, 112–14
 social issues, 131–2
 steel, 121
 substantive obligations, 117–36
 tariffs, 117–18
Johnson, Allen, 154
Johnston, Kellie, 19
Jordan–US FTA, 30, 146, 150, 190

Kearney, A. T., 81
Keith, Minor, 45
Koizumi, Junichiro, 111, 112, 114, 117

Korea, 11, 37, 76, 111, 218
Kyoto Protocol, 131

Lagos, Ricardo, 62
Laos, ACFTA and, 193, 197, 203
legal personality, 217, 222
Lesotho, 97, 101–2
Liechtenstein, 97, 109
Lipsey, Richard, 81
Loos, François, 150

Madrid Protocol, 53
Malaysia
 ACFTA and, 193, 197, 198, 220, 221
 Australia FTA, 37
 Japan FTA, 111, 113
Mankiw, Gregory, 172, 207
Mekouar, Aziz, 147
MEUFTA
 agriculture, 86
  beef, 89
  quotas, 91
  review, 96
  tariffs, 91
 assessment, 94–6
 automotive industry, 83–4, 90–1
 background, 74–5
 compatibility with WTO
  anti-dumping, 92
  dispute settlement, 93–4
  general exceptions, 92–3
  safeguards, 92
  SPS measures, 92
  technical barriers, 92
 competition, 93
 dispute settlement, 93–4
 economic effects, 137, 138
 entry into force, 74, 86
 FDI in Mexico and, 81–3, 83–4
 financial services, 84–5, 88, 88–9, 94
 goods, 90–4
 government procurement, 93
 motivations, 79–80, 83–4
 NAFTA model, 88
 negotiations, 85
  chronology, 87
 quotas, 91–2
 rules of origin, 86, 91
 safeguards, 92
 services, 84–5, 94

INDEX

structure, 90
substantive obligations, 90–4
tariffs, 86, 90–1
trade statistics, 76–80
Mexico
  See also NAFTA
  1910 Revolution, 74
  2003 elections, 117
  automotive goods, 77, 83–4, 120
  democratic reforms, 83
  economic effects of JMEPA, 141–2
  economy, 75, 86, 95
  emerging markets and, 81, 83–4
  FDI, 75, 83–4, 124, 142
  financial services, 88–9
  FTAs
    Central America, 76
    China, 76
    European countries, 94
    European Union. *See* MEUFTA
    foreign direct investment, 81–3, 83–4
    hub-and-spoke, 81
    strategy, 76, 141
  government procurement, 140
  history, 74
  independence, 74
  Japan FTA. *See* JMEPA
  manufactures, 78
  Maquiradora system, 140, 142
  NAFTA disputes, *Metalclad,* 125
  NAFTA effects
    automotive industry, 83
    FDI, 75
    financial services, 84
    food imports, 76–7, 119
    significance, 95
    trade increase, 137
  office and telecom equipment, 77
  oil production, 79
  Program of Sectoral Promotion, 140
  tariffs, 117
  trade
    agriculture, 78–9
    chemicals, 79
    Japan, 137
    pharmaceuticals, 79
    policy-making, 89
    statistics, 76–80
    textiles, 78
    United States, 77, 137, 138, 141

treaty hierarchy, 88
treaty powers, 88
WTO disputes, 80, 89
Middle East FTA, 146, 190
Miyahara, Jenji, 116
Morocco
  See also US–Morocco FTA
  EU Association Agreement, 147
  financial services, 175
  government procurement, 163
  labour laws, 182
  labour productivity, 159
  tariffs, 147
  US investment, 148
  US investment treaties, 150, 166
  US trade, 144, 147–8
Muhammad, Sultan Sidi, 145
Muhammad VI, King of Morocco, 149, 150
Myanmar, 193, 197, 203

NAFTA
  creation, 46
  dispute settlement
    blocking formation of panels, 94
    choice of forum, 93, 212
    investor-state model, 128
    US attitudes, 170
  effects on Mexico
    automotive industry, 83
    FDI, 75
    financial services, 84
    food imports, 76–7, 119
    significance, 95
    trade increase, 137
  financial services, 89
  investment disputes, 29
  model, 88, 128
  rules of origin, 83, 161
Namibia, 97, 101–2
Napoleon III, 74
natural resources, GATT, 34
Netherlands, 82
New Zealand, 14, 37
Nicaragua, 47, 56
  See also CAFTA–DR–US
North American Agreement on Environmental Cooperation (NAAEC), 55
Norway, 97, 98, 109
Novelli, Cathy, 149–50, 151, 153

Oman, 146
Orendain, Eduardo, 121
Oxley, Alan, 29

Pacheco, Abel, 56
Panama, 47
Philippines, 113, 193, 196, 220
plant varieties, UPOV, 53
Poland, 81
Portillo, Jósé López, 74
Portman, Rob, 34
Portugal, 86
Prebisch, Raul, 45
predatory pricing, 206–7
prison labour, GATT 1994, 34

Qi Jingfa, 218

Robles, Edna Ramírez, 94
Rubins, Noah, 29
Russia, 76, 81

SACU
  See also EFTA–SACU FTA
  customs union, 100
  economic development, 106
  membership, 97
safeguard measures, value, 209
Salinas de Gortiari, Carlos, 74
Santander, 82, 85
Saudi Arabia, 79
Scotiabank, 82
services. See GATS
Severino, Rodolfo, 217, 218
Shaw, Malcolm, 222
Singapore
  ACFTA party, 193, 197
  Australia FTA, 14, 36, 201–4
  FTA 'spaghetti bowl', 201
  Japan FTA, 111, 199, 201
  US FTA, 16, 48
Siriwardana, Mahinda, 36
Smallberger, Wilhelm, 99
Solis, Ottón, 57
South Africa
  bilateral investment treaties, 104–5
  black economic empowerment, 105
  EFTA–SACU FTA and, 98, 102
  EU–SA TDCA, 98, 99
  government procurement, 105
  new generation issues, 104

SACU and, 97, 100
  trade with Switzerland and Norway, 97
'spaghetti bowl', 200–1
Spain, 82, 86, 144
Stockholm Convention (1960), 99
Stoler, Andrew, 6
sustainable development, WTO and, 34
Swagel, Phillip, 206–7
Swaziland, 97, 101–2
Switzerland
  EFTA membership, 97
  EFTA–SACU FTA
    agricultural offers, 109
    negotiations, 102
  Generalized System of Preferences, 98
  Japan FTA, 113
  trade with South Africa, 97

Taiwan, Mexico FTA, 76
Tanner, John, 146
Telstra, 27
terminology, 6
Thailand
  ACFTA and, 193, 221
  Australia FTA, 14, 36
  farming sector, 196
  Japan FTA, 111, 113
  WTO complaints, *EC – Sugar Subsidies*, 17
trade remedies, economic theory, 206–9
trademarks, Madrid Protocol, 53
treaties
  definition, 215
  treaty-making powers of International
    Organizations, 215–16
Trebilcock, Michael, 206–7, 208
TRIMS, 168
TRIPS
  copyright, 179
  Doha Declaration on TRIPS and Health, 33
  trademarks, 179
  TRIPS-plus agreements, 30, 53, 178
Tunisia, 145
Turkey – Textiles, 95, 191

United Fruit Company, 45
United Kingdom
  Central American influence, 44
  FDI in Mexico, 82
  trade with Morocco, 144
United States
  agriculture, 8, 50

Caribbean Basin Initiative, 45–6, 51
Constitution, Takings Clause, 168
counter-terrorism, 144, 145, 146
cultural exceptions and, 23
FDI in Mexico, 81, 82
FTAs
   Australia. *See* AUSFTA
   Bahrain, 146, 191
   CAFTA–DR–US. *See* CAFTA–DR–US
   Chile, 16, 30, 48
   Honduras, intellectual property, 30
   Israel, 146, 190
   Jordan, 30, 146, 150, 190
   Korea, 11
   Morocco. *See* US–Morocco FTA
   Singapore, 16, 48
immigration, 48, 191
intellectual property rights, importance, 30
McKinley Tariff Act, 44
Mexico and
   FDI, 81, 82
   Metalclad, 125
   trade, 77, 137, 138, 141
   WTO dispute, 89
Middle East policy, 145–6, 190
Morocco and
   investment, 148
   investment treaties, 150, 166
   trade, 144, 147–8
national security, 8
ratification of CAFTA–DR–US, 56
steel protectionism, 8
trade
   Australia, 6–7
   Central America, 47–8
   European Union, 76
   Mexico, 77, 137, 138, 141
   Morocco, 144, 147–8
WTO disputes
   Mexico – Taxes on Soft Drinks, 89
   with Australia, 7
UPOV, 53
US–Morocco FTA
   administration, 185
   agriculture
      administration, 159
      beef, 158
      citrus, 157
      corn, 158
      export subsidies, 159
      Morocco's market access, 157–9
      negotiations, 151, 153–4
      olives, 157
      poultry, 158–9
      safeguards, 159
      significance, 148
      sugar, 157
      US market access, 156–7
      wheat, 158
   bribery and, 184
   chemicals, 156
   customs cooperation, 161–2
      textiles, 161
   dispute settlement, 185–7
      amicus briefs, 170
      choice of forum, 185
      consultations, 185
      environmental protection, 184
      financial services, 174
      investment, 169–71
      labour protection, 182
      non-violation complaints, 185
      panels, 185–6
      potential for disputes, 190
      rules of procedure, 186
      telecommunications, 177
   economic impact, 188
   electronic commerce, 177–8
      customs valuation, 178
      non-discrimination, 178
   entry into force, 188
   environmental protection, 183
      dispute settlement, 184
      investment, 169
   exceptions, 187–8
      balance of payments purposes, 188
      conformity with WTO, 187
      security, 187
      taxation, 187
   financial services, 174–5
      dispute settlement, 174
      exceptions, 174–5
      nationality requirements, 174
      non-discrimination, 174
      self-regulation, 174
   foreign policy impetus, 144–6
   government procurement, 163–6
      exclusions, 164, 166
      negotiations, 152
      overview, 163–4
      procuring entities, 165
      scope, 164

US–Morocco FTA (cont.)
   thresholds, 165–6
   information technology, 156
   intellectual property, 178–81
      copyright, 179–80
      digital piracy, 179–80
      enforcement, 181
      geographical indications, 179
      Internet service providers, 181
      patents, 180–1
      pharmaceuticals, 180–1
      trademarks, 179
      TRIPS-plus, 178
   investment, 166–72
      capital transfers, 168
      definition, 164
      dispute settlement, 169–71
      due process, 169
      environmental and labour laws, 169
      expropriation, 167–8, 187
      nationality requirements, 169
      non-conforming measures, 171
      non-discrimination, 167
      performance requirements, 168–9
      scope, 166
      security exception, 169
      standards of treatment, 167
      transparency, 169
   Joint Committee, 185, 189–90
   labour protection, 181–3
      dispute settlement, 182
      investment, 169
      Labour Cooperation Mechanism, 183
   market access, 155–6
   motivations, 144–7
   national treatment, 155–6
   negotiations, 148–54
      1st round, 151–2
      2nd round, 152–3
      3rd round, 153
      4th round, 153
      5th round, 153
      6th round, 153
      7th round, 153–4
      8th round, 154
      agriculture, 151, 153–4
      future, 189–90
      government procurement, 152
      groups, 150
      labour issues, 152
      players, 149–50
      textiles, 152, 190
   pre-existing investment, 148
   pre-existing trade, 147–8
   safeguards, 162–3
      agriculture, 159
      compensation, 162–3
      textiles, 160
   sardines, 156
   services, 172–4
      electronic commerce, 177–8
      financial services, 174–5
      GATS compatibility, 172–3
      negative listing, 173–4
      telecommunications, 175–7
      WTO conformity, 191
   significance, 144
   substantive obligations, 155–88
   tariffs, 155–6
   technical barriers to trade, 162
   telecommunications, 175–7
      competition, 175
      dispute settlement, 177
      interconnectivity, 176
      network access, 176–7
      universal service, 177
      value-added services, 177
   termination procedure, 188
   textiles, 159–61
      customs cooperation, 161
      economic impact, 188–9
      future negotiations, 189–90
      negotiations, 152
      rules of origin, 160–1
      safeguards, 160
      tariffs, 156, 160
   transparency, 184
   WTO conformity, 190–1
Usabiaga, Javier, 120, 142

Vacarro brothers, 45
Vaile, Mark, 9, 16, 19, 34, 36
Venezuela, oil exports to US, 79
Vietnam, 113, 193, 197, 203
Villalobos, Angel, 115
Volkswagen, 82

Walker, Ignacio, 63
Workman, Willard, 146
WTO
   audiovisual debate, 24
   Cancún Ministerial Conference, 111

disputes, US–Australia, 7
DSU, 39, 136
GATS. *See* GATS
GATT. *See* GATT 1994
Government Procurement Agreement, 163
improvements on, 6
jurisprudence, 212
safeguards, 205
   developing countries, 206
sustainable development, 34

TRIMS performance requirements, 168
TRIPS. *See* TRIPS

Yamazaki, Ryuichiro, 115

Zedillo, Ernesto, 86
Zemurray, Samuel, 45
Zhu Rongji, 193
Zoellick, Robert, 9, 8, 29, 145, 146–7, 149, 150, 150–1, 151, 154

For EU product safety concerns, contact us at Calle de José Abascal, 56–1º,
28003 Madrid, Spain or eugpsr@cambridge.org.

www.ingramcontent.com/pod-product-compliance
Ingram Content Group UK Ltd.
Pitfield, Milton Keynes, MK11 3LW, UK
UKHW030659060825
461487UK00010B/893